AUSTRALIA AT THE POLLS

AUSTRALIA AT THE POLLS

The national elections of 1975

Edited by Howard R. Penniman

American Enterprise Institute for Public Policy Research
Washington, D. C.

Library of Congress Cataloging in Publication Data

Main entry under title:

Australia at the polls.

   (AEI studies ; 142)
   Includes index.
   1. Australia. Parliament—Elections—Addresses,
essays, lectures. 2. Elections—Australia—Addresses,
essays, lectures. 3. Australia—Politics and government
—1945–   —Addresses, essays, lectures.
I. Penniman, Howard Rae, 1916–   II. American
Enterprise Institute for Public Policy Research.
III. Series: American Enterprise Institute for Public
Policy Research. AEI studies ; 142.
JQ4094.A8   329′.023′9406   77-949
ISBN 0-8447-3239-7

AEI studies 142

Printed in the United States of America

CONTENTS

PREFACE

1   **THE AUSTRALIAN POLITICAL SYSTEM**
Leon D. Epstein   **1**

    The National Setting   2
    Federalism and the Constitution   6
    The National Government   10
    Parties 20
    Elections   27
    Constitutional Crisis   37

2   **THE RISE AND FALL OF WHITLAM LABOR:
THE POLITICAL CONTEXT OF THE
1975 ELECTIONS**   *Patrick Weller* and *R. F. I. Smith*   **49**

    Changing Political Patterns   49
    Liberal-Country Party Government
        in the 1960s   52
    The Rise of Whitlam Labor   54
    June 1974 to June 1975:
        The Beginning of the End   66
    June to November 1975: The Decline
        and Fall of the Labor Government   70

3   **THE LABOR CAMPAIGN**   *D. W. Rawson*   **77**

    The ALP: Traditions and Innovations   77
    The Course of the Campaign   89
    The Trade Unions   96
    Finances—Before and After   98

4 THE LIBERAL PARTY Michelle Grattan 103

The Background 103
The Liberals in Opposition 112
The Liberal Campaign 131
Victory and Its Aftermath 140

5 THE COUNTRY PARTY Margaret Bridson Cribb 143

Organization 145
The Country Party between 1970 and 1975 147
The Campaign 150
Conclusion 156

6 THE ROLE OF THE MINOR PARTIES
Paul Reynolds 159

Minor-Party Formation 159
Minor-Party Survival 161
1975: A Watershed 165

7 THE MEDIA AND THE ELECTIONS
C. J. Lloyd 171

The Australian Mass Media 172
The Buildup to the 1975 Campaign 178
Bias and the Journalists' Strike 181
The Media and the Campaign 198
Some Final Thoughts 208

8 OPINION POLLING AND THE ELECTIONS
Terence W. Beed 211

A Concentrated Press and a
  Concentrated Population 211
The Record of Australian Opinion Polls 218
The 1975 Election 229
Conclusion 253

9 AUSTRALIA'S FOREIGN POLICY AND THE
ELECTIONS OF 1972 AND 1975 Owen Harries 257

Background to 1972 258
The Whitlam Years 264
The Return of the Coalition 272
Conclusion 275

10 THE ELECTORATE SPEAKS—AND AFTER
Colin A. Hughes 277

Long-Term Electoral Patterns 278
Electoral Patterns in 1975 296
Labor's Prospects 303
The Broad Implications of 1975 309

APPENDIX A Politics and the Constitution:
Twenty Questions Left by Remembrance Day
David Butler 313

APPENDIX B The Vote and the Count 337

APPENDIX C A Summary of Australian National
Election Results, 1972–75 *Richard M. Scammon* 351

CONTRIBUTORS 359

INDEX 361

PREFACE

Australia at the Polls: The National Elections of 1975 is another in the series of studies of national elections in selected democratic countries to be published by the American Enterprise Institute for Public Policy Research. The volumes that have been published thus far cover important elections of 1974—the two parliamentary elections in Britain, the Canadian general election, the French presidential election, and the House of Councillors election in Japan. In addition, a volume discussing the parliamentary elections in Denmark, Norway, and Sweden in 1973, 1975, and 1976 has recently appeared. In progress or planned are studies of the Italian and German elections of 1976, the referendum on British entry into the Common Market, the 1976 referendum and 1977 election in Spain, and the Israeli parliamentary election of 1977.

Australian voters went to the polls in December 1975 to elect the entire membership of both the House of Representatives and the Senate. This was the second time in nineteen months but only the fourth time in Australian history that such a "double dissolution" had occurred. The constitution requires members of the House of Representatives to face another election within three years of attaining office. Senators, elected from six states, by contrast, normally can expect to serve out fixed terms of six years.[1] (Their terms are staggered so that half the senators face election every three years.) When the Senate has blocked legislation passed by the House twice with an

---

[1] Unlike the terms of senators from the six states, the terms of senators from the Northern Territory and the Australian Capital Territory expire "with each dissolution of the House of Representatives." Frank L. Ley, *Commonwealth Electoral Procedures*, Australian Electoral Office (Canberra: Australian Government Publishing Service, 1976), p. 37.

interval of three months, however, the Senate may be dissolved along with the House.

Comfortable margins are not uncommon for the victorious party in the House of Representatives because elections are held in 127 single-member districts—a system that, as Colin A. Hughes points out in Chapter 10, often exaggerates the winner's edge in the popular vote. On the other hand, the proportional representation system under which five (after double dissolutions ten) senators are elected at-large from each state and two each from the Northern Territory and the Australian Capital Territory tends to distribute seats much more evenly between the major parties in the Senate. In 1975 the Liberal-National Country party (L-NCP) coalition won 54.1 percent of the popular vote and ninety-one seats (71.7 percent) in the House of Representatives, while the Australian Labor party (ALP) gained 42.8 percent of the votes but only thirty-six seats (28.3 percent). In the Senate races the major parties won roughly the same relative share of the votes, but the L-NCP margin over the ALP in that body was an undramatic though solid thirty-five to twenty-seven with the remaining two seats going to outsiders.

The 1975 Australian elections, however, will be remembered not for the smashing L-NCP victory but for the constitutional issues raised by the manner in which the elections were brought about. For six months prior to the dissolution of Parliament, the Labor government of Gough Whitlam was plagued by continuing scandals which drove the prime minister to reshuffle his government and fire prominent ministers. Public criticism of the government opened the way for Malcom Fraser, the newly elected head of the Liberal party and leader of the opposition coalition, to call on the opposition's one-vote majority in the Senate to "block supply" (that is, to refuse to vote funds required to keep the government operating) with a view to forcing early elections. The constitution's language on the power of the Senate to stop appropriations is not clear, but in practice the Senate never previously had prevented the passage of appropriation measures. The Senate began to vote against appropriation measures in mid-October and by early November it appeared possible that all government expenditures could be halted by year's end for want of funds.

A second and perhaps even more controversial constitutional issue was raised when Governor General Sir John Kerr dismissed the Labor government on November 11 and named Fraser caretaker prime minister until elections could be held. The Senate promptly voted to appropriate the needed funds, and both houses of the legislature were dissolved by the governor general. No other governor general in the history of Australia since independence had ever taken upon himself the sole responsibility for dismissing the prime minister and dissolving Parliament.

ALP leaders reacted vigorously to the actions of both the Senate and the governor general, denouncing them as unconstitutional and a threat to the democratic system itself. Some constitutional law authorities joined in the criticism. A majority of Australians also reacted negatively both to the blocking of supply by the Senate and to the dismissal of the government by the governor general. Briefly public support for Whitlam and the ALP increased, but by December 1—about half-way through the electoral campaign—Fraser and the L-NCP had regained a commanding lead that held up through the election. A majority of Australian voters (whatever their views on the constitutional issues, which may trouble Australian politics for decades to come) were not prepared to vote for a scandal-ridden government and particularly a government associated with a very high rate of inflation and a rapid rise in unemployment. The argument that the actions of the Senate and the governor general endangered the democratic process apparently lost force for some when the only obvious result of those actions had been to take the whole matter to the voters for decision.

Twelve authors, ten of them from Australia, have contributed essays to this volume discussing the issues and events leading up to dissolution, the campaign and election, and some of the consequences flowing from the election. Leon Epstein in the introductory chapter describes the Australian political system for readers who are not well acquainted with this special variant of the British parliamentary model. Patrick Weller and R. F. I. Smith provide the political context within which the 1975 election occurred. D. W. Rawson, Michelle Grattan, and Margaret Bridson Cribb contribute separate chapters on the major parties—Labor, Liberal, and National Country. Paul Reynolds describes the lesser parties and their roles in Australian elections. Terence W. Beed discusses Australian public opinion polling organizations and their findings about the political views of the people before and during the campaign. C. J. Lloyd describes the Australian media and analyzes their role in the election. Owen Harries examines the impact of the elections of 1972 and 1975 on the nation's foreign policy. Colin A. Hughes, in the concluding chapter, discusses the outcome of the elections and some prospects for the future of Australian politics.

An article by David E. Butler that raises and carefully analyzes constitutional and related issues surrounding the 1975 dissolution is reprinted in Appendix A. In Appendix B excerpts from an Australian Electoral Office publication describe and illustrate in detail the voting systems used in Australia. Richard M. Scammon provided the electoral data in Appendix C.

Beverly Shurr and Lorraine Millard of the Australian Embassy in Washington, D.C. have earned the special thanks of the AEI staff by providing countless bits of information needed in preparing this study for publication.

HOWARD PENNIMAN

1
THE AUSTRALIAN POLITICAL SYSTEM

Leon D. Epstein

Australia belongs to the small and hardly growing number of nations that regularly conduct competitive elections. Along with New Zealand, it is the southwestern Pacific outpost of Western-style constitutional democracy and specifically of a British-derived political order. Accordingly the Australian political system is significant even without its distinctive features—of which one, bicameral parliamentary government, became salient in 1975.

This chapter is designed for non-Australian readers, primarily but not exclusively Americans, who are unfamiliar with Australian government and politics.[1] For their purposes, it stresses the relation of a parliamentary system, particularly the Australian variant, to parties and elections. It does so by comparing parliamentary-cabinet government in general with the American separation of powers, and the relatively familiar British, or Westminster, model of parliamentary-cabinet government with the special Australian form. Beyond these institutional or structural comparisons, the chapter describes certain other characteristics of the Australian political system that are most relevant for understanding the 1975 general election. Many important characteristics, however, cannot be described here at all, and others can be noted only briefly. Fortunately readers can find much more

[1] Having only recently had the chance to study Australian affairs, I can hope that my own previous unfamiliarity serves as an adequate reminder of the need to explain certain elementary points that Australians often take for granted. Insofar as my unfamiliarity has diminished, I owe much to the helpfulness of my colleagues in late 1975 at the Department of Political Science, Research School of Social Sciences, Australian National University, and particularly to the Australian specialists Robert Parker, Colin Hughes, Don Rawson, Peter Loveday, Patrick Weller, Robert Smith, and Campbell Sharman. My visit to Australia was made possible by fellowship support from the Australian National University and the Australian-American Educational Foundation.

information and analysis in texts and other first-rate publications chiefly by Australian political scientists.[2] The present essay is a substitute for such works only to the extent that it helps those for whom the 1975 election study is their first substantial introduction to Australian politics. Australian readers, especially, may want to move on to subsequent chapters unless they are curious about the comparative perspective of an American observer.

The chapter has two main themes. One, obviously crucial as election background, is that government is based both on a written constitutional document—a phenomenon familiar to Americans, as are the legalist means of interpreting such a document—and on unwritten constitutional conventions whose observance depends, as does much of the British constitution, on their continued acceptance by politicians and their publics. Conflict between these two elements of the Australian system was at the heart of the crisis leading to the 1975 election. The second principal theme is the maintenance, in the electorate and in Parliament, of stable, strong, and cohesive party alignments backed by substantial organizational structures. Politics in Australia, not wholly but much more than in the United States, is party politics.

The National Setting

Thirteen million Australians—a population no larger than Pennsylvania's—live on an island continent as large as mainland United States. Nevertheless, Australia is a highly urban and suburban nation: two-thirds of its people live in cities of over 100,000 inhabitants and another fifth in smaller urban centers. Moreover, the two largest metropolitan centers, Sydney and Melbourne, together have over 5.5 million people. Three other large cities (Perth, Adelaide, and Brisbane) have a total population of 2.5 million. All five of these are coastal cities as well as state capitals. Apart from Perth, very distant

---

[2] The best-known text, on which I have relied for much basic information, is L. F. Crisp, *Australian National Government* (Hawthorne, Victoria: Longman, 1974). Also widely available is a shorter introductory book especially useful for non-Australians, J. D. B. Miller and Brian Jinks, *Australian Government and Politics* (London: Duckworth, 1971). A newer, broadly conceived text is Hugh V. Emy, *The Politics of Australian Democracy* (Melbourne: Macmillan, 1974). Worth mentioning also in the category of general works are three excellent readers: Henry Mayer and Helen Nelson, eds., *Australian Politics: A Third Reader* (Melbourne: Cheshire, 1973); Colin Hughes, ed., *Readings in Australian Government* (St. Lucia: University of Queensland Press, 1968); and Richard Lucy, ed., *The Pieces of Politics* (South Melbourne: Macmillan, 1975). For Australia generally, not just its politics, see the valuable and readable "Second to None: A Survey of Australia," *Economist*, vol. 258 (March 27, 1976), pp. 1-42 (supplement).

in Western Australia, these major centers, along with nearly adjacent urban concentrations, constitute a population belt—known as the boomerang coast because of its shape—that stretches, with some breaks, for about 1,600 miles from Adelaide and Melbourne in the south around to Sydney and Brisbane on the east and north. There are simply no major inland cities. The largest "inland" city is Canberra, the new, completely planned national capital, but its population is still less than 200,000 and it is only about 100 miles from the eastern coast.

Plainly, Australia has nothing like the American Midwest of the Great Lakes and the Mississippi Valley. Not only is there no industrial heartland in the interior of the Australian continent, but neither is there an inland combination of favorable soil and rainfall that could support a large agricultural population. Only in patches near the coast can there be numerous family farms resembling those of the midwestern United States. Even the less intensive agricultural use of the land, for wheat, sheep, and cattle raising, occurs mainly within a few hundred miles of the sea. So does the production of sugar and tropical fruits in the north. Most of the rest of the continent is a sparsely inhabited desert or near-desert whose pockets of population are often linked to important mining enterprises. Australia's inland population has always been small compared with its coastal concentrations. Yet the vast territorial expanse is of considerable historical importance in understanding the country and its people. For Australians, living on the edges of so large and sparsely populated a continent, the bush and the "outback" have pervaded the national consciousness more fully than the wild west has occupied the American mind. And inland Australia is economically important. Not only does it have mineral wealth, but its dry but better-than-desert section a few hundred miles from the coast has long been significant for the sheep-raising and wool production that for a century has provided Australia's largest and most famous export.

Thanks to its successful wool production as well as its mineral wealth, Australia is a rich country despite the barrenness of much of its territory. Australia's gross national product per capita ranks it among the dozen wealthiest countries in the world. The working class, heavily concentrated in cities, is prosperous even by the high standards of developed Western nations. Australian workers secured their prosperity relatively early because of the limited labor supply; a nation so remote discouraged mass European immigration at the same time that the government practically excluded Asian immigration. Protective tariffs against imported manufactured goods and strong trade unions, deeply entrenched since the nineteenth century, have also played a part in raising the standard of living of the work force.

This is not to say that wealth is evenly distributed. Successful Australian capitalists, not just foreign investors, have been the special beneficiaries of economic development, especially since World War II. Some of the most conspicuous Australian wealth has long been based on agricultural land owning. Sheep and cattle-raising enterprises developed and have remained, for understandable economic reasons, as large-scale units rather than family farms. The owner of this kind of enterprise is a distinctive and important Australian landholder. Called a "grazier," he seems to combine the social characteristics of the Texas rancher and the British country gentleman. His business proprietorship resembles the Texan's, though his property is called a station, not a ranch, but his social and political status is much more firmly established. Indeed, in Australian politics the grazier plays an accepted role much more like that of Britain's landed aristocracy. Yet neither the graziers nor any other Australian group constitute a traditional ruling class in the older British or European sense. Class consciousness there surely is, as everywhere, but there is also an especially strong egalitarian ethos, long observed as an Australian characteristic, and a rate of upward occupational mobility that appears even higher than that of the United States.[3] Australia's dominant if not exclusive political tradition has been democratic, often in radical or progressive form. Preceding large-scale industrialization, the tradition apparently "congealed" a fragment of the nineteenth-century British society from which the nation derived.[4]

The British origins of almost all of Australia's population during the formative years, indeed until 1945, can hardly be overemphasized. "British," however, means not just English but also Scottish, Welsh, and notably Irish. From its early settlement, Australia has been an Anglo-Irish country with a large Catholic minority. Continental Europeans, constituting a very limited proportion of the pre-World War II population, responded in large numbers to the Australian government's encouragement of immigration after 1945 and to the economic expansionism of the 1950s and 1960s. They became an important diversifying element in Australia's population as it grew from under 8 million in 1947 to the 13 million of the early 1970s.

---

[3] Leonard Broom and F. Lancaster-Jones, "Father-to-Son Mobility: Australia in Comparative Perspective," *American Journal of Sociology*, vol. 74 (January 1969), pp. 333-42.

[4] Richard Rosecrance, "The Radical Culture of Australia," chap. 8, p. 300, of Louis Hartz's insightful comparative study, *The Founding of New Societies* (New York: Harcourt, Brace & World, 1964).

Of the approximately 2.5 million immigrants who arrived in Australia between 1947 and 1970, over half came from continental Europe (and most of the remainder from the British Isles). Still, of course, Australia's people are overwhelmingly European rather than Asian. "White Australia," long openly proclaimed as national policy and rigorously, even ruthlessly, enforced, is still a reality, despite anti-racist concessions both in legal terminology and in the actual admission of limited numbers of qualified Asians. With no likelihood of an early large-scale immigration of Asians and with only a small, though no longer entirely neglected or abused, minority of dark-skinned aborigines, Australia is for the foreseeable future an island of European peoples in Asian seas.

As a European settlement, and still a chiefly British settlement, Australia is very young even by American standards. Fully "discovered" only late in the great explorations of modern European history, the island continent had no white settlers until the British government began using Australia as a penal colony at the end of the eighteenth century and no large immigration of nonconvict settlers until the middle of the nineteenth. As in America a few centuries earlier, the British settlement of Australia developed in separate seaboard areas, each of which became a colony with its own governing authority and commercial center. Much more heavily than the American colonies, however, the Australian settlements required governmental enterprise and capital for the development of inland areas. Limited though such development was by harsh climatic conditions—perhaps, indeed, because it was thus limited—each colonial government tended to become a strong central authority on which people depended for a variety of public works. There is not the same individualist antigovernment tradition in Australia as there is in the United States. This difference cannot be attributed exclusively, however, to the more difficult physical circumstances of Australia. It may also reflect the fact that the nineteenth-century British settlers of Australia were more ready to accept active governmental authority than were the earlier settlers of the American colonies. Australia was settled by a people already experiencing the industrial revolution and its accompanying demand for the exercise of a regulating governmental authority.

In another more directly political sense, Australia has the marks of a new country. It is literally a twentieth-century nation. The six Australian colonies, though achieving democratic self-government separately in the late nineteenth century, did not join to establish the federated Commonwealth of Australia until 1901. Thus, the national history is especially short, which may help explain the absence of generally venerated national heroes. Australia has no Washingtons, Jeffersons, or Lincolns. Of course, no national revolution ever took place against British imperial authority. Self-government and federation came by peaceful negotiation unlikely to reveal heroic acts. Even Australia's significant participation in two world wars, despite victories and tragic heroism, made no individual commander a universally accepted national leader. Nor did the writing of the Commonwealth's constitution produce an Australian equivalent of James Madison. Several founding fathers, particularly Alfred Deakin, are familiar to Australians interested in their national history, and their names, along with those of early explorers and colonial governors, have been given to schools and suburbs. But none is treated, yet at any rate, as a national hero. Perhaps the veneration of patriotic figures will always be un-Australian. Reflecting either their egalitarian ethos or a cynical, knocking spirit, Australians like to "cut down the tall poppies." Whatever the reason, the Commonwealth's founding fathers and their constitutional document do not achieve the universal veneration of their U.S. counterparts.

Federalism and the Constitution

For Australia, as for the United States, Canada, or any other nation established by the consent of its regional components, a written constitution provides not only the structure of a central authority but also the distribution of governmental powers between central and regional authorities. Australia's constitution deals with both these matters in considerable detail. It is definitely a legal document, carefully drafted by lawyers to limit the national government and preserve for the six states many of the significant powers they had exercised as self-governing colonies. Coming only at the turn of this century, Australian federation brought together much more modern political societies than did the union of the American states in the late eighteenth century. The most highly developed Australian states, New South Wales and Victoria, already had large urban populations, and their colonial parliaments had responded to problems associated with such populations. Significantly, the states also had substantial bureaucracies that had developed from active colonial administrations. Then as now, local authorities were limited in scope. Moreover, Australian colonial governments had been heavily democratized for several decades before 1900, notably introducing manhood suffrage in advance of many Western nations. Thus the colonial, now state, political leaders had popular bases of support and opposition. Among these were strong labor parties and associated trade unions, organized among miners and shearers on large sheep stations as well as among city workers.

The relatively advanced political and economic status of the pre-federation Australian colonies may help to explain the establishment of a surprisingly limited national authority in 1901. Originally, of course, the development of strong separate governments was a consequence of geographical distance. The continent was settled and most conveniently managed throughout the nineteenth century from the six distinct seaboard capitals. Even in 1901, when railroads (first built on different gauges in different states) were used along with sea and preautomotive road transport, continental travel remained slow and difficult enough to justify decentralization. Only with the advent of the airplane and electronic communication over half a century later would "the tyranny of distance" sharply diminish.[5] But the new mid-twentieth-century circumstances, while conducive to the considerable growth of central authority, have not overcome the limitations imposed by the states in the constitutional structure created in 1901.

The residual strength of states' rights is a hard though curious fact. Generally speaking, Australia does not have the heterogeneity often associated with a federal system. Its states do not coincide with ethnic, linguistic, or religious units, as the provinces do in Canada or the cantons in Switzerland. Nor are any of the Australian states, singly or as a group, set as sharply apart by their social institutions as the southern states have been from the rest of the United States. Rather, the Australian nation is remarkably homogeneous as compared with Canada, the United States, or even Great Britain. The continent was settled almost everywhere, originally and for most of its history, by people overwhelmingly from the British Isles, many of whom moved freely from colony to colony despite distance. They established the pattern of Australian life and culture before the immigration of large numbers of continental Europeans, which has taken place only in recent decades.

Australia seems to have a national uniformity in so many important respects that the tenacity of its federal structure often surprises foreign visitors. The lawyers who wrote its constitution deliberately circumscribed the powers of the central government in order to make their document acceptable to the states. And judicial authorities have often interpreted the constitution so that national powers, notably

---

[5] The phrase serves as the title for an ingenious, highly readable analysis by Geoffrey Blainey, *The Tyranny of Distance* (Melbourne: Sun Books, 1966).

with respect to economic policies, remain more limited than those of the U.S. government under the generous judicial opinions of the U.S. Supreme Court in the mid-twentieth century. For example, the Australian national government does not have the power to fix prices and incomes in peacetime. For it to obtain that regulatory authority would require a constitutional amendment—sought, without success, in 1973.[6] Most other attempts to amend the constitution, usually designed to increase the powers of the federal government, have also failed to gain the necessary popular referendum majorities (over half of the total national vote *and* over half of the votes in each of four of the six states). Of thirty-two amendment proposals submitted to the electorate by Parliament between 1901 and 1974, only five were approved.[7] The results might well suggest popular support if not for states' rights, at least for limiting the national government; on twenty-four of the thirty-two proposals, a majority of the national vote has been opposed to constitutional change.

Yet substantial changes have occurred in the federal relationship, even if seldom by formal amendment of the constitution. The most striking and consequential strengthening of the national government has been financial. Preempting income-tax revenue during World War II and then continuing to do so in peacetime, the national government has obtained the resources both to develop its own programs and to determine, through its allocation of funds, the nature of many state programs.[8] By 1975, the Australian states, while still responsible legislatively and administratively for a wide range of services, were weakened as initiators of policy, probably more so in many respects than American states. A symbolically significant sign of a changing federal relationship is the decision of the national government between 1972 and 1975 to call itself the Australian government rather than the Commonwealth government, as it is labelled in the constitution. Nevertheless, the states remain constitutionally and politically capable of resisting the growth of national powers. Resentment of centralization, especially by the peripheral states, played a part in the election campaign against the Labor government in 1975. State governments hope to arrest, or even slightly reverse, the centralizing trends by securing a greater share of the income-tax revenue through lump-sum grants.

---

[6] C. J. Lloyd and G. S. Reid, *Out of the Wilderness* (North Melbourne: Cassell, 1974), pp. 298-305.

[7] Crisp, *Australian National Government*, chap. 2.

[8] Ibid., chap. 5.

The federal feature of the Australian constitution that needs special emphasis here is the existence of the Senate as a second parliamentary chamber along with the House of Representatives. The nomenclature itself, interestingly identical to the U.S. terms, reflects the conscious adaptation of the federal model with which the Australian founding fathers were most familiar and which they preferred to the then apparently more centralized Canadian model.[9] In particular, the Australian Senate was supposed to be a states' house that, like the U.S. Senate, would have equal numbers of members from small and large states—at first six senators from each of six states, and later ten from each of the six (plus, in 1975, two from each of two territories). Again like the U.S. Senate, the Australian second chamber was given by the constitution legislative powers nearly equal to those of the House of Representatives.

From the start, Australian senators were popularly elected in statewide constituencies, as American senators have been only since 1913. Despite the unequal populations of the several states, in Australia, as in the United States, senators derive from their election democratic credentials of a kind that cannot be claimed by Canadian senators, who are appointed, or by the predominantly hereditary British lords. These credentials would seem to have made it easier for the Australian Senate to assert the considerable powers granted by the constitution. The Senate could also draw, however, on the Australian experience with important second chambers in the colonial and state governments. As in the United States, bicameralism was familiar in Australia before its use at the national level. And it remains operative in five of the six Australian state governments. This suggests that the Senate, while established to represent states as states, might well survive as a second chamber representing other interests more plainly than those of the states themselves. It is certainly true that politically the Senate has long divided mainly along party lines rather than along strictly state lines. No more than in the United States does the chamber originally designed to give small states equal representation with large states turn out to be primarily an arena for clashes between states.

---

[9] J. A. La Nauze, *The Making of the Australian Constitution* (Carlton, Victoria: Melbourne University Press, 1972), pp. 16-17, 27-28. In addition to this scholarly historical account, there are the famous commentaries by convention participants, John Quick and Robert Garran, *The Annotated Constitution of the Australian Commonwealth* (Sydney: Angus and Robertson, 1901); the more recent standard work, R. D. Lumb and K. W. Ryan, *The Constitution of the Commonwealth of Australia Annotated* (Sydney: Butterworths, 1974); and several first-class constitutional analyses by Geoffrey Sawer and P. H. Lane, among others.

The National Government

Only some of the most significant working rules of the national government are to be found in the Australian constitution itself. Apart from specifying national powers, the constitution establishes the legislative, executive, and judicial structures. But it does not spell out legislative-executive relations in the American manner. Instead, these relations are assumed to rest on parliamentary conventions derived from British and colonial experience. Without knowledge of these conventions, one would surely fail to understand the political system. The constitutional document appears to give executive power to a governor general, appointed by the British monarch as her representative, and to a council of ministers of state named by the governor general. Furthermore, the constitution grants the governor general, in behalf of the monarch, a share of the legislative power otherwise vested in the Senate and House of Representatives. But just as the British monarch had lost the reality of such executive and legislative powers long before 1900, so in Australia the authority formally granted to the governor general has been assumed from the start to be mainly exercised in his name by a prime minister and other cabinet ministers responsible to the elected Parliament. Furthermore, the very appointment of the governor general, while formally made by the British monarch, has come to be regarded as the choice of the Australian prime minister, who suggests the person to be appointed. British monarchs are expected to follow the suggestion of the prime minister, and indeed they have done so by appointing the governor general for a fixed term (ordinarily five years) and by acquiescing in the recent custom of appointing Australians rather than Britons to the position. Also, and the point is of great potential significance, British monarchs are assumed to accept the principle that they should dismiss a governor general when an Australian prime minister so advises.

Parliamentary Democracy. The Australian constitution specifies that ministers, serving as political heads of administrative departments, must be members of either the House of Representatives or the Senate (or become members within three months of their ministerial appointments). There is, however, no constitutional mention of a prime minister or a cabinet as such nor of the way in which prime minister and cabinet are to be held responsible to Parliament. Australians, like Britons, have simply taken for granted, or occasionally learned from authoritative texts, that prime minister and cabinet derive their positions and authority from the support of a majority of the members of the lower house. Now, as it has been for many years, that majority is ordinarily held by a party or a combination of parties that has won its control in a parliamentary election. The governor general in Australia, like the queen in Britain, is supposed to appoint as prime minister the accepted leader of the majority party and then to confirm the prime minister's choices for other ministerial posts. The possibility that a governor general could choose as prime minister anyone other than the leader of a House majority is limited in the sense that such a prime minister would lack the parliamentary support necessary to govern and so to remain in office (unless a new election provided him with a majority). In this system, as in the British tradition generally, parliamentary support is crucial for the prime minister. Without it, his government could be denied "supply"—the appropriation of money—to carry out its functions. And while the denial of supply is thus the ultimate parliamentary weapon against a prime minister, other means are also available to force the government either to resign or to hold a new election. The House majority can vote censure or no-confidence motions, or simply turn down a major government proposal. As in Britain, parliamentary government means that the tenure of the political executive depends on a legislative majority that an American president does not require in order to stay in office.

There has never been any doubt about Australia's acceptance of this crucial parliamentary convention with respect to the power of the House of Representatives. A majority in that chamber has always been essential to the government. This is another way of saying that the prime minister and his cabinet represent the leadership of the majority party, or of the majority party coalition, in the House of Representatives. In practice, the government's support in the House is continuous. Its policies are those of its party majority in the House. Regularly the majority of representatives confirm their support for the government by voting in favor of its measures and against opposition party motions.

No such majority support for the government is required in the Senate. The prime minister and his cabinet can and do survive the defeat of their proposals by the Senate. In fact, defeat of this kind becomes likely when the party majority in the Senate differs from that in the House of Representatives—as it has for substantial periods in Australian history. Of course, the situation is frustrating when a government, backed by its House majority, fails to secure Senate enactment of its proposed legislation, for Senate disapproval cannot simply be overridden by subsequent vote of the House.

Nevertheless, the prime minister and cabinet—that is, the leadership of the majority party in the House—can remain in executive office despite Senate defeats. Or, to be more exact, they can remain in office without holding an election if they wish to do so and if their Senate defeats do not involve the denial of supply.

Here we reach the constitutional question that became crucial in 1975. Should the Australian Senate, possessing legislative powers substantially equal to those of the House of Representatives in other respects, also exercise the power to deny supply and so be able to jeopardize the tenure of prime minister and cabinet? On this point, the language of the constitution, while hardly conclusive, seems to allow the Senate the power to deny supply. With respect to both appropriation and taxation measures (and no other measures), Article 53 specifically precludes Senate origination and amendment. But the constitution is silent as to Senate rejection, deferral, or refusal to pass money bills. Perhaps an intention to preclude Senate blockage of supply and other money measures ought to be inferred from the constitutional provisions that prohibit the Senate from amending such measures, allowing it only to request changes that the House can make if it sees fit to do so.[10] But the more prominent argument advanced against Senate blockage of supply when the issue arose in 1974–75 was not based on the language of the constitution. Rather, it was based on parliamentary tradition. The opponents of Senate blockage contended that an unwritten constitutional convention or custom made it politically illegitimate for a second chamber to exercise such power in a British-style parliamentary system. Britain's second chamber, the House of Lords, had been specifically restrained in this respect since 1911, and the Australian Senate, powerful in so many other ways, had existed for three-quarters of a century without blocking supply. At the state level, it is true, Australian upper houses had upset executive authority by blocking supply as recently as 1947 and 1952. But these state experiences, while of consequence, did not themselves establish precedents for the national government.

Belief in the illegitimacy of Senate blockage of supply rested on more than the record of disuse. Parliamentary democracy, it was thought, ought to work so that the executive remained in office so long (and only so long) as it had the confidence of a majority of members of the more popularly elected house. In Australia, "the more popularly elected house" has always been the House of Representa-

---

[10] From a reading of successive constitutional drafts, Sir Richard Eggleston, a former judge, argued that the framers of the constitution intended to preclude Senate blockage of supply. See his letter to the Melbourne *Age*, December 5, 1975.

tives. Its members, now 127, are elected from constituencies which in constitutional principle are supposed to be roughly equal in population and which in practice generally are so despite some debatable variations. Thus the House of Representatives can claim to be the "people's house" at least to a greater degree than the Senate. And the matter of degree is significant, even though Australian senators are chosen by popular vote. The considerable disparity in population of the states, each electing the same number of senators, suggests one obvious sense in which the Senate is the less popularly based body. Also, the constitution provides six-year terms for senators, with half elected every three years, in contrast to a maximum three-year term for representatives. Thus, after an election the House can claim to have a fresher popular mandate than the Senate, half of whose members would ordinarily have been elected three years earlier.

An American reader will quickly note that the U.S. House of Representatives similarly appears to be more popularly based than the U.S. Senate. Like their Australian counterparts, members of the U.S. House of Representatives are elected both more frequently (and all at the same time) and by more nearly equal populations than U.S. senators. Yet, especially in recent decades, not much has been made of these differences in the United States. Certainly they do not provide the basis for the U.S. House to make a persuasive claim to a popular mandate superior to that of the U.S. Senate. Even the one constitutional advantage given to the U.S. House, the sole authority to initiate revenue measures, does not in practice confer upon the House any greater power than the Senate exercises. Of course, the U.S. Senate can amend revenue measures, as it can any other measures, while the Australian Senate is expressly denied such power over revenue measures and appropriations.

The difference between the constitutional powers of the two senates points to the unmistakable fact that the Australians did not intend to make their two legislative chambers virtually equal in all respects. However much the founding fathers believed that they needed a powerful upper house in order to conciliate state interests, they were also committed to a parliamentary tradition that gave primacy to a lower house. Notably, that primacy meant that the lower house, through its elected partisan majority, determined the composition and the tenure of prime minister and cabinet. It is hard to imagine that the framers intended to make the executive authority responsible to both chambers in the sense of needing majority support in the Senate as well as in the House in order to take and hold office. Such an order of things would have been decidedly un-British in its dubious practicality. Since different partisan majorities often control the two houses, a party government has to be based on one house or the other. And most certainly that has meant the lower house in Australia as it has elsewhere in British-style parliamentary systems. The principle is only confirmed by the practice, established as a constitutional convention in Australia before it was in Britain itself, that the prime minister should be a member of the lower house—shifting there from the Senate (as one did in 1968), if necessary, upon assuming office. His cabinet includes senators, often in important positions, but it is drawn more heavily from the House of Representatives.

Dissolution. Consistent also with British parliamentary tradition is the Australian constitutional provision for the dissolution of the House of Representatives before its maximum term (three years) has expired. Legally the governor general is given the power to dissolve the House, but it has been understood, despite the absence of a constitutional provision qualifying his exercise of this power, that the governor general would actually dissolve the House, requiring an election of a new House, only on the advice of the prime minister. It has also apparently been understood that the governor general would be obliged to grant a dissolution when so advised. Hence, like the British prime minister, the Australian prime minister has an important tactical option: to submit his government (really his party majority in the House) to the electorate at a time of his choosing instead of waiting out the maximum term of years.

The early dissolution option, in Australia and in Britain, did not develop just because of its political usefulness for prime ministers. Rather it seemed implicitly desirable in a system that makes executive authority dependent on a parliamentary majority. The prime minister's majority might cease to exist before the end of his term of office because of partisan defections within the three-year period. To be sure, the prime minister could then resign in favor of someone else commanding a majority in the same House. But such a majority does not always clearly exist. A new election provides the opportunity for the original prime minister to restore his parliamentary majority or for an alternative leader to secure a new majority. In other words, the power to dissolve under such circumstances is a democratic means of trying to remove the uncertainty and instability of executive authority. The justification for early dissolution is less plain, however, when a prime minister with a solid parliamentary party majority simply finds it politically expedient to call a general election before the full House term has expired. Given the strong and cohesive parties functioning in the Australian House of Representatives, this is more likely to occur than an important shift in the relative strength of the parties in the House.

Under the Australian constitution, there is another and more unusual aspect of the dissolution power. Not only the House, but also and simultaneously the Senate may be dissolved, submitting all of its members to election for new terms.[11] Senate dissolution, which can only occur along with House dissolution, has a different and more limited basis from that which underlies the more frequent dissolution of the House alone. The Senate may be dissolved when it has refused to approve legislation passed by the House on two occasions three months apart. In this case dissolution is conceived as a means to resolve a deadlock between the two chambers, or what is really a deadlock between a prime minister, heading a government based on a majority of House members, and a hostile partisan majority in the Senate. Given such a deadlock, the decision to dissolve has in practice been the prime minister's, although the constitution formally grants to the governor general the "double-dissolution" power, just as it grants him elsewhere the power to dissolve the House alone. The governor general has been expected to follow prime ministerial advice here as on other political matters, neither ordering double dissolution on his own nor refusing to order it when he receives a request based on the constitutionally required facts. Thus, a prime minister can secure double dissolution only when Senate and House disagree in the manner described in the constitution.

Even if the constitutional condition is met, a prime minister may not call for double dissolution since it forces him to risk his House majority, and so executive office, in the same general election at which a new Senate majority is sought. A prime minister might well calculate that it is better to tolerate continued Senate disapproval of the government's and the House's legislation than to hold a general election in political circumstances unfavorable for retention of a House majority. On the other hand, a prime minister reasonably confident of retaining his House majority may be tempted by a double dissolution even if he is less certain of winning a new Senate majority. With a fresh electoral mandate in the House of Representatives, the prime minister can probably resolve, in favor of the governing party, the precipitating deadlock between the two houses even without

---

[11] When the whole of the Senate is thus subject to election at the same time, the top five winning candidates in each state are awarded the six-year terms, and the next five the three-year terms.

control of the Senate. The constitution provides for a joint sitting of members of both chambers if, after a double-dissolution election, the Senate continues to refuse to approve the proposed legislation passed again by the House of Representatives. And in this joint sitting, where passage is possible by an absolute majority of the combined membership, the government's majority in the larger House is likely to prevail over the opposition's majority in the Senate.

So the government did prevail in 1974 after a double-dissolution election returned a Labor majority (though reduced) in the House but not in the Senate. The Labor government was able to use the joint sitting to enact the six bills (but only those six bills) on which the Senate and the House had previously disagreed. Interestingly, the joint parliamentary sitting of 1974 was the first in Australian history. The only two previous double dissolutions had resolved House-Senate deadlocks by returning the same partisan majorities in both houses. The first of these, in 1914, produced majorities against the prime minister who had initiated the double dissolution, and the second, in 1951, majorities for the prime minister. Unlike the 1974 Labor government, which after the joint sitting again faced a Senate in which it lacked a partisan majority, the victorious governing parties of 1914 and 1951 controlled both houses. Thus they had much the same capacity to enact their legislative programs as they would have had in a unicameral parliamentary system or in a de facto unicameral system, like Britain's, that allows a lower house to override an upper house.

The point remains that the Australian system does not guarantee that a government, based on a lower-house majority, will have the capacity to enact its legislative program. The constitution unquestionably gives the Senate the power to disapprove of a wide range of legislative measures, and the Senate's elected character makes it politically possible for this power to be exercised by an anti-government majority. For twenty-two of the first seventy-four years of Australian history, the governing party had only a minority of the seats in the Senate. To be sure, in most of those years considerable government legislation was nevertheless enacted, with only infrequent resort to double dissolution. The absence of a governing party majority in the Senate has not historically led to the obstruction of all or even many proposals, either by an opposition-party majority in the Senate or by a looser Senate majority including independents or minor-party members along with the principal opposition party. Yet the Senate's power to defeat government proposals on important occasions has certainly been a political reality in Australia.

16

Senate, House, and Cabinet. Significantly, Senate power seemed to loom larger than it ever had before in the decade preceding 1975. Perhaps this was because in most of these ten years no party had an absolute majority of Senate seats. In a closely divided chamber, independent and minor-party senators often held the balance of power. First, the Liberal-Country party coalition government had to govern without a partisan Senate majority, particularly between 1967 and 1972 when it held less than half of the Senate.[12] Then from 1972 to 1975 the Labor government confronted a similar but much more concerted pattern of opposition. The absence during much of this decade of a partisan Senate majority for either the government or the opposition was new in Australian experience. It is often attributed to the delayed effects of the change, in 1949, to a form of proportional representation for Senate elections. Explained at least partially in a later section of this chapter, this electoral system enables some independents and minor-party candidates to become senators at the same time as it makes it difficult for either of the two major parties to obtain many more Senate seats than its main rival. The effect of the system is to make it less likely, though not impossible, for a party to secure control of both the Senate and the House (as did the Liberal-National Country party coalition in 1975).

During the decade in which the Senate was not controlled by a government majority it became a more politically consequential body than it had been during most of its existence. The change was noticeable in the 1967–72 period when Labor, out of executive office since 1949, used the Senate as a forum for criticizing the government and occasionally, when it had enough allies, for defeating government proposals. Senate standing committees, covering a wider range than the very restricted House committees, were developed and used with some effectiveness. Once, in 1970, the Labor leader, Gough Whitlam, and the Labor leader in the Senate, Lionel Murphy, went so far as to speak of rejecting a government money bill in the Senate and so of forcing a general election.[13] Although it did not actually take this step, the Senate behaved much more independently of the govern-

---

[12] G. S. Reid trenchantly analyzes the Senate's growing role in "The Trinitarian Struggle: Parliamentary-Executive Relations," in Mayer and Nelson, eds., *Third Reader*, pp. 513-26. Another excellent short work on the same subject is Jenny Hutchison, "The Senate," in Lucy, *Pieces of Politics*, pp. 407-17. J. R. Odgers, clerk of the Senate, is the author of an important work detailing the powers of that body, *Australian Senate Practice* (Canberra: Parliament of the Commonwealth of Australia, 1972).

[13] *Commonwealth Parliamentary Debates: House of Representatives* (Canberra: Australian Government Publishing Service) vol. 68 (June 12, 1970), p. 3496; and *CPD: Senate*, vol. 44 (June 18, 1970), p. 2647.

ment than did the House of Representatives.[14] It was natural for this to be the case if only because the governing party lacked a majority in the Senate. Party discipline alone, even if it had been as strict in the Senate as in the House, could not have kept the Senate in line with the government. In addition, however, even government-party senators displayed slightly more freedom than did government-party representatives.

Well before the late 1960s, the House of Representatives had become a highly disciplined party-dominated body. Its members, belonging almost exclusively either to the Liberal-Country party coalition or to the Labor party, voted as party blocs in support of or in opposition to the government. In practice, such voting must mean a regular and automatic parliamentary majority for the government. The House, under these circumstances, plays little public part in checking executive authority. As the limitations of the House's role became increasingly apparent, the Senate might well have been encouraged to assert its power. At any rate, the House of Representatives appears, much more than the Senate, to be the "prime minister's house," even as it is also the "people's house." [15] Not since 1941, when two independent representatives, happening to hold the balance of power, ceased to support a government, has the House itself voted a prime minister and his cabinet out of office.

Finally, with respect to the structure of the national government, a little more should be said about the executive authority since there is no doubt about its predominance in relation to the House of Representatives and ordinarily also in relation to the Senate. The prime minister, holding his office as leader of the party possessing a House majority (or of the largest party in a coalition possessing a House majority), has become leader in the first place as a result of an election by his party's representatives and senators, voting together in a party meeting. His leadership and thus his prime ministership can be terminated by the same parliamentary party that elected him, and that did in effect happen to a Liberal prime minister in 1971. Note that such an internal party process, though involving only members of Parliament, is very different from a House vote against a government of the kind that occurred, as observed, in 1941. In any event, for a governing party to withdraw its support from the prime

[14] Emy, *Australian Democracy*, pp. 294-96, discusses the several reasons for the executive's lesser control of the Senate.

[15] Lloyd and Reid, *Out of the Wilderness*, p. 182, summarizes definitively: "Party discipline is strong and persistent in the House of Representatives and opportunities for sustained opposition are few."

minister in this way is a decidedly exceptional occurrence. The fact that it occurred at all serves mainly to remind us that a prime minister does need to retain the support of his parliamentary party in order to remain in office.

There are usually good political reasons for parliamentary party members to keep their leader in office. Moreover, a substantial number of these parliamentary party members, and almost all of the most important members, are ministers appointed to their offices by the prime minister (although in the Labor party a prime minister is able only to assign particular ministries to those representatives and senators elected by their fellow Labor members of Parliament—the powerful party caucus).[16] Cabinets vary in size. Labor cabinets tend to be large mainly because of internal party arrangements, including the caucus's election of the cabinet. Thus, Whitlam's government in 1975 had twenty-seven ministers, twenty from the House and seven from the Senate. Fraser's Liberal-National Country party coalition government started 1976 with only twelve cabinet ministers, plus twelve other ministers outside the cabinet (thus, a "cabinet" of twelve, but a "ministry" of twenty-four); of the twenty-four, eighteen were representatives and six were senators (with, coincidentally, an eighteen-to-six ratio of Liberals to National Country party members). Almost invariably, federal political practice dictates cabinet representation for each of the six states.

Regardless of their party, state background, or particular house membership, government ministers will have made their way to executive office through parliamentary careers. Neither prime ministers nor other cabinet members are recruited directly from outside Parliament—not from business or other nonpolitical occupations or even from state government offices. Of course, some ministers, before becoming members of Parliament, have pursued careers involving administrative or comparable responsibility. And some members of Parliament have previously served in state parliaments and state executive offices. But it would be most exceptional for a state minister to move to a national ministerial post without a substantial intervening period of national parliamentary service. With access to executive office thus limited in practice, governments can seldom draw upon whatever potential talent and experience in administrative management exists outside Parliament. It is by no means clear that the kinds of abilities revealed by a strictly parliamentary career are the most relevant for ministerial performance. Yet, especially when a party

[16] Ibid., chap. 6, is an account of the relations of the Labor caucus with the Whitlam government.

comes to office after a long period of opposition (twenty-three years for Labor in 1972), the government is necessarily composed of individuals most unlikely to have had the chance to display anything but their abilities as parliamentary debaters, campaigners, and internal-party tacticians.

Parties

Postponing until now the separate consideration of Australian parties has meant the discussion of governmental institutions without much appreciation of the political agencies whose activities so greatly influence the functioning of these institutions. Only enough has been said so far to indicate that parliamentary parties are crucial to the relations between Senate and House, prime minister and cabinet, and prime minister and Parliament. Much the same could be said about any parliamentary system, but Australian parties dominate the political process to an unusual degree and in certain distinctive ways. Their domination is not new. Nor is there anything very new about the particular parties that dominate Australian politics. In fact, their electoral alignment reflects patterns of voting behavior that have persisted over several decades.[17]

Electoral Alignment. Loosely speaking, party competition since 1909 has been between the Australian Labor party (ALP) and a non-Labor combination. The latter, although a continuous electoral force, has undergone several name changes and has been composed of two parties for the last half century. Since World War II, the larger of the two non-Labor components has called itself the Liberal party, thus readopting its pre-World War I name in preference to its interwar labels, National and United Australia. As it was in the past under other labels, the Liberal party appears to be conservative, rather than liberal in the American sense. It is the principal political vehicle of the business community and of the urban and suburban middle class.[18]

---

[17] The largely unchanged shape of Australian electoral politics since 1910 is the principal theme of Don Aitkin, *Stability and Change in Australian Politics* (Canberra: Australian National University Press, 1976). See also Don Aitkin and Michael Kahan, "Australia: Class Politics in the New World," in Richard Rose, ed., *Electoral Behavior: A Comparative Handbook* (New York: The Free Press, 1974), pp. 437-80.

[18] Apart from selections in readers noted above, scholarly works on the Liberal party are scarce. The best known is Katherine West, *Power in the Liberal Party* (Melbourne: Cheshire, 1966). More limited in scope, but filled with information and insight concerning the party in a single important state, is Peter Aimer, *Politics, Power and Persuasion: The Liberals in Victoria* (Melbourne: James Bennett, 1974).

It also has some support in rural areas, but not nearly as much as the National Country party (NCP). Calling itself just the Country party until 1975, what is now the NCP has been the main parliamentary representative of farmers, country towns, and the embattled nonmetropolitan way of life since the 1920s.[19] It has been able to win and hold many rural seats in the House, sometimes against Liberal as well as Labor opposition, and to win Senate seats usually on joint Liberal-National Country party (L-NCP) tickets.*

Holding, as it usually does, nearly one-sixth of the representatives (thanks partly to rural overrepresentation in relation to population), the NCP is ordinarily essential for any non-Labor parliamentary majority. So it was from 1949 to 1972. Only after a landslide victory, of which 1975 provides the sole recent example, do the Liberals alone have over half of the seats in the House (but not in the Senate, even in 1975). Naturally the NCP is most consequential after a close election: when the Liberals win only a little more than one-third of the House seats, the non-Labor majority is slender and within it Liberals outnumber NCP representatives by not much better than two-to-one. But generally the NCP has been so crucial to a viable non-Labor government that the NCP and the Liberals have functioned as a national parliamentary coalition almost continuously since the 1920s.

The two non-Labor parties, while maintaining separate parliamentary as well as separate extraparliamentary organizations, have worked together both in opposition and in government. Their coalition governments are headed by the Liberal leader; characteristically the NCP leader serves as deputy prime minister. Other ministerial positions are distributed between the two parties but often in favor of the Liberals by a ratio of three-to-one even when Liberals do not outnumber NCP representatives by that ratio. Especially since 1949, the L-NCP coalition has been strikingly durable, forming the basis for twenty-three years of government (1949–72) and then for three years of opposition until the coalition's return to power at the end of 1975. Strains most certainly exist between the NCP, now often associated with the more conservative causes, and the Liberals, now heavily suburban, but the strains may be no more difficult to handle than those containing similarly disparate groups within a single party.

---

[19] Among several useful studies of this distinctive Australian party is Don Aitkin's empathic, *The Country Party in New South Wales* (Canberra: Australian National University Press, 1972).

* Editor's Note: For consistency, the name of the non-Labor coalition has been abbreviated as L-NCP throughout the volume, even though the Country party only adopted the name National Country party in 1974.

In a sense, the L-NCP arrangement is just a different type of coalition from that represented by a single large and equally diverse party. Judging by the electoral record since World War II, the two-party coalition is a highly successful conservative political force.

On the other side, though it has held national office for only three years since 1949, the ALP is a longer-lived political entity than either of its coalition opponents, and it receives more popular votes, even in most of its losing years, than does its principal opponent, the Liberal party. The ALP has an impressively reliable bedrock voting strength that has dropped as low as 40 percent of the total popular vote at only one House general election (1966) during all of its losing years after World War II. Its relations with the massive Australian trade-union movement give it a capacity to survive frequent defeats. Furthermore, it has had its victories at both national and state levels. Indeed, the ALP's successes are striking because they started so early relative to those of European labor parties. Not only did the ALP achieve office in state governments around the turn of the century, but in 1910 it was able to form a Commonwealth government based on majorities in both houses of Parliament. The ALP was again in national office during the first years of World War I, the depression years of 1929–32, and the eight years between 1941 and 1949—apart from its recent 1972–75 period of office. Its early successes were plainly those of a working-class party. Even more than the present-day ALP, whose parliamentary leadership is heavily middle class, the party of the first half of the twentieth century was the political wing of the trade-union movement. Many of its parliamentary members were themselves from trade-union ranks, and the extraparliamentary organization was based, as it still is, principally on the affiliation of trade unions.[20] Although never revolutionary or even clearly socialist in a Marxist or any other sense, the ALP has always been a class party. Not only has it identified itself with the interests of manual workers, but it has cultivated a spirit of "working-class fraternity."[21]

With the long-established competition between the ALP and the L-NCP coalition dominating the electoral arena, especially in 1975, other parties require only brief attention. Still, for almost twenty years beginning in the mid-1950s an additional party did play a significant competitive role. This was the Democratic Labor party (DLP), a heavily Catholic and strongly anti-Communist group that

---

[20] D. W. Rawson, *Labor in Vain?* (Croyden, Victoria: Longmans, 1966), treats the ALP's development incisively, comparatively, and carefully. Other helpful works on the ALP are numerous.

[21] The phrase is from Emy, *Australian Democracy*, p. 376.

emerged from the ALP after bitter factional conflict. At one of its high points, the DLP managed to secure over 9 percent of the total votes for the House of Representatives (and almost 15 percent in the State of Victoria). Without electing any representative of its own, the DLP had enough votes in certain House districts so as adversely to affect ALP candidates.[22] The DLP did better for itself in Senate races, electing five senators in 1970 and thus in that year, as it had earlier, holding the balance of power in the second chamber. Losing all of its Senate seats in 1974, failing to win any in 1975, and dropping off sharply in House contests in both 1974 and 1975, the DLP appears finally to have spent its force.

The former prominence of the DLP, however, shows at least that it is possible for new parties to rise under the Australian electoral system. In particular, as noted earlier, the election of the Senate by a form of proportional representation provides opportunities for candidates outside the two major blocs to win seats in the upper house. In 1974 and 1975 not only were independent senators elected (one in each year), but also the Liberal Movement, a centrist breakaway from the Liberal party in South Australia, elected and reelected its leading member to the Senate. Otherwise, however, neither the Liberal Movement nor any other new party has been successful in a national election recently, or more than moderately successful in a state election. Several older minor parties, including persistent leftist movements, regularly run candidates and conduct campaigns without winning or seriously expecting to win. The two major party blocs, which together polled over 95 percent of the total House vote in 1974 and 1975, now appear capable of attracting and retaining their overwhelmingly decisive shares of the Australian electorate.

Organized Membership. The Liberals, the NCP, and the ALP, then, are the party organizations of principal concern. Outside of Parliament, each of the three has a membership organization that is basically federal. Reflecting Australia's constitutional structure, each national party is a federation of state parties. Members, joining parties locally in their electorates (constituencies), are thus directly involved in state organizations, represented by councils, conferences, and executive committees, and only indirectly in the national or federal bodies. The latter are composed of delegates from the state organizations. Structurally, the federative arrangement, with its lack of a large central staff, is similar to that of parties in the United States,

---

[22] P. L. Reynolds, *The Democratic Labor Party* (Milton, Queensland: Jacaranda Press, 1974), analyzes the party's role through the early 1970s.

but the dues-paying memberships of Australian state parties resemble British and European party memberships rather than the looser organizational patterns characteristic of American parties.

Membership numbers are fairly substantial. During the early 1970s, the Liberals have had about 100,000 members (in all of their state branches), and the NCP almost that many. The ALP count is more complex; the party's individual membership through local branches has been about 55,000, but almost 1.5 million additional "members" have been affiliated through their trade unions.[23] The affiliation is really by trade unions as such; they pay party dues on behalf of their members. Significantly, Australian unions affiliate with state party organizations rather than with national or local units (whereas British unions maintain their Labour party affiliation at both national and local levels). Given the immense disparity between the numbers of trade-union affiliated members and the numbers of direct individual members, it is obvious that trade unions, and more specifically their leaders, can dominate the ALP's state party organizations and, through them, the national organization as well. Moreover, the ALP structure is such that control of the state organizations provides great leverage over party branches in the several electorates of a state. At all levels the unions' leverage is increased by special trade-union financing of ALP campaigns over and above the funds regularly received from the affiliated dues-paying membership.

The integration of the trade unions in the ALP is not the only organizational difference setting off one Australian party from the others. The ALP especially differs from the two coalition parties in the extent to which its extraparliamentary organization plays a policy-making role and openly enforces discipline among the party's parliamentary representatives. Symbolizing the relationship is the ALP's requirement that its candidates pledge, if elected, to carry out the principles of the party platform and to vote in accord with decisions taken by a majority of the ALP's parliamentary caucus. To be sure, Liberal and NCP members of Parliament now actually behave as though they were similarly bound and seem almost as likely as ALP members to lose their extraparliamentary party support if they seriously deviate from their parliamentary party positions. Yet party discipline remains less clear-cut in principle for the non-Labor parties than for the ALP, and perhaps less likely to be carried to the point of actual expulsion of

---

[23] The membership figures, together with other organizational data, come from Lex Watson, "The Party Machines," in Mayer and Nelson, eds., *Third Reader*, pp. 339-65, and from updating, particularly of candidate-selection methods, supplied by Judith Walker of the Department of Government at the University of Sydney.

an offending member. More significantly, the Liberals and the NCP, unlike the ALP, assign only very limited policy-making roles to their external organizations. The power to make party policy is meant to reside with the elected representatives and senators and, in practice, with their parliamentary leaders—explicitly so in the Liberal party. Nevertheless, the extraparliamentary organizations may influence the policies that the non-Labor parliamentary leaders decide to adopt. Influence from state organizations flows through the federal party organization, and also, especially within the NCP, directly to parliamentary leaders.

The three party organizations not only differ from each other; each of the three also varies considerably from state to state. On the non-Labor side even the names of state branches of a party occasionally differ, and within all of the parties the state organizations have their own distinctive rules, composition, and practices. This is consistent with the fact that they have always been concerned with state as well as national government. Though they come together in federal party councils, conferences, and executive committees, where the national parliamentary party leaders exert great influence, the state parties (and state parliamentary party leaders) remain substantial centers of power even in national politics.

Candidate Selection. The importance of state party organizations is illustrated by their role in the vital matter of selecting (or, in Australian usage, "pre-selecting") parliamentary candidates. As in other Western democratic nations apart from the United States, in Australia party organizations themselves select the candidates to be presented to the voters at general elections. No intervening government-conducted direct primary allows ordinary party voters to determine which candidates should bear the party label. Party voters, in order to play a part in selecting their candidates, must be members of the party organization. In this strictly organizational matter, each state party determines the relationship between its own central authority and party branches in the state's electorates. State parties customarily establish some method for central approval of candidates selected by their branches, and many state parties also provide, in different ways, for substantial involvement of their leaders or delegates in the actual candidate-selection process at the level of the electorate. In these and other respects, each major party (ALP, Liberals, and NCP) has certain distinguishable national tendencies but not by any means a single candidate-selection practice uniformly applied from state to state. Nor, within each state, does a particular party select its candidates in the same way for House, Senate, and state legislature. Generalizing about candidate selection is, therefore, hazardous. It is common for candidate selection to be entrusted to a body of party representatives elected by the organizational members for this purpose. Often, however, a party council or executive committee elected for various organizational purposes is entrusted with candidate selection—or the selecting body combines representatives from an existing party authority with specially chosen delegates. But regardless of how the body is constituted, its members, often numbering 50 to 100 dedicated party activists, usually see, hear, and question several prospective candidates before balloting to determine their choice.

There are two major deviations from the representational method, in two quite different directions. The first, which increases the participation of nonactivists, involves a plebiscite of party members in a given electorate (for the House or state legislature). Once widely used especially by the ALP, the plebiscite gives the entire dues-paying membership the opportunity to ballot for its party's candidate. This procedure is hardly identical with the American direct primary, however, since the plebiscite is run by the party, not the government, and only an actually organized membership is able to cast ballots. In any event, the plebiscite method has lost ground in recent decades. It is difficult to administer fairly because of uncertain and fluctuating party membership lists, and political leaders appear to regard it as less likely than other methods to produce satisfactory candidates. Accordingly, candidate selection by plebiscite now tends to be replaced by some form of the representational method.

The second deviation from the representational method of candidate selection increases the direct or indirect powers of the central executive authorities of the parties at the state level.[24] Candidate selection by party executives is by no means new, and it may be no more dominant now than in the past. Moreover, it is, in a sense, a variant of the representational method: even a state executive authority, while it is composed of leaders rather than of more numerous delegates, is itself a representative body chosen by party branches and affiliates. Either the state party executive or some similarly chosen (though perhaps larger) state council or conference is used to select Senate candidates for their statewide constituencies. For House candidacies, the state party authority, although it occasionally intervenes directly in the selection process, is more likely to be represented, in various ways and to various degrees, on the candidate-selection body otherwise chosen from party branches in the relevant electorate. By

[24] Rawson, *Labor in Vain?* p. 23.

one means or another, there is an opportunity here for party leaders, definitely including national parliamentary party leaders, to exert influence through state organizational channels. Such influence, however, is not equivalent to full control over candidate selection. Leaders may be resented and effectively resisted in this area as elsewhere.

Whatever their recent changes and continued variations, Australian methods of candidate selection can be understood as an important component of strong and cohesive political parties. Because the political parties are strong, their organizations effectively select the candidates. And because of this organizational authority, the parties have another means for maintaining their strength. Certainly the methods of candidate selection used in Australia are conducive to party cohesion among elected representatives—members of Parliament owe their party candidacies and so their elections to the organizations that selected them to run. Getting elected as an independent, while legally possible, is rarely practical, especially for the House (where only one independent has won a seat since 1949). Major-party support is almost always required as a first step toward election to Parliament, and party loyalty is the price exacted for it. No doubt, such loyalty is willingly and freely given by most of those who want to be party candidates and party representatives in Parliament. And there are many reasons, besides any fear of retaliation by the organization, for parliamentary party members to maintain their cohesion. Nevertheless the capacity for retaliation by the organization, every parliamentarian knows, is implicit in the party's control of candidate selection. It is taken for granted as part of the political system.

Elections

Australia has a well-deserved reputation for innovative election procedures. The plebiscite method of candidate selection might be considered one of these procedures except that it belongs, in Australia as it does elsewhere outside of the United States, to the realm of parties as private associations rather than to the area of government-operated elections. Also, while the plebiscite is of diminishing importance, most of Australia's innovative election procedures are durable illustrations of the national effort to secure full and equitable popular participation.

General Characteristics. In the nineteenth century, the Australian colonies pioneered the use of the government-provided secret ballot— hence the name "Australian ballot" when this now-familiar form was adopted in the United States. Australia's twentieth-century electoral innovations, however, have remained more distinctive, especially in comparison with the practices of the other English-speaking democracies. Compulsory voting is the best-known of these. Following widespread use of compulsory registration of voters and one state's experience with compulsory voting, the Commonwealth made voting in national elections a legal obligation in the mid-1920s. Adult citizens (now all over eighteen years of age) are subject to fines for failing to cast ballots unless they can successfully claim that illness or other unavoidable cause prevented them from voting. Voter turnouts, in consequence, are above the 95 percent mark. Neither parties nor candidates have to exert any of their campaign effort to get out the vote. It is even possible that parties have supported compulsory voting in order to be relieved of the task of getting their voters to the polls. The non-Labor parties may benefit from this system because it brings greater numbers of women to the polls than would be likely to vote under a voluntary system, and women tend to be less pro-Labor than men. The ALP may have good reason to favor compulsory voting, however, as long as working-class voters seem likelier than heavily middle-class electors to require organizational mobilization in a voluntary system.

On the other hand, the ALP suffers from a particular provision of the Australian voting law, namely the requirement that a voter put a number beside the name of each candidate (except one, assumed to be the voter's last choice), instead of simply marking an "X" beside a single name. The practice of numbering candidates to indicate voter preference follows from the distinctive Australian election methods yet to be explained. For the time being, it is enough to say that the preferential voting arrangement, employed in different ways for the House of Representatives and the Senate, increases the likelihood that the voter will cast an invalid ballot. The voter must indicate preferences for all but a last choice among the listed candidates, and this means putting numbers beside the names of as many as forty to over sixty candidates in a statewide Senate race (but no more than about three to six in a House contest). Unless the ballot is thus fully marked, it will not be counted for any candidate for the particular Senate or House contest. Australians call an incompletely marked ballot "informal," as opposed to a "formal" or valid ballot. Over 10 percent of the ballots in most Senate elections have been classed as informal, and they appear to come disproportionately from ALP constituencies where working-class voters are thought to have special trouble following official ballot instructions or their own party's "how-to-vote" cards advising as to the ordering of preferences. Understandably the ALP has sought to change the election law so that voters would no longer have to indicate all of their preferences (many of which are unlikely to be consequential anyway) in order to cast formal ballots.

In addition to the ALP's partisan reason for wanting a change, it could well be argued that the present law involves a curious contradiction of purposes: it requires all eligible citizens to register and to vote, regardless of their level of interest and information, yet it makes voting so complicated that many of those compelled to go to the polls are unable to cast valid ballots. This contradiction, however, is not such as to wipe out the advantages of compulsory voting. Even with 10 percent casting informal ballots, the effective number of voters remains very high—85 percent of the total eligible electorate. And the 10 percent figure is an unusual feature of certain Senate contests, particularly in the recent double-dissolution elections at which states elected all ten of their senators on one ballot. In House contests, the proportion of informal ballots is much smaller, rarely exceeding 3 percent. On the whole, Australian voters, accustomed to preferential voting in state as well as national elections, cope very well with their electoral burdens. Moreover, a voter's correctly completed House ballot is counted even if at the same election he casts an informal Senate ballot. Finally, it should be noted that, while most informal ballots are assumed to be cast inadvertently, some may be deliberately mismarked or not marked at all by citizens who wish to protest against the political system or all of its parties and candidates. The law can do no more than require the citizen to go to the polls and receive a ballot; it cannot, without violating the secret ballot, require that he cast a valid, or formal, ballot.

Although it is not an innovation, one other Australian electoral practice deserves attention because it differs drastically from the practices of the United States and most other nations: Australian ballots do not contain party labels, but only the names of candidates. In this respect, there is no official governmental recognition of the overwhelmingly important role of parties in the electoral process. Australian law does not go even as far as British law, which since 1970 has permitted each candidate to list his party or other political identification beside his name on the ballot. The Australian voter who wants to cast his ballot for his party's selected candidates (as most Australian voters surely do) must get his cues from party sources. Hence, the how-to-vote cards distributed by the parties are of crucial importance in enabling voters to give first preferences to their own party's candidates and to assign lower preferences to candidates of other parties in the order most compatible with their party's calculated electoral purpose.

Indeed, the relevance of party cues is as apparent in Australia as it is in the United States. By requiring the numbering of several or even many candidates, though for a limited number of legislative offices, Australia produces a ballot just as bewildering, without party labels, as the long American ballot can be when (as in many municipal elections) it carries no party labels. Australian parties solve the problem by publishing how-to-vote cards in newspaper advertisements and flyers during the election campaign and distributing them at the entrances to polling places on election day. Voters are allowed by law, and encouraged by their parties, to take their how-to-vote cards into the voting booths.[25] They need them. The next step, already taken by one state, is to put the how-to-vote cards on official display in each voting booth.

The House. The election of the House of Representatives, like the election of the Senate, deserves specific attention. Representatives are chosen in single-member districts ("electorates" or "divisions," in Australian usage) intended to be roughly equal in population, though in fact they deviate somewhat in certain instances. Among the reasons for deviation are delays in parliamentary reapportionment and a disputed 20 percent tolerance used deliberately to overrepresent the dispersed populations of rural areas. In itself, the single-member district system resembles that used in both American congressional and British parliamentary elections. With only 127 district representatives, the Australian House is relatively small. Its size can be increased by parliamentary action but only in conjunction with an increase in the size of the Senate since the constitution specifies that the number of House members shall be, as nearly as practicable, twice the number of senators (now sixty-four). The three-year House term, as observed earlier, is a maximum that can be shortened by a decision, ordinarily the prime minister's, to dissolve the House and call a general election (with or without a Senate election at the same time). The three-year maximum is itself a short term (compared to Britain's five-year maximum for the House of Commons, for example), and it is not surprising that about two-thirds of the Houses elected in Australia's history have served between two and one-half and three years before dissolution. The exceptions, however, are numerous enough to indicate considerable flexibility in election timing.

[25] Laurie Oakes and David Solomon, *Grab for Power* (Melbourne: Cheshire, 1974), pp. 478-89, describes how nearly foolproof a party can make its how-to-vote advice.

So much is relatively familiar from the experience of other parliamentary regimes. The Australian novelty lies in the method of election in each of the single-member districts. Called simply preferential voting by Australians, who adopted it nationally in 1918 after its use in half of the states, the method also goes by the name of "the alternative vote" in other nations. The latter term is more descriptive since the House election method is but one form of preferential voting. It is a notably ingenious means to ensure that the winner of a single-member district election will have an absolute majority (over half) of the total vote even if three or more candidates so divide the vote as to produce no majority winner under our usual counting procedure. Instead of seeking a majority winner through a run-off election between the two leading candidates, the Australian method produces a majority winner in the original contest. This is done by counting the preferences that voters have been required to enumerate on their ballots.

At the initial stage of the election count, all the first preferences are tallied to determine whether any of the candidates has a majority and has accordingly won election without taking into account any other preferences. This is often the case in many House districts (three-quarters in 1974). Obviously, first preferences are sufficient to determine a winner when there are only two candidates. But even when there are several, the district may be so heavily populated by voters of a given party that its candidate is almost certain to secure over half of the first preferences. In fact, safe seats are numerous enough so that very large majorities of first preferences are not unusual no matter how many candidates happen to stand.

There remain, however, a substantial number of districts in which majorities seldom emerge on the first count. What happens in these districts can best be explained by illustration. Suppose that four candidates are running in a district and that the first tally has not produced a majority winner. The election officials then tally the second preferences marked on the ballots cast for the candidate (here called "Z") who secured the *fewest* first preferences. When these second preferences are distributed among the other three candidates, a majority winner may emerge—that is, a candidate whose first preferences and newly assigned second preferences add up to over half of the total formal votes. If this result is not achieved, the next step is to count and distribute the second preferences of the third-place candidate ("Y"), along with the third preferences on ballots whose first preference was Z and second preference Y. The consequence of this count must be a majority for one of the two remaining candidates.

Note, however, that the majority winner at the end of this process may not be the candidate who had the most first-preference votes on the original count.[26]

Among the practical political consequences of preferential voting for the Australian House is the possibility for closely aligned parties to run competing candidates without helping the opposition. The Liberal and National Country parties, for example, can both run candidates in a given district without the risk of an ALP victory on a simple plurality in a three-cornered race. Such a victory, based on less than half of the total vote, is precisely the kind of result that the preferential device is intended to preclude. Of course, this eventuality could also be precluded by the Liberal and National Country parties' agreeing on a single candidate to oppose the ALP (assuming that no other candidates were running). But often there are intense local interparty disputes that make it expedient for both the Liberals and the NCP to present candidates. Given the election system, the two parties can maximize the chances for victory of one of their candidates by urging party voters to designate the coalition partner's candidate as their second choice. The same advantage exists for a single party that, because of internal rivalries, is unable or unwilling to agree on a single candidate in a given constituency. In such a situation, the party organization can present two candidates, asking and expecting party voters to allocate their first and second preferences between the two party choices. Although this practice is now uncommon, it has been used in the past particularly by the NCP.

A somewhat different use of the House's preferential voting procedure, but one that was notably effective for almost twenty years, is illustrated by the tactics of the DLP, the right-wing group that broke off from the ALP. Fielding candidates in many House districts where it had no serious chances of victory itself, the DLP nevertheless has often secured a substantial minority of first preferences, presumably from voters traditionally loyal to some kind of labor cause, and at the same time has persuaded such voters to assign their second preferences to non-Labor candidates (usually Liberals).[27] Both the purpose and the result of this maneuver, particularly in the 1950s and 1960s, has been to make it more difficult for ALP candidates to win election despite pluralities of first-preference votes. Understandably such outcomes appear discriminatory in the eyes of the ALP, most significantly

---

[26] Crisp, *Australian National Government*, p. 144, explains the counting method by means of a detailed example.

[27] Reynolds, *Democratic Labor Party*, pp. 48-71.

when they have been numerous enough to make the difference between ALP and L-NCP control of the House.

With its grievances under preferential voting, the ALP for a time proposed a return to the old simple-plurality, or first-past-the-post, election method that remains so well established in Britain and in American congressional contests. The proposal, however, may well fade away along with the DLP. It is not clear that preferential voting will always work against the ALP, and even when it does, there are principled arguments as well as partisan ones in favor of retaining the method. It does, after all, honor the choices of a majority, expressed through preferences, for a particular party candidate. There seems nothing inherently undemocratic about blocking the election of a candidate who has a plurality of the vote but who is, in effect, opposed by a majority who prefer one or more of the other candidates.

One last word should be said about the preferential method. It has proved to be entirely compatible with stable, majority-party control of the House of Representatives—defining majority-party control to include the L-NCP coalition as well as the ALP. One or the other combination has regularly had a reliable House majority, certainly since World War II and almost always since the introduction of preferential voting. The system may have made it a little easier for the NCP to maintain its existence as an electoral force, separate from but working with the Liberals, though it cannot be said to have caused the development or most of the success of the National Country party. The NCP could function, though a little differently, in simple-plurality elections and could probably win most of the rural seats that it now holds. At any rate, the NCP's relations with the Liberals have been close enough, despite occasional tensions, to provide as much stability of parliamentary support for coalition governments as the Labor party provides for its governments. And, as noted earlier, the House support in each case is disciplined and cohesive. Moreover, it is *majority* support. The House's preferential system has not been conducive to the election of minor-party candidates or independents.

The Senate. Senate elections are much more complicated in their results as well as in the methods by which they are conducted than House elections. Always elected from multimember state constituencies, since 1949 senators have been chosen (ordinarily five at a time from each state but ten at a time when there is a double dissolution) by a form of proportional representation employing a device known as the single transferable vote. Called PR-STV, the method (adopted as early as 1907 for Tasmanian Assembly elections) is similar to that used in Ireland but it differs substantially from the more familiar party-list proportional representation of several continental European nations. The latter merely requires voters to check the name of a single party; seats are then allocated to the candidates of the respective parties in accord with the proportion of votes each party list has received. Australia achieves a similar division of seats as between parties, but it does so much less directly. Voters cannot simply check a party list since no party label appears on the ballot. It is true that each party can and does group its candidates on the ballot in a column carrying a given letter of the alphabet (A, B, and so forth). Yet voters, although made aware of which column is their party's by the omnipresent how-to-vote cards, cannot cast valid ballots merely by checking one of these columns. Instead, as described earlier, voters must number their individual candidate choices. Most voters, assumed to be party followers, first write down the lowest numbers for their own party's candidates, doing so in accord with party recommendations on how-to-vote cards and, in effect, on the ballot, where each group list is ordered as the party wishes. Thus the official blindfold hardly precludes effective party voting, despite the difficulties that some voters have in following the required procedures. The Senate ballot is reproduced in Appendix B of this volume.

Counting the votes to determine Senate winners is an intricate process, specified in the relevant electoral laws (and in Appendix B of this volume) but here described only in general terms. The basic element in the process is the establishment of a quota of votes necessary for individual election in each state (and since 1975 for the Northern Territory and the Australian Capital Territory, each of which now has two senators).[28] The quota is such as to require the equivalent of 16.67 percent of the formal vote for a candidate to be elected in a five-member election and 9.10 percent in a ten-member election. For a party to elect three of its candidates when five senators are being chosen, it must receive 50.01 percent of the vote; for it to have six elected out of ten, 54.55 percent. The quota (that is, the number of votes corresponding to such percentages) may be achieved strictly on first-preference votes—as it is in fact by each major party's head-of-the-ticket candidate. But it can also be achieved, as it must often be,

---

[28] To arrive at the quota, the standard PR formula is: total first-preference votes ÷ (seats + 1) + 1. Odgers, *Senate Practice*, pp. 46-51, describes the details of the Australian Senate's election method. Other works more readily available in the United States and Britain also explain PR-STV; a clear brief account appears in the article, "Electoral Systems," by Stein Rokkan, *International Encyclopedia of the Social Sciences* (New York: Crowell Collier and Macmillan, 1968), vol. 5, pp. 7-19.

through the distribution of preferences. For instance, when a state's ten Senate seats are being filled at a single election (as in 1974 and 1975), a party will succeed in electing six of ten senators if at least 54.55 percent of the voters mark "1" beside the name of that party's first-ranked candidate and then add the numbers "2" through "6" beside the names of the party's next-ranked candidates. Victory here occurs because the preferences flow with a waterfall effect from the top candidate down, successively filling the quotas of the lower candidates until six have been elected. This distribution of preferences for Senate elections is different and much more involved than the distribution for House of Representatives elections.[29] Only when the full number of senators to be elected is not settled by the continuing process of distribution from the top down is a move made to count the second and subsequent preferences on the ballots of those candidates who received the fewest votes.

Even from so limited an exposition of PR-STV, its major political consequences can be understood. Given two contending parties of roughly equal electoral strength, Senate elections are almost certain to provide each party with nearly equal numbers of senators rather than to exaggerate one party's slight electoral advantage, as do election methods that allow the winning of numerous marginal seats. This consequence is plain in Australian experience. The ALP and the L-NCP coalition have, in fact, ordinarily had much more nearly even numbers of senators than of representatives. There can be no large-scale turnover of senators from one party to the other. To be sure, when five senators are chosen in each state, one party must (without independent and minor-party successes) win three seats no matter how nearly equal the other party is in electoral strength. But the chances of the same party's winning three-out-of-five seats in five or more of the six states are not usually high. Thus a party majority in the Senate, if it occurs, is predictably small. And it has not always existed, as observed in the discussion of the Senate's power, because of another consequence of the election method.

This is the success of minor-party and independent candidates. For candidates who can win at least a substantial minority of votes, access to the Senate appears to be easier than access to the House, where every winner must receive a majority. To obtain 9.10 percent of the vote in a ten-member race, or even 16.67 percent in a five-

---

[29] The number of a Senate winner's second preferences actually allocated is equal to that winner's surplus of first-preference votes over the quota. From the ballots of candidates elected from such a surplus, a similar distribution of preferences can next take place.

member race, is not nearly so high a hurdle as is majority election in a single-member district. The way is open not only to candidates of a party the size of the DLP (which held Senate representation continuously from 1956 to 1974), but also to candidates whose followings, notably in smaller states, rest either on personal appeal or on state-oriented political issues. Admittedly, not many of these candidates have been successful. Even the opportunity they have under PR-STV has not been sufficient to disrupt massively or durably the electoral dominance of the two major forces, the ALP and the L-NCP combination.

But the successes of minor-party or independent candidates need not be numerous in order for them to be crucial in a Senate elected in such a way that the major parties will have nearly equal strength. The DLP and the independents held the balance of power in the Senate during the late 1960s and early 1970s. Nor is the balance-of-power possibility the only important consequence of the Senate's election method. Another, obviously of prime importance in 1974–75, is that the Senate, because its election does not reflect the same swing in electoral support as does the House's election, may well remain in, or fall into, the hands of a majority hostile to the House majority and so to the government. Of course, PR-STV is not the sole cause of that outcome. The fact that senators are elected from different constituencies and often at different dates from representatives must also be taken into account, as must the fact that only half of the Senate is normally up for election at three-year intervals.

A few other features of Senate elections need to be noted because of their bearing on the events of 1975. Senators are chosen to represent states, and, although the basic procedures for their election are established by national law, there is some state involvement in the process. In particular, state governments must participate in the legal steps that lead to an election. While it can usually be taken for granted, the willingness of each state government to hold a Senate election is technically necessary before the election can take place at the time recommended by the national prime minister and accepted by the governor general. Moreover, state governments are empowered to fill casual Senate vacancies arising because of death or retirement of senators before the expiration of their terms. The convention, at least from 1949 through 1974, was to allow the party whose senator was being replaced to decide who should be appointed, thus honoring the party division produced by PR-STV even though the state government itself might be in the hands of a different party from that of the relevant senator. But because in 1975 two state governments appointed non-ALP senators to fill ALP vacancies, the status of the convention is now in doubt. Like certain other more important conventions, this practice may no longer prevail.

Constitutional Crisis

The truth is that the Australian political system cannot now be described as it would have been before 1975. Although it is too early to declare that the system has been permanently altered, there is little reason for confidence that it will function according to all of the rules that, before 1975, political scientists assumed to be in effect. Perhaps the force of these rules had been overstated. At any time the written constitution might have been legally interpreted so as to override accepted parliamentary conventions. It was so interpreted in 1975, and this chapter has been written to provide not just a general background in Australian politics but also, specifically, a framework in which to understand the constitutional crisis preceding the 1975 election.[30] That crisis was itself momentous even apart from its connection to the election. In the exciting month from mid-October to mid-November, and in a different way during the following month's election campaign, there came into public view certain ambiguities and contradictions implicit in the operation of the political system. At one level, a conflict existed between a legally interpreted written document and a set of parliamentary conventions, and, at another level, a conflict between two strong and highly disciplined political party forces, each in effective control of a legislative chamber whose separate powers could not be reconciled with those of the other chamber as long as party lines held firm. The firmness of those party lines, nearly inconceivable in an American Congress, is just what an appreciation of Australian politics should lead us to expect.

The Strategic Situation. A brief summary of the political circumstances of 1975 is also essential for understanding the crisis. Prime Minister Gough Whitlam's ALP government, in office since late 1972, had survived the May 1974 double-dissolution election, which preserved its House majority without producing a similar Senate majority. But by mid-1975 it had suffered a massive loss of popular support, as demonstrated in public opinion polls and in a House by-

---

[30] The interpretation of the crisis presented in this chapter owes much, despite its departures therefrom, to Robert Parker's "Thoughts on the Constitutional Crisis," an impressive paper produced for an Australian National University seminar almost immediately after the astonishing events of November 11 and subsequently published by the R.I.P.A. (A.C.T. Group), *Newsletter*, vol. 3 (February 1976), pp. 14-20.

election (to fill a vacated seat). The ALP government's unpopularity was at least partly a result of continued high inflation and of growing unemployment. The combination of these economic misfortunes was not uniquely Australian in 1975; yet the government was held responsible by a people accustomed, since World War II, to almost continuous prosperity accompanied by more modest rates of inflation. Moreover, before late 1975 the Whitlam government did not appear to have a program designed to cope with inflation or unemployment. At the same time, in mid-1975, the government's competency if not its integrity, came under sharp and sensational attack with the disclosure, by the press and the opposition, of a strange, secretive, and possibly unconstitutional effort, through suspect intermediaries, to borrow US$4,000 million * of Arab oil money, apparently to be used to purchase Australian mineral rights owned by multinational corporations.[31] By July, the disclosure had led Whitlam to dismiss from his cabinet one leading ALP politician, Jim Cairns, who was accused of withholding information about his involvement in a related negotiation. On the other hand, the prime minister defended and retained in his government Rex Connor, who as minister for minerals and energy had conducted the controversial loan negotiations but who then seemed to be charged with nothing worse than a mistaken and abortive (though not unpopular) policy initiative. Just before mid-October, however, Connor too faced the more serious political charge that he had continued loan negotiations after the date in May at which they had been officially terminated. When Connor's initial denial of the charge failed to hold up in the face of documentary evidence produced by the broker with whom he had dealt, Connor too was forced to leave the cabinet.

The timing here is important. Just after Connor's resignation, in mid-October, the Liberal leader, Malcolm Fraser, announced the decision of his party and of the NCP to block supply in the Senate as a means to bring about a general election.[32] Perhaps the decision would have come even without the Connor case. The ALP government remained far behind the L-NCP coalition in public opinion surveys, and there was every reason to believe that it would remain behind for

---

* Editor's Note: Throughout the volume, dollars means Australian dollars unless otherwise stated. An Australian dollar was worth approximately US$1.00 on January 17, 1977; during the period under discussion, it was approximately US$1.25.

[31] H. W. Arndt, "The Economics of the Loan Affair," *Quadrant*, vol. 19 (September 1975), pp. 11-15.

[32] The press conference at which Fraser made his announcement is reported in the *Australian*, October 16, 1975.

several months. It seemed unlikely that the government would recover its popularity until the economy had also recovered, and this, it was thought, would not happen until the government's new economic policies—wage-price indexation to limit inflation and generally moderate, orthodox budget measures—had been in effect for about a year. Politically, therefore, Fraser had cause to force an election in late 1975 even without the fillip of the Connor resignation. His own party organization and certainly the NCP, which had vital interests of its own to protect, favored an early election.

Yet Fraser knew that risks were involved in seeking to employ Senate power, for the first time in Australia's national history, to force an election on a prime minister supported by a solid House majority. Fraser himself, upon assuming the Liberal leadership a few months before, had spoken of the Senate's power to withhold supply as reserved for a government that was "reprehensible" rather than merely politically objectionable.[33] Also, he had to take note of the fact that another non-Labor Senate, partly by threatening to block supply, had helped to produce the May 1974 election. To force the ALP government to the polls a second time within three years of its initial victory might well strike all but the strongest L-NCP partisans as unfair. Balanced against that calculation, however, must have been more than the desire, important though it was, of the L-NCP leaders to go to the polls while their electoral prospects were good. One has to allow for the possibility that they and their followers were convinced, as they claimed to be, that continued ALP government meant irretrievable disaster for the country. If so, the L-NCP leaders would not be the first or the last politicians to equate their own office-holding with the national welfare.

In announcing on October 15 the coalition's intention to block supply, Fraser was depending on a very bare L-NCP margin in the Senate. In a chamber whose maximum membership was still sixty, there were at the time only fifty-nine sitting members because one non-Labor appointee to what had been an ALP seat faced a legal challenge that kept him from serving. Of the fifty-nine, two (including the other non-Labor appointee to an ALP seat) were independent of the two main party groups; both of these senators refused to vote to block supply. With the twenty-seven ALP senators, there were thus twenty-nine votes against blockage—and thirty L-NCP votes in favor. The thirty votes sufficed, however, for the L-NCP coalition to move successfully and repeatedly to defer the passage of appropriations bills as they were presented to the Senate each week between mid-

[33] Melbourne *Age*, March 22, 1975.

October and mid-November. Deferral, rather than rejection, was the coalition's chosen tactic, perhaps because of the reluctance of a few senators to vote actual rejection or perhaps (as the Liberal leadership claimed) because deferral could more readily be changed to passage at the propitious time.

The thirty to twenty-nine margin to defer was possible only as a result of a vacancy that a non-Labor state government had refused to fill with an appointee belonging, as had the dead senator, to the ALP. Hence it was possible for the ALP to assert, as it did dramatically and often, that deferral was being voted over a dead man's body. With that senator's vote, the ALP could have produced a tie and so a defeat for deferral of supply. But it would still have been unable to *pass* the appropriations bills, provided the thirty L-NCP senators all voted negatively, since a tie would have effectively prevented passage.

The narrowness of the margin in the Senate affected strategy in another respect. It tempted Prime Minister Whitlam in 1975 to believe that an early half-Senate election, due anyway before the end of June 1976, might change the Senate balance in the ALP's favor with respect to the passage of supply. Generally, senators newly elected from the six states would not take their seats before July. But in 1975 two were due to be seated immediately to fill the casual vacancies that had been subject to temporary appointments. So also were four new senators to be elected for the first time from the territories. The ALP was virtually certain to win one seat in each territory, given the application of PR-STV to a two-seat constituency. In addition, it could at least hope to win both of the casual vacancies if its candidate ran a sixth in each of the relevant states—admittedly a chancy proposition.[34] And the ALP expected that an independent defector from the Liberals, former Prime Minister John Gorton, could win the non-Labor senatorship in the Australian Capital Territory.[35] With Gorton's promise to vote to pass supply, and with four new ALP senators (one of whom, however, would replace the appointed independent who was voting against deferral) and only one new L-NCP senator, the thirty to twenty-nine margin would be tipped to

[34] Awarding the casual vacancy to the sixth leading candidate follows from the law which, logically enough, gives the regular six-year terms to the first five winners and the shorter fill-in term to the next ranking candidate. In each of the two relevant states an even split of six seats between the two parties was anticipated, which meant that the ALP would have been able to win the casual vacancy only by avoiding so much success as to give it three winners among the first five.

[35] The expectation appeared reasonable for a half-Senate election, although Gorton's actual defeat in the December 13 double-dissolution election makes dubious even the earlier expectation.

thirty-one to thirty-three. Or, if one of the pro-supply candidates failed to win, there would be a thirty-two to thirty-two Senate, at least precluding continued deferral. But all of these calculations were most uncertain. Predicting election results was obviously a gamble. And, in this case, the gamble was compounded by the apparent unwillingness of non-Labor state governments, including the two involved in the casual vacancies, to issue writs for an early half-Senate election even if the national government were to propose that they do so.

Nevertheless Whitlam retained a half-Senate election among his options throughout the crisis, apparently assuming that the governor general would be obliged to follow the prime minister's advice to call such an election. The half-Senate election could be a kind of referendum on the blockage of supply, a popular judgment of the Senate's action, preferable, in the government's view, to allowing the Senate to force a House election as the L-NCP coalition wished. Moreover, in the three or four weeks after mid-October, Whitlam's chances of winning a quasi-referendum on the blockage of supply appeared to improve. However unpopular his government had become on other grounds, he secured majority support for his attacks on the L-NCP use of the Senate to deny the government the funds with which to function. Whitlam, himself a lawyer, was at his most persuasive in Parliament and in public meetings when he argued for the preservation of British-style constitutional conventions.[36] The ALP launched a national campaign to discredit the Liberals' maneuver; signs, bumper stickers, and buttons carrying the words "Shame, Fraser, Shame" were widely distributed. On the ALP's side of the argument were many members of the academic community, kindred intellectual spirits working in the news media and the arts, and a large slice of the articulate public not otherwise notably pro-ALP. Opinion polls, almost immediately after mid-October, began to show popular majorities against the blockage of supply, and at the same time substantial gains for the ALP in response to questions about voting intentions. By early November, the ALP and the L-NCP coalition stood nearly even in some polls, in sharp contrast to the situation a month or so earlier. Fraser's popularity had gone down and Whitlam's up.[37]

---

[36] Whitlam's effective rhetoric may be sampled from his Curtin lecture at the Australian National University, printed in the *Canberra Times*, October 30, 1975, and also from his parliamentary speech on October 21, 1975, *Weekly Hansard: Representatives*, no. 20, pp. 2305-09. Fraser's response of the same date is a good example of opposition arguments, pp. 2309-11.

[37] Poll data are from the Melbourne *Age*, especially October 30-31 and November 1, and from polls summarized in the *Bulletin*, vol. 97 (November 22, 1975), p. 13. Chapter 8 in this volume provides closer analysis of the poll data.

The Issue. In fact, during late October and the first ten days of November, Whitlam and the ALP appeared to have won the battle: public opinion seemed to support the constitutional convention that a hostile Senate cannot legitimately force a government, holding a House majority, to resign or to call a new House election. Whatever the letter of the constitution might allow, it seemed that most Australians preferred the Westminster tradition that made prime minister and cabinet responsible to one house rather than to two. One must say "seemed" since the December election results raise questions about the intensity and durability of this preference. Perhaps many—at least many nonintellectuals—who moved to the ALP's side in the first weeks after mid-October simply wanted government to function and perceived the L-NCP coalition as obstructive. Once the obstruction had finally led to an election and so to the elimination of the obstruction, there may have ceased to be anything so objectionable in the coalition's behavior as to influence their voting.

Despite the eventual outcome, there was a time during the crisis when popular opinion seemed to press for a Liberal backdown. It is again a tribute to party cohesion that no coalition senator did back down. Something can also be said for Fraser's own tenacity in refusing to concede defeat when the polls turned against his decision. In early November, he retreated only so far—and possibly just for tactical reasons—as to propose a compromise under which the coalition would pass supply provided Whitlam agreed to a House election, along with a half-Senate election, before the end of June 1976.[38] But Fraser's concession of six months beyond the election date he had originally hoped for was not enough for Whitlam. The ALP prime minister wanted a much more decisive constitutional and political victory than he could claim if he agreed to a House election date imposed by the opposition. He could still believe that Fraser would soon be forced to capitulate completely or that a half-Senate election without a House election would settle the issue favorably for the government.

Time now became critical. Through early November, the government had managed without passage of the appropriation bills. By administrative action, only some mainly symbolic economy measures had so far been taken. But soon, probably in another month, without parliamentary authorization to spend, the government would have been unable to meet its financial commitments or to pay its employees. Whitlam and other government ministers alternated

---

[38] Fraser's compromise is contained in a statement published in the Melbourne *Age*, November 4, 1975.

between emphasizing the difficulties of the impending shortage of funds and assuring the nation that the government could manage somehow—by borrowing from banks or by asking its creditors and employees to wait for their money. Either way, the government would plainly depart from one basic principle of the parliamentary system: it would seek to remain in office and to function without the full legal authorization represented by the passage of supply legislation.

To be sure, the Whitlam government argued that it had the only parliamentary authorization that ought to be required according to the canons of democratic legitimacy, namely the support of the House. In its eyes, the Senate—really the tenuous L-NCP majority in that body—was usurping power by interpreting the language of the Australian constitution so as to contravene modern British-derived practice—the cherished Westminster model. Here the issue was fairly joined. The L-NCP coalition could admit that it was thus contravening practice insofar as such practice was based on virtually complete adherence to the Westminster model. But the coalition's view of the Australian system was that it did not rest so exclusively on the Westminster model as to preclude an exceptional Senate action to block supply. True, the action was decidedly exceptional in that the Senate was effectively blocking supply for the first time in the three-quarters of a century of Australian national history. But the power to do so, it could be argued, had always been implicit in the constitution. Whitlam himself was cited as having accepted its legitimacy in 1970 when he seriously discussed the proposed blockage of an L-NCP government's money bill by an ALP-DLP majority in the Senate.

Breaking the Deadlock. All of the arguments on both sides had been well aired by the second week of November. Both Whitlam and Fraser, and their party followers, refused to surrender. Compromise through negotiation, either directly or through separate consultations with the governor general, Sir John Kerr, had not succeeded. Unless an election were announced within a few days, there could be none before Christmas, and probably none would be feasible before late January or early February. By early 1976, the government's funds and perhaps its credit, too, would have run out unless the L-NCP coalition responded to mounting pressures, as its critics projected it would, and finally passed supply. With such prospects, Whitlam indicated on November 11 that he would advise the governor general to call a half-Senate election. But, as we well know, before Whitlam could formally tender that or any other advice on that day, the governor general dismissed him, appointed Fraser as a "caretaker" prime minister committed to undertake no policy initiatives before an election, and secured Fraser's agreement to the Senate's passage of supply in return for a double-dissolution election. (This type of election was technically possible under the constitution because of House-Senate disagreement on several pending bills.)

These sweeping acts, by a presumably ceremonial representative of the British Queen, stunned Whitlam and the ALP. Most Australians were surprised, too, and so was the rest of the Western democratic world. We have long been accustomed to the pattern by which English-speaking parliamentary democracies, in Britain or overseas, have politically powerless and so politically neutral heads of state. Little attention has been paid to their legally established authority, even when it appears to be specified in a constitutional document like Australia's. Whatever the technicalities, the authority of the head of state seemed safely atrophied from disuse and from observance of the democratic convention requiring the head of state to follow the advice of a prime minister commanding a parliamentary majority. Lawyers, it is true, occasionally discussed the "reserve powers" of a monarch or a governor general, implying that these powers might be used in an extraordinary situation. But the nature or the relevance of any such reserve powers has hardly been clear.

Whitlam was not alone in assuming that the governor general was supposed to follow only the prime minister's advice, even if that advice were to resolve the crisis by the highly uncertain means of a half-Senate election. At the time of his decision to take this measure the prime minister was only somewhat more confident of the governor general's compliance with it than were most students of parliamentary government. He might have had a personal basis for his confidence. Whitlam had had the opportunity to talk with Sir John Kerr both before and during the crisis weeks. Furthermore, Whitlam was the prime minister who, the year before, had recommended Kerr's appointment to the Queen, and what lay within the prime minister's gift—the de facto appointment—also lay within his power to take away by request to the Queen. But Whitlam had such power only as long as he was prime minister. Once dismissed himself, as he was so suddenly, Whitlam could no longer act officially against the governor general. Kerr, by moving swiftly and decisively, had preempted any possibility of his own dismissal.

In this and in many other respects, the governor general's deed of November 11 remains controversial and incompletely explained. Even if he thought that only double dissolution could solve the crisis, might not the governor general have first asked Whitlam to consider this as an alternative to dismissal? Did Sir John Kerr refrain from making such a suggestion because he thought Whitlam so determined to avoid a general election that he would, if given time as prime minister to think over the proposal, telephone the Queen to obtain a new governor general? If Kerr so reasoned, he might well have acted as peremptorily as he did not just to save his own position but also to avert, as he saw it, an intolerable prolongation of the crisis and an unfortunate involvement of the Queen in Australian affairs. Whether or not Kerr had good cause to dismiss Whitlam, there can be no doubt that by doing so the governor general appeared to have intervened in an even more partisan way than he would have done by securing Whitlam's reluctant assent to a double dissolution.[39] His assent would at least have left Whitlam in office, with the material and psychological advantages of incumbency, during the election campaign. Even if he had chosen this course, however, the governor general would have played a definitely political role. Threatening a prime minister with dismissal as a means to obtain a general election, just as surely as the actual dismissal, would have involved a significant break with the constitutional convention that in political matters the governor general should follow the prime minister's advice.

Whatever the ingredients, then, of the governor general's decision making, there can be no doubt that to obtain the double dissolution he had to override a long-entrenched convention against the use of his legal authority under the constitution. In this his action paralleled the Senate's—and it is significant that it followed from his acceptance of the validity of the Senate's use of its power. Sir John Kerr's statement of November 11 was unambiguous on this point. The Senate, he said, "undoubtedly has constitutional power to refuse or defer supply to the government." And, he added, "a prime minister who cannot obtain supply . . . must either advise a general election or resign. If he refuses to do this I have the authority and indeed the duty under the Constitution to withdraw his commission as prime minister." [40] For good measure, the governor general explicitly drew the distinction between Australian bicameralism, with its federal basis, and the British pattern.

Altogether, the governor general's actions, like those of the Senate, rested on the supremacy of written constitutional law over

---

[39] David Butler persuasively states this point in "Politics and the Constitution: Twenty Questions Left by Remembrance Day," *Current Affairs Bulletin,* vol. 52 (March 1976), pp. 4-18, reprinted as Appendix A in this volume.

[40] From Sir John Kerr's official statement, reported verbatim in the *Sydney Morning Herald,* November 12, 1975.

constitutional convention. It is worth noting that Kerr had been a distinguished lawyer and chief justice of a state supreme court before becoming governor general and that the only person whom he mentioned having consulted on his decision was the chief justice of Australia. The practice of basing the settlement of a political dispute on essentially legal reasoning is familiar enough in American experience, though we might expect the decision to come from a court. But this is not the usual British way of settling such matters. Those Australians (including some constitutional lawyers) most deeply devoted to the British model of parliamentary institutions found the governor general's action, like the Senate's, at odds with their understanding of the mainsprings of the political system.[41]

A distinctively Australian variant of parliamentary government emerged from the events of 1975. Until the Senate actually blocked supply and, through the governor general, forced an election—which the blocking parties won—there was at the very least great doubt whether the Senate could effectively or legitimately use its disputed legal authority. Now the Senate's power to force an election must be regarded as resting on experience as well as law. Yet the future of this power is still uncertain. Frequent use, when an opposition controls the Senate, is unlikely because it would appear politically counterproductive in a nation accustomed to stable government. Even occasional use may be avoided despite the success of the L-NCP coalition in 1975. The same favorable circumstances will not necessarily recur.

Generally, the Senate remains controversial in the Australian political system. The ALP has often wanted to abolish it altogether. And many Australians would prefer, through custom or constitutional amendment, to concentrate power in a single popularly elected chamber and so in the leadership of the party whose majority controls that chamber. From that standpoint, the Senate seems an obstacle, or potential obstacle, to the majority will because it is less popularly based than the House. But the Senate cannot be as readily dismissed on democratic grounds as can a second parliamentary chamber whose membership is by appointment or inheritance. Australian senators are elected by popular vote even though their constituencies are much

---

[41] For example, see *Death of the Lucky Country* (Ringwood, Victoria: Penguin Books Australia, 1976), in which Donald Horne, one of Australia's best-known journalists and social critics, bitterly attacks the several forces, including the governor general, who brought about the general election and the defeat of the Whitlam government. In another book published soon after the crisis, C. J. Lloyd and Andrew Clark emphasize that the governor general acted contrary to expectations, particularly Whitlam's, at a time when there was a growing belief that the Liberals would soon back down. *Kerr's King Hit!* (Sydney: Cassell, 1976).

more unequal in population than those of representatives in the House. The Senate, therefore, is in a stronger position than the British House of Lords to exert power against a government resting only on a lower-house majority. And when that power is exerted so as to force a general election, it is difficult to argue (as the ALP learned during the 1975 campaign) that the general election is itself undemocratic.

2

THE RISE AND FALL OF WHITLAM LABOR: THE POLITICAL CONTEXT OF THE 1975 ELECTIONS

Patrick Weller
R. F. I. Smith

Changing Political Patterns

The political context of the 1975 elections cannot be simply described. The elections took place in dramatic circumstances after a period of unusually intense political activity that had disrupted and disoriented previous patterns of Australian politics. In 1972 a Labor government had been elected after twenty-three years of Liberal-Country party rule. Labor's three years in office were characterized by a series of political upsets and scandals which overshadowed the party's proposals for reform. Both houses of Parliament were dissolved in May 1974, and again in December 1975. Australian electors were called to the polls three times in as many years.

After the 1974 elections the economy declined markedly and Labor's troubled attempts to deal with unemployment and inflation revealed how fragile was its command of the processes of government. In this it shared the experience of many similar governments faced with these two problems, for the *conjunction* of which economic theorists had no agreed explanation, let alone remedy. An orthodox, post-Keynesian solution of either problem only made the other worse. By the end of 1975 the effects of scandals, economic difficulties, reactions to some of Labor's more considered and substantial but still controversial policy initiatives, and the activities of an emboldened and increasingly ruthless opposition, had generated widespread uncertainty and apprehension. The apprehensive included those who feared the dissolution of Labor's initiatives in fields previously

We would like to thank Robert Parker, Leon Epstein, Colin Hughes, and Peter Loveday for their comments on an early draft of this paper.

49

neglected by Liberal-Country party governments as well as those who felt threatened by Labor's activities.

Much of what happened during the years 1972–75 challenged prevalent understandings of both the normative and the pragmatic rules of the game in Australian federal politics.[1] As the political battles intensified, each party tried to gain advantage by putting existing institutional machinery to new uses. This raised complex questions about what were proper and what were effective political tactics. The stratagems employed by both sides conflicted with many people's understanding of the working of parliamentary government in a federal system. Specifically, they raised questions about the role of the Senate (in which Labor did not have a majority), the means of resolving deadlocks between the two houses of Parliament, and the role of the governor general that were debated in an atmosphere of excitement and tension. Once the process had started, each side contributed to it. Labor tried to establish the legitimacy of its actions by developing and publicizing interpretations of the constitution favorable to itself. It also tried to ignore some of the institutional restrictions that had customarily been observed by governments, at first in order to implement particular policies and then simply in an effort to stay in office. The Liberal and National Country parties, meanwhile, used similar methods in attempts to cripple the government and bring it down.

The double dissolution in 1974 arose from Labor's reactions to L-NCP opposition in the Senate to government legislative proposals. Labor welcomed a dissolution as a chance to gain a majority in both houses and to show the opposition that it had continuing popular support. But Labor failed to win control of the Senate; the dissolution of both houses in 1975, after the opposition in the upper house had deferred consideration of the budget bills and the governor general had dismissed the Labor administration, was regarded by Labor supporters with bitterness. The election was called against the government's wishes, at a time when Labor was unpopular and the government nominally had half of its term still to run. The importance of the 1975 election lies not only in the details of voting trends, although these have their interest, but also in the manner of its

---

[1] These terms are used here in the sense suggested by F. G. Bailey in *Stratagems and Spoils* (Oxford: Blackwell, 1970). Valuable accounts of the politics of the period have appeared in C. J. Lloyd and Andrew Clark, *Kerr's King Hit!* (Sydney: Cassell, 1976), Laurie Oakes, *Crash Through or Crash: The Unmaking of an Australian Prime Minister* (Melbourne: Drummond, 1975), and Paul Kelly, *The Unmaking of Gough* (Sydney: Angus & Robertson, 1975). Further books threaten to appear.

calling and in the implications of this for the future conduct of politics. The election was part of a successful bid for power by the L-NCP coalition after the Labor party had blundered repeatedly. Labor gave the coalition parties ample opportunity, and they took advantage of it. Even Labor partisans agree that Labor's performance in office was poor in many respects and that, however questionable the manner in which it was called, the election was run fairly. But neither the magnitude of the L-NCP victory nor the resolution of the deadlock over the Budget can resolve all doubts about the pattern of events in 1975.

The period from 1972 to 1975 has been widely regarded as a period of change. Activity and unrest, however, are not in themselves change. Change is "a difference of the pattern of events over time. It is the replacement (in part or in whole) of one such pattern by another, within the same area or unit."[2] The creaking of branches in a strong wind is not the same as the falling of a tree. Certainly the amount, scope, and intensity of political activity in the 1970s was unusual—to find a similar period of questioning, debate, and potential for change one has to look back to the war and postwar years of the 1940s. Moreover, political patterns *have* changed to the extent that what were once significant rules of the game can no longer be taken for granted.[3] The turmoil of recent years has also left a substantial increment of bitterness in the ALP—a party already replete with the cynicism engendered by over three-quarters of a century of direct and acute experience of human fallibility. And in the course of challenging the Labor government, the Liberal and National Country parties questioned, in a manner unknown to the non-Labor parties since the 1930s, not only the role of the federal government in public policy but also the role of government at every level. How deep-seated any of these changes will prove to be is not yet clear.

The purpose of this paper is to explore these questions by outlining the main events of the confrontation between the ALP and the L-NCP coalition in 1975. It should be noted, of course, that to focus on the parties' responses to the unfolding of events is necessarily to consider in less depth many other important factors.

---

[2] Anthony D. Smith, *The Concept of Social Change* (London: Routledge & Kegan Paul, 1973), p. 152.

[3] Colin Howard, Hearn professor of law in the University of Melbourne, has concluded "that basic shifts of power have taken place which create a serious potential threat to stability of government." See "The Constitutional Crisis of 1975," *Australian Quarterly*, vol. 48 (March 1976).

Liberal-Country Party Government in the 1960s

In 1965 Sir Robert Menzies, Liberal prime minister since 1949, retired.[4] Although the Liberal and Country parties won a striking victory at the 1966 elections, the government shortly afterwards lost its grip on the terms of political debate. Since the split in the ALP in 1955, the government coalition had generally been able to keep Labor on the defensive. It had made much of foreign policy issues on which Labor took controversial stands and was often divided. At the 1961 elections the effects of measures restraining credit had brought the government unexpectedly close to defeat, but it had recovered quickly and had defeated Labor soundly at an early election for the House of Representatives called by Menzies in 1963. From then on elections for the two houses of the national Parliament were held at different times. This helped to increase the prominence of the Senate[5] and also meant that Senate elections, trailing House of Representatives elections by approximately a year, became midterm tests of party support—disrupting the cycle of government policy making in the process. Indeed, the results of the Senate election at the end of 1967 may be taken as marking the beginning of the Liberal decline.

The problem of the L-NCP coalition government from the late 1960s to the 1972 election came partly from within the coalition itself and partly from external sources. By the late 1960s the government was aging. Menzies, who had first been prime minister in 1939, had been an important catalyst both in the collapse of the non-Labor forces during the 1939–45 war and in their revival with the formation of the Liberal party in the middle 1940s. His retirement in 1965 tested the coalition's adaptability. None of the leaders who succeeded Menzies was able to maintain the confidence and cohesion of his party or the respect of his coalition partners. Harold Holt was in difficulties at the time of his disappearance while swimming in rough surf in 1967. John Gorton, Holt's successor, had built up his reputation while government leader in the Senate and failed to make an effective transition to the lower house. As prime minister he further unsettled a government already unsure of itself. He questioned established policy orientations but had an unpredictable personal style and was unable to propose firm alternatives

---

[4] Events in recent Australian political history may be followed in the "Political Review" in *Australian Quarterly* and in the "Australian Political Chronicle" in *Australian Journal of Politics and History*. For the basic texts on Australian politics see the references listed in chap. 1.

[5] See David Solomon, "The Senate," in Henry Mayer and Helen Nelson, eds., *Australian Politics: A Third Reader* (Melbourne: Cheshire, 1973).

to the policies he criticized. In some of his approaches to policy—his apparent preference for centralist and interventionist solutions, for example—Gorton particularly alienated right-wing Liberals dedicated to states' rights and free enterprise. His considerable personal charm was evident both before and after his term as leader of the government but proved a slender resource while he actually held the office. William McMahon, inhibited from contesting the leadership after Holt's disappearance by the opposition of Sir John McEwen, then leader of the Country party, was no more successful. Indeed, after his election some Liberals even canvassed the possibility of deposing him and bringing Gorton back. As a minister, and especially as treasurer, McMahon had established a reputation for mastering his responsibilities and for working hard. But as prime minister, without a strong department and a clear brief to support him, he was unable to manage the multiple roles he was called upon to fill. He worked harder than ever but was unequal to the challenge of maintaining consensus in the government while finding new issues and symbols with which to fight off a reviving Labor party.

The problems of the Liberal leadership contrasted with the transfer of power within the Country party, the Liberals' coalition partner. As Sir John McEwen neared retirement several younger Country party ministers aspired to replace him, all of them at least as tough as McEwen in defining and pursuing their objectives, if not yet as versatile. In 1971 one of them, Doug Anthony, succeeded McEwen as leader. Within the government the presence of Country party ministers, who were often both embarrassingly specific in their demands and obdurate in seeing that they were met, was a frequent source of irritation. In the early 1970s, it was notably so.

Besides the problems of leadership and coalition unity, the circumstances requiring adaptive responses from the Liberal and Country parties included trends in international affairs and changes in the context of domestic politics and administration. As U.S. intervention in Vietnam, supported with enthusiasm by the Liberals and exploited electorally by them in 1966, dragged on, the government's advantage over Labor in foreign policy drained away. By the time of the election in 1969 Labor was able to turn the issue against the government. The direction that U.S. attitudes towards China were taking, meanwhile, added to the coalition's embarrassment. The visit to China by President Nixon in 1972 legitimized in retrospect the visit that opposition leader Gough Whitlam had made to China in 1971. The balance of advantage in foreign affairs, in terms of Australian internal politics, thus shifted strategically in Labor's favor.

Meanwhile the government's performance in domestic affairs was receiving increasingly critical attention. As prime minister, Menzies had taken over many of the policies evolved by Labor during and immediately after the war. Under his government they were allowed to run on and run down; they were seldom expanded or amplified. Menzies did not introduce many new themes in domestic policy. By the late 1960s it had become obvious that much of the legacy of the 1940s was exhausted. Menzies's bequest to his party was to present it with a challenge to develop new domestic stances at a time when international trends were working to its disadvantage. The length of his government's time in office had also contributed to a loosening of the Liberals' ties with their supporting interests, especially in business. Whereas the leaders of the Country party not only maintained their links with rural interests but also tried to build connections with manufacturing and mining interests, the Liberals grew away from their old supporters and failed to find new ones. Liberal ministers came to depend more and more on their public service (civil service) advisers. They had the habit of ruling, but they allowed their political instincts to become blunt. Thus, by 1972 the coalition had lost its sense of direction. The hapless McMahon's desperate attempts to provide leadership had no effect. One of his statements during his last months in office epitomized the condition of the government: "Our attitude is a clear one; as yet we have not made up our mind definitely as to what our policy should be." [6]

The Rise of Whitlam Labor

During this period the Labor party was rehabilitating itself as an effective opposition after many fruitless years of internal conflict. It both contributed to and exploited the revival of interest in domestic policy. Its rise was identified with the character and style of its leader, Gough Whitlam, a middle-class lawyer without trade union experience who had succeeded Arthur Calwell in 1967. Whitlam's activities as leader compelled attention. His errors were as impressive as his successes. His was a brittle leadership—brilliant, industrious, and enthusiastic, but also infuriating, headstrong, and tactless. He was careless of the details of otherwise magnificent stratagems and on occasion showed disconcerting misjudgment in party matters, especially when it came to maintaining internal party cohesion and

[6] *Australian Financial Review*, June 21, 1972. This was in reply to a question at a press conference during McMahon's Asian tour in 1972 on Australia's attitude to the Strait of Malacca.

working within the party's tortuous rules and related traditions. In 1968 Whitlam nearly lost the leadership to Jim Cairns when Whitlam resigned impetuously during a struggle to allow Brian Harradine, a controversial delegate from Tasmania to the federal executive of the party, to take a seat at executive meetings. Whitlam tried to force members of the parliamentary party to identify his stand on this issue with the value of his leadership. By reelecting him only narrowly they declined to do so. But Whitlam also had his successes. Assisted by men skilled at "getting the numbers," he secured the reconstruction during 1970 and 1971 of the ALP branch in the state of Victoria,[7] noted throughout the 1960s for its ability to embarrass the national leadership by taking unpopular and self-consciously left-wing stands. Whitlam's biggest achievements in opposition were in conducting election campaigns, harassing the government in Parliament, and developing party policy. By the 1972 election he had inspired the rewriting of the party's platform and had outlined a distinctive set of policies incorporating themes that he had pioneered in his early work as a backbencher in the 1950s. These placed a marked emphasis on the needs of urban dwellers and paralleled a concentration of electoral effort on the outer suburban areas of Sydney and Melbourne. Specific policies were addressed to welfare and distributive considerations and proposed extensive government action on social security, the provision of medical and health care, the problems of the cities, and education. In all of these areas Whitlam drew on the work of experts and professionals. He also made much of the capacity and responsibility of the federal government to intervene in fields constitutionally the responsibility of the states. These included many of the areas he had picked out for special attention by a Labor government.

Whitlam's policies played a prominent part in mobilizing support for Labor at the 1972 elections.[8] The ALP campaign was effective (and expensive), though it did not run as smoothly as some liked to think it had in the heady months immediately after victory. Labor took office with a small but comfortable majority of nine in the

[7] See Eric Walsh, "Broken Hill and After—An Exercise in Self-Destruction," *Australian Quarterly*, vol. 42 (December 1970); Judith Walker, "Restructuring the A.L.P.—N.S.W. and Victoria," *Australian Quarterly*, vol. 43 (December 1971); R. F. I. Smith, "Victorian Labor since Intervention," *Labour History*, no. 27 (November 1974).

[8] For accounts of the 1972 election see Henry Mayer, ed., *Labor to Power* (Sydney: Angus & Robertson, 1973), and Laurie Oakes and David Solomon, *The Making of an Australian Prime Minister* (Sydney: Cheshire, 1973).

House of Representatives, but from the beginning it was in a minority in the Senate.

Whitlam took over as prime minister with a speed that startled McMahon, who had expected a more leisurely and decorous transfer of power. Until final figures for the election were settled and the Labor caucus could assemble to elect the new cabinet, Whitlam and his deputy Lance Barnard divided portfolios between them and ruled as a duumvirate. This was a period of dramatic activity when Whitlam used administrative powers to give effect to party policy. Military conscription was ended; draft resisters were released from prison; the People's Republic of China was recognized. However, even at this early stage questions about his style as prime minister were asked. The duumvirate pointedly excluded the leader and deputy leader of the party in the Senate. It was suggested that Whitlam should have included them in his initial team even though his relations with the leader in the Senate, Lionel Murphy, later appointed to the High Court, were not good. Whatever Whitlam had done in the weeks immediately after the election, he could not have satisfied all his critics. If he had waited for a cabinet to be elected he might well have been accused of adopting too casual a pace. But the period of the duumvirate later came to epitomize for some of Labor's opponents all that they resented about his prime ministership.

The Problems of Office. Even after the election by the Labor caucus of a twenty-seven-member cabinet and the establishment of systems of cabinet and caucus committees, Labor's approach to the opportunities and responsibilities of office continued to reflect Whitlam's own style. But now this was combined, often uneasily, with the talents and ideas of other ministers and the traditions and procedures of a party for which the problems of office had an explosive potential. It is important for an understanding of Labor's performance to examine its special preoccupations and sensitivities, the specific assumptions on which its approach to office was based, and the capabilities and weaknesses of its machinery for making and carrying out decisions. Labor has held office at the federal level only at long intervals and, except in the 1940s, only briefly; it has had more experience in opposition than in government. But the methods and rules for gaining and holding positions within the party develop skills that are of limited use in official positions. The early experiences of the party inspired a distrust of leaders and parliamentarians that has been internalized by many activists and incorporated in party rule books and procedures. To succeed in office Labor ministers had to adapt to the challenges of governing, yet also to retain the support of individuals and party institutions that did not share the experience of governing. It is especially important for a Labor prime minister to pay conscious attention to maintaining his support not only in the parliamentary party but also in the extraparliamentary organization. This is tedious and time consuming, but in the Labor party a leader, no matter how good his performance, is never automatically granted respect and allegiance.

The assumptions underlying Labor's approach to office were not clearly articulated by the leading members of the party, but as the Whitlam government proceeded they became more plain. Although Labor spokesmen had criticized the Liberal and Country party government's unwillingness to make changes, they assumed that a Labor government would operate in the same stable atmosphere that had characterized much of the period of L-NCP rule. Nevertheless, once in office Labor ministers, all anxious to make their mark, rushed to do— and even more, to say—things that worried sections of the population. They underestimated the extent to which a Labor government, however mild and cautious, would disturb existing expectations and procedures—and they totally misjudged the effects of an activist one. The state governments, in particular, were not disposed to cooperate with Labor. Many of Whitlam's most cherished proposals depended on the states' accepting a new disposition of resources, determined and supervised by the federal government. This would enhance the already strong position of the central authority. The states must neither resist federal proposals nor challenge the federal government's superior access to finance. Labor also underestimated the extent to which the non-Labor parties would succeed in identifying support for themselves with the protection of what they presented as states' rights. Labor's expectations about non-Labor's more general response to losing office were contradictory. On the one hand it was thought that the Liberal and Country parties would be content to sit out one or two terms in opposition and concede to Labor the right to determine the timing of election contests. But on the other there was a fear of what the coalition parties might do which strengthened Labor's desire to implement its program as quickly as possible. At first Labor supporters feared less that the coalition parties would force an early election than that they would be able to regroup sufficiently to win the next normal one. This latter fear became stronger as time passed, as did the belief that the L-NCP forces would use any means to bring down the government. One such means, of course, was blockage of supply bills by the non-Labor majority in the Senate. At first it was widely assumed that a newly elected government's legislation would be passed, substantially as presented, by the Senate as well as the House. But this was soon shown to be wrong. There was also tension between Labor leaders in the House of Representatives who believed that the Senate should at most play a subsidiary role in the processing of legislation, and other Labor leaders, like Senator Lionel Murphy, who had helped build up the Senate during the 1960s and who wanted not only Labor's legislation to be passed but also the status of their house to be maintained.

Labor's most critical assumption was that the economy would be tractable. Since the 1940s a low level of unemployment and low levels of inflation had been regarded as essential for any government wishing to stay in office. If unemployment reached 2 percent of the work force, criticism of the government swelled. In 1972 the government was faced with a sluggish economy and shifting international exchange rates. Labor took office with the effects of the 1972 Budget (expansionary, but too slow to save the McMahon government) and the failure to revalue the Australian dollar (the result of stiff Country party resistance) still working through the economy. Significant sections of primary industry, which had been in recession since the late 1960s, experienced a strong upswing in the second half of 1972, and some business leaders, tired of the indecisiveness of the post-Menzies coalition governments, found a change of government not unwelcome. In early 1973 unemployment, which had risen during 1972, receded and the new government could claim that it had made a good start in economic management. But this was fortuitous. Labor had little understanding of trends in other Western capitalist economies and of their significance for Australia. Nor did it appreciate the likely effects of the large increases in federal government spending entailed by its program. Furthermore, it underestimated the ease with which shifts (or foreshadowed shifts) in government policy, especially in sectors used to preferential treatment, could disturb and upset business interests. Even after the level of inflation had begun to attract critical attention, many ministers still regarded pressing on with their own plans as more important than making sure that these plans were founded on a firm economic basis. Whitlam himself, like Menzies, had no great interest in economics and gave his government no leadership in this area.[9] This is not to suggest that Labor could

---

[9] Of Menzies, L. F. Crisp has written: "As a first-class barrister he was always, and more particularly under pressure in crises, admirably capable of immersing himself to such purpose in his brief that he could preside masterfully over Cabinet or Parliamentary consideration of national economic policy. But I do not believe that *economic* policy-making or co-ordination *as such*, much less their

necessarily have foreseen and corrected all, or even any, of the economic difficulties that later plagued it; merely that it did not at the outset identify economic management as one of the most significant tasks before it.

Prime Minister, Cabinet, and Caucus. In addition to problems arising from Labor's style of organization and the assumptions underlying its approach to office, Labor had difficulty in making good use of the central institutions of government.[10] Its approach to making and carrying out decisions reflected the problems we have just described. The government lacked a sense of collective strategy. Individual ministers differed in their awareness of the need for a strategic view even of their own departments, and few tried systematically to coordinate departmental responsibilities with the course of government policy. The cabinet had a limited capacity to assess the government's overall position and to make adjustments in policies as circumstances changed. Furthermore, any opposition finds that the information available to it on taking office makes its election proposals and commitments seem unsatisfactory. Later it has to develop new policies while in office. The role of the cabinet in tackling such difficulties (of which Labor had many) is critical, and the functioning of the cabinet was a problem throughout Labor's period in office.

One of the most common criticisms of the Labor cabinet was that it was too large. Members of the Labor caucus had decided to keep the number of ministers at twenty-seven, the same number as in the McMahon ministry, but not to divide these into a small cabinet of twelve or thirteen and an outer ministry, as had been usual under the L-NCP governments since the 1950s. A cabinet of twenty-seven had obvious drawbacks (at cabinet meetings if every member spoke even briefly an hour or more was taken up), but merely cutting its size would not have resolved questions about who should be named to cabinet positions, how the prime minister and members of the cabinet should regard each other, and what the relationships should be between the cabinet and cabinet committees, the caucus and caucus committees, and other party institutions. These questions were sharp-

more detailed ramifications, held any great measure of intrinsic charm for Menzies. His principal interests lay elsewhere." It has often been remarked, by public servants as well as other commentators, how well this characterization also applies to Whitlam. See L. F. Crisp, "Central Co-ordination of Commonwealth Policy-making: Roles and Dilemmas of the Prime Minister's Department," *Public Administration* (Sydney), vol. 26 (March 1967), p. 38.

[10] For an excellent review of the government's problems see two long articles by John Edwards in the *National Times*, November 11-16, 1974, and November 18-23, 1974.

ened by Labor's traditional distrust of its leaders and its desire for caucus control of the parliamentary leadership on the basis of a platform and policy laid down by the party's national conference and interpreted where necessary between conferences by a national executive. When these considerations were combined with Labor's attempts to introduce changes in many fields of public policy simultaneously, a selection of cabinet ministers whose talents in administration varied widely, and a prime minister who, although a dedicated party member, had always had ambiguous relations with the party machinery, the stage was set for institutional incoherence.

Labor's attempts to control its leaders with institutional hobbles produced a system that had worked well enough in opposition. But in office it required sensitive handling. This was especially true of the role of the caucus.[11] In opposition, members of the Labor caucus could know about and express views on most matters of importance to the parliamentary party. Moreover, they could define these matters in terms of Labor rules and traditions. But in office the nature and volume of government business, along with the transformation of the caucus executive into a cabinet with roles and responsibilities extending beyond the caucus room, generated tensions and misunderstandings. The caucus could not see everything that came before the cabinet and make decisions on it, yet it was unwilling to settle for seeing only what the prime minister and other ministers thought fit. The ministers, and especially the prime minister, meanwhile, did not want to face the party caucus every time a controversial matter had to be decided. The demands of the caucus also exasperated some of the government's advisers, both public servants and outside consultants. Periodically caucus members expressed their frustration by reversing or holding up government policy on matters that could be used to symbolize caucus supremacy. Such actions received much unfavorable publicity. More significant were relations between ministers and the relevant caucus committees. Some caucus committees were too large to permit effective discussion and some were avoided or manipulated by ministers; attempts by ministers to stifle dissent by monopolizing discussion were not uncommon. But where ministers took caucus committees into their confidence, arranged briefings by departmental officers, and made sure that departmental matters requiring cabinet decisions were understood by committee members, useful interaction between the party views expressed by caucus members and the advice given to ministers by other sources

---

[11] Patrick Weller, "Caucus Control of Cabinet—Myth or Reality," *Public Administration* (Sydney), vol. 33 (December 1974).

could take place. Clearly, to adapt caucus procedures to the needs of office took effort and understanding on all sides. Workable relations between cabinet and caucus would not emerge automatically.

Labor and the Public Service. Relations between Labor and the federal public service also varied widely. Like governments in other complex, Western, capitalist societies with governmental systems descended from the British model, the Australian federal government, whether controlled by Labor or the Liberals, and whether it recognizes the fact or not, has problems in harmonizing party political with bureaucratic forces. The incapacities of the McMahon government left the public service expectant and with a measure of good will toward Labor. But well before the end of the new government's term of office substantial sections of the public service, especially at senior levels, were complaining of confusion, low morale, political attacks on the service, bureau shuffling, and attempts at bypassing public service advice. The attitudes of Labor ministers and members of Parliament toward the public service were contradictory.[12] On the one hand, there was the view that the federal public service was a competent, loyal bureaucratic machine and that it should be treated not only carefully but warmly; on the other, that the service was slow moving and conservative and that officers at senior levels had served the Liberals too long to adapt readily to Labor's requirements. These views were distributed unevenly among the Labor ministers and in particular cases individual emphases changed. Whitlam's first minister for labor began by improving public service conditions to set the pace for conditions in the private sector but later turned on senior public servants as privileged "fat cats." The prime minister himself blew hot and cold—praising public servants in public but criticizing them trenchantly in private. Labor's ambivalence was not simply proof that the party did not know its own mind, however. The public service was uneven in quality and adaptability. There were indeed public servants who had little sympathy for Labor's objectives and who showed little imagination in trying to achieve them. Moreover, the public service consisted of sets of organizations with their own systems of incentives and patterns of power. How to assess the capacities and preferences of different sections of the public service and to devise methods that elicit the desired responses to requests from the party in office is a problem for any government.

[12] Labor attitudes to the public service may be sampled in the Melbourne *Age*, April 12, 1973; August 25, 1973; August 28, 1973; November 10, 1973.

At first Labor set out to strengthen the capacities of ministers and to widen the range of advice presented to them. The Whitlam government redistributed responsibilities among the existing departments and created new ones—such as the Department of Urban and Regional Development—to fit its own priorities. The new government also created several advisory commissions with a variety of charters; set up a large number of commissions of inquiry, including in mid-1974 a commission to examine the public service itself, the Royal Commission on Australian Government Administration;[13] and allowed ministers to expand their personal staffs and hire advisers and consultants from outside as well as inside the public service. However, this did not always produce the expected results. Some of the new departments had insubstantial responsibilities and seemed designed for the tailenders of the cabinet or, in one case, for a minister whose real responsibilities lay in managing parliamentary business. Later in the life of the government, changes in ministerial responsibilities led to some random bureau shuffling. The range of advisory commissions and their styles of operating also created problems. While some shunned publicity and drew whatever staff they needed mainly from the departments working in the same policy fields, others, whether by ministerial intention or their own ambition, made controversial public reports and seemed to consider themselves in competition with the related departments. The distribution of functions between departments and advisory commissions was not clear; nor was it clear whether the implications of rivalry between them had been thought through and a strategy based on competition developed. The intention of strengthening ministers by strengthening their staffs was fulfilled to the extent that more staff were available to support their ministers in a variety of service roles, but staff who tried to develop "counter-bureaucracies" came to grief.[14]

One of Labor's intentions had been to try to bypass public service institutions that did not view policy needs in the way that

13 The deliberations leading up to the establishment of the royal commission also illustrated Labor's ambivalence about the public service. The first calls for an inquiry were made by Labor backbenchers in early 1973; the inquiry was not established until June 1974.

14 On ministerial staff see the different views expressed in Roy Forward, "Ministerial Staff of the Australian Government 1972-74: A Survey," and J. M. Anthony, "The Politics of the Bureaucracy and the Role of Ministerial Staff," both in Roger Wettenhall and Martin Painter, eds., The First Thousand Days of Labor (Canberra: Canberra College of Advanced Education, 1975); R. F. I. Smith, "Ministerial Advisers," in Report: Royal Commission on Australian Government Administration, Appendix vol. 1 (Canberra, 1976); and Sir Henry Bland, Public Administration—Whither? (Canberra: Royal Institute of Public Administration, A.C.T. Group, 1975).

Labor did. Where no major institution existed, as in urban and regional development, a new department could be set up. But where departments were already entrenched the government encountered difficulty. It learned the hard way that in such cases there are no short cuts. Unless departments understand a government's wishes and organize themselves to meet them, resources are wasted and conflicts take place. One important departmental reorganization was attempted: in the second half of 1974 the prime minister began reorganizing the Department of the Prime Minister and Cabinet.[15] John Menadue, in the 1960s Whitlam's private secretary and later an executive with the Murdoch newspaper group, succeeded Sir John Bunting as head of the department. Also the Priorities Review Staff, established in 1973 to examine forward economic trends and later used as a team skilled in analysis to tackle all manner of difficult problems, was brought into the department; a new unit—the Policy Co-ordination Unit—with a special concern for federal-state relations was set up; and a departmental capacity to give the prime minister advice on economic matters was developed.[16] Whitlam's dependence on his private office decreased as his department's capacities were expanded. The changes in the prime minister's department attracted considerable attention and contributed, belatedly, to the coordination of government policy in other fields as well. These included economic policy and patterns of public expenditure. But in contrast with the Department of the Prime Minister and Cabinet, the Department of the Treasury, despite several proposals for reconstruction and bifurcation, was left untouched. Labor's problems with the Treasury form a distinct and disturbing subtheme within the story of its attempts to manage a declining economy. Some of these problems will be considered below. For the moment it is sufficient to note that not until the last of the three Labor treasurers took over did Labor's use of Treasury's undoubted resources of information and analysis become purposeful.

For all that, during 1973 and early 1974 the government avoided serious trouble and generally received the benefit of the doubt. This was a time of excitement and initiative as ideas on social welfare, cities, health and medical care, tariffs and protection policy, and other ideas resisted during the 1960s by the L-NCP government were

---

[15] See Allan Barnes, "Happy Revolution around the P.M.," Melbourne *Age*, October 3, 1975; and F. A. Mediansky and J. A. Nockles, "The Prime Minister's Bureaucracy," *Public Administration* (Sydney), vol. 34 (September 1975).

[16] An earlier attempt to provide this had been made under Prime Minister J. B. Chifley in 1949 but had been wound down when Labor lost the election in that year. See Crisp, "Central Co-ordination."

incorporated into ministerial statements and government policy. The prime minister also made much of his attempted redirection of Australia's role in foreign affairs. The lack of coordination in some areas of government activity could be dismissed as the inevitable and pardonable result of the party's inexperience in office and its attempts to make up for lost time.

In the area of economics a number of decisions made in this period stand out: the restructuring of the Tariff Board to establish the Industries Assistance Commission (covering assistance to primary as well as secondary industry), a 25 percent cut in tariffs, and the handling of the report of the task force, chaired by Herbert Coombs, on the expenditure patterns of the previous government. In 1973 these actions were widely praised as indicating the government's commitment to economic rationality. Later, when the economy slumped, however, the tariff cut was blamed for all manner of ills and the Coombs task force report became an embarrassment. At first it aroused the hostility of interests (rural interests were especially aggrieved) which saw their government assistance marked for withdrawal—even before the government had decided on specific recommendations. Then, when the consequences for government popularity of cutting back on previous commitments aroused concern among the Labor leaders, the extent of government backtracking was clear to see. The Budget of 1973 was unexciting and, as far as steering the economy goes, neutral. However, the government later began a zigzag course in economic affairs, first taking decisions and then, under pressure of events, reversing them.[17] It was reluctant to come to terms with the problem of inflation and sought refuge in soft and ineffective options. One of these was to seek a constitutional amendment to give the federal government power to control prices. But the legislation submitting the matter to referendum was passed in the Senate only after the Democratic Labor party had succeeded in altering the amendment so as to also give the federal government the power to control incomes. At this, large sections of the trade union movement were horrified. Both proposals, when put to the people in December 1973, were defeated. In 1973 the government also suffered badly at a by-election for the seat of Parramatta, retained by a Liberal candidate, after it had made an unpopular decision to locate a new airport nearby. At the time this seemed to be no more than a tactical blunder. Later it would be seen to be part of a wider pattern.

---

[17] See John Edwards's articles in the *National Times*, cited in note 10.

The L-NCP in Opposition and the 1974 Elections. After twenty-three years of government, the transition to opposition had a traumatic effect on the Liberal and Country parties, particularly in the early months when they assumed that they would be in opposition for at least six years. In their leadership election they rejected the candidates who might be regarded as divisive in favor of Bill Snedden, a man apparently without convictions beyond a belief in consensus. Snedden managed to keep the party together when many feared it would distintegrate; but his positive achievements were few. He was unable to get the party working together or to match Whitlam on the floor of the House. The Country party too had its problems. At the state level some branches considered union with the DLP, but the alliance proved short-lived and ineffective. As long as the party's rural support remained solid and no redistribution of electoral boundaries was accepted, its future was assured. In Parliament the leading Country party members adapted quickly to opposition and were to be the Labor government's toughest opponents.

In the first eighteen months the two opposition parties elected separate executives, but they still voted together on almost all occasions. Gradually they used their numbers in the Senate to amend, then reject, Labor legislation. In September 1973 Anthony, the Country party leader, first broached the idea of using the Senate to withhold supply and force an early election. The activities of the non-Labor senators caused a sense of frustration to develop which erupted in the "Gair affair." A half-Senate election was due in May 1974, and, in the hope of engineering Labor control of the Senate, Whitlam appointed Senator Vince Gair, long-time leader of the DLP, as ambassador to Eire; Whitlam expected, of course, that the Labor candidate would win Gair's seat.[18] But the mechanics of the operation were bungled and before Gair formally resigned, the Queensland premier instructed the state governor to issue the Senate writs. Gair's seat thus became a casual vacancy which would be filled by the state parliament.

At the same time the Liberals whipped up a feeling of moral outrage about the Gair affair and decided to break with convention by using their numbers in the Senate to delay supply. Whitlam, who had contemplated calling a double dissolution in the previous few months, took up the challenge and at the first technical step to stop supply asked the governor general to dissolve both houses.

The 1974 election campaign was dull—as one commentator put it, " '72 champagne recycled from the dustbin." The Liberals were

---

[18] See *New Accent*, April 26, 1974, and Melbourne *Age*, April 11, 1974.

not ready for it. The new national policy research unit, formed to provide assistance in policy development, had not yet got off the ground. The L-NCP policy statement, grandiosely called *The Way Ahead,* was dreamed up by some of the party's leaders in a five-day work session. It was a "me-too" document, accepting many of Labor's initiatives, but without coherence or logic. For his part, Whitlam pleaded for a "fair go," repeating the promises of 1972 and asking for time to fulfill them. In the campaign Snedden forced Whitlam to discuss inflation, but then the consumer price index figures for the March quarter fortuitously showed a slowing of inflation and allowed Whitlam to argue that he had inflation beaten. The Labor government was returned, but with its majority reduced from nine to five in the House of Representatives and without the majority it so badly needed in the Senate.

June 1974 to June 1975: The Beginning of the End

In retrospect the election of 1974 was to be the highpoint of the Labor party's reign. Whitlam became the first Labor leader ever to win two successive federal elections; the election victory was heralded as a reaffirmation of the government's mandate. But in fact it fell far short of that. Without a majority in the Senate, the government could still not get its legislation accepted, and as the economic climate deteriorated the Senate obstructed more and more of the important bills.

The historic joint sitting of the House and Senate allowed the Labor party to pass the six bills that had been the official cause of the double dissolution, and Medibank, a controversial scheme for financing medical and hospital care, became law. But this was a rare victory. The economic problems that would eventually cause the government's downfall plagued the cabinet. Figures produced in the week after the election showed that inflation was still soaring; the small rise in the consumer price index of the January quarter, which Whitlam had cited so frequently during the campaign, proved to have been a false dawn. Unemployment increased consistently, from under 100,000 at the time of the 1974 election to over 300,000 in late 1975.

Labor ministers were faced with the classic dilemma of any reformist government. They believed that they had to continue to develop their new programs because they were electorally committed to them; yet at the same time their economic advisers were arguing against any further increases in public expenditure. Further, financial restraint caused unrest in the caucus as many backbenchers, acting out their traditional role as the self-appointed conscience of the party, opposed measures that might reduce the flow of benefits to their supporters.

Within a week of the election Whitlam and his close advisers had been warned by the Treasury of the parlous state of the economy. The Treasury put a case for stringent measures that included rises in income tax, in the excise on petrol, and in postal charges. Eventually the Treasury's ideas were accepted by Whitlam's inner circle, who produced a "mini-budget," but this the cabinet rejected, allowing only the new postal charges and a rise in the pension rate. As a weapon designed to counter inflation, the mini-budget was a farce, but the ad hocery that spawned it continued throughout the budget process in 1974 and was indicative of the Labor government's approach to planning and decision making.

When the cabinet began to formulate its own budget strategy, the Treasury continued to argue for tough measures and a budget surplus. Most ministers remained wedded to an expansion of public spending, and the 1974 budget process began a long and often bitter confrontation between the Treasury and the ministers. As one correspondent described it:

> The week of the Budget Cabinet saw a situation emerge where virtually open war was declared between the public servants of the Treasury and the Government ministers who had to take responsibility for rational economic policy. It led to the appointment of a special committee of mainly outside advisers, headed by Dr. H. C. Coombs, to provide the Government with some alternative proposals to the single course of action upon which the Treasury Department insisted. The warfare was so open that the civil servants and the politicians were seeking public allies. The Treasury fed information on the content of confidential Cabinet Submissions to uncritical journalists, senior Cabinet Ministers talked openly about the disagreements with the Treasury, and made no secret at all of their disenchantment with its role.[19]

In the original background papers presented to the week-long cabinet meeting that determined the shape of the Budget, the Treasury argued for a surplus of $320 million. Its advice was, possibly deliberately, ambiguous, and, as some ministers quickly calculated, its recommendations were in fact likely to lead to a surplus of around

---

[19] *Australian Financial Review*, November 5, 1975.

$1,320 million. Nevertheless, the demands for moderation were rejected so completely that there was no restraint of expenditure proposals and the 1974 Budget finally led to a massive increase in the government's plans, particularly in areas like education and urban development. This dispute was the best (or worst) example of poor relations between Labor ministers and the public service. It epitomized a problem that bedevilled the whole administration.

In these budget disputes the demands for an expansionist policy had been led by Jim Cairns. After the election, the caucus had reelected the twenty-six ministers who survived, showing a conservatism that depressed those who had hoped that some of the proven failures would be discarded. But the caucus did choose a new deputy prime minister. The loyal but uninspiring Lance Barnard was replaced by Cairns, leader of the left, advocate of civil rights, acknowledged champion of the anti-Vietnam moratorium marches of the late 1960s and early 1970s, the man who publicly argued that principle was more important than office. Cairns is one of the greatest enigmas of the Labor government; he promised much in opposition but failed in government, at least in part because he failed to translate his soaring visions into administrative sense.[20]

Cairns had challenged the Treasury's economic plans in the 1974 Budget and in November he was given the job of treasurer. Rumors, totally unfounded, even suggested that he would challenge Whitlam for the prime ministership. In February 1975, at the biennial Labor party conference, he was at the height of his power. Amidst the undistinguished debates, two incidents stand out. First, the conference resolved that a department of economic planning should be founded, and Cairns fully supported such a challenge to the Treasury's hegemony. Then, in one of the keynote speeches, Cairns argued that, as Australia had a mixed economy, the government had to give greater support to the private sector. This public change of emphasis was all the more remarkable in that it was Cairns who had announced it.

The First Whiffs of Disaster. Yet even at this high point of Cairns's career the seeds of his and the government's disastrous decline could be seen. In December, despite a public furor, Cairns appointed as his private secretary Juni Morosi, a notably good-looking grandmother in her early forties, who had come to Australia from the Philippines. At first much of the comment referred to her looks, but it became

[20] In his book, *The Quiet Revolution* (Melbourne: Gold Star, 1972), written while Labor was still in opposition, Cairns tried to describe the type of society he wanted to achieve.

more serious. She had been connected with a series of companies that had collapsed, and her husband also held government appointments. Even more significant, she controlled access to the treasurer. Cairns's influence had depended on his close ties with the caucus. These were now cut; it became difficult to gain admission to his office, and he lost sympathy and support.

At the same time Cairns's reputation as a minister declined. As an advocate of spending or a proponent of broad schemes he had been effective; but as treasurer, in a job where detailed paperwork was required and restraint was needed, he was not a success. Unable to refuse good causes, he became known as "Dr. Yes." By the time the loans affair broke, his reputation was in tatters.

Several other disasters had also hit Labor in the months between October 1974 and June 1975. In an election for the Northern Territory Legislative Assembly, Labor won no seats at all; in a Queensland state election it won only eleven seats and 36 percent of the vote. Then when Darwin was devastated by a cyclone on Christmas Day 1974, Whitlam flew back from Europe to view the ruins, but only briefly; he quickly resumed his tour of Greece and was widely criticized for seeming so keen to get away from Australia again.

In March Lionel Murphy, leader of the Labor party in the Senate, was appointed to a vacancy on the High Court. The Liberal premier of New South Wales announced that—as Murphy's seat in the Senate had been vacated for political reasons—he might not follow the usual convention of appointing a Labor nominee to replace Murphy. Despite ineffective disapproval from Snedden, still Liberal leader, the premier finally appointed a "political neuter," the elderly mayor of a country town. This nominee would vote eventually against withholding supply, but the precedent was created. When a Queensland Labor senator died later that year, the CP state premier selected to replace him an anti-Whitlam puppet who masqueraded as a good Labor man. Although at the time of the constitutional crisis this second nominee was not sitting because his position had been legally challenged, the failure to appoint a Labor man gave the opposition the numbers they required to withhold supply. Again the non-Labor forces were to break long-standing conventions in their attempts to destroy the Labor government.

Yet, despite a barrage of disasters and incompetence, despite the raging inflation and rising unemployment, Whitlam's reputation as a campaigner still held. In February many Liberals were talking of stopping supply but feared that, if they did, Whitlam would once again pull the election out of the fire.

June to November 1975: The Decline and
Fall of the Labor Government

The Loans Affair. Although the "loans affair" was only revealed to public scrutiny in June 1975, its history can be traced to a meeting of the Executive Council on the previous December 13.[21] Then, unknown to Parliament and indeed to many members of the cabinet, the Executive Council had given the minister for minerals and energy, Rex Connor, the authority to try to raise a loan for temporary purposes of US$4,000 million. After the initial authority lapsed, a second Executive Council meeting renewed Connor's authority to raise a loan this time of US$2,000 million. The idea of such massive loans had been suggested late in 1974 and was supported in particular by Cairns and Connor. In theory, since any loan for permanent purposes needed the authority of the Loan Council, the loan to be raised was to be considered for temporary purposes. But its real purposes were never clearly defined; there was some vague notion of "buying back the farm," of allowing the government to secure equity in most of the large mineral developments. Yet even after the plans were exposed to public view, no one explained precisely what the massive loan would have been used for; it was a case of getting the money first and then deciding what to do with it.

The decision to raise the money was itself an important step. But even more important was the ministers' decision to raise it through unusual channels. Instead of using the Treasury's overseas contacts in New York, London, and Switzerland, Connor and the permanent head of his department, Sir Lennox Hewitt (who had formerly been head of the Prime Minister's Department), worked through shady characters on the edge of the business world who earlier had indicated that money might be available. These foreign "funny money" advocates promised that the money was almost certainly available if only the Australian government would commit itself slightly more specifically. In retrospect it seems likely that the money was never available; the great irony of the loans affair is that the Labor ministers, blundering around without any thought of personal gain, were taken in by vague promises and destroyed themselves without raising a cent.

The most publicized of these funny money merchants was Tirath Khemlani, a London-based Pakistani who had previously dealt in

---

[21] For details on the loans affair, see particularly Lloyd and Clark, *Kerr's King Hit!* All the newspapers, particularly the Melbourne *Age*, ran detailed coverage of the revelations.

commodities. He had entered the money business only in response to rumors that the Australian government was interested in raising "a massive loan." At one stage the Treasury did check Khemlani's credentials with Scotland Yard (an unauthorized, if reasonable, inquiry that was regarded in some circles as part of the Treasury's conspiracy when it was made public), but only discovered that he neither had a criminal record nor was an undischarged bankrupt. Scotland Yard's clearance did not confirm whether Khemlani was a man to be trusted in such a transaction or even whether he had any capacity to raise vast sums of money.

The first public intimations of these strange loan-raising efforts were made in the House on May 20. In reply to a question asked during a scheduled question period by the deputy leader of the opposition and based reputedly on evidence leaked from the Treasury about Connor's loan-raising activities, Whitlam abruptly announced that Connor's authority to raise the loan had been revoked. Then, owing to a further series of leaks, again reputedly direct from the Treasury, and to some skillful investigative reporting, particularly by the Melbourne *Age*, more facts gradually came to light. They appeared slowly enough to keep the sensational affair in the headlines for weeks on end. It soon became public knowledge that Cairns had also issued four letters to various acquaintances authorizing them to make inquiries on behalf of the Australian government into the possibilities of raising loans. One of these letters was very general in its scope, being addressed merely "To Whom It May Concern."

When three of these letters came to light, Whitlam reshuffled his cabinet, shifting Cairns from the Treasury on the ground that the issuing of the letters was an indiscretion that disqualified him from holding the post of treasurer. Cairns had further been discredited by the revelation that his son, who was his electorate secretary, had used his position on the treasurer's staff to his own advantage in business dealings in Fiji. Cairns chose the portfolio of environment and conservation, thus associating himself with the new cause of the 1970s.

On June 4 Cairns was asked in the House whether he had offered a commission to his intermediaries in any of the letters. He denied categorically that any such promise had been made or that he had authorized his contacts to do anything but make inquiries. Then on June 10 the fourth letter became public; it specifically promised a 2.5 percent brokerage fee in terms that clearly conflicted with Cairns's denial of June 4. On July 1 Whitlam finally sacked Cairns on the ground that he had misled Parliament.

It had always been assumed that the leader of the Labor party had the power to reshuffle ministers but not to dismiss them. Whitlam now proved that, if the prime minister could retain the support of the party caucus, he could sack ministers whose errors were great enough. In the next caucus meeting Cairns stood for the vacancy caused by his own dismissal. In effect he forced the party to choose between himself and Whitlam, for it was inconceivable that Whitlam would have allowed Cairns to be reinstated. In fact Cairns only got a third of the votes and Whitlam's actions were endorsed.

In an attempt to defuse the issue Whitlam recalled Parliament, then in recess, for a one-day session. He tabled a massive number of papers, none of which implicated any minister other than Cairns. But the opposition was still looking for evidence that would involve Whitlam. In the Senate members of the opposition used their numbers to call six public servants before the bar of the Senate, but under instruction from their ministers the public servants refused to answer any questions. One Adelaide builder who had acted as an Australian contact for Khemlani was also called, but provided no new information. For a time it looked as though the loans affair had finally run its course.

The Bass By-election and Labor's Attempts To Close Ranks. In the midst of this furor, the Labor party met a shattering by-election defeat. Lance Barnard, the minister of defense and, before June 1974, the deputy prime minister, had become tired of politics, particularly as he felt that Whitlam might have lobbied harder on his behalf when he had been challenged by Cairns. He wanted to retire and asked Whitlam to redeem a promise made earlier of a diplomatic post. Barnard resigned and was later appointed ambassador to the Scandinavian countries. The by-election that was held for his Tasmanian seat of Bass caught the Labor party totally unprepared. Its national reputation was in tatters, the state Labor government was equally unpopular, and the local party organization was nonexistent. The Labor party had no strong candidate, and the man it chose to run proved unbelievably inept. By contrast the Liberal party had carefully courted the Tasmanian electors and, two months before the by-election, had chosen a personable ex-colonel who, even though he was new to Tasmania, was hard working and presentable.

Although a number of Labor ministers went to Tasmania to campaign on behalf of their candidate, the Labor party was annihilated. A swing of almost fourteen percentage points reduced the Labor party's vote from 54 percent to 40.2 percent. The defeat was as traumatic for Labor as their victory was encouraging to the Liberals. The federal secretary of the Labor party wrote a devastating critique of the events leading up to the by-election, of the performance of the government, and of the lack of organization of the Tasmanian party. Of the Labor government he commented:

> It is seen as an incompetent and confused administration and this largely among traditional Labor supporters. Those who have indicated in the polls that they would desert us in an election are in my view not the traditional swinging voters exclusively, but traditional Labor voters who feel an acute sense of disillusionment and betrayal.

In devastating style, he concluded: "We look like a party of junketeers who don't expect to be in office often or long." [22]

For two months after Bass the Labor party desperately tried to improve its electoral image. A reshuffling of the cabinet brought forward some of the party's ministerial successes; caution, pragmatism, and a greater acceptance of the private sector replaced the fuzzy ideological approach of many of the older members of the party. A new system of cabinet committees replaced the earlier ones which had been allowed to wither away after the 1974 election. These committees were tighter, more exclusive, backed by high-powered groups of officials and heavily influenced by the revived Department of the Prime Minister and Cabinet. By late August 1975 the government had begun to develop some internal cohesion and was facing up to the problems earlier created by deficient machinery. The August Budget introduced by the new treasurer, Bill Hayden, emphasized restraints on the growth of public expenditure and was widely regarded as responsible. Fraser announced that, given the current state of information, the Budget would be passed. While some welcomed this stand, others in his own party and particularly the leading members of the Country party were quick to point out the qualification and to argue that Fraser had not ruled out the possibility of an election.

The Crisis. The polls showed that the Labor government was still unpopular and that the Liberals would gain a landslide victory if an election were held. Fraser publicly agonized over stopping the Budget. He consistently looked for a pretext that would justify the opposition's taking advantage of its numbers in the Senate and was probably about to argue that the whole performance of the govern-

---

[22] The *National Times* (August 11, 1975) published the whole report, which had been intended, of course, for internal party consumption only.

ment was extraordinary and reprehensible, when the loans affair reerupted and the Labor party played into his hands. Khemlani, disappointed that his authority had been revoked, flew to Australia, and telex messages in his possession showed that Connor had continued to be involved in loan-raising negotiations after May 20. Whitlam thereupon sacked Connor for misleading Parliament and, after a stormy meeting, the caucus endorsed the prime minister's action. The scandal was all that the Liberals required. Since the opposition had an effective majority in the Senate after the premier of Queensland had broken yet another convention by replacing a deceased Labor senator with a man opposed to the Labor government, Fraser announced that the opposition would defer the Budget until an election was announced.

In announcing this decision Fraser emphasized that, since the Senate had the constitutional right to reject the Budget and since the government's performance had been so bad, it was only fitting that the voters should be allowed to pass judgment. The supremacy of Parliament, he claimed, required that, if a government could not get supply through Parliament, it should immediately go to the people. By contrast Whitlam adopted his usual strategy of trying to crash through obstacles. He claimed that by convention the government depended on a majority in the lower house for its existence and that since his party had never been defeated there he would continue to govern and would send his budget bills up to the Senate until it agreed to pass them.

At this stage, and for the remainder of the crisis up to November 11, Whitlam assumed that the governor general would act only on the advice of his ministers, and Whitlam has since declared that at no time was he given any indication by the governor general that this would not happen. Publicly Whitlam claimed that the governor general would act only on advice, an assumption that proved to be totally unwarranted. Fraser challenged this interpretation; he argued, with the support of some lawyers in his party, that the governor general could act independently to break the deadlock and indeed might even be obliged to dismiss Whitlam if he insisted on governing without supply.

For four weeks the deadlock continued. The polls began to show a swing back to Labor as Whitlam and his supporters addressed mass meetings throughout the country. Rumors that Liberal senators were about to cross the floor and let the budget bills pass were common, but, although some senators only gave qualified support to blocking supply, none seriously suggested that he would change sides. Nor was that surprising. Any such action would have meant the loss of Liberal endorsement and thereby political suicide.

In an atmosphere of crackling tension, each side used Parliament as a forum to attack the other. At one stage Khemlani flew back to Australia again but, though he brought several suitcases of documents, he produced nothing that could implicate Whitlam. At the same time Whitlam hinted that he might call a half-Senate election which, as even Fraser feared, might conceivably give the government a temporary majority in the Senate.

Since no federal government had previously attempted to govern without supply, no one knew how long money would last. In some departments it was lasting better than others; in all it seemed likely to run out by mid-December, at which time the government would be unable to pay the public servants' salaries. Several alternative arrangements were explored, including a system of guarantees by the government to cover vouchers issued by the banks in lieu of pay until the crisis ended. But none of these alternative schemes had been thought through by November 11.

On November 7 Fraser offered a compromise. He said that he was prepared to pass the Budget if the government agreed to hold a general election at the same time as the next half-Senate election, which had to be held before the end of June 1976. Early on November 11 he put this proposal to Whitlam, who rejected it. Whitlam then proposed to the Labor caucus that a half-Senate election be held and obtained caucus approval for this step. He telephoned the governor general, told him of his plans, and made an appointment to have that decision ratified. Instead, when he arrived, Whitlam was given, without comment, the notice of his own dismissal. It had obviously been drafted long before that morning. Kerr later revealed that he had received advice from the chief justice of the High Court, himself a former Liberal attorney general and cousin of Liberal lawyer and member of the House of Representatives Bob Ellicott, who was another of Fraser's closest advisers during the crisis. As soon as Whitlam left, Fraser was appointed caretaker prime minister. He was instructed to make no appointments, dismissals, or changes in policy and to call an immediate election.

By an incredible oversight the Labor leaders in the Senate were not told of the dismissal immediately. As scheduled they brought the bills before the Senate at 2:15 p.m., and these were immediately passed. Fraser was thus able to announce in the House at 2:34 p.m. that he was prime minister, had supply, and was about to recommend a double dissolution. Although the House passed a vote of no-confidence in his government, the governor general refused to see the speaker of the House bearing the message of that vote until his secretary had read the announcement of the double dissolution on the steps of Parliament House at 4:45 p.m. Despite the angry scenes outside Parliament, the situation was irreversible. Parliament was dissolved; the Labor party's dismissal was irrevocable, its defeat inevitable.

3

THE LABOR CAMPAIGN

D. W. Rawson

The ALP: Traditions and Innovations

The defeat of the Australian Labor party government in December 1975 was characteristic of the state of the party at that time and perhaps of the Australian political system in general. It was accompanied by strange and apparently portentous events; but, for better or worse, the outcome left very little changed in any fundamental way. In the aftermath of the election, Labor was out of office in the federal Parliament—as usual. It was still the largest single Australian party and there seemed no chance of its disappearing or being replaced by any party of a different type; it could already feel that its prospects of returning to office were quite real, in the medium rather than the short term, but also that they depended as much upon the prospective errors and ill-luck of its opponents as on any changes for the better in Labor's own methods of operation—all of which was very much the normal state of affairs.

An Unsuccessful Party. In short, the "constitutional crisis" of November–December, which was the proximate cause of Labor's downfall, soon proved to be just that—a crisis involving the constitution or, more precisely, the respective roles of the two houses of Parliament and the governor general. Those important but not truly fundamental functions and relationships, it is true, may never be the same again. But they are, and have already been shown to be, peripheral to the operation of the party system and, more specifically, to Labor's place within it. If Labor can in the near or distant future win and hold the support of a clear majority of voters, there is no reason why it should not be able to deal with such problems as those that caused its downfall in 1975. This is a big "if"—but then it always has been.

Over three generations, Australians have grown used to seeing the ALP out of power, but to outside observers this situation is surprising since the ALP was by a large margin the world's first successful Labor party.[1] By what may or may not be coincidence, all the Labor parties which today are among the major actors in their respective countries appeared, at opposite ends of the earth, within a period of a mere five years or so around the year 1890. The origin of the party in Britain is not entirely clear-cut and in New Zealand even less so, but it can at least be said that in Britain the Independent Labour party, one of the important constituents of the Labour party to come, was established in 1893, and there were premonitions of Labor political activity in New Zealand in 1891, though the appearance of a united Labor party was much delayed. Of this small group of Labor parties, the Australian party made much the most rapid progress. With the federation of the country itself, the party operated as a federal body from 1900 on, though outside of Parliament it remained a loose confederation of state parties for many years and it is still a far from unified body.

By 1910 Labor had gained majorities in the federal Parliament and in two of the states, and by 1915 it had gained majorities in all the states except Victoria, where it has always been much less successful than elsewhere. Thus, Labor can be said to have achieved electoral victory in Australia some twenty years earlier than in any other country.

This did not mean, however, that Labor came to dominate Australian politics, either electorally or ideologically, as it can be said to have dominated Swedish politics throughout the middle of the twentieth century. Ever since 1910, the ALP has remained one of the most important Australian parties and for more than half a century—since around 1920 when the formation of the Country party divided the non-Labor side—it has been the country's largest party. Nevertheless, it has usually been in opposition. In federal politics, Labor has been in power for a total of only eighteen years since 1910, and the Whitlam government of 1972–75 was the first Labor administration since 1949. In state politics the party has on the whole fared better, though there was a brief period in the late 1960s when none of the six states had a Labor government. Even during most of the term of the Whitlam government there were Labor state administrations

---

[1] This point is discussed in the author's "The Life Span of Labour Parties," *Political Studies*, vol. 17, no. 3 (September 1969).

only in South Australia and Tasmania, two of the three smaller states. Many adjectives can be used to describe the history of the ALP, but one of the least arguable is "unsuccessful." In this sense, despite all the unique aspects of the election of December 1975, its result—a Labor defeat—was much more characteristic of the party's history than the Labor victories in 1972 and 1974.

The ALP and Socialism. We have in Australia, then, a Labor party which developed well in advance of similar parties elsewhere and which has survived without serious challenge throughout this century but whose electoral record has, on the whole, been one of failure. There are various possible explanations of this paradox. One hypothesis, however, can be ruled out without much hesitation: the ALP has *not* lacked popularity because it has been an extreme socialist party or because it has threatened to transform society along traditional radical lines. Although the word "socialization" has occurred in the party's policy statements since 1921, it has never been clear precisely what the term has meant—but it has not generally been interpreted as involving the total or even the widespread nationalization or public ownership of industry. In both word and deed, the ALP has avoided any commitment to a predominantly socialist economy or society as those are understood in Western Europe. The public ownership of businesses of a developmental kind has a long history in Australia, and Labor governments have had a share in establishing and maintaining government business enterprises in areas like transportation, communications, and fuel and energy supply. However, the non-Labor, antisocialist parties have done even more in this direction, simply because they have spent much longer periods in office.

In rather special circumstances, a Labor government in 1947 tried to nationalize the trading banks, this being one of the rare occasions on which a Labor government sought to take over a profitable industry. The attempt was frustrated by legal action, which produced a judgment by the High Court of Australia, upheld by the Judicial Committee of the Privy Council, which made it extremely difficult for the federal government to nationalize an industry unless it could first secure the amendment of the constitution—a process that in Australia has been notoriously difficult.[2]

The attempt to nationalize the banks and a somewhat earlier attempt to nationalize the airlines, which was similarly frustrated by a legal challenge, were not characteristic of the ALP, either before or

---

[2] See L. F. Crisp, *Australian National Government* (Melbourne: Longman, 1974), chap. 2.

after 1947. For at least the first century and a half of white settlement in Australia, government characteristically assumed extensive responsibilities, irrespective of the ideologies of the political protagonists. Geographic circumstances made necessary large and unprofitable expenditures on railways and on water and electricity before private investors could expect a profitable return, and largely for this reason Australian governments of all complexions assumed responsibility for many such industries. Labor governments were as likely as others to involve themselves in such fields, but (with individual exceptions) they were not very much more likely to do so.

Yet the theme of socialism was as prominent in political contention in Australia as elsewhere in the first half of this century. In part this was because socialism in a relatively strict sense—involving, at the very least, the public ownership of most large industries—was always a goal of large sections of the Labor party, though never of those who formed Labor governments or decided what those governments would actually do. There was always a strong section of the party outside Parliament that was ready to advocate a comprehensive socialist transformation of industry and society, and if they were not strong enough to dominate their own party they were quite strong enough to alarm their opponents. The formal policies of the ALP were sufficiently radical to give satisfaction to its socialist members, though in fact the party was not even formally committed to securing the public ownership of all major industries except for a brief period between 1921 and 1927. The attempts in the late 1940s to nationalize the airlines and the banks not only failed but provoked judicial interpretations of the constitution which made any subsequent large-scale nationalization unlikely. Nevertheless, the fear of socialism remained, and in the 1970s the unrestrained, enterprising, swashbuckling style of the Whitlam government persuaded many antisocialist Australians that such a government would somehow manage to get around the constitutional barriers to nationalization.

There was, let it be said, nothing in the record of the Whitlam government from first to last to justify such fears; but the terms of the argument about socialism had changed significantly since the 1940s. In the 1970s there were rational and important non-Labor leaders who believed that the ALP was actively seeking to bring the major part of the economy under public ownership within, say, ten or fifteen years. Moreover, it was no longer necessary to believe this to perceive socialism as a real issue between the parties. This change was due to the non-Labor parties rather than to the ALP. During the period of non-Labor predominance and economic growth of the 1950s and 1960s, the Liberal and Country parties ceased to accept that it was necessary for government to provide the prerequisites of secondary industry, especially in the form of transportation and energy. As late as 1950, an L-NCP government in Victoria nationalized the town gas industry in that state for the familiar and characteristically Australian reason that the industry needed more rapid expansion than its private owners were likely to find profitable. This move was on a par with earlier non-Labor decisions to establish state-owned monopolies in railways in the mid-nineteenth century and in electricity production and distribution early in the twentieth. It was, however, the last venture of its kind. The development of the economy had now reached a point where it was possible to secure the development of all basic industries by private capital. For the non-Labor parties, this was both desirable and possible. For Labor it was not obviously desirable, especially since Labor often sought more rapid development, or development of a different kind, than private industry would find acceptable.

So it was that in the 1970s the old catchwords, socialism and nationalization, not only retained some life but even became somewhat more apposite than in the past, as the non-Labor parties moved away from the assumption (which antisocialists had always found uncomfortable, if sometimes necessary) that the development of Australian industry required the direct participation of government. Some of the activities of the Whitlam government—such as the establishment of a Pipeline Authority to build and maintain pipelines for the transporting of natural gas and other fuels from the (private) companies that produced them to the (predominantly private) firms that consumed them, or the encouragement of the Australian Atomic Energy Commission to take an active part in the search for uranium— might seem, on the face of it, to be examples of a time-honored, non-partisan tradition of Australian governments. In fact they were not, because the non-Labor parties had tacitly, and no doubt thankfully, moved away from that tradition.

The ALP and the Unions. The role of government in the economy is one area in which social change affected the Labor party by altering assumptions about what was and was not a matter of interparty conflict. Other such changes affected the party more directly. In a sense the most fundamental of these was the position of the affiliated trade unions within the party. It was fundamental in the sense that a Labor party is necessarily a party to which unions belong and that change in this area is, as it were, basic by definition. On the face of it, there had been few surprising developments in this respect. Although the records of the Labor party have been in some respects inadequate and the party has often been secretive about its own structure, we can say that in the early 1970s the role of trade unions was very much as it had been for the previous sixty years. Nevertheless, there had also been changes, some obvious and others more subtle.

About 58 percent of Australian employees in 1975 were members of trade unions.[3] This meant that Australia was one of the world's most unionized countries, though it was a good deal less so than Sweden and a few others. Of these unionists, numbering almost 2.5 million, about two-thirds belonged to unions which were affiliated with the ALP.[4] With rare exceptions, the individual members had little opportunity to indicate whether or not they approved of this arrangement, since the unions normally paid their annual affiliation fees to the party out of ordinary union funds and were not required (as unions are in Britain) to give members who disapproved the option of "contracting out" of payments used for political purposes.[5]

All of this probably changed relatively little between the 1920s and the early 1970s. The principal reason for the numerical strength of Australian unionism since early in this century has been the existence of comprehensive state and federal systems of compulsory industrial arbitration, which in general have encouraged and in a few cases have compelled employees to belong to unions. As a result, much of this membership was apathetic and some of it reluctant. Certainly it was always assumed that a considerable proportion of trade unionists did not support the Labor party at elections since otherwise the party would have been virtually unbeatable. Most estimates, in recent years supported by the evidence of public opinion polls, placed at about one-third the proportion of unionists who usually voted for other than Labor candidates.[6]

From the beginning, therefore, there was a considerable gap between the model of a unionized working class which endorsed the

---

[3] Australian Bureau of Statistics Bulletin 6.24, *Trade Union Statistics: Australia December 1975.*

[4] D. W. Rawson, *A Handbook of Australian Trade Unions and Employees' Associations*, 2nd edition (Canberra: Australian National University Press, 1973), p. 17.

[5] See Cyril Grunfeld, *Modern Trade Union Law* (London: Sweet and Maxwell, 1966), pp. 218-314.

[6] A national sample of 1,000 unionists interviewed in May 1976 included 57 percent who said that they would vote for the ALP "if an election were held tomorrow." However, this is probably a lower proportion than at most periods in the past. This figure comes from as yet unpublished research by the author.

Labor party as a natural extension and instrument of trade unionism itself and the Australian reality of a partly conscripted trade union membership many of whom declined to support the party even as voters, though they might be compelled, through their union membership fees, to make some contribution to its running expenses. By the 1970s, moreover, there was some evidence that this gap between model and reality had grown wider over a long period and was widening more rapidly as time passed. The only system of public opinion polls that extended far enough into the past to make the study of trends possible suggested that there was a long-term tendency for manual workers to turn away from the ALP—though considerable majorities of them continued to support it. On the other hand, there was a compensating tendency for other occupational groups, especially white-collar workers, to become more favorable to the ALP.[7]

This might not have produced any great anomaly if the white-collar workers who were slowly tending to move towards the ALP had also been joining unions affiliated with the party, so that the only real change would have been a blurring of the distinction between manual and nonmanual employment, in its political implications as in much else. What actually happened, however, was not so simple. There was a tendency, though it asserted itself rather slowly, for manual and nonmanual unions to cooperate more closely and for an increasing proportion of unionists to belong to the major national trade union federation, the Australian Council of Trade Unions (ACTU). But there was not any clear tendency for this to be accompanied by a continuing movement of unions into affiliation with the ALP. In the main, those unions that had always been affiliated with the party remained affiliated, but the party gained few new union adherents.

Though there might be some tendency for manual trade unionists, the party's strongest supporters, to move away from the ALP, this trend was slow and only somewhat modified the political allegiances of individual manual workers. By and large, manual trade unionists still voted Labor in 1975 as they had for nearly seventy years. However, it did not follow that they necessarily endorsed the partisan role of their unions. On the contrary, there was evidence that most trade unionists, even if they themselves voted Labor or even if their unions were affiliated with the ALP, believed that their organizations should avoid permanent commitment to any party and

[7] See Murray Goot, *Policies and Partisans: Australian Electoral Opinion 1941 to 1948* (Sydney: University of Sydney, Department of Government and Public Administration, 1969), pp. 95-96.

certainly should avoid affiliation with a party.[8] It is not easy to be sure whether this attitude, which also seems to be characteristic of British trade unionists,[9] is a new development; but, new or old, it suggests that the very idea of a Labor party is unpopular even among those who, as unionists and as individual voters, are the Labor party's principal supporters.

All this might seem to suggest that in recent years the ALP and the Australian party system in general had become highly unstable and liable to rapid change if not dissolution. Yet anyone seeking direct evidence of a loosening of traditional ties between the ALP and the main body of trade unionism would have found little in 1975. In some respects, the ties seemed closer than ever. For the first time, the president of the ACTU, Robert J. Hawke, was also the federal president of the ALP, the latter being an honorific but not insignificant position. Similarly, in the largest state, New South Wales, the secretary of the state branch of the ACTU, John Ducker, was also president of the state branch of the ALP. Although the organization of the party had been restructured in several states during the previous ten years, in each case the representatives of the trade unions had been given or had retained majority representation on the bodies which ultimately controlled the party in the state. Put to the crucial test of an election that the party seemed certain to lose and which it in fact lost heavily, the trade unions not only gave Labor resolute and expensive support but did so without arousing any serious criticism or hostility within their own ranks.

This discrepancy between an apparent movement away from partisan commitment by rank-and-file unionists and the retention, or even strengthening, of the party ties of their organizations is paradoxical but not very difficult to explain. The majority of unionists, who favored Labor themselves but thought that their unions should "keep out of politics," were inactive union members. Often they only tepidly opposed their union's party ties—perhaps were even unaware of them. The active minority of union members were much more likely to be concerned with political questions and to see their union as a means of pursuing their own political goals, whether self-interested or otherwise. Though the financial support which the unions gave to the ALP was vital to the party, it made up a very trivial proportion of union subscriptions.

---

[8] See D. W. Rawson, "The Paradox of Partisan Trade Unionism: The Australian Case," *British Journal of Political Science*, vol. 4, part 4 (October 1974).

[9] David Butler and Donald Stokes, *Political Change in Britain* (London: Macmillan, 1969), p. 168.

While it is therefore possible to point out some important ways in which the ALP was becoming out of step with the attitudes of rank-and-file unionists, it is not obvious that this was (or is) causing any serious weakness in the party's operation. Union officials continued to be prominent and active within the ALP and union funds continued to sustain it, perhaps never more so than during the 1975 campaign. The long-term loosening (rather than severing) of the allegiance between many unionists and the party that was taking place, meanwhile, contributed to the generally increasing volatility of the electorate: in the 1970s unionists, like other voters, were more likely than ever before to change their votes under the influence of immediate and personal considerations.

The weakening of the links between the ALP and the rank-and-file unionists had long had an important influence on the composition of the parliamentary Labor party and its activities in office: it had enabled highly educated men of professional background to rise rapidly to positions of leadership within the party. This development, very obvious in the federal Parliament and somewhat less so in some of the states, had emerged long before Whitlam took office in 1972, but Whitlam's own career was the prime example of the process. From the time of his election as parliamentary leader of the ALP in 1967, Whitlam had been pointing out, to audiences likely to be sympathetic, that the ALP could no longer be considered an anti-intellectual party or one in which highly educated people found it difficult to advance. Of the five candidates for the party leadership the year Whitlam won, four (Whitlam, Cairns, Crean, and Beazley) were university graduates, the only nongraduate being Daly who, like the others, served in Whitlam's ministry. While not all of the four graduates shared Whitlam's upper-middle-class background, all had entered the federal Parliament from professional occupations. The predominance of the highly educated and professionals was even more marked among the younger Labor members of Parliament elected for the first time in 1969, 1972, and 1974.[10]

This would certainly have produced serious conflict within the party had the newcomers risen at the expense of the full-time union officials and the most politically active union members who had looked to the Labor benches in Parliament as one avenue of promotion for themselves. But in fact, just as most of the unions retained their allegiance to the party, so the party continued to provide an opening

[10] See Michelle Grattan, "The Australian Labor Party," in Henry Mayer and Helen Nelson, eds., *Australian Politics: A Third Reader* (Melbourne: Cheshire, 1973), p. 403.

for this relatively small group of union activists. Though they tended to be overshadowed and increasingly outnumbered by the university-trained professionals, they continued to control a reasonable proportion of Labor's parliamentary seats, including many of the safest. Those who made way for the new men were not the union officials but rather all the rest of the traditional Labor constituency. It was the manual workers who did *not* have records of consistent union activity and a mixed bag of other common people—small farmers, small businessmen, and so on—who tended to be pushed off the Labor benches through the 1960s and 1970s.

Party Discipline. One other long-term Labor adjustment to social change, which had its effect on the Whitlam administration and hence on the election campaign, needs to be mentioned. The ALP had been unique among the world's Labor parties, which often tended to emphasize the importance of rank-and-file participation, in its insistence that rank-and-file sovereignty should be maintained even at the expense, if need be, of the autonomy of the Labor members of Parliament. It was one of the few democratic parties in a democratic system to assert bluntly that its members of Parliament were properly subject to direction from extraparliamentary organizations speaking in the name of the rank and file and that such direction might extend beyond general matters of policy to particular questions of parliamentary tactics. It was true that the actual intervention of party leaders into the affairs of the parliamentary party was regarded by both as a last resort and that when it was attempted it commonly led to the temporary disruption of the party and the removal or defection of its parliamentary leaders. It was also true that attempts to discipline parliamentary leaders in this way had been more characteristic of state than of federal politics. The ALP's own organization was so concentrated at the state level that it was many years before its lightweight federal organizations were able to challenge the powerful ALP federal politicians.

Nevertheless, the balance did shift. In 1950 the party's federal executive successfully induced the Labor members of the federal Parliament to change their course on one matter, and the threat that it would do so again in 1963—the issue this time being whether the party should categorically oppose the establishment of an American military communications base in Australia—was real enough to acutely embarrass the parliamentary leaders. (Whitlam was then deputy leader to Arthur A. Calwell.)

It was in the nature of politics that challenges to the parliamentary leaders of this kind were most likely to come from the left of the party and to be electorally unpopular. The Labor politicians, as professional judges of electoral opinion, were not likely to require urging on in a course that they could see would bring an electoral dividend. So, from the time he became parliamentary leader in 1967, Whitlam conducted a spectacular and hazardous but ultimately successful struggle against two related pressures: left-wing control of the party machinery, especially in the state of Victoria, and the power of the extraparliamentary machine to control the Labor members of Parliament. The machine, at the federal level, could not be made simply a handmaiden of the politicians, but its power to threaten their independence could be virtually removed. And, since the party's federal organizations were made up principally of delegates from each of the states, the taming of the party section in Victoria would help safeguard the autonomy of federal members of Parliament while at the same time improving the party's electoral prospects.

Even by 1969, when Labor made such electoral gains as to be obviously in the running for office when the next opportunity should arise, the left wing of the party had been pushed into a subordinate but by no means powerless position. The party's federal authorities —the biennial national conference and the smaller national executive which met several times a year—had undergone only minor reforms, but these were enough. In particular, by introducing a substantial proportion of state and federal politicians to these bodies, who held their positions ex officio, the reforms had reduced almost to the vanishing point the likelihood that these organizations would become rods for the back of the federal leader and his associates.

The ALP on the Eve of the Election. So it was that, with a minimum of formal change, the Labor party that held office after 1972 had become a very different body from the ALP that had held office decades before. It was a much more free-wheeling and unpredictable national organization than in the past. It was certainly less distinctive and harder to characterize. It was even less a socialist party than in the past, if that term implies advocacy of the predominantly public ownership of industry; but just as the opponents of Labor had become more antisocialist in their actions as well as in their aspirations, it could be argued, Labor was increasingly socialist in terms of the party contest which it faced. Its parliamentary members were less subject to the threat of intervention or control from the organizational wing and the party's reputation rested more completely and more obviously with the parliamentary party than in the past. The breaking down of old assumptions and the sheer passage of time since there had been a federal Labor government meant that the ordinary Labor politicians had very little in the way of precedent or convention to guide them in determining their relations with the Labor cabinet and specifically with the prime minister. The union officials and activists had a lesser role than in the far-off days of earlier Labor governments, but they were not squeezed out of all positions of patronage and importance, and since most of them were pragmatic men with nowhere else to go in politics, they were a good deal more content than many previous generations of union officials had been. There was a very small federal office of full-time officials and staff who were young, products of the new and hazardous but in the main successful era of Labor politics which had begun with and was symbolized by the emergence of Whitlam as leader.

The eventful and increasingly disappointing record of Labor in office is covered in another chapter in this volume. It will suffice here to note briefly the condition of the party at the time of the 1975 election campaign in the light of the long-term trends which have been discussed. In the main, those trends persisted through the victory and disappointment of the 1970s as they had previously persisted through defeat and high hopes. The Labor government elected in 1972 did not attempt the nationalization of existing industries but, for reasons that have already been explained, this did not prevent it from being denounced as socialist by its opponents. The conflicts and reshuffling that occurred in the ministry did not indicate any reaction against the predominance of leaders with university education and, in most cases, with no background in the trade unions. The trade union officials themselves showed little discontent and there was no sign of a demand, which had marked some previous Labor governments, for the unions to try to increase their control over the party if not to virtually remake it. Though by 1975 Whitlam had lost a good deal of his popularity among the electorate at large and had disappointed or annoyed some of his parliamentary colleagues by his failure to consult them adequately, there was no serious sign of the appearance of any alternative leader; and, as was soon to be shown, his popularity among the more active and committed Labor voters was unabated. The party's extra-parliamentary machinery remained very weak in financial resources, especially at the federal level, and the burden that fell upon its federal staff, especially the national secretary, David Combe, was heavy at the best of times and likely to become impossibly taxing in a crisis.

Such were the circumstances when, on November 11, 1975, the Labor party found its government dismissed from office and had to face, at short notice, a campaign for both houses of the federal Parliament.

The Course of the Campaign

The 1975 campaign was, of course, conducted under circumstances that seemed unusual to the point of unreality; but the important word is "seemed." In retrospect, the electoral situation began to return to "normal" from the moment of Whitlam's dismissal. The long-term trend had been for the government to lose popularity since mid-1974 because of the country's increasing economic difficulties and the government's own lack of cohesion and image of failing competence. The Bass by-election and the consistent record of the opinion polls had illustrated this clearly enough.[11] The opposition's decision to hold up supply had temporarily reversed this trend and, as far as can be judged, was either downright unpopular or caused serious misgivings among all but the most bitter opponents of the government. But the reason for this unpopularity was not altogether clear. It had little to do with constitutional principles such as the relations between the two houses. It did not even have much to do with hazier principles such as the notion that the government was threatened with immediate breakdown because of a deadlock initiated by the opposition. When the deadlock was broken—and almost irrespective of *how* it was broken—the pattern of sagging support for Labor which had developed over more than a year would reassert itself. The deadlock was broken by extraordinary means—the dismissal of the government—and this made necessary another extraordinary, though short-lived, arrangement, rule by a minority government pending an election. But basically the dismissal of Whitlam ensured that ordinary processes of government would be restored within a matter of weeks. An election would be held, a government would be elected, and normal political processes would resume. Voters could again consider which party they thought most likely to produce a competent administration, and that was not the Labor party.

Labor was in an impossible position. All it could do was seek a strategy which would minimize its defeat and, for those able to look further ahead, give it the greatest opportunity for some kind of comeback in the future. Even so, the best strategy, or rather the

11 For an account of the Bass by-election and its implications see pp. 72-73 in this volume.

least bad one, was not self-evident. Emphasis on the "crisis" and the action of the governor general was a dwindling asset, but no one could be sure just how fast it would dwindle. Emphasis on Labor's improved performance in economic affairs during mid-1974 could not save the government but might prevent its being remembered by future electors as totally incompetent.

In the event, the party probably emphasized the crisis too much and for too long. It might have done better to give more weight from the outset to the party's new-found economic caution and reliability. But this is entirely a matter of speculation. It must not be forgotten that all that was at stake was the margin of defeat, and perhaps only the details of that margin.

As in many crisis elections, the visible part of the campaign included displays of great enthusiasm for both sides, with Labor receiving even greater apparent support than its opponents. For a time, Labor's denunciation of Fraser and of Kerr and the growth of unprecedented popular demonstrations in support of the ALP seemed to sustain each other. As long as large, frenetically enthusiastic pro-Labor crowds kept appearing, obviously moved much more by the government's dismissal than by any more sober thought that it had belatedly shown economic responsibility, the temptation to emphasize the crisis was irresistible.

Whitlam's Appeal. Even before the official opening of the campaign, Whitlam addressed huge and enthusiastic crowds in four states. On November 24 there was an open-air lunch-time meeting in a Sydney park, attended by an estimated 30,000 people. The same night the campaign was officially opened at a meeting in a huge Melbourne building called the Festival Hall, usually used for boxing matches and pop music concerts. The building held 8,000 people, and many more could not get in. Whitlam's speech, half an hour of which was televised across the country, was the focus of this unique occasion.[12] In the purely formal sense, it was a speech in which the government, like many others before it, "stood on its record." Whitlam duly listed many of his government's new measures, including some of those that had been defeated in the Senate. There were the usual and quite legitimate appeals to sectional interests of one kind or another—to pensioners, city dwellers, farmers, women, aborigines. Such appeals were set in a framework which implied, without openly admitting it,

---

[12] The text was reproduced in full in many publications. The quotations that follow are from the printers' union journal *PKIU State News*, vol. 7, no. 10 (November-December 1975).

that the government's overall economic policy might have been deficient in the past but that this had now been corrected. The phrase "the Hayden Budget," repeated several times, suggested, without actually condemning Hayden's predecessors, that Labor's economic policy was now in safe hands.

In his policy speech, Whitlam argued that Labor was now in a better position than its opponents to produce economic recovery. Sustaining such an argument was obviously a formidable task after the events of the previous three years, but Whitlam's attempt did not lack cogency. He argued that recovery depended on the success of the policy of wage indexation and that the policy of indexation required, in turn, "the greatest restraint, responsibility, discipline, goodwill and co-operation from employees." These had been forthcoming because employees had been willing to accept moderation in wage claims, believing that a Labor government's social reforms would more than compensate them for the "false and temporary advantages foregone in excessive wage demands." A non-Labor government, it was implied, would cause the unions to return to "excessive wage demands" with disastrous effects on the rates of inflation and unemployment.

That the argument was cogent did not necessarily mean that it was valid, unless one accepted the view, which Whitlam was unable to state directly, that the party's economic policies and attitudes had fundamentally changed during 1975. If union wage demands can ever properly be described as excessive, they could have been under Whitlam's administration in 1973 and 1974. During these two years, the number of working days lost in industrial disputes had been almost as high as the total for the four preceding years of non-Labor government. Nor, for better or worse, had these disputes been in vain. There had been a considerable increase in the proportion of the gross national product going to wage and salary earners. It was obviously difficult, to say the least, for Whitlam to argue that these trade union successes during the early period of his government had been unfortunate or mistaken and that henceforth his administration would try to prevent any further redistribution of national wealth—the more so since Hawke and other union leaders were pointing to the employees' increased share of the gross national product as one of the government's successes and a reason why it merited continued union support. Yet the events of 1973 and 1974 were fresh enough in most people's minds to raise a serious doubt as to whether Labor, even with the evidently competent Hayden and James McClelland in the ministries most directly concerned, would really secure trade union moderation.

Faced with the difficult task of presenting Labor as having recently become the party of economic competence and responsibility without openly admitting that it had ever been anything else, Whitlam followed the orthodox strategy of taking the offensive. It was the opposition, he argued, that had been economically irresponsible, in general by refusing throughout his term to give Labor an opportunity to put its policies into effect and in particular by blocking supply, a maneuver that had prevented the benefits of the Hayden Budget from being felt and had produced economic dislocation and uncertainty. Hence the constitutional crisis was related to the problem of economic stability. Whitlam argued, correctly enough, in his speech at the Festival Hall that inflation and unemployment were worldwide problems, and, much more dubiously, that his government "was as successful as any comparable government in dealing with them. But," he went on, "my government alone has had to wage this war in the face of economic sabotage by its political opponents."

All this sounds much like an orthodox policy speech in which a party leader boosts the record of his own administration, blames his opponents for what went wrong, and suggests, if necessary, that he will do better in the future, without specifically conceding past failures. It is true, as commentators noted, that the speech contained no specific undertakings for future action, but it was not unknown for Australian party leaders to confine their campaign appeals to descriptions of their own achievements and of the villainy of their opponents.

This sketchy account of Whitlam's speech, while it accurately reports the candidate's policy stands, barely suggests the spirit of the occasion. At the time, what Whitlam said seemed almost irrelevant. The meeting, part of which was televised, was the occasion for a demonstration of feverish support. The candidate's speech skillfully blended serious argument with a rousing appeal to the emotions, and these ran so high as to almost obliterate reason.[13] Nevertheless, Whitlam's speech provided some basis for the rational as well as the emotional course of the campaign. The two elements were nicely combined in one early passage:

> The shame of the past six weeks must be wiped away. In those shameful six weeks, a stacked Senate went on strike against a Budget vital to Australia's welfare and the nation's economy. The nation and the nation's elected government were held to ransom. And by those means, the

---

[13] Very little of the more solid content of the speech was included in the section of the speech that was televised.

elected government in full command of the confidence of Parliament was deposed.

There, in miniature, was Labor's appeal. It was based principally on the claim that the Whitlam government had been brought down by shameful means; but there was also the claim that Labor had brought forward a sound and beneficial Budget, which had been aborted by (to turn an unpopular term to Labor's advantage) a Senate "strike."

The Issues: Constitutional Crisis or Economic Recovery. From the beginning of the campaign, then, Labor had the options of emphasizing the constitutional question, the party's recovered economic competence, or the two in conjunction. The difficulty was that these two issues were not linked in the minds of the voters as they were in the minds of Labor spokesmen and that each might appeal to a different section of the electorate. The constitutional questions were undoubtedly responsible for the unprecedented enthusiasm that continued to greet Whitlam and other party spokesmen at meetings, for a ready flow of financial support from trade unions and individuals, and for a rapid increase in Labor party rank-and-file membership. But these manifestations of support for the ALP, though unprecedented in recent party history and involving many thousands of people, nevertheless affected only a small proportion of the voters. Most people, whatever the Labor spokesmen might say or do, rapidly lost interest in the constitutional question once it was plain that some sort of effective government was likely to emerge from the general election. Even at the start of the campaign, all the indications from the public opinion polls suggested that Labor would be defeated. As the campaign proceeded, some polls showed clearly that, in the minds of the voters, the constitutional crisis was dropping out of sight and the management of the economy was becoming the most prominent issue.[14] During the last two weeks of the campaign, Labor made some attempt to switch its own emphasis towards the economic management issue.

In all of Whitlam's election campaigns, but especially in this one, the leader's own statements and movements had a crucial place. However, the campaign of 1975, despite the anachronistic revival of huge public meetings, was still modern enough to rely heavily on centralized media propaganda, especially campaign broadcasts on television. The party's centralized propaganda, by far the most expensive part of the campaign, was devised by the Sydney advertising firm of Mullins, Clarke and Ralph in the light of their consultations with federal party officials, Whitlam and his staff, and one of the principal market

---

[14] See *National Times*, November 16-23, 1975.

research organizations and pollsters, Australian National Opinion Polls (ANOP). During the early weeks, Labor's campaign in the media emphasized almost exclusively the constitutional crisis. This was largely because the surveys of ANOP had not suggested much hope for any alternative emphasis. The agency produced a series of low-keyed television advertisements which sought, through the mouths of officials of a variety of homely community organizations and sporting groups, to assert the impropriety of removing leaders from office by unorthodox means. A variety of prestigious but unexpected people were introduced to defend the Whitlam government and condemn the methods used in its removal. These temporary spokesmen for Labor included not only many of those prominent in the arts but even the former Liberal prime minister, John Gorton, who had relinquished the seat he had held as a Liberal from Victoria and was now seeking (unsuccessfully) election to the Senate from the Australian Capital Territory as an independent. This was part of a general strategy of making the most of the very large, though far from sufficient, number of individuals who had been mobilized on the Labor side by the manner of Whitlam's removal from office. The party quietly orchestrated a series of "spontaneous" declarations of support for Labor in newspaper advertisements by a variety of occupational and social groups.

The shift in emphasis toward the economy in the later stages of the campaign probably had little effect. Any positive credit that Labor might have received in this area probably depended on the reputations of Hayden and James McClelland, who were duly given greater exposure. More persuasive was Labor's argument that the Liberal and National Country parties were unlikely to produce better results for the economy, but here Labor's opponents, by refusing to discuss specifics, presented Labor with few opportunities to drive the point home.

Impending Defeat. Overall, and especially for the first two weeks, the Labor campaign proceeded on two quite different levels which gave rise to quite disparate impressions. Outwardly it was enthusiastic and, by every yardstick except the opinion polls, extraordinarily successful, centered on the improper removal of a viable government. But beneath the surface, it was an almost unrelieved failure, dominated by the bad long-term record of the Whitlam government in economic policy. As the campaign drew to a close, the gap between the two contenders lessened considerably, though it by no means dispersed. The public opinion polls, consistently against Labor, began to convince all but the most devoted partisans that the ALP could not win. The size and conviction of the crowds at Labor meetings diminished perceptibly, though both remained almost fantastically high by the standards of the Labor campaigns of the 1950s and 1960s.

The campaign closed with what was to have been the climactic Labor rally on the lawn outside Parliament House, Canberra, on the evening of Wednesday, December 10. This was the last night before the election on which radio and television propaganda could legally be broadcast, and the party had saved a large share of its time allocation from the Australian Broadcasting Commission for the occasion.[15] And this was the place where, on the afternoon of November 11, several thousand angry Canberrans had gathered spontaneously upon hearing of the Whitlam government's dismissal. Now, a month later, every effort had been made to attract a huge crowd to the "Rally for Democracy."

The event was not, in the ordinary sense, a failure; indeed, at any other election, it would have been considered a resounding success. About 7,000 people came; they duly cheered Whitlam, Hawke, and others. If there had been twice as many, it might have seemed that perhaps the opinion polls were wrong or that some last-minute swing was under way. As it was, the cool breeze that passed through the crowd, blowing out most of the candles that had been handed out, carried with it not only the scent of roses from the adjoining gardens but also the chill of defeat.

The campaign continued for the two days of the "electronic blackout," fully reported in the press. Just before the vote, there was another huge turnout for Whitlam in Melbourne, a crowd of 15,000 at an open-air meeting. By this point the opinion polls had been unanimously predicting a heavy Labor defeat for more than two weeks. Some party spokesmen questioned the reliability or applicability of some polls and even the cooler heads found it hard to believe, after such a campaign, that the defeat could be as heavy as was being predicted and as in fact it was. Nevertheless, there was a double meaning to Whitlam's remarks at the end of the Labor campaign. He told the crowd: "I can understand that many Australians, especially young Australians, must be wondering after the events of November 11 whether reform is possible in our society. I ask you not to lose faith. I ask you to remain vigilant for democracy."[16] The words were not inapposite assuming the return of a Labor govern-

---

[15] On the radio and television "blackout" in the last days of the campaign see note 42, chap. 7 in this volume.

[16] Melbourne *Age*, December 12, 1975.

ment the following day. But they were also addressed to the possibility that the disappointments and frustrations of Labor supporters were about to be compounded by electoral defeat. At the end of it all, the faith of Labor supporters in the efficacy of their support for the party was to be put to a much more severe test than the hostility of the Senate and the actions of the governor general; it would have to withstand rejection by the electorate and the return to opposition.

The Trade Unions

The circumstances of the campaign ensured that the trade unions would strongly support the Labor party, and they probably did so with greater conviction and unanimity than at any previous election. It was by no means self-evident that this help would be forthcoming. Previous Labor governments had often disappointed the unions, and the same might well have been said of Whitlam's government had it survived for its full term. From the changes in the cabinet in mid-1975, it seemed likely that the good times for employees and their organizations had come to an end. Clyde Cameron, minister for labor and immigration until June 1975, had been regarded by the unions as "their" minister, in spirit and in deed, as well as because he was himself a former union official. His replacement by James McClelland, against Cameron's bitter protests, was regarded as indicating the beginning of an era which, if not actually antiunion, would be much less favorable to union claims than the preceding one. There was less hostility to Hayden among the union officials, but it was clear from the time of his Budget in August that he too would preside over conditions less to the liking of the unions than those that had prevailed when Crean and later Cairns had been treasurer.

Even before the holding up of supply by the Senate, less anxiety about these developments was expressed by the unions than might have been expected from the political record of Australian unionism. This was partly because the benefits which Labor had brought to the unions and their members were substantial and recent, while any change in government policies remained largely potential. Even more important, most sections of the union leadership had very lively fears of what would follow the return of a non-Labor government, especially with Fraser as prime minister. Earlier in the year, before he had become leader of the Liberal party, Fraser had been the principal influence behind a new statement of Liberal industrial relations policy. The new policy proposed what were delicately described as "consequences" for those who defied the decisions of industrial arbitration authorities. To union officials, this could only imply the return of the hated "penal powers," under which unions had been fined heavily for striking or taking other forms of direct action. These had been in abeyance since 1969 when united union opposition had made them unworkable; but the union officials had no wish to fight that battle over again to an uncertain outcome.

An election under ordinary circumstances, therefore, would have found the main body of the unions lining up behind the ALP, though in many cases without much enthusiasm and to the accompaniment of a good deal of private grumbling. The constitutional issue changed this situation, prompting instead virtually unanimous and much more effective union support from the ALP. A special meeting of the executive of the Australian Council of Trade Unions on October 23, after the Senate had begun to block supply, called on the unions to provide financing and personnel "in any election arising out of the present crisis." What was envisaged at that time was a half-Senate election. The eventual outcome, an election for both houses following the dismissal of Whitlam by the governor general, ensured that such support would be more readily forthcoming than ever in the recent past.

For many officials and active members of unions, the change of government appeared to be not only a setback for the interests of their members but also a particularly open and shocking instance of ruling-class dominance and trickery. This attitude came most naturally to the minority of union leaders who supported one of Australia's three Communist parties ("national," "pro-Soviet," and "pro-Chinese"). To them, the fighting of an election on such an issue was, among other things, a useful educational experience for the majority of unionists who did not accept the inevitability of class rule. However, variants of such views were held by many other people in the unions—and outside of them—who could not be called revolutionary in any strict sense. Even those unions which did not belong to the Labor party, including most of the unions of teachers and of public servants, had good reason to regard Labor as having been favorable to their interests, both industrial and professional. It was not surprising that unions and union leaders now rallied very strongly to the party, though over a long period Labor's parliamentary leadership had increasingly been made up of people of nonunion background; though the party's popularity (as the election result showed) was at a low ebb among the voters in general and probably among rank-and-file members of unions; and though the indications immediately preceding the dissolution had been that the Whitlam government was turning away from prounion policies.

Donations from state branches of unions to the ALP funds in their respective states appear to have been more widespread and larger than usual; the $4,000 donated by the New South Wales branch of the Printing and Kindred Industries Union, with about 25,000 members, was probably typical.[17] In addition, many unions organized the collection of individual donations from members. Sydney members of the Waterside Workers' Federation were asked by their union to give $5 each and, this being a small, militant, and cohesive organization, this goal was probably more or less achieved. What is more remarkable, unions not affiliated with the ALP became involved. The Council of Australian Government Employees, made up principally of white-collar employees of the federal government whose organizations were formally nonpartisan, set up an Australian Government Unionists' Committee for Gough Whitlam, while the Australian Broadcasting Commission Staff Association, another nonpartisan union, was said to have received about $1,000 in donations for the party early in the campaign.[18]

Finances—Before and After

Attempts by the Whitlam government to oblige parties to disclose the sources of their financial support had been defeated by the non-Labor majority in the Senate. Ironically, this means that little is known of Labor's own successful efforts at fund raising for the campaign to restore Whitlam to office. On the other hand, all too much has come to light about one unsuccessful venture.

The responsibilities connected with party financing were divided between state and federal party organizations, with the former making contributions to the federal funds. The plural "funds" is used advisedly, since one such fund, the larger, was controlled by the party's national officials and another by the federal parliamentary leaders. In both New South Wales and Victoria, the state organizations had to face the prospect of state parliamentary elections early in 1976 and were therefore unable, even in the exceptional circumstances of the 1975 election, to devote all their resources to the federal campaign. This was particularly true in New South Wales, where the party had good prospects of victory at a state election (which in fact it won) in May 1976. Early in the campaign, the New South Wales

---

[17] PKIU State News, November-December 1975.
[18] Sydney Morning Herald, November 22, 1975.

secretary of the party said that $150,000 had already been raised in the state but that this was only half of what the state organization was required to raise.[19] Most of the new money, it was said, was in small amounts and the party received less than usual from business sources. No matter how the figures were juggled, it was not possible to see how the ALP could organize a national campaign that would be at all comparable with those of its opponents.

A False Move. It was in these circumstances that the most bizarre aspect of the Labor campaign occurred, though it had no practical effect at the time and was not known to the public until the election was over. This was the party's attempt to obtain additional funds from sources in Iraq. In retrospect, the whole venture seems almost incredibly foolish. Seeking funds from any overseas source would have been hazardous, and seeking them from an Arab source was bound to revive, more intense than ever, all the suspicions raised by the "Arab loans affair." Though there was never any suggestion that the party would be prepared to change its policies on the Middle East or anything else in return for Iraqi funds, the whole venture would certainly be seen, inside the party as well as by the public, as carrying inescapable anti-Israeli overtones. Hence it had to be kept secret, not least from Hawke, the notably pro-Israeli national president of the party. The intention of the instigators of this operation was that the whole affair should be kept quite separate from the party's other financial dealings and records and that it should be known only to a handful of people. But, like the Whitlam government's attempts to raise the Arab loans, this new transaction involved strange and unreliable intermediaries whose attachment to the party was, to say the least, dubious and who were likely to turn against it if the operation did not succeed.

There are several long published accounts of this strange story, compiled after the affair had come into the open and had been discussed in detail by the party's national executive in March 1976.[20] The essential facts do not appear to be in dispute. At the first meeting of the party's national campaign committee after the dismissal of Whitlam, on November 16, the left-wing "anti-Zionist," Bill Hartley, one of the members of the national executive from Victoria, raised with Whitlam and Combe the possibility of obtaining a large sum for the party from Arab sources. It was decided by these three that it

[19] Ibid.

[20] A good account is in Paul Kelly, *The Unmaking of Gough* (Sydney: Angus & Robertson, 1976), chap. 24.

was worth making an approach and that this should be done through a Sydney businessman, Reuben F. Scarf, who had many commercial contacts in Arab countries. However, the contact was actually made not with Scarf but with one of his employees and associates, Henri Fischer, who, to introduce a strange twist, some years before had written for a short-lived journal of the extreme right and whose political views, so far as he had publicly expressed them, were anti-socialist, anti-Zionist, and, it was alleged, anti-Semitic. Fischer had later dropped his public political activities but there was, to say the least, no reason to think that he was a Labor supporter or a man on whose loyalty the party could depend, especially in so delicate and dubious a matter as this.

Fischer's dealings were initially with Hartley alone, but he also met Combe and Whitlam before departing for Baghdad, where he had discussions with officials of the Iraqi government and of the Ba'ath Socialist party. On his return he reported that a sum of US$500,000 and possibly more would be made available to the ALP by the Ba'ath Socialist party. After some delays, two Iraqi emissaries arrived in Sydney on December 8, having obtained entry visas from the Australian embassy in Tokyo, where they had said that they wished to discuss the establishment of an Iraqi consulate-general in Sydney. They had discussions with Fischer, Hartley, and Combe, which apparently were encouraging enough for Combe to arrange for additional press and television advertising during the last days of the campaign.

On December 10, at their insistence, the Iraqi emissaries met Whitlam over breakfast at Fischer's apartment, but apparently no discussion of money took place until the candidate had departed. Then the emissaries left for Tokyo, accompanied by Fischer, leaving Whitlam, Combe, and Hartley with the belief that their discussions had been satisfactory and that the sum of US$500,000 would be forthcoming. Three days later, extra advertising notwithstanding, the election resulted in the devastating defeat of Labor.

The possibility of investing half a million dollars in a party that had no prospects of holding office any time soon no doubt took on a different light when viewed from Baghdad. During January and into February, as the deadlines for paying the campaign bills came closer, Combe and Hartley received equivocal encouragement from Fischer, who was at that time in Baghdad and later in London. For a time Fischer's messages were cheerful and Combe, in a further exotic twist to the story, departed for a family holiday aboard a Soviet cruise ship. However, the acute financial problems facing the firm of Mullins,

Clarke and Ralph because of the party's nonpayment of bills finally made it necessary to reveal the whole story to other party officials, including Hawke. There was then a meeting of party officers, including Combe who interrupted his cruise, and it was decided that the party would not accept the Iraqi money should it be offered. The immediate problem was solved by a bank overdraft; the party would simply have to raise the money from its Australian supporters. There is no question of the sincerity of the officers' decision to repudiate any foreign financial support, but by the time they reached that decision the prospect of the Iraqi funds' actually materializing must have seemed very small.

Even in February, the story was known only to a few people, but that was soon altered. Fischer himself, apparently changing sides, contacted Rupert Murdoch, the newspaper proprietor whose papers had become most vehemently opposed to Labor, and gave him the whole story. The story broke publicly on February 25, immediately placing in jeopardy the positions of Whitlam, Combe, and Hartley. In the event, all three retained their positions after a variety of meetings and maneuvers too complex to be detailed here. The vital decision was taken by the party's national executive at a long meeting on March 5–7, which is worth noting not only because it wound up this particular strange tale but also because it had wider implications for election finance.

The Party's Response. The executive stated in its long resolution that it could "only condemn in the strongest terms" the actions of Whitlam, Combe, and Hartley.[21] They had committed "grave errors of judgment," both in entertaining the idea of overseas financial contributions at all and in not telling the other federal officers what was going on. However, the executive also made two points in palliation. One concerned the nature of the election and the party's way of handling its finances: whatever errors of judgment had occurred could be explained in part by "the extraordinary circumstances of the recent election" and by the "excessive pressure and responsibility" which had been placed on the national secretary in matters of fund raising. (It might be added that the division of responsibility between the secretary and the parliamentary leader, each in charge of a separate fund, did little to diminish the burden on either; this uncertain division of authority was, if anything, likely to produce further troubles.) The executive also declared its intention to review the

---

21 The national executive's resolution and the story of the problems leading up to the meetings of March 5-7 are summarized in the *Australian Financial Review*, March 8, 1976.

whole question of election finances, with what outcome it still remains to be seen.

The executive's second palliation was broader. It pointed out that Labor had been "the only party in this country to espouse disclosure of sources and public funding of election campaigns." (It had been Labor's belief, of course, that the ALP would obtain a relative advantage from such disclosure in that many of the heavy contributors to the nonsocialist parties, forced to reveal the amounts of their donations, would be caused considerable discomfort by speculation as to their motives.) Had Labor's proposals to force public disclosure of funds not been defeated by its opponents in the Senate, the party would have been saved the consequences of the bad judgment of those who had sought to act on its behalf on this occasion—and, more generally, election financing would have come under public scrutiny so that improper or undesirable pressure of any kind, even the appearance or possibility of such pressure, would have been restricted.

The episode was, in a sense, a fitting epilogue to the Whitlam government. In the area of campaign finance, as in others, Labor had good intentions that it would have put into effect had it not been for the hostile majority in the Senate. But when it came to the reality of electoral financing it was Labor, not its opponents, that was exposed. Its errors appeared to be due not to any evil let alone criminal intent, but to haste, bad judgment, and the absence of teamwork and mutual trust.

4

THE LIBERAL PARTY

Michelle Grattan

Before its defeat in the December 1972 election, the Liberal party, in coalition with the Country party, had ruled Australia continuously at the federal level for twenty-three years. Non-Labor governments had been in power nationally for all but sixteen years since federation in 1901. During the L-NCP coalition's most recent spell in opposition, 1972 to 1975, the Liberal party underwent a policy reassessment, power realignment, and organizational shakeup greater than any since the party's formation in the 1940s. To understand the party that went into the 1975 election it is necessary to know something of its history and nature and to examine in some detail this "time in the wilderness."

The Background

The Liberal party is the last of a series of Australian conservative parties.[1] Several times, and most spectacularly in the 1940s the conservative forces have broken up, regrouped, and changed their

---

[1] For material on the Liberals, see Katherine West, *Power in the Liberal Party* (Melbourne: Cheshire, 1965); Peter Aimer, *Politics, Power and Persuasion* (Melbourne: James Bennett, 1974); Hugh V. Emy, *The Politics of Australian Democracy* (Melbourne: Macmillan, 1974), chap. 15; Louise Overacker, *The Australian Party System* (New Haven: Yale, 1952), chaps. 7 and 9; Louise Overacker, *Australian Parties in a Changing Society 1945-67* (Melbourne: Cheshire, 1968), chaps. 7, 8, and 10; L. F. Crisp, *Australian National Government* (Croydon: Longman, 1973), chap. 9; Ray Aitchison, ed., *Looking at the Liberals* (Melbourne: Cheshire, 1974); C. J. Lloyd and G. S. Reid, *Out of the Wilderness: The Return of Labor* (Melbourne: Cassell, 1974), chap. 11; Paul Kelly, *The Unmaking of Gough* (Sydney: Angus & Robertson, 1976), passim; Ken Turner, "The Liberal 'Iceberg'," in Henry Mayer and Helen Nelson, eds., *Australian Politics: A Third Reader* (Melbourne: Cheshire, 1973), pp. 368-85.

name. On two occasions—after splits in the Labor party over conscription in World War I and over economic policy in the depression—the anti-Labor party digested sections of the former Labor government, and former ALP men became conservative prime ministers.[2] By the early 1940s, however, the non-Labor government was in disarray, torn by internal strife and fights with the Country party. Between 1939 and 1941 there were several different combinations of the United Australia party (UAP) and the Country party, headed by UAP leader Robert Menzies and Country party leaders Earle Page and Arthur Fadden. In October 1941 the precarious hold of the then Country party-UAP government in power ended when two independents withdrew their support; a no-confidence motion on the government's budget proposals was carried and a Labor government was commissioned. This was the beginning of eight years of Labor rule, Labor's longest continuous period in federal office. The non-Labor forces were decimated at the 1943 federal elections and in that year Labor governed all of the states except Victoria and South Australia: by 1945, for the first and only time since 1915, six of Australia's seven governments were under Labor rule.

In late 1944, when the conservative forces were at their lowest ebb, Menzies gathered together the shattered remnants of the UAP and other conservative groups for two conferences which resulted in the formation of a new political party. This was to be antisocialist, but its stress must be positive, Menzies told the delegates from eighteen organizations who attended the first unity conference in Canberra. On too many questions, Menzies said, the UAP had been in the position "of the man who says 'no'." The new party should strive for a "true revival of liberal thought which will work for social justice and security, for national power and national progress, and for the full development of the individual citizen, though not through the dull and deadening process of socialism."[3] The young party won comfortably in 1949, swept to power by the increasing unpopularity of a Labor government loath to relax wartime controls, such as petrol rationing, and under seige over an abortive attempt to nationalize the private banks.

---

[2] William Morris Hughes, Labor prime minister from October 1915 to November 1916, served as the National Labor group prime minister from November 1916 to February 1917 and then as the Nationalist party prime minister from February 1917 to February 1923. Joseph Aloysius Lyons, former minister in the Scullin Labor government, was United Australia party prime minister from January 1932 to April 1939.

[3] Overacker, *Australian Parties*, p. 175.

Just as the Liberal party's creation was very much the work of Menzies,[4] so its decline, which ended in the 1972 defeat, reflected the aftermath of Menzies's dominance. After resigning from the federal Parliament, a former government whip, Henry B. Gullett, said: "the Menzies government is ninety percent Menzies."[5] Its founder presided over the Liberal government—with one very near defeat in 1961 during the economic recession—until his retirement in January 1966. The country's relatively steady economic growth, Labor's disarray, and Menzies's skillful exploitation of the "Communist scare" issue of the cold war years contributed to the Liberals' success.

However, Menzies's supremacy within the party created a severe leadership vacuum in the years following his retirement. The party that had known no other leader for the first twenty-one years of its life was to have five between 1966 and 1975. Menzies had removed all those whom he perceived as potential threats to his own position. His chosen successor, Harold Holt, who had won a landslide victory in the 1966 "Vietnam" election, was already losing support when he was drowned while surfing in December 1967. Holt's successor, John Gorton, chosen by the party mainly for his "image" and presumed ability to make a good public and television showing against the new Labor leader, Gough Whitlam, sparked serious ideological division within the party, especially over his more centralist approach, and alienated some sections by his "shoot from the hip" political style; many believed that he lacked the self-discipline for the job. When Gorton was displaced in March 1971 by William McMahon,[6] already past his political prime, the party was well on its way to political defeat and torn by factional fighting. By the 1972 campaign, the L-NCP coalition was tired and lacking in ideas, and McMahon's leadership had little support either within the government or among

---

[4] In her first book on the Australian party system, published in 1952, Overacker points out that in the early years there was widespread dissatisfaction with Menzies's leadership within the Liberal party and that after the Liberals failed to gain office in 1946 some suggested that a new leader should take over. Menzies at that time, like Malcolm Fraser later, was saddled with an unfavorable image acquired in earlier political battles—that of a destructive troublemaker and a man who lacked the "common touch" (Overacker, *Australian Party System*, pp. 267-68). Electoral success, however, established and consolidated Menzies's supremacy.

[5] H. B. Gullett, "Parliamentary Government in Australia," in John Wilkes, ed., *Forces in Australian Politics* (Sydney: Angus and Robertson, 1963), p. 91. H. B. Gullett was chief whip for the L-NCP government in the federal Parliament from 1950 to 1955.

[6] Gorton used his casting vote against himself after a tied vote in the party room on a confidence motion on his leadership. See Alan Reid, *The Gorton Experiment* (Sydney: Shakespeare Head, 1971), pp. 437-43.

the electorate at large. He was no match for the articulate and persuasive Whitlam. The issues of the 1950s and 1960s, including communism and the Vietnam War, were fading or turning sour, and the country's economy was worse off than it had been for a decade. The Liberals could not put forward policies to match the programs for young suburbanites which Labor under Whitlam had been evolving and selling since 1967, nor could it approach the flair of the ALP's "It's Time" campaign.

The Nature of the Liberal Party. The Liberal party is ideologically a coalition ranging from highly conservative to liberal with a small "l"; organizationally, it is a federation of six state parties and a federal party. While it draws its basic financial support from the business and professional sector and has its electoral base in the middle classes, it pitches its appeal in wider terms and frequently portrays itself as the "nonsectional" party of Australian politics. (For the occupations of Liberal M.P.s since 1949 see Table 4-1; for membership data on the six state parties see Table 4-2.)

As in all conservative parties, power flows downwards. The leader, together with his senior colleagues, dominates the parliamentary party, which jealously guards its independence against any direction from the outside organization. In a Liberal government the prime minister chooses his own ministers, in contrast to his ALP counterpart, whose ministry is elected by the party caucus.[7] After the 1975 victory, Prime Minister Fraser set up an elaborate network of backbench party committees which review proposed legislation, but the role of the "party room" (the equivalent of Labor's caucus) in determining policy when the Liberals are in government is still only persuasive and advisory, rather than formal and decisive like that of the caucus in the Labor party. On the other hand, Liberal M.P.s very occasionally use the ultimate sanction of crossing the floor on an issue.[8] The basic disciplinary weapon of the party's extraparliamentary organization is still the power to choose candidates and so to withdraw party endorsement from any dissident member or senator;

---

[7] But note that in the Victoria state government most members of Liberal cabinets are elected, though a Liberal premier retains the right to nominate a couple of them.

[8] In April 1976 six Liberal senators crossed the floor to defeat a move by the new Liberal government to abolish the funeral benefit for pensioners. In December 1976 the government was forced to back down on its proposed changes to the Australian Broadcasting Commission because nearly a dozen Liberal members said they would oppose them.

Table 4-1

OCCUPATIONS OF LIBERAL MEMBERS OF HOUSE OF REPRESENTATIVES, 1949–75

Occupation	1949		1963		1969		1975	
	Percentage	Number	Percentage	Number	Percentage	Number	Percentage	Number
Professionals (including teachers and accountants)	32.7	(18)	44.2	(23)	43.4	(20)	50.0	(34)
Farmers, graziers	16.4	(9)	9.6	(5)	17.4	(8)	13.2	(9)
Party officers, officials of employer groups, political consultants	—	—	3.8	(2)	6.5	(3)	5.9	(4)
Company directors, business executives	30.8	(17)	25.0	(13)	19.5	(9)	16.2	(11)
Owners of small businesses	9.1	(5)	11.5	(6)	6.5	(3)	7.3	(5)
Management and economic consultants	1.8	(1)	3.8	(2)	6.5	(3)	5.9	(4)
Blue-collar workers	—	—	—	—	—	—	—	—
White-collar workers	7.2	(4)	—	—	—	—	—	—
Housewives	1.8	(1)	—	—	—	—	—	—
Members of armed forces	—	—	1.9	(1)	—	—	1.4	(1)
Total	100.0	(55)	100.0	(52)	100.0	(46)	100.0	(68)

Note: Years refer to elections at which members won their seats. Percentages may not add to 100 because of rounding.

Source: Australian Press Services, *Guides to Federal Parliament* (published privately); Australian Government Publishing Service, *Australian Parliamentary Handbooks*; Joan Rydon, *A Biographical Register of the Commonwealth Parliament, 1901–1972* (Canberra: Australian National University Press, 1975); personal inquiry.

Table 4-2

MEMBERSHIP AND STAFF OF LIBERAL PARTY BRANCHES,
BY STATE, OCTOBER 1975 AND SEPTEMBER 1976

| State | Number of Branches | | Member-ship | Number of Full-Time Staff |
	Metro-politan	Rural		
October 1975 [a]				
New South Wales	314	174	23,165	51
Victoria	207	214	33,498	34
Queensland	166	48	9,580	18
South Australia	97	170	34,195	22
Western Australia	63	104	16,073	15
Tasmania	(not available)		6,308	9
Total	847	710	122,819	149
September 1976 [b]				
New South Wales	328	171	39,068	50
Victoria	210	203	38,416	34
Queensland	146	54	10,983	15
South Australia	104	166	34,014	21
Western Australia	71	109	21,220	26
Tasmania	(not available)		8,193	11
Total	859	703	151,894	157

[a] The federal Liberal party had a full-time staff of nineteen at this date.
[b] The federal Liberal party had a full-time staff of twenty at this date.
Source: Liberal party Federal Secretariat.

this, however, while it may be useful as a threat, is difficult and clumsy to apply in practice.[9]

The tremendous authority which the Liberals vest in their leader derives both from the philosophical and organizational nature of the party and from the Menzies reign. The other side of the coin is the demand that the leader deliver electoral success—or be replaced by someone who, in the opinion of the party, can. Bill Snedden, elected federal leader after the 1972 defeat, sowed the seeds of his own overthrow when he mistimed the forcing of the May 1974 double

[9] During the constitutional crisis there were strong mutterings that any senator who deserted on the budget vote would face party retribution, and certainly senators who were opposed to rejecting supply feared that they would be axed by their state divisions.

dissolution, and he ensured his removal by his poor performance vis-à-vis Whitlam in late 1974 and early 1975. Even the anticipation of a leader's defeat can be enough to remove him: the New South Wales party tossed out Premier Thomas Lewis in early 1976 when a state election was looming because it regarded him as an electoral liability.

The Liberal party is organized primarily around personalities and the pursuit and maintenance of power. While there are internal doctrinal differences, they are not as hard and fast as those that divide the ALP, and regroupings take place across hazy and shifting ideological boundaries without those involved feeling too much unease with their new bedfellows. Thus Malcolm Fraser, whose views placed him on the conservative wing of the party, helped John Gorton, on the left wing of the party, to power in 1968—and was a prime force in his removal in 1971. If a leader is perceived as strong, and able to give direction to the party and deliver the electorate, the party will support him regardless of ideological qualms: Fraser came to power with the support of many who would have considerable differences with him on matters of policy.

But while the Liberal party's ideology is less rigorous and easily described than the ideology—or ideologies—of the ALP, while it is more often a rallying cry than a detailed prescription for action, it has certain identifiable negative and positive strands. It is "antisocialist," stresses "individual initiative," and uses the rhetoric of free enterprise. It preaches the decentralization of power and the federal system. It prefers to look to the individual rather than the state as a source of economic development and initiative. Yet a strand of "welfarism" runs through it: Liberal party conservatives advocate state help to the "needy," while liberal Liberals advocate something closer to the Labor variant, that is, very active government participation in services and welfare. In international affairs, the Liberals have had a dependent mentality, placing more emphasis on Australia's weakness and need for powerful friends than on its potential as a significant middle power. The party's very pragmatism should perhaps also be included as an aspect of its ideology: first and foremost, it is concerned with running government. Thus, the Liberals' commitment to free enterprise did not inhibit successive Liberal governments from accepting and extending the Australian norms of government intervention in the private sector to provide both services and subsidies. Their belief in federalism did not stop pre-1972 Liberal federal governments from eroding state powers for practical and electoral purposes. The battles over financial relations which

Liberal premiers had with Liberal prime ministers, especially Gorton, were just as bitter as those they had with Labor Prime Minister Whitlam. Menzies's promise in the 1963 election campaign of federal aid for secondary school science buildings and equipment was to take the government into direct school funding and pave the way for massive education funding by the Labor government a decade later.

The Liberals' 1972–75 opposition period had its effect on ideology and policy, on the parliamentary party's relations with the organization, and on the organization's own structure and role. When the Liberals had been in power, they had basically allowed public servants to dominate policy creation: in opposition the party had to come to grips with formulating policy without the resources of the bureaucracy behind it. It also had to decide in what terms to pitch its electoral appeal. After the 1972 defeat, the conservatives within the Liberal party tended to argue that it had lost its traditional principles and had moved too far towards Labor, while the party's left wing felt it had become conservative and out of step with modern thinking and the young voter. In 1974 the Liberal leader, Snedden, tried to capture the middle ground by accepting many of Labor's initiatives; his was basically a "me too" policy except in the area of economics, where the tax cuts he proposed were later taken over by the victorious Labor government. Circumstances and the ideological inclinations of Fraser combined in 1975 to produce a Liberal policy which stressed the differences between the Labor and Liberal alternatives and the tough options which the Liberals told the people were needed to restore the ailing economy. The formal policy renewal process which went on inside the party, including the updating of the federal platform, was important not only as an electoral maneuver but also as psychological rejuvenation, as therapy for a party in the process of coming to grips with opposition.

As the Liberals' electoral fortunes had declined, the party organization had become more and more assertive; while they were in opposition, it flexed its muscles.[10] The party organization never made any real attempt to change the power relationship between itself and the parliamentary party—that is, to increase M.P. accountability to the party machine on the Labor model—yet its awe of the Liberals in Parliament diminished after the 1972 defeat. The party organization

---

[10] "As the party moved from secure and stable government under Menzies, to shaky and faction-ridden government under Gorton and McMahon, to opposition under Snedden, so the function of the organizational wing has changed from passive support to active policy making and direction." Dean Jaensch, "The Liberal Party and Change," in Richard Lucy, ed., *The Pieces of Politics* (Melbourne: Macmillan, 1975).

reminded them that their weaknesses and divisions had caused defeat, and it demanded that note be taken of its opinions, such as its long-standing disapproval of the Liberal governments' tendency to increase the power of the central government. The party's federal president, Robert Southey, spoke out plainly after the Liberal defeat of December 2, 1972:

> The personal ambitions and feuds inside the parliamentary Liberal party since the death of Harold Holt have been deadly and destructive. That sort of conduct must be buried with the past. If it is not, the organization's authority over [the endorsement of] candidates may have to be employed ruthlessly.

Southey said the transition from government to opposition substantially altered the role of the Liberal organization:

> What I particularly have in mind is that in these changing times, the parliamentarians will need to be responsive to the mind and the will of the organization so that the policies espoused by the Parliamentary Party become a true reflection of the organization's outlook, which is very representative. . . .[11]

Despite its determination to resist any encroachments on its power, the parliamentary party was forced to look to the organization's secretariat, whose functions had atrophied while the Liberals were in government, to provide it with the research backup it now needed. The possibility of operating policy and communications units outside the secretariat was eventually abandoned in favor of merging such units with it. By 1975 the secretariat had become an efficient vehicle for gathering and distilling information and disseminating propaganda. In this upgrading of the secretariat, the Liberals looked to experience overseas, especially to that of the British Conservative party. The hiring in 1974 of Tony Eggleton, former press secretary to four Liberal prime ministers, first to head the planned communications unit and later to become the party's federal director, also strengthened the secretariat's links with the parliamentary party. Eggleton was highly regarded by both Snedden and Fraser; he worked out of the office of each for a time and played a key role in the 1974 and 1975 campaigns. His personal influence and rapport with Fraser ensured a continuing input from the secretariat in the early days of the new Liberal government in 1976.

---

[11] *Daily Telegraph*, December 5, 1972.

One academic observer wrote of the Liberal party in the mid-1960s: "Except in a strictly formal sense, there is no such thing as the Liberal Party of Australia which, in practice, is a composite of seven Parties. . . ."[12] Nowhere was this more true than in national election campaigns, where the state divisions of the party went their own ways even to the extent of employing their own advertising agencies. The experience of Labor's 1972 campaign and the strong drive to win back government prompted an enormous strengthening of the federal party's hold over campaigning. By late 1973 the party had appointed a national advertising agency: by the time of the 1975 campaign there was a formidable national election organization which ran with military precision and liked to use military jargon.

The Liberals in Opposition

As the 1972 elections approached, most members of the L-NCP coalition government saw the inevitability of defeat, but when it came few were psychologically or practically prepared for it. None of the fifty-eight Liberal and Country party House of Representatives members returned in 1972 had previously sat in opposition. Senior party members lost the ministerial staff and public service support on which they had come to rely. The general secretary of the New South Wales division, J. J. Carlton, described the early reactions of some of them to being out of office:

> It is surprising how much it affected them and how much they did not realise what the changes would be like. A lot of them wandered around like headless chooks [chickens] for a long time, not having departmental heads to call on, and people to arrange their itineraries, and I think some of them had even forgotten how to use a telephone—not all of them.[13]

James Killen, who had been a minister in the Gorton government, summed up the situation:

> For the Liberal Party, defeat was an utterly demoralising blow. After three years of bitter and schismatic struggle, during which time appeals for reconciliation were spitefully ignored, the loss of government was bewildering. It would be a gross piece of dishonesty to pretend that in the months that followed December, 1972, recrimination was not given a savage role.[14]

---

12 West, *Power in the Liberal Party*, p. 261.
13 Quoted in Lloyd and Reid, *Out of the Wilderness*, p. 310.
14 *Australian*, December 14, 1973.

With the divisions of the past in mind and fearful that the party might self-destruct, as the UAP had, the Liberals chose a consensus man to replace McMahon. Billy Mackie Snedden, forty-five, unexciting, ideologically gray, but disliked by no one and able to exert a unifying influence, was elected party leader by one vote after a tied vote out of a field of five candidates. Snedden, who had been deputy party leader and treasurer in the Liberal government, had come from a struggling working-class background and obtained a law degree under the ex-servicemen's rehabilitation scheme. Though Snedden was an affable man, insecurity was a basic trait of his personality, and his need to prove himself was to contribute to his subsequent downfall. His new deputy was Phillip Lynch, thirty-nine, former minister for labor and national service, and a management consultant before entering Parliament. Lynch too was from relatively humble origins and a Catholic in a traditionally WASP party.

While defeat made the organization more assertive, it also led to some experimentation within the parliamentary party. The party decided to elect the members of its parliamentary executive, rather than have them appointed by the leader. This was an experiment with which Snedden did not agree but which, wisely, he did not fight. A year later, as the party saw itself approaching closer to government, it was abandoned.

Defeat also quickly affected relations between the Liberals and their former coalition partner, the Country party, generating some early friction. For many Liberals, especially the more progressive members from urban constituencies, the L-NCP coalition was a marriage of convenience rather than of choice: they resented being tied to a party that could be strident in its sectional demands and hardline-conservative on social issues. During the 1960s the alliance had been kept smooth at the national level by the skillful management of Menzies and the Country party's leader John McEwen, who, for his part, was eager to broaden the Country party's image against the day when the erosion of the rural population would eat away the party's natural base. However, at the state level, most notably in Victoria, relations between the two organizations were traditionally very bad, and this was exacerbated by opposition. Even at the federal level there had been a damaging wrangle within the government in December 1971 over the parity of the Australian dollar, during which Douglas Anthony, McEwen's successor, had threatened to take the Country party out of the coalition. After the 1972 defeat, the Liberals were angered at statements from Anthony and his deputy, Ian Sinclair, which blamed the Liberals for the debacle. Anthony announced that the two parties would operate separately in opposition. The early days saw some unseemly squabbling about whether Anthony or Lynch would be the second most important person in the opposition and receive the staffing and accommodation perquisites that went along with the position. The two parties held separate meetings and each appointed its own committees and spokesmen to cover the gamut of policy. Tensions at the organizational level flared from time to time, notably in Victoria and Queensland, where there were major rows over the order of Liberal and Country party candidates on the Senate ticket, and in Victoria over the contesting of seats against sitting Country party or Liberal members.

Within Parliament, although a basic harmony remained, one spectacular clash occurred in late 1973 when the Country party broke with the Liberal party over its attempt to block funds for schools in an effort to get a better deal for the wealthier private schools. The Country party, always electorally pragmatic, saw the danger in having to defend wealthy schools to a skeptical electorate. It negotiated a deal with the government and crossed the floor, voting with Labor to pass the schools' funds.

During the 1974 campaign Anthony embarrassed the Liberals by publicly supporting an increase in oil prices, which was contrary to opposition policy, and by declaring that the ninety-day price freeze that Snedden was advocating would not work for fresh foods. In 1975 attempts by the Country party to revive its organization in Tasmania were perceived by the local Liberals as a threat. However, the days of opposition made it clear to both parties that they must work closely together to regain government: before the 1974 campaigns they had moved back into close working relations with a joint policy for the election, and a formal coalition was set up after the election.

The Policy Review, 1973–75. The reassessment of Liberal policy, which Prime Minister McMahon began in a last-ditch effort to rescue his dying government, proceeded in opposition on two linked fronts: within the parliamentary party and in the organization.[15] The review took time to get into full swing but gradually it became more systematic. In early 1973 Snedden appointed about a dozen policy com-

---

[15] See Graeme Starr, "Preparing for an Election: The Liberal Party's Policy Review, 1972," in Henry Mayer, ed., *Labor to Power* (Sydney: Angus & Robertson, 1973). The Liberal party distinguishes between its *platform* which contains the general philosophical commitments and goals of the party and is the responsibility of the organization, and its *policy*, which contains fuller and more immediate and specific commitments and is the responsibility of the parliamentary party.

mittees within the parliamentary party, backing up the areas covered by frontbench spokesmen. These committees were to examine government actions, prepare policies, and establish liaison with the party organization and specialists within the community. The party also began a review of its platform, a thin and general document which had basically survived from the 1940s with some revisions in 1960 and 1971. Deputy Leader Lynch chaired a Platform Review Committee of equal numbers of Liberal members of Parliament and organization representatives and representing all state and ideological factions. This group reported to the Joint Standing Committee on Federal Policy, which links the parliamentary party and the organization and is chaired by the parliamentary leader. Letters were sent to all branches of the party asking for ideas: each branch was asked to fill in a questionnaire, which included a wide range of policy headings, and to call a special meeting to discuss policy. Sixty-five percent of the branches replied to the questionnaire. Each person on Lynch's Platform Review Committee was given specific policy areas to handle and was instructed to produce a draft document. The committee then considered and rewrote these drafts and asked the parliamentary party's policy committees for opinions. Revised drafts were sent to the state divisions and to federal M.P.s. The platform review thus involved all levels of the party and in itself had a unifying effect. With the calling of the premature election, the platform was published in draft form, although it was not until October 1974 that it was formally ratified by the Federal Council.

The new platform, seventy-five pages to the old sixteen, although (unlike Labor's platform) still only advisory to the parliamentary party, was a comprehensive and detailed document.[16] Its eight main sections covered government, Australia in the world, the law and the individual, the welfare of the individual, the community, economic development, and "into the 1980s." Some forty subsections ranged through federalism, administration, censorship, aborigines, leisure, culture, consumer affairs, the economy, overseas investment, primary industry, and a host of other topics. The new platform, with a modern painting to replace the staid blue cover of the old version, dropped the preamble that had declared the document to be "a programme for a people whose highest ideals are inspired by a belief in God." In general, the influence of the party's middle-of-the-road elements was evident, as was the passing of some of the old preoccupations of

[16] See *The Official Federal Platform of the Liberal Party of Australia*, as approved by the Federal Council, May 31, 1971, and Liberal party of Australia, *Federal Platform*, as approved by the Federal Council, October 1974.

the cold war era. Although the new document contained the odd reference to the evils of communism, this subject did not rate a separate section; the outmoded version, by contrast, had called for "unremitting opposition to Communism as the enemy of human freedom and the most unscrupulous opponent of religion, civilised government, law and order, peace and national security" and a multi-fronted campaign to widen "the public understanding of the aims and activities of Communism." [17] The disguised defense of the "White Australia Policy" [18]—a policy that had started to break down under the Holt government—disappeared, as did reference to the policy of encouraging British-stock immigration in order to preserve "our national heritage." The revised platform reflected the new issues of the 1970s, including technology and conservation. Provisions stressing the need to control foreign investment and recognizing the rights of aborigines to a traditional life style (rather than simply calling for their assimilation) reflected both the times and the changes that the Labor government had made. The platform also showed the party's disenchantment with the centralist trend of government that had been promoted particularly by Labor, but also by former Liberal governments.

The old platform had not attempted to spell out the Liberals' federalist commitment in more than general terms. The Liberals' aim, it had said, was "To maintain the Federal system of Government with the division of powers and functions between State Governments and the Commonwealth Government as most conducive to the progress and well-being of Australia and its citizens, the development of Australia's territories and resources, and the democratic protection of the freedom of the individual." [19] The new platform was the first and major step in the evolution of the new federalism that was to be a central policy of the 1975 campaign and of the early months of the Fraser government. The party committed itself to "Financial arrangements between the Commonwealth and the States to provide adequate and assured sources of revenue with which to carry out their constitutional responsibilities, such sources to provide the States with substantial income under their own control." [20] It went on to spell out "The guaranteeing of an adequate proportion of Commonwealth personal income tax revenue for the purpose of the States, such

---

[17] *Official Federal Platform*, 1971, p. 3.

[18] Explicit reference to this policy had already been eliminated from the Liberal platform by the 1960s.

[19] *Official Federal Platform*, 1971, pp. 4-5.

[20] For this and subsequent references, see *Federal Platform*, 1974, p. 7.

proportion to be determined by arrangement between the Commonwealth and the States." In a reaction against the use of the tied-grants section of the constitution, which had mushroomed under Labor, the new Liberal platform provided that grants to the states should be "free of restrictions in detail that infringe on the right of States to determine policy in their areas of responsibility."

A substantial part of the work on the platform had been done by May 1974. On the policy side, by early 1974 the parliamentary party's policy review was just starting to produce results and the whole process was fairly uncoordinated. Considerable work had been done in the economic area by Snedden and Lynch. The party had announced in early 1973 that it would establish a policy research unit which would work closely with the parliamentary party and its leadership to develop policies. The unit was to be separate from, but under the general auspices of, the secretariat. It would be directed by a research group, chaired by Snedden, which would report to the joint standing committee on policy. But it was not until January 1974 that Timothy Pascoe, who had qualifications in engineering, economics, and business, was appointed director of the unit. The three-man research staff at the secretariat was busy with the platform review. The result was that, when the opposition forced the 1974 double dissolution, it was caught without its own detailed policies ready. A 136-page policy document, *The Way Ahead*, was put together for the election in a frantic week-long meeting over Easter. Though quite impressive, this document drew heavily on Labor initiatives, and the speed of its production meant no one had much in the way of a personal commitment to its contents.[21]

After the 1974 elections the policy unit was merged into the general secretariat and Pascoe became the party's federal director. The secretariat adopted what one of its research members termed a "conduit" role, bringing together shadow ministers, backbenchers, and outside experts for seminars on major policy areas. Each was attended by about twenty people and each cost the party about $1,500 to $2,000. Liberal party policy research manager Ian Marsh described the process:

> A typical working party began with a discussion of the assumptions underlying the possible range of objectives, moved on to consider the specific goals that might guide policy, then identified the issues most needing action by government, and concluded with a review of the role and policy options available to the Commonwealth Govern-

---

21 *The Way Ahead*, Liberal party, March 1974.

ment. These working parties provided the information from which draft policy papers could be developed as all outside participants provided written summary notes on the particular topics on which they were to lead discussion. . . .

Participants did not necessarily have a formal association with the Liberal Party, although a shared commitment to liberal values helped to avoid ideological wrangling. Instead, groups were assembled to satisfy two criteria: first, to ensure that individual participants had original and practical suggestions on the particular matters on which they were asked to lead discussion; second, that the group as a whole contained protagonists for the current major alternative approaches to policy in the area being considered.[22]

The fleshing out of Liberal policy on federalism illustrates the process at work. The party's Federal Council had established a joint committee of federal and state parliamentary leaders and organization representatives, chaired by Lynch, to find a tax-sharing formula. Lynch asked Senator John Carrick to make preliminary recommendations. The secretariat assembled a working party consisting of three visiting academics from the Australian National University's federal financial relations center (including one with recent experience of Prime Minister Trudeau's major reform of Canada's federal arrangements), a law professor, two economists, a political scientist, and two others experienced in local government administration and training. Several senior M.P.s also took part. The document which emerged from this meeting was later recast by Senator Carrick into a more "political" form and was put through the parliamentary party's executive.

After Fraser became leader he established in April 1975 a Policy Co-ordination Committee chaired by Lynch. The committee, Fraser said, would assist him "by adopting roles as my watch-dog and my devil's advocate in the development of policy proposals." Ian Marsh, in his essay on Liberal policy making, comments:

> The establishment of this committee represented renewed endorsement of the principle that Opposition represented a 'sabbatical' period during which new policy proposals could be developed. The committee's task as the leader's watch-dog and devil's advocate was interpreted to involve setting a timetable for policy development and seeing it was observed. . . .

---

[22] This quotation and the material and quotations in the rest of this section are from Ian Marsh, "Policy Making in the Liberal Party: The Opposition Experience," *Australian Quarterly*, June 1976, pp. 5-17.

This committee also ensured policy papers were adequate in logic and content and were consistent between areas. . . .

Finally, in keeping with the debauched state of the economy, the committee also had to ensure that new spending commitments were kept at the absolute minimum.

Policy papers went from shadow ministers through this committee, then to the shadow cabinet, and finally to the party room. By November 11, 1975, nine major policy statements—on the economy, federalism, foreign affairs, education, foreign investment, and social welfare—had been cleared by the committee, the shadow cabinet, and the party room and had been publicly issued; eight more—covering, among other topics, the environment, housing, and aboriginal affairs—were waiting to go to the shadow cabinet, and ten others had had some consideration from the Policy Co-ordination Committee.

The 1974 Elections and the Fall of Snedden. In 1973–75 the Liberal and Country parties had a power that oppositions in democratic countries rarely possess between elections: the ability to frustrate government measures of which they disapproved and, ultimately, the ability to throw the government out of office. Both of these derived from the opposition's effective control of the Senate. Before the 1974 double dissolution, this control depended on the help of the DLP, but after the 1974 election the coalition had the numbers to block any legislation. The opposition used its strength readily: it did not accept the proposition that the government had a mandate for any specific item in its program, nor did it take for granted that the Labor government would necessarily serve out the conventional three-year term. The Senate became a battleground for government and opposition from the earliest months. After the "raid" in March 1973 by the attorney general, Senator Murphy, on the headquarters of the Australian Security Intelligence Organisation in Melbourne, the Senate censured Murphy and set up its own inquiry into the affair.[23] By the end of 1973 the opposition had rejected or failed to pass legislation for Labor's proposed universal health scheme, electoral legislation to reduce the allowable variation between electorates from 20 percent to 10 percent (which would have cost the Country party three or four seats), the Australian Industry Development Corporation bills, the petroleum and minerals authority and offshore control legislation, the trade

---

[23] On March 15, 1973, Senator Murphy paid a late night visit to the Australian Security Intelligence Organisation office in Canberra, seeking information about Croatian terrorists. Angered by a document he found there, Murphy flew to Melbourne next morning and arrived at ASIO's headquarters with Commonwealth police, who sealed the files.

practices bill, and referendums to alter the constitution. Although only 27 out of 256 bills had been rejected or deferred, they included key aspects of Labor's program.

The opposition's "obstruction" in the Senate was such that by the end of 1973 Prime Minister Whitlam was flirting with the possibility of a double dissolution in the hope of getting his legislation through the subsequent joint sitting. Several factors were pushing the opposition towards an election. The government's popularity was sliding considerably in the latter part of 1973, and this trend had been reflected in the Liberals' comfortable win in the Parramatta by-election in September after a former Liberal minister, Nigel Bowen, was appointed to the bench. By the end of the year Snedden was becoming confident that the opposition, under his leadership, could win an election. As two commentators wrote, "The defeat of two referendums [in December]—to give the federal government constitutional power over prices and incomes—and his own performance in the referendum campaign gave him a false impression of what was likely to happen in a general election. He and his staff underestimated the difference between a referendum campaign and the real thing." [24] Snedden's own need to establish his leadership position authoritatively within the party made him anxious for an early election. He was under no immediate threat, but his leadership throughout 1973, though it had improved, had been uninspiring. His chief virtue was that he held a potentially warring party together and encouraged the expression of different points of view; but he tended to overact and could not match Whitlam in Parliament. A good election win, either in the Senate poll due in the first half of 1974 or in a general election, would give his leadership the stamp of authority that victory accords Liberal leaders. The Country party made no secret of its eagerness for a general election: above all, the NCP feared the effects of a redistribution (redistricting) under Labor's proposals, and its leader, Anthony, was studying the option of forcing an election by September 1973.

Whether and how quickly these factors alone would have induced the opposition to break with convention and reject supply can never be known. Without the "Gair affair" the opposition would have had to initiate the convention-breaking that was to characterize 1974–75; at the earliest, it would probably have waited until the government had presented its 1974 Budget, when its own policies would have been in better shape and the economy in a clear recession. By so doing

---

[24] Laurie Oakes and David Solomon, *Grab for Power: Election '74* (Melbourne: Cheshire, 1974), p. 183.

it would have ensured victory and Snedden would have saved his leadership. Instead, Snedden reacted emotionally to Labor's appointment of DLP Senator Gair to an ambassadorship in a bid to improve the government's position at the forthcoming half-Senate election. Snedden later reportedly told one of Whitlam's staff that the move to reject supply had resulted from Country party pressure: "The reason we did it was that there was a half-Senate election due. We thought you might gain control of the Senate and get your redistribution through. Doug Anthony told me we had to do all in our power to prevent the redistribution." [25] Within the Liberal camp there was some soul searching about the move: senior member James Killen spoke out against it in the party room. But the emotionalism of the Gair affair drowned the doubters' voices: the decision began the paradox of the Whitlam years, during which "the conservative parties cast themselves in the role of constitutional radicals." [26]

The premature rejection of supply left the Liberals only half prepared for the 1974 campaign. Their revamped campaign committee had begun planning as far back as September for both the half-Senate election that was due and the possibility of a double dissolution. It had commissioned several surveys which had shown that inflation was an issue to be stressed in any campaign. But the policy-making process was lagging and only a few policies had been released or were ready for release when the election was called. A week-long meeting was needed to draft the policy manifesto for the campaign.[27]

The key to the Liberals' campaign was the attack on inflation. Snedden proposed a $600 million tax cut to give leadership for a program of voluntary wage and price restraint. He also promised that a Liberal government would reduce the rate of growth in federal government spending. Snedden warned that if these measures did not work "we would take the further step of a short-term prices and incomes freeze in conjunction with State Governments." [28] His economic package met with trenchant criticism from economic journalists, and he was pursued by the media at daily press conferences for details

---

[25] Quoted in Laurie Oakes, *Crash Through or Crash: The Unmaking of a Prime Minister* (Richmond: Drummond, 1976), p. 141.

[26] Kelly, *Unmaking of Gough*, p. 270.

[27] For a description of this meeting, see Oakes and Solomon, *Grab for Power*, chap. 17.

[28] Campaign opening speech by the leader of the opposition, April 30, 1974. Snedden said it would be "necessary for a Liberal-Country Party Government to play its part in providing for tax relief if the unions and employers are to be asked to moderate their wage and price claims."

of what would be cut. Too often he allowed himself to be drawn into debates on the specifics of what a Liberal government would do, and an apparent contradiction emerged between the promise of spending restraint and the Liberals' takeover of many of Labor's initiatives. In the vital second week of the campaign, Snedden made the mistake of spending too much time in the outlying states, away from the main centers of Melbourne and Sydney. In the 1975 campaign, Malcolm Fraser would show that he had absorbed both lessons.

The closeness of the election result ensured Snedden's survival as leader for the immediate future. But despite the worsening economic crisis and the increasing unpopularity of the government, Snedden's popularity and performance deteriorated markedly over the months. In March 1974, 41 percent of a national sample had approved the way Snedden was handling his job and 46 percent disapproved. The proportion that disapproved was 52 percent in September and above 60 percent at the time of Snedden's overthrow in March 1975.[29] The process involved the classic syndrome of decline: the increasing press and public criticism of Snedden's performance itself contributed to his inability to cope. His verbal gaffes culminated in his statement at a businessmen's lunch on November 15:

> I'll tell you why I should be leader of the Liberal party—I'm the best—that's why I should be. I can give leadership to my team and they will all follow me. If I asked them to walk through the valley of death on hot coals they'd do it. Every one of them trusts me. Everyone recognises my political judgment and, if I say something must be this, it will be. That's why I'm leader.[30]

The first challenge to Snedden's leadership was led by a young former academic, Tony Staley, whom Snedden had appointed as one of his parliamentary secretaries in 1973. Staley was also close to the aspirant, Malcolm Fraser. The challenge came out of the blue, with Fraser leaving all initiatives to his sympathizers. Staley and five others, after taking soundings within the party, went to Snedden and suggested he should resign in favor of Fraser. Snedden rejected the suggestion, but word of the move had leaked out, and a vote was precipitated in the party room on November 27. Although the coup was defeated, the Fraser forces mustered about twenty-six votes out of a total of sixty-two—a substantial number considering that they had little support from senators. Snedden was to hold on for another

---

29 Gallup Polls reported in *Sydney Morning Herald* April 19, 1974, and Melbourne *Sun-News Pictorial*, March 15, 1975.
30 Quoted in Kelly, *Unmaking of Gough*, p. 45.

four months but after this point he was a lame duck leader. Fraser's supporters were making it clear that it was only a matter of time before Snedden would be deposed. Early in 1975 Snedden confronted Fraser and extracted a declaration of loyalty from him, but the form of words did not preclude any future challenge; indeed it was at once interpreted in some sections of the press as opening the way to such a challenge. Meanwhile, Fraser was building up his reputation with speeches and appearances, always careful to underplay his role as pretender and leave the work of promoting his candidacy to his political henchmen. The situation came to a head during March as party colleagues watched Prime Minister Whitlam ridicule Snedden and tear him to pieces on the floor of the House. When Parliament broke for a brief recess it was clear that Snedden could not last. A Snedden supporter and senior frontbencher, Andrew Peacock, precipitated the resolution of the leadership crisis when he publicly called on Snedden to hold a party meeting and ask for a vote of confidence so that divisive speculation could be ended.

Peacock's stand left Snedden little choice but to call a meeting. Always unwilling to face the fact that he had strong opposition within the party, Snedden had left lobbying too late, and anyway Fraser had the numbers sewn up, although Snedden retained considerable support within the organization, especially the state branches in Victoria and Tasmania. At the party meeting on March 21, veteran backbencher W. Wentworth moved to have the leadership declared vacant. In the subsequent leadership ballot, Snedden stood and so stopped Peacock, who would not oppose him, from running. Fraser won easily, thirty-seven to twenty-seven. How critical was the role of leadership in the party was shown by the rallying around Fraser: Liberal M.P.s were relieved to have found someone they believed could give them direction, even if they did not always fully approve of where he might take them.

Malcolm Fraser and the Run to Power. John Malcolm Fraser, forty-four, broke the pattern of Liberal party leadership in several respects. Of the party's six leaders since 1944, he was the first to be drawn from the heart of the rural "establishment." Fraser and Gorton were the only nonlawyers out of the six. Born into a wealthy grazing family and educated at private schools and Oxford, where he studied politics, philosophy, and economics, Fraser entered the federal Parliament in 1955 as member for the district of Wannon in Western Victoria. An M.P. from the age of twenty-five, Fraser had been a professional politician all his life. After ten years on the backbench he was made minister for the army in January 1966. When Gorton became prime minister, Fraser was promoted to the ministry of education and science and into the cabinet; later he took over defense. In all of these posts Fraser was regarded as a strong and competent minister who insisted that his department do what *he* wanted, yet who did not hesitate to go "down the line" for advice. At first a confidant of Gorton, Fraser later fell out with his chief in part over Gorton's alienation of the states. The differences between the two men erupted spectacularly in March 1971, when Gorton did not attempt to prevent a newspaper report that the chief of the general staff, Sir Thomas Daly, during a meeting with Gorton, had accused Fraser of extreme disloyalty to the army and its minister, Andrew Peacock. Fraser resigned from the ministry and in a bitter speech denounced Gorton, saying, "I do not believe he is fit to hold the great office of Prime Minister, and I cannot serve in his government." [31] Gorton lost the prime ministership as a result of these events, and Fraser spent five months on the backbench before Prime Minister McMahon brought him back to the ministry.

This background is important to the style Fraser adopted in his bid for power in 1974 and 1975 both within the party and in the wider context of the national campaign. Fraser's devastating attack against Gorton earned him deep enmity and suspicion in some sections of the party. Gorton himself, who was now nearing the end of his parliamentary career and in fact resigned from the Liberal party in 1975 to run for the Senate as an independent, used every opportunity to attack Fraser and attempt to thwart his ambitions. After Fraser won the leadership, South Australian Jim Forbes refused to serve on his frontbench. Fraser's concern about his "wrecker" image accounts for his extreme caution in his challenge to Snedden. At all times Fraser avoided any direct attack on Snedden. He left the running, and especially the undermining of Snedden in the early part of 1975, to his allies. An extreme illustration of Fraser's anxiety that his past record might work against him was his reported reaction when he was first told in November of the plan to promote him for the leadership of the party: according to Staley, Fraser's reply was, "Oh my God, don't talk to me about it. I can't bear to think of this." [32]

Fraser's politics and his political style, which emerged in the leadership struggle and later on in the preelection period, are an often confusing mixture of ideology and pragmatism, of seemingly firm intentions followed by quite different actions, of expediency clothed

---

[31] Quoted in Reid, *Gorton Experiment*, p. 432.
[32] Quoted in Kelly, *Unmaking of Gough*, p. 50.

in principle. His conservative political values have been called the "clearest and most comprehensive ideology of Federal (Liberal) leaders since Menzies."[33] Central to his value system are the role of the individual, struggle, self-improvement, and small government. He values, and he judges that the electorate values, predictability and certainty. Fraser derives much from Toynbee's view that the decline of civilizations is due to weaknesses from within. The core of the Fraser ideology emerges in a lecture Fraser gave in 1971:

> life is not meant to be easy. . . . We need a rugged society, but our new generations have seen only affluence. If a man has not known adversity, if in his lifetime his country has not been the subject of attack, it is harder for him to understand that there are some things for which we must always struggle. Thus people or leaders can be trapped to take the easy path. This is the high road to national disaster. There are many strands to the maintenance of will—a society which encourages individual strength and initiative, an understanding of events, ability to bear sacrifices, an understanding that there are obligations that precede rights and a belief that work is still desirable.[34]

One of Fraser's chief concerns is that government should not seek to provide a full range of services itself, but should allow the individual the opportunity and choice to dispose of his own income and make his own decisions wherever possible. He is suspicious of general welfare programs, which he sees as sapping individual initiative, but he has a concept of the deserving poor and believes that welfare should be concentrated on this group and directed toward establishing them in a position of self-help. In many ways Fraser is the radical conservative: he does not simply resist change—or, like the pre-'72 Liberal government, seek to slow its pace—but instead wants to remold society in a new and distinctive direction; his commitment to federalism illustrates this point. Yet at times what seems most distinctive about Fraser is his sheer ability to ditch ideology and take whatever course appears to be the most practical at the time, regardless of personal values or previous commitment. The Liberal government's reversal in 1976 of its election promises on the abolition of the prices justification tribunal, the modifications of its proposed union ballot legislation, and the setting up of a government commer-

---

[33] Peter Tiver, *ANU Reporter*, April 30, 1976. See also Tiver's "On the Conservative Side of Liberalism: The Political Ideology of Malcolm Fraser," ANU Work-in-Progress Seminar, 1976.

[34] Quoted in Kelly, *Unmaking of Gough*, p. 137.

cial health insurance fund, were among the most spectacular examples of what Fraser describes as "flexibility." [35] Fraser is the most Menzian of the Liberal leaders since Menzies, the man he looks to and admires. Fraser's strength and toughness were among his most attractive traits to a party that had become directionless; they distinguished him from Snedden. Significantly, he gained support from the progressive as well as the conservative sections of the party.

After his election in March, Fraser immediately set about consolidating his position. He moved to pacify the Tasmanian branch, heavily pro-Snedden, which had been muttering about a possible split if Snedden were overthrown. He quickly established a decision-making system in which real power rested in a core of about ten Liberal and Country party leaders who met frequently—a pattern which carried over significantly into government when many important decisions were made by meetings of the leaders plus two or three other key ministers. Fraser was personally closer to Country party attitudes and values than previous Liberal leaders, which later made for a very unified coalition relationship in the first year of government, despite the fact the Liberals now had a majority in their own right in the House of Representatives.

A New Election? Within hours of becoming leader, Fraser moved to defuse speculation about another premature election. However, the ambiguity of his statement, which only showed up later, was to set the tone for his and the opposition's comments on an election. Fraser said:

> I generally believe that if a government is elected to power in the Lower House and has the numbers and can maintain the numbers in the Lower House, it is entitled to expect that it will govern for the three year term unless quite extraordinary events intervene. I want to get talk about elections out of the air so the government can get on with the job of governing and make quite certain that it is not unduly distracted in these particular matters.

But he went on:

> If there are questions when an election might be held or when someone might want to do something about it, I would

---

[35] Labor set up a universal health scheme which gave basic coverage to everyone. In addition, people could buy extra coverage from private funds. The Liberal government in 1976 modified this scheme, introducing a levy and a provision allowing people to opt out of the basic scheme and buy commercial coverage from a private fund or from the government's new commercial insurance fund.

not be wanting to answer that particular question or trailing my coat about what our tactics or approach would be. If we do make up our minds at some stage that the government is so reprehensible that an opposition must use whatever power is available to it then I'd want to find a situation in which we made that decision and Mr. Whitlam woke up one morning finding that he had been caught with his pants well and truly down.[36]

As in his avowal of loyalty to Snedden in February, his comments in August on the passing of the Budget, and his commitment to wage indexation in the election campaign, it was the "fine print" that counted.

Within weeks Fraser had the perfect trial run for a general election. When the government provoked the Bass by-election by making Lance Barnard an ambassador, it handed Fraser the opportunity to test the political water and establish his own leadership by electoral success. The by-election came at the best time and in the best place for the Liberals. Snedden had assiduously cultivated Tasmania, where Labor held all five House seats. The state had been badly hit by the tariff cut and the rural slump. The poll came just after Treasurer Cairns's demotion over the loans affair and the attendant cabinet reshuffle. The local Liberal organization already had its candidate off and running while a fighting and fragmented local ALP machine was still selecting its candidate. The compromise candidate Labor eventually chose pleased no one and was unable to stand the scrutiny of the national press, who descended to study Bass as a mirror of the nation. Fraser campaigned on the point that Bass was indeed a microcosm of Australia and that its people had a chance to register the nation's discontent with the Labor government. The result was a landslide swing to the Liberals: Labor's vote fell from 54 percent in May 1974 to 36.5 percent in June 1975, while the Liberals polled 57.6 percent. The result—combined with Cairns's sacking from the ministry a few days later in another installment of the rapidly escalating loans affair—redoubled the pressure for an election. The Liberal organization stepped up its plans for a possible early election, and demands mounted within the organization for the Budget to be rejected.

However, the Budget itself presented the party's growing pro-election lobby with some problems. The reshuffling of the Labor cabinet had brought to the fore the "economic rationalists" headed by Treasurer Bill Hayden, and the Budget he produced contained the

---

[36] Quoted in Kelly, *Unmaking of Gough*, pp. 131–32.

same basic thrust that the opposition advocated: it tried to rein in spending and make some impact on the mounting deficit. In reply, Fraser set out in an "alternative Budget" the general lines of the policy he was to sell through the rest of the year and in the campaign. He promised that a Liberal government would index personal and company taxes over three years at an estimated cost of about $2,500 million, a policy supported by the unions but opposed by the Treasury because of the drain on revenue. Among the special incentives to get the private sector moving, Fraser advocated a 40 percent investment allowance and the suspension of the system of quarterly company tax payments for the duration of the economic crisis. The alternative program was "based on no increase in the deficit and this will be made possible by a reduced rate of government expenditure." Fraser listed economies which he said would save $1,000 million, although a Treasury costing for the government put them at $560 million. The savings policy had three prongs: a zero-growth limit on the public service, special administrative economies (cutback of the urban and regional development department and abolition of the media department, the prices justification tribunal, and the legal aid office) and a reduction in capital and other expenditures (including sale of the Pipeline Authority project and suspension of the capital advance of the Australian Industry Development Corporation).

Two days after the government had presented its Budget, Fraser moved apparently to try to end speculation about its rejection. He said on television: "With the knowledge we have at the moment, at this stage, it will be our intention to allow the passage [of the Budget] through the Senate." [37] Fraser's office issued a transcript of this statement and drew journalists' attention to it as an indication that the Budget would be passed. However, within a day Anthony, in a television interview, pointedly referred to the qualification in Fraser's statement. He set a pattern for the coming weeks, when the Country party exerted maximum pressure on the Liberals for an election, at the same time asserting that the Liberals had to be satisfied before a move was made. The opposition appeared to be casting around for "reprehensible circumstances" when Fraser made much play of a letter from Hayden to Whitlam saying that additional supply might have to be sought for Medibank and the Regional Employment Development Scheme. In fact, the "leaked" letter had been in opposition hands for some weeks, and its contents were routine, but it fueled the rapidly overheating election fire.

---

[37] Allan Barnes, "Fraser Says Too Much or Too Little," Melbourne *Age*, September 18, 1975.

Fraser's statements contained everything needed to encourage rather than discourage speculation. On Sunday, September 14, he said: "I have never promoted speculation about elections. I have sought to end that speculation." On Monday, he asserted on television that election speculation could encourage business confidence because businessmen might think there was going to be a change of government. In what was typical of the Fraser double line at this time, the television interview continued:

> Question: You are still in favour of the present government running its full term?

> Answer: I don't think that can be said, no, because the government is so unpredictable. Nobody knows what's going to happen. There could be another loans affair, they might get rid of another Treasurer. . . . I believe really that the sooner there can be responsibility returned to government, the better. But you've got to balance that against the constitutional practices, or the conventional practices, which have generally determined how long governments will last.[38]

The proelection hand was strengthened when Queensland Premier Bjelke-Petersen broke convention after the death of a Queensland Labor senator and replaced him by an appointee hostile to the government. This reduced Labor's numbers by one and gave the opposition enough votes to pass a positive motion deferring the Budget, rather than simply rejecting it. This development would be important if the government tried to "tough out" a blocking of the Budget. If the governor general were to step into such a situation, the opposition would need to be in a position to deliver supply. The Liberals' surveys were giving the opposition every encouragement to reject the Budget: results of the party's opinion polls showed support at a high level, and one telephone poll indicated that the opposition would only lose about 3.5 percent of those who intended to vote Liberal if it broke convention again and blocked the Budget. It would still be swept into government. To be weighed against this was the fact that a number of Liberals, especially in the Senate, were deeply worried about the propriety of blocking the Budget.

The Crisis. The crunch came when the Liberal Federal Council met on the weekend of October 11-13. Detailed soundings were taken of party opinion in discussions outside the formal meeting, and a

---

[38] The quotations in this paragraph are from ibid.

group of officials and politicians drew up a table of possible outcomes that could follow if the Senate rejected supply, including a decision by the government to call a half-Senate election or to try to "tough it out." At the Federal Executive meeting on October 10, Fraser had canvassed the opinions of all division presidents about an election. Only Peter Hardie from Victoria had stood out against the crisis but he said he would abide by whatever decision the parliamentary party took. The president of the Young Liberals, Chris Puplick, supported Hardie. On the day of the meeting a High Court judgment was delivered which pushed the Liberals further towards the rejection of supply. The court decided that legislation granting the two territories two senators each was valid. This gave the government the chance, albeit remote, of temporarily controlling the Senate and putting through its redistributions and electoral reforms, a move the opposition wanted to prevent at all costs.

Fraser's speech to the Federal Council on Sunday canvassed the election options and the proprieties. His staff steadfastly maintained that he had still not made up his mind about the rejection of supply but there seemed little chance to draw back now. Then, within forty-eight hours, the government delivered the final "reprehensible" circumstances for which the opposition had been searching. Documents published in a newspaper on Monday, October 13, showed that Minister for Minerals and Energy Connor had misled Parliament about his loan-raising efforts. Connor resigned from the cabinet on Tuesday morning, and that afternoon the opposition leadership unanimously decided to defer the budget bills due to be voted on in the Senate that week. Fraser contacted executives of major newspaper chains and told them the decision would be announced the next day: he was rewarded with editorials saying the government must go. On Wednesday the shadow cabinet and full party meeting endorsed the decision.[39] Only two senators, Allan Missen (Victoria) and Don Jessop (South Australia), expressed doubt in the party room. But they made it clear they would not defect on the issue.

So began the constitutional crisis, a long seige that was to try the nerves of Liberal backbenchers and test Fraser's authority within the party. On October 17 frontbencher Robert Ellicott, who was to be Fraser's close adviser in the crisis and later was rewarded with the attorney generalship, issued a press statement which he sent to Government House outlining what he saw as the role of the governor general in the crisis and his power to sack a prime minister. Mean-

---

[39] At the meeting of the shadow cabinet, Fraser asked each member individually for his opinion about blocking supply. All agreed to it enthusiastically.

while Fraser predicted, before a rally of 12,000 in Melbourne on Sunday, October 19, that the governor general would intervene "quite soon" to resolve the crisis.[40]

On Sunday, November 2, federal and state Liberal and NCP leaders met for a summit in Melbourne. At this meeting the opposition decided it would maintain its stand in principle but go to the governor general with a compromise to show its good faith. The compromise was that the opposition would pass supply immediately on condition that a general election was called by the government in six months. These moves only increased the government's confidence that the opposition would back down, a view held by more and more members of the dispirited Liberal ranks as public outrage against the blocking of supply swelled, apparently building up Labor's support. Both Missen and Jessop were speaking in the party room against continued deferral, and there was strong pressure from the party's division in Victoria to back down. But the leadership did not waver, and the Liberal leadership "ethic" meant that this strength was decisive.

The next weekend Fraser proposed a meeting between the government and opposition leaders to which the prime minister agreed. However, the meeting, which took place on the morning of November 11, ended in stalemate. The prime minister told the three opposition leaders, Fraser, Lynch, and Anthony, that he would call a half-Senate election. The three went from this meeting to a joint meeting of their parties; incredibly, they did not announce Whitlam's decision. It had been decided to "play it cool" at the party meeting in an effort to contain backbench anxiety. Lynch told a press briefing afterwards, "We believe events will work themselves out. We believe that the present course is sound for reasons which will become apparent to you later." [41] Within hours this confidence was vindicated: Fraser was summoned to Government House and sworn in as caretaker prime minister.

The Liberal Campaign

Planning and Organization. Within weeks of the May 1974 election, the Liberal party staff planning committee met to begin work for the next election. The meeting brought together the federal director, the six state secretaries, the federal public relations manager, and the

---

[40] Kelly, *Unmaking of Gough,* pp. 276-77.
[41] Ibid., p. 294.

research manager. They had before them papers on contingency planning for an election. At the latest, the next Senate poll was two and a half years away; another snap double dissolution could come much earlier. The organization men began discussing the preparation of media schedules and deciding which issues should be given priority by the advertising agency. A mock itinerary for the leader, worked up in late 1974, was reviewed every two months. Several organizational men who had worked for the McKinsey management consultant firm and the highly efficient Tony Eggleton saw to it that before the end of 1974 a "campaign bible" was drawn up. This looseleaf folder contained a checklist of everything that would be needed in an election and covered possible ways of opening the campaign, kinds of publications required, control and direction of the campaign, the team to support the leader in the field, and the leader's itinerary. The advertising agency Berry Currie was asked to produce a model media program, setting out the breakdown between different types of media, the papers and television stations that would be used, a program for marginal seats, and cost estimates. Each time the staff planning group met in the following months, it discussed the current political situation and reviewed the plans. From the end of 1974, the party commissioned surveys of opinions on issues, party preferences, and leadership support as part of its contingency planning.

In May 1975, the party decided to change its advertising agency and sought agency bids. The firm of Masius Australia was selected and took over in early September. The agency was asked to draw up schedules and costings for both a half-Senate and a general election campaign. They began working up dummy television advertisements on issues including the economy, unemployment, the government's inability to manage affairs, and its lack of integrity. This preparation was well under way by November 11.

On Thursday, November 13—two days after the Labor government was sacked—the staff planning committee met in Canberra with representatives of Masius. The next morning the Federal Campaign Committee, comprising the Staff Planning Committee, plus the leader, his deputy, the Senate leader, the federal president, the past president, the federal treasurer, and one state president, met. It approved the basics of the "Turn on the Lights" campaign, to which the party's federal executive gave its imprimatur that afternoon. Thus, the Liberals were off and running well ahead of their Labor opponents, who were still stunned by the dismissal.

The early planning had paid off. At these meetings the agency had presented advanced mock-ups for press advertisements on the economy, sixty- and thirty-second radio spots, television advertisements, and the "Turn on the Lights" jingle (which was sung to those present to guitar accompaniment). The "Turn on the Lights" slogan had been devised by the agency. It was a gift to the cartoonists and was easily ridiculed by opponents—one left-wing weekly came out with the front-page statement, "Okay, Turn on the Lights (we can't trust the bugger in the dark)"—but apparently it caught on. In a pamphlet on the slogan, Masius said later: "The reason it succeeded was simply that it interpreted the Liberal promise of revival in suitably evocative terms." In contrast, according to Masius, Labor's "Shame, Fraser, Shame" and "Right the Wrong" had the fault of being negative: "No benefits were offered, and that's about as fundamental a mistake as can be made in marketing." [42]

The party had told the agency it wanted a slogan that was forward looking but also conjured up Labor's failures. One suggestion that came from the Liberals themselves was "Revive Australia"; "Let's Live Again" was also tossed around. Over the two days of meetings in early November, the agency presented its slogan in the context of a three-stage campaign. The campaign would open with a basically negative phase centering on the government's mistakes, whose theme would be the "Three Dark Years of Labor." The second stage, when the jingle would be introduced, would be more positive and emotive, setting out what the Liberals would do as well as harking back to Labor's record. The final stage would concentrate more strongly still on selling Liberal policies and personalities, with only occasional reminders of Labor's record. The meetings of Friday, November 14, approved a plan for a sixty-second "time capsule" advertisement devoted to the history of the Labor government and several radio advertisements. It was decided that the radio advertisements would start the next Wednesday and the agency would complete the "Three Dark Years of Labor" capsule advertisement over the weekend so that it could go on the air at the end of the following week.

The 1975 Liberal advertising campaign was both more quickly paced and more flexible than earlier Liberal campaigns because it was under national control. Previously, each state secretary had had to approve any change in advertisements. This had been a problem even in 1974, when some steps had been taken to centralize the management of the campaign. In 1975 ali authority was vested in Eggleton, as federal director of the party. The advertising campaign was also more extensive than ever before.

---

[42] "Turn on the Lights: Anatomy of a Slogan," pamphlet from Masius Australia.

Table 4-3

USE OF COMMERCIAL TELEVISION AND RADIO,
BY PARTY, 1975 CAMPAIGN

Party	Radio		Television	
	Cost	Percent	Cost	Percent
Australian Labor party	164,599	36.02	643,958	34.6
Liberal party	187,921	41.11	748,122	40.2
National Country party	80,719	17.66	202,292	10.9
Liberal Movement	1,521	.33	—	—
Australian party	2,267	.50	—	—
Democratic Labor party	6,626	1.45	138,341	7.4
Other	13,416	2.93	128,560	6.9
Total	457,069	100.0	1,861,273	100.0

Note: Table includes expenditures, in Australian dollars, for the broadcasting of campaign advertisements and political speeches by commercial stations.
Source: *Hansard*, June 2, 1976, pp. 2904-2905.

The Liberals outspent Labor on both radio and television. According to official figures, the Liberal party and its supporters on its behalf spent $748,122 on buying television advertising and $187,921 on radio time (see Table 4-3). This represented 40.2 percent of the total funds spent by all parties on television advertising time (compared with the ALP's 34.6 percent) and 41.11 percent of total spending on radio time (compared with the ALP share of 36.02 percent). In addition, the Liberals spent at least another $100,000 on production costs. The total Liberal national advertising campaign, including both electronic and press advertising but excluding agency fees, cost about $1.25 million, according to party sources.[43]

The Key Role of Headquarters. The most novel feature of the Liberal campaign was the establishment of a vast campaign headquarters, in constant touch with Fraser and Eggleton (who was traveling with him) and with the advertising agency. It ran a monitoring service of the media and transmitted telexes and facsimile documents. The party had asked Masius to look for a site for such a center in Melbourne close to the agency's offices. Suitable premises were found in

---

[43] The official figures come from *Hansard*, June 2, 1976, pp. 2904-05. The party does not provide a full costing of the campaign. The production figure is an estimate, based on discussions with party officials.

Queens Road, and after the opposition moved to block supply, Eggleton rented most of one floor of the building. On the morning of Tuesday, November 11, the final arrangements were made for the installation of the communications equipment. A week before the formal campaign opened, the center was fully operating and the party's national staff had moved down from Canberra.

"HQ," as the Liberals called their headquarters, was run by Timothy Pascoe, now secretary of the Victoria division. It was a vast communications center with a forty-extension switchboard, six telex machines, three telephone facsimile machines, a dozen color television sets, eating and sleeping facilities for workers, and its own letterhead. The center oversaw the national organization of the campaign and was open twenty-four hours a day, manned by about thirty Canberra party employees and volunteers. On the wall was a master plan showing the ministers' locations and contact points. Fraser had told his ministers not to make private campaign commitments because the central office was coordinating itineraries.

Whenever possible, Fraser got back to Melbourne at night. He was then able to operate from his Melbourne home, and Eggleton could meet with the campaign staff and Masius. The demands of the campaign meant that these meetings were sometimes held at all hours of the night. At HQ the day began around 4:30 a.m., when Geoff Allen, a former press secretary to Snedden, put together a report of what had appeared in the media. A staff meeting, normally held between 6:00 a.m. and 7:00 a.m., looked at assessments of the media from all capital cities, as well as reports from small "intelligence groups" that were meeting in each state capital to react to the campaign. Each of these groups included half a dozen people—perhaps a housewife, a student, a banker, and so on—representing a cross section of the population. By about 7:30 a.m. Pascoe was on the telephone to Eggleton, giving him a rundown and assessment of the morning's meeting, and Eggleton then briefed Fraser. A summary of the morning's press came through on the telex. The Fraser party used telexes in state Liberal offices or hotels when necessary and carried its own facsimile machine on the campaign trail.

HQ edited speeches delivered by prominent frontbenchers and sent out the new points in them for members and candidates throughout the country to use. A list of HQ's functions included supervision of tactics, analysis and assessment of the course of the campaign and what the opposition was doing, speaker control, publications, communications, media, advertising, monitoring, liaison with overseas groups in London, Port Moresby, Wellington, Kuala Lumpur, and

Singapore (the party had been badly organized to pick up absentee votes in London in 1974), and advance work for the parliamentary leader. Two advance men traveled ahead of the prime minister's party to ensure that all arrangements had been made. They also prepared and transmitted information about the local electorate to the traveling party.

On the Hustings. The method of their assuming office gave the Liberals both disadvantages and advantages in the campaign—but the latter quickly predominated. On the negative side, the drawn-out constitutional crisis and the dismissal of Whitlam precipitated mass demonstrations throughout the country which seemed to indicate a tide of sympathy for Labor and made many Liberals anxious, particularly before the supply crisis was resolved. On the other hand, there was a feeling in the air that Labor must have done something reprehensible for the governor general to have sacked it. Moreover, the Liberals fought the campaign as the government, with all the material and psychological advantages that entails. The "caretaker" terms of the commission did not stop the new government from using what evidence it could dig up against its predecessors and hinting at what it did not in fact produce. The Liberals had at their disposal the immense resources of government, ranging from expert advisers in the public service to ministerial cars and VIP planes. In contrast, Whitlam, always particular about documentation, found himself deprived of the files he had left in the Prime Minister's Department; during the campaign, the staff traveling with him often lacked vital information and statistics on which to base speeches and replies to Fraser.

The new government lost no time using their access to Treasury information to score off Labor. On November 12, the day after Whitlam was dismissed, Fraser said Treasury briefings had convinced him that the economy was in far worse shape than previously revealed. He did not back up the allegation but told television reporters he would soon make a full statement. The treasurer, Lynch, instructed his department to consider where government spending could be cut after December 13 and how the new tax scheme, introduced in the Labor Budget and due to come into effect on January 1, could be changed. Insisting on this point, Fraser said many people did not realize how much economic damage the former government had done; it would take three years to undo, he claimed.[44] The active use

---

[44] See *Australian Financial Review*, November 13 and 14, 1975, and Melbourne *Age*, November 14, 1975.

being made of public service information provoked unease among some sections of the bureaucracy: within the Treasury two senior officials complained to the head of the department, and sixty-eight middle-ranking officials formally protested in a letter to the governor general, Sir John Kerr, that the government had broken the caretaker guidelines. The officials asked Sir John to spell out his guidelines for the government in considerably greater detail and said they were concerned that the government's behavior could prejudice the principle of public service impartiality. However, Lynch simply asserted that he was seeking normal departmental advice and information. The Liberals had no intention of not cashing the bonus they had been handed. Fraser went on television to attack Labor's economic administration, claiming that the ALP's Budget would have led to more inflation and higher unemployment, although the promised revelations about where Labor had misled the people failed to materialize. The Labor party replied with allegations that unemployment would soar to a million under a Fraser government and that health, construction, and other vital programs would be axed.

By the time the campaign formally opened the following week, the parameters for the debate of the next three weeks had been set. The caretaker government would use all its armory to discredit Labor on the economy and its administration, while Labor would stick to the constitutional crisis for the early part of the campaign, later broadening its attack to include the Liberals' economic package and their intention to cut back on Labor's program. The Liberals banked on the expectation that the constitutional crisis would fade in people's minds as their economic instincts came to the fore, and this calculation proved correct. A poll of swinging voters (party switchers) over the weeks before polling day showed a steady rise in the proportion who saw the economy and inflation as the main issue and an inverse movement in the proportion who said the constitutional issue was the main thing in the election.[45] The Liberals' assessment was further boosted by the criticism which the Whitlam policy speech received from the media for failing to make any commitments for the future and concentrating instead on the constitutional arguments. The Liberal campaign, due to open on Tuesday, November 25, a day after the Labor campaign, was delayed two days when Fraser contracted influenza. The delay helped rather than hampered the Liberal cause. It gave the party extra time to polish the supplementary economic statement which was to accompany and back up the policy

---

[45] Published in *National Times*, December 8-13, 1975, p. 14. The poll was taken on November 19-20, 26-27, and December 3-4, 1975.

speech. It also left the Labor party in a vacuum: the Liberals would be most vulnerable when forced to justify the details of their program, and Labor could make little headway with that line of attack until the policy statement was delivered. In fact, embargoed copies of the Liberal speech had been released and had reached the ALP but Whitlam, though he referred to it in passing, would not launch a full-scale attack on its details before the speech had been delivered. Fraser also got a good deal of "human interest" publicity from his flu when the front pages of the nation's newspapers carried pictures of him in bed. In the meantime, he released a statement asserting that the 1976 forecasts of the Organization for Economic Cooperation and Development (OECD) would show Australia to have the second highest inflation rate of any OECD country. When questioned by a journalist he confirmed the figure of 15 percent. The statement apparently embarrassed OECD, and later Fraser had to retreat somewhat from the figure.[46]

The Policy Speech. On Thursday, November 27, two days late, Fraser delivered his policy speech. Its prime thrust was to boost business profitability and investment. It looked to an investment-led recovery to bring down the inflation rate and restore economic health. "A sustained and permanent revival in employment," Fraser said, "will not be secured through private consumption expenditures. . . . A consumption-led revival would be fragile and short-lived. The essential ingredient in a soundly based economic recovery is a revival in private investment." [47]

Among the benefits for business which the policy promised were a 40 percent investment allowance as well as an accelerated depreciation allowance, suspension of quarterly company tax collections for the duration of the economic crisis, changes in tax rules that the Liberals considered unfair to small companies, indexation of company taxation over three years, and abolition of the Prices Justification Tribunal. For the wage earner, Fraser promised to index personal income tax in a three-year program starting with the next Budget, support the wage indexation agreement, reintroduce the home savings grants scheme, and introduce a special rebate for child care for single-parent families. The package for the rural sector included reintroduction of the superphosphate bounty, assistance to the beef industry, and relaxation of the tight eligibility provisions

---

[46] See Melbourne *Age*, November 27, 1975.

[47] *Policy Speech*, Malcolm Fraser, November 27, 1975, published by the Liberal party.

for unemployment assistance to farmers. There was to be "an end to Government extravagances and excesses. . . . Economies can and will be made in Government spending without disrupting essential programmes, or programmes for which contracts have already been let," Fraser said. The supplementary statement said that new cabinet and administrative machinery would be immediately established to review government spending. This review would have three objectives: to seek economies which could be speedily implemented in areas of waste and extravagance, to lay the groundwork for a program to ensure maximum economies in the next Budget while maintaining the real value of spending on essential education, health, welfare and urban programs, and to set in train an ongoing review to operate for the full three years of the economic program. The policy speech mentioned the constitutional crisis and Whitlam only briefly: Whitlam was the man who had "tried to rule without Parliament . . . the man who took Australia the first significant step on the road to dictatorship."

The Fraser plan had the advantage of being positive, but it was vague when it came to costs and what existing programs would be cut. Fraser was to admit that many of the major proposals for reviving business had not yet been costed. He said the speed with which some promises could be introduced depended largely on "the success of our efforts to rein in Labor's mad extravagances." [48] Fraser was well aware of the traps he could be caught in on costs and cuts. His strategy was to refuse to be pinned down on specifics. The result was that the press—who had successfully pinned down and so helped to undo Snedden in 1974—conducted a constant battle to try to nail Fraser on details, both of his own program and of the future Labor program. But Fraser, with victory in sight, wanted to enter power as untrammeled by specifics as circumstances would permit: he refused to give a timetable for the introduction of the measures he proposed; he constantly promised that "essential" programs would not be cut and declined to spell out what was "essential"; he stressed curbing waste and extravagance but the only examples he gave were relatively minor, if sensitive, such as Whitlam's trips. Fraser also adopted the technique of holding separate press conferences for television and newspaper reporters. This meant that he could present his views on television in prepared statements without the public's seeing him subjected to the tough, even haranguing and hostile, questions tossed up by the members of the Canberra press gallery who traveled with him

[48] Ibid., p. 5.

on the campaign trail. Fraser's confidence that he could get away with such tactics was soon vindicated by the opinion polls.

By the start of the second week of the campaign the poll conducted for the *Age* showed that the L-NCP coalition had an 8.3 percentage point lead over Labor, with support for the coalition at 52.3 percent compared to 44 percent for Labor. The polls indicated that most voters saw inflation as the main issue, which is what the Liberals had banked on. A Gallup Poll also showed that Fraser was far outstripping Whitlam in personal popularity—59 percent to 41 percent.[49] Despite his rather awkward public style, Fraser was trouncing the seasoned Labor campaigner whose natural forte was the hustings.

Victory and Its Aftermath

The coalition was swept back to power with a fifty-five seat majority in the House of Representatives and clear control of the Senate. The Liberals had a majority in their own right in the lower House; however, Fraser was quick to allay any suggestion that the coalition might be broken. The Labor party's share of first-preference House votes was 42.8 percent, down 6.5 percentage points since the 1974 elections. The Liberal-National Country party coalition polled 53.1 percent, up 7.2 percentage points. This was divided up between 41.8 percent for the Liberals and 11.3 percent for the Country party. The coalition made a near clean-sweep of all the outlying states—a reflection of Labor's tendency to overconcentrate on the large metropolitan centers in the east. The coalition won every seat in Tasmania and all but one in Queensland and Western Australia, dramatically reflecting the extent to which Labor had alienated the rural vote and those who feared centralism. They also won back the vital ring of outer suburban seats around Melbourne and Sydney which had responded to Labor's "It's Time" issues in 1972.

The 1975 campaign was a classic case of a government's losing an election rather than an opposition's winning it. Fraser was correct in his calculation that people would differentiate between passing judgment on the way in which Labor had been dismissed and deciding who they wanted the next government to be. Fraser's contribution to the victory was to give the Liberals a sense of direction and confidence in the months before the election, and, by his political toughness, to steady their nerve when public opinion seemed to be going against them. When achieved, the victory at the polls established Fraser in

---

[49] Melbourne *Age*, December 3 and 4, 1975; Melbourne *Sun-News Pictorial*, December 6, 1975.

true Liberal style in a very powerful position within the cabinet and the party. His domination of the cabinet was reinforced by his penchant for taking a detailed interest in most policy areas, a characteristic that was soon to bring him criticism.

The new government immediately set about its cost-cutting exercise and showed itself willing to ditch any election promises which were found to conflict with its overriding goal of bringing inflation under control. Fraser knew that he and the government would ultimately be judged on their handling of the economy—and his retaining power within the party for the long term depended on his winning a favorable judgment. However, a year after their massive victory, the Liberals were encountering some tough economic and political hurdles. Their fight against inflation was set back by the decision to devalue the Australian dollar caused by a rush of speculative capital out of the country. Unemployment remained high and the huge backbench turned out to be vocal and restive on a range of issues. At the time of writing, the Liberals' success in the vital economic battle is far from clear.

5

THE COUNTRY PARTY

Margaret Bridson Cribb

The agrarian movement, though part of the North American political experience as well as the Australian, has had a more lasting effect in Australia than in Canada and the United States. Here, agrarian politics have shaped one of the major national parties. The Country party or National Country party [1] was born out of the deep resentment felt by the farming communities against economic and social insecurity and injustice, its advent on the political scene hastened by the shift from a simple majority voting system to one of preferential voting in 1918.[2] The party's ability to retain an independent status and identity within successive coalition governments, as it has done since 1923, can be traced to a felicitous combination of political circum-

---

[1] To avoid creating unnecessary confusion in the minds of readers I have used *Country* as the name for the party throughout this study. I have done this with great reluctance, however, as the name *Country party* is no longer strictly accurate. Since 1975 the party at the national level has been called the *National Country party of Australia*; the Queensland branch, since 1974, *National party of Australia*. In the 1975 elections, party candidates in New South Wales, South Australia, and Western Australia stood under the banner of the *National Country* party; those in Victoria, Queensland, and Tasmania were called *National* party candidates, and those in the Northern Territory were designated as *Country Liberal* party candidates.

[2] The definitive work on the origins of the Country party in Australia and its subsequent history to 1929 is B. D. Graham, *The Formation of the Australian Country Parties* (Canberra: Australian National University Press, 1966). The importance of the preferential voting system for the Country party lay in the fact that both Liberal and Country party candidates could stand in an electorate without splitting the non-Labor vote, provided that they exchanged preferences with each other. This exchange of preferences, part of the electoral agreement between the two parties, is widely publicized and printed on "how-to-vote" cards handed out to voters outside the polling booths and is generally followed by the voters in marking their ballot-papers.

stances and to the energy, astuteness, and hard-nosed bargaining abilities of its national leaders. As a parliamentary force, the Country party has exploited to the fullest extent possible the Liberal party's need for its undivided support and has pursued the coalition strategy mapped out for it by its early leader, Earle Page. The Liberal-Country party coalition has been based not only on self-interest, however, but also on a close ideological affinity between the two non-Labor parties.

As spokesman initially for the farm organizations, which were themselves an amalgam of class politics and the politics of sectional interest as both related to the rural sector, the Country party developed a restrictive view of the political process and a tendency to see politics in black and white terms.[3] Government policies and activities were measured exclusively against the yardstick of rural interests. The party's ideology was simplistic in its substance, pragmatic and single-minded in its application. It embodied seemingly contradictory beliefs, advocating the greatest amount of freedom on the one hand and protection for the rural sector on the other, freedom from direct government intervention in and interference with the affairs of the primary producers, and protection for their industries and compensation to cushion the impact of economic down-swings.

Since its entry into national politics, the Country party has been able to place the requirements of the rural sector high on the list of government priorities, with favorable results. It has presided over the erection of a complex infrastructure of supports and subsidies within the primary industries and has fought a protracted delaying action against any serious rationalization or reorganization of these. It must be said also that the Country party has held parliamentary seats and ministerial portfolios inflated both in number and importance in relation to the level of electoral support it has received at national elections.

For much of its history the Country party has been bedevilled by two inherently conflicting pressures: its need to participate in a coalition if it is to have any real political power at the national level and its insistence, based on grass-roots sentiment, upon retaining its independent status. Efforts to reach any permanent agreement with the Liberal party on policies, electoral arrangements and strategy, and so on have consistently failed. This is the cause of much of the internecine quarreling which breaks out from time to time between the coalition parties. Repeated offers of amalgamation from the Liberals have been rejected, yet the fear remains within the Country

---

[3] On the farm organizations, see Graham, *Australian Country Parties*, pp. 31-46.

party that the Liberals will govern in their own right if the magnitude of their electoral success is ever sufficiently great.[4] This accounts for the Country party's obsessive interest in any proposed changes to the electoral and voting systems which do not contain specific safeguards for its interests, particularly since demographic changes in Australia's population are already eroding the base of its voting support.[5]

Organization

Contrary to its own propaganda and to its official name—National Country party, as of 1975—the Country party, strictly speaking, is not a national party. Unlike the major parties, it has contested at most only a third of the seats at national elections (44 out of 127 in 1975), and for much of its history it has not been able to maintain a vigorous, independent organization in each state. In South Australia, for example, the Liberal and Country parties merged in 1932 and only since 1963 has an independent Country party branch been reconstituted, while in Tasmania the branch of the party, in its present form, is little more than a year old.

Federalism wedded to a system of strong, highly disciplined political parties has produced, in the case of the Country party, a loose national organization superimposed upon a number of autonomous state parties.[6] Each state branch has full control over the selection of the party's candidates for national as well as state elections, over financing the day-to-day operations of the state organization, and even over the provision of much of the money required for election campaigns.

While the constitutional arrangements and organizational framework of the state branches are generally similar, there are marked differences in practice and in the level of success achieved by the party from one state to another; much of this, in turn, affects the

[4] At the December 1931 elections, the United Australia party—predecessor of the present Liberal party—obtained an absolute majority in the House of Representatives. Coalition negotiations with the Country party broke down and it was excluded from the government until the September 1934 elections when the United Australia party lost its absolute majority. At the 1966 elections, the Liberals came within two seats of obtaining an absolute majority in the House.

[5] Census figures for June 30, 1971, showed 64.5 percent of Australia's population living in major urban areas, 62 percent in the state capitals, 21.06 percent in other urban areas, and only 14.31 percent in rural areas. *Official Year Book of Australia* (Canberra: Australian Bureau of Statistics, 1973), vol. 59, p. 137.

[6] For detailed accounts of the state Country parties see S. R. Davis, ed., *The Government of the Australian States* (Sydney: Longmans, 1960), and John Rorke, ed., *Politics at State Level—Australia* (Sydney: University of Sydney, 1970).

performance of the party nationally.[7] The variations themselves stem from dissimilarities in the history and development of the branches and from factors such as geographic, social, political, and economic diversity between and within the states themselves. The marked contrast between the Queensland and Western Australian branches at the present moment is a pertinent example. In Queensland, the Country party has been in office continuously since 1957 as senior partner in a coalition government. State party officials have taken up with enthusiasm the national leader's call for expansion and change and have promoted with initiative and drive a campaign to alter the party's image and broaden its electoral appeal. The state branch changed its name in 1974 to National party of Australia (Queensland branch) and contested seats outside historically recognized areas.[8] In the 1974 state elections the party swept within an inch of being able to govern in its own right; it won a national seat from Labor the same year and three more in 1975.

In Western Australia, on the other hand, all attempts to stem the Country party's rapid decline have failed. Though remaining a very junior partner in a coalition government, the party has been losing electoral support so rapidly that it now has no representative in either house of the national Parliament other than a solitary senator who barely scraped home in 1975. The very existence of the Western Australian branch of the Country party is now clearly at stake.[9]

Country party policy is arrived at essentially through mutual understanding and consultation between the leaders of the parliamentary party and those of the organizational wing. Because the party has not had to harbor within its ranks a wide range of views and ideological beliefs it has suffered little of the internal conflict endemic in the major parties, although on occasion clashes between primary-producer interests have been reflected within the party. The parliamentary leader operates untrammelled by any constitutional right of the party membership to bind his hands on policy or strategy. This is not to deny the strength and power of the state organizations in the party set-up as a whole, but rather to suggest that the balancing position within the political system that the Country party has held

---

[7] For a detailed account of the organizational infrastructure of the Country party, see L. F. Crisp, *Australian National Government* (Melbourne: Longmans, 1965), pp. 216-25.

[8] Margaret Cribb, "Queensland Politics," *Current Affairs Bulletin*, vol. 51, no. 11 (April 1975), pp. 23-31.

[9] The state "Political Chronicles" in the *Australian Journal of Politics and History* provide a continuous assessment of the current political situation in each of the Australian states.

for half a century, together with its sectional representation, has necessitated a solidarity, a strict discipline, and a cohesion of all sections of the party behind the leader more easily arrived at in this party because of the close concordance of the ideas and beliefs of its members.

The Country Party between 1970 and 1975

The importance of the first half of this decade for the Country party lay in the party's relations with the Liberals, in its reaction to much of the program of the Whitlam governments, and in the self-reappraisal which the party undertook while in opposition.

The internal dissension which racked the Liberal party from the death of its leader, Prime Minister Harold Holt, in December 1967 until 1975 was specific to that party, but its successful resolution was in no way assisted by the behavior of the Country party. The Liberals accepted the interdict of John McEwen, the Country party leader, that his party would not serve in a coalition headed by the deputy Liberal leader, William McMahon. This not only put an end to that gentleman's candidacy for the prime ministership on that occasion but also was indicative of the power wielded within the coalition by the Country party leader. The intransigence of the Country party both in and outside the cabinet was not helpful to the subsequent prime ministers, John Gorton and McMahon, either, as they strove to project an image of strong and purposeful leadership. On such matters as aboriginal policy and the vital issue of the proper exchange rate for the Australian dollar, Gorton and McMahon were forced to give in to Country party demands. On several occasions the Country party threatened to withdraw from the coalition in order to have its way.[10]

While the coalition was in opposition after December 1972, relations between the two parties deteriorated even further. Bitter quarrels in Victoria over electoral arrangements were reflected at the national level. There were clashes, too, over the rival claims of Doug Anthony, by then Country party leader, and Phillip Lynch, deputy Liberal leader, to the not inconsiderable perquisites of the office of deputy leader of the opposition. These were compounded when the Liberal leader named a comprehensive shadow ministry from among the Liberal parliamentarians alone, depriving Country party members of portfolios which they considered it their prerogative to shadow.

---

[10] Laurie Oakes and David Solomon, *The Making of an Australian Prime Minister* (Melbourne: Cheshire, 1973), pp. 35-43, 75-76, 79-89.

In time, however, wiser counsel prevailed and the two parties drew closer together in a joint endeavor to bring down the Labor government. The Country party was unabashedly in favor of obstructing the government in the Senate and of forcing it to the country in 1974 and 1975. Its leaders participated actively in the Gair affair and other controversial actions taken by Labor's opponents in those years.[11]

The Country party adjusted more quickly than the Liberals to being out of office. The leadership change occasioned by McEwen's retirement early in 1971 had been made smoothly, with the selection of Anthony, deputy leader since 1966, as his successor. A member of the House since 1957, son of a former federal minister, and a minister himself since 1963, Anthony was only forty-one years old when he stepped into McEwen's shoes. Anthony was a prosperous farmer who projected a youthfulness, charm, and ingenuousness that masked an astute political awareness, tough-mindedness, and a proven ability to count the numbers accurately. Though initially inclined to overproject a "simple farm boy" image, he has recently taken on a more serious and thoughtful mien.

Using the foundations laid by McEwen in 1966 to create a wider-based party embracing the secondary as well as the primary producer, Anthony began the task of building a national identity for the Country party.[12] He initiated a thorough review of the party platform and launched a huge fund-raising and membership drive. Party members were polled directly by the leader on a variety of issues and proposals, including a name change for the party and the feasibility of developing an antisocialist alliance with the Liberals and the Democratic Labor party. Amalgamation talks were actually begun with the latter, though only in the Western Australian and Queensland branches was any enthusiasm shown for a merger. In Western Australia a National alliance between the two parties was unsuccessful and short-lived, and the poor performance of the Democratic Labor party in the 1974 elections cooled the ardor of the Queenslanders for the marriage. The revitalization of branch organizations in South Australia and Tasmania also date from this period.

Many of the Whitlam governments' policies and actions produced intensely adverse reactions in the rural areas. The interests of the

---

[11] C. J. Lloyd and G. S. Reid, *Out of the Wilderness: The Return of Labor* (Melbourne: Cassell Australia, 1974), and Laurie Oakes and David Solomon, *Grab for Power: Election '74* (Melbourne: Cheshire, 1974). See also chap. 2, p. 65, in this volume.

[12] On McEwen's contribution see Don Aitkin, "The Australian Country Party," *Australian Politics: A Third Reader*, eds. Henry Mayer and Helen Nelson (Melbourne: Cheshire, 1973), p. 423.

primary-producing sector, including the extractive mining industry, were threatened by a variety of governmental measures that ranged from the abolition of all exploration and mining share subsidies to the cessation of the superphosphate bounty. Rural interests also became bitter over the loss of concessions granted by earlier coalition governments. High on their list of grievances were the cutting back of the petroleum products subsidy in rural areas, increased postal and telephone charges, and the pruning of airline service to rural locations made necessary by increased fuel costs and air navigation charges.

The Labor government's electoral legislation directly threatened the Country party itself. Only one segment—the Commonwealth Electoral Bill (No. 2, 1973), which removed some of the cushioning for the party against the elimination of Country party seats through redistribution (redistricting)—had passed into law by the time Labor was defeated in 1975, but the Country party opposed the whole of the electoral reform program in both houses of Parliament with tenacity and bitterness.[13] The fear that the proposed changes, if implemented, would place the party's very existence except as a rump group in jeopardy was the Country party's primary motivation for forcing Labor to an election by refusing to pass the Budget in the Senate. It is fair to say, however, that a large part of the legislative and administrative program of the Labor government even beyond electoral reform ran counter to the philosophy of the Country party and the interests of its supporters. Its overwhelming desire to see the Labor government turned out of office was due not only to the Country party's need to quash the electoral changes or to the adverse effects of Labor's policies on the rural and mining sector, but also to an unshakable conviction that the Labor government was a socialist government, implementing a socialist program.

---

[13] The Commonwealth Electoral Bill (No. 2, 1973) reduced the margin for departure from the quota in an electoral redistribution from the 20 percent allowable since 1902 to 10 percent. It also revoked the three criteria for the redistribution commissioners, which had been inserted in 1965 under pressure from the Country party. These were: disabilities arising out of remoteness or distance, the density or sparsity of population of the division, and the area of the division. The Electoral Laws Amendment Bill (1974) sought to implement wide-ranging reforms in the electoral system, the most controversial of which was the replacement of the preferential voting system by an optional preferential marking of the ballot paper. A further Electoral Bill (1975) provided among other things for the limitation of electoral expenditure and the public disclosure of the sources of funds made available to political parties and candidates. See *Commonwealth Parliamentary Debates: Joint Sitting* (Canberra: Australian Government Publishing Service), August 6, 1974, pp. 4-44; *CPD: House of Representatives*, November 13, 1974, pp. 3444-3454, November 25, 1974, pp. 3966-4000, February 12 and 13, 1975, pp. 131-316; *CPD: Senate*, November 26 and 28, 1974, pp. 2721-2942.

When the Whitlam government was returned to office after the May 1974 election, neither Anthony nor the leader of the Liberal party was prepared to admit that the coalition had been defeated or that the government had a mandate.[14] Thus, it was not really surprising that a new election was staged only a year and a half later. This time the Liberal party was led by Malcolm Fraser, and the change was warmly welcomed by the Country party. In the person of Fraser, the Liberals appeared to have one last chance to achieve internal unity and to reclaim the government benches in the next term. As a wealthy grazier and member of the "landed gentry" whose family had been part of the rural establishment for many years, Fraser is the first of his kind to lead the Liberal party. His perception of the political process, as illustrated by the history of his rise to the leadership of his party, is more akin to that of the Country party leadership than to that of many Liberals. As successful primary producers, Fraser and the Country party leadership have much in common, and it is to be expected that this fact alone will contribute to a closer working relationship between the leaders of the two parties than has been possible in recent years.

The Campaign

The remarkable frequency of national elections between 1972 and 1975, together with the usual round of triennial contests at the state level, placed exceptional strains on the campaign funds of all the political parties. Under normal circumstances, the Country party depends on membership fees, fund-raising social activities, business enterprises such as fattening and selling cattle,[15] and direct donations to cover its operating and electoral expenses. The primary producer has traditionally provided much of the party's revenue. Recently, however, substantial (some would allege, massive) financial support has come from the mining industry, which has contributed mainly to the Queensland branch and the national organization. Again in Queensland, where the Liberal party is in the doldrums, some prominent members of the business and financial communities have thrown their support behind the Country party. Consequently, though publicly crying poverty, the party did not lack the money to mount an expensive and sophisticated election campaign in 1975.

---

[14] *CPD: House of Representatives*, July 10, 1974, p. 84, and Melbourne *Age*, May 30, 1974.

[15] This is a scheme whereby some ranchers earmark a number of beasts for the Country party, run them with their own herds and, when they have been fattened and sold, hand over the net profit from their sale to the party treasury.

After its successful trial run in 1974, the Country party's organization was finely tuned and ready long before December 1975. The federal secretariat had been strengthened by the appointment of a research officer and a marketing director and, although the branch organizations in the states were of an uneven standard, the party's strength lay where it counted most, in the eastern states, with the Queensland organization being the most effective political machine of them all. The party's membership drive and the political climate of the time had produced a marked increase in national membership. By the election date party membership had surpassed 100,000, according to party figures.[16]

The Candidates. In 1975 some state branches—notably that of New South Wales—still used the plebiscite or preselection ballot of party members in each electorate to choose its candidates. Several other methods of candidate selection were used elsewhere, practice sometimes varying from one electorate to another. The Victoria branch used selection by electoral councils, while in Queensland a combination of the council and plebiscite methods came into play, together with a third procedure that had been used to good effect in state elections: this was the practice of seeking out an "ideal" candidate and persuading him (where necessary) to join the party and stand for election under its banner, backed by its organization. In several electorates the party made use of still another constitutional arrangement, unique to itself: this was the endorsement of two candidates in a single electorate. Its purpose was to maximize support for the party by winning for it the personal followings of both candidates. Dual endorsement was used in the Tasmanian seat of Franklin and the Queensland seat of Dawson. In the latter, one of the Country party candidates, Raymond Braithwaite, defeated the sitting member, Rex Patterson, minister for the Northern Territory in the outgoing Labor government.

In keeping with its design to alter the party's image, the Country party noticeably modified its candidate type in this election. Until very recently its typical candidate was male, a farmer or grazier with little or no higher education, who had had extensive local government experience as a shire councillor or council alderman and who had probably held official positions both in an appropriate primary-producer association and in the Country party organization itself. The background of the five sitting members who were up for reelection in Queensland conformed closely to this pattern; in New

[16] *Sydney Morning Herald,* December 3, 1975.

South Wales the majority of the sitting members could be similarly categorized.

The change in the candidates' general backgrounds, occupations, educational levels, and areas of prior experience was most marked in Queensland. The nine new contestants in 1975 were, respectively, a clearing contractor/grazier, a real estate agent, the director of an equipment-leasing company, an accountant, a foreman in a coal mine, a tourist resort owner who was also a retired permanent army officer, and three businessmen, one of whom had direct pastoral connections. Five of the nine had at least some higher education, only one had served in local government, and two had experience in the party organization. Candidates in other states were split almost evenly between those who conformed to the traditional pattern and those who did not. Of the six incumbent Country party senators at the time of the election, just one, a medical practitioner from Queensland, was not a primary producer, and his election dated only from 1974. While Western Australia put up almost a full team of farmers, the Senate candidates in other states covered an occupational range that included a senior public servant, a teacher, a solicitor, a motel proprietor, and an engine driver of a six-engined coal train. Overall, the candidates were younger than their predecessors, and four women were given places in Senate teams. In choosing its candidates the party as a whole is now clearly less interested in honoring the claims of primary producers with long years of voluntary service to the party than it is in finding well-known, popular members of the local community who have been actively involved in commercial and service organizations.

Issues and Tactics. The Country party adopted "Let's Get Australia Back on Its Feet" as its campaign theme, along with "There's More to Australia than Sydney and Melbourne." Party strategy was to capitalize, if possible, on the marked swing away from Labor in the rural areas at the 1974 elections by hammering home the message that the Whitlam government had alienated and neglected the rest of Australia in order to further the interests of Sydney and Melbourne, where its own political strength lay. Opinion polls taken before the constitutional crisis had shown popular support for the government at its lowest point since Labor had taken office; thus, the Country party's other tactic was to remind voters of specific government policies which had acted to their personal detriment. General government mismanagement was stressed, the constitutional crisis and the coalition parties' role in it minimized or ignored.

Since Fraser was prevented by illness from opening the coalition's campaign on the appointed date, the honor fell to Anthony. The specifics in his speech, delivered in Brisbane on November 26, were directed to the rural sector and the mining industry.[17] They promised a return to life as it had been under earlier Liberal-Country party governments, the maintenance and extension of rural reconstruction schemes and supports, and, for the miners, a return to a political climate which encouraged exploration and development, with tax write-offs for oil exploration and a special investment allowance for developmental projects. The rigorous pruning of government expenditure promised by the coalition would clearly not be made at the expense of the Country party voter. Neither then nor later, however, did Anthony refer to coalition plans to restore the concessions that the rural sector had already lost. Questioned on this, he said that these cuts could only be restored when the economy was in a better condition. Rural voters didn't expect anything more, Anthony said, because the Country party hadn't promised it, but at least they knew it had "sympathy for their cause." [18]

In this election the Country party was in the fortunate position of canvassing that portion of the electorate where the tide had already observably turned against Labor [19]—and the shift of support away from Labor could be expected to continue. It was left to the Liberal party to specify what the coalition, if it won, would do to curb inflation and unemployment and to court the cities. At the national level there was a good deal of mainly informal cooperation between the two parties and their campaign officials. Anthony personally directed the Country party's national campaign, which was coordinated by the federal secretariat working with the state campaign directors. His leadership was, in the opinion of party officials, his most impressive to date. Extensive use was made of the media, particularly the press, where the Country party ran full-page advertisements. There was a perceptible change, however, in the tone and content of these and of Anthony's speeches as the campaign developed. A low-key recounting of Labor's failures in office, delivered "more in sorrow than in anger," was replaced by declamatory indictments of the "corrupt" Whitlam government as a threat to democracy, a government bent on smashing the power of Parliament and one

---

[17] J. D. Anthony, *Policy Speech*, November 26, 1975; published by the National Country party secretariat, Canberra, 1975.

[18] *Australian*, December 1, 1975.

[19] Malcolm Mackerras, "City vs Country: Analysis of 1974 Election Results," *Politics*, vol. 9 (November 1974), pp. 195-99.

that incited disruption and fostered trade union lawlessness. The further Anthony traveled away from the capital cities, the more his campaign developed the momentum and intensity of a religious revival that equated the evils of Labor with those of socialism and communism. Not a subtle orator, Anthony tended to grossly oversimplify complex issues, but his style on the hustings was well received. Like the leaders of the major parties in this election, of course, he was preaching for the most part to the converted, the party faithful.

The state branches ran individual campaigns, independent of those of the Liberal party organizations. These covered the state capitals and the rural areas and placed great emphasis on country radio and the provincial press, the media through which the branches believed they could most effectively woo the voters. There were marked differences among the state campaigns. In Queensland, for example, the party commissioned a private survey from the Roy Morgan market research organization to discover which issues a sample of the electorate considered important; the party used the results as a guide in planning its strategy.[20] So confident was the state machine of its ability to correctly interpret the issues and gauge the style to which Queenslanders would best respond that early in the campaign it cut off the flow of directives and literature from the national organization and took over sole responsibility for the whole of the campaign in Queensland. In many ways this was but an extension of the tough, rough, and hard-hitting campaign style which had been honed to a fine edge of efficiency in the 1974 state election. The Queensland branch took a much stronger, more emphatically antisocialist line than that of the party branches in other states.

The Results. The Country party was confident that it would improve its position.[21] While it was some time before the final results of the vote were known, especially in two Queensland seats ultimately snatched by the Country party from Labor ministers, it was clear before election night was over that the Liberals had won by such a landslide that they would be able to govern in their own right should

---

[20] The record of the Labor government was the issue rated most important by the sample. Results of the survey are held by the National party of Australia (Queensland branch), Brisbane.

[21] The public opinion polls, which had been showing the combined Liberal-Country party team with over 50 percent of the vote, did not provide a separate assessment of Country party support. The party's optimism was based on the results of a private survey it had commissioned, together with the feedback it had been getting from party workers in the electorates.

154

they choose to do so, having won 68 seats in a House of 127, to the Country party's 23.

On balance the Country party itself appeared to have done well, with three new wins in Queensland more than counterbalancing the loss of a seat in Victoria to the Liberals and an increase in national voting support of only .2 percentage points.[22] It should be noted that the party stood more candidates in 1975 than ever before; the increase in Senate representation from six to eight, however, was more the result of felicitous positioning of Country party candidates within the joint teams on the ballot paper than of increased electoral support. In Western Australia, for example, where the Country party ran an independent team, the party's share of the vote dropped by almost 4 percentage points and the only successful candidate, Senator Thomas Drake-Brockman, was fortunate to retain his seat. Indeed, a breakdown of Country party results by state for the House of Representatives tells a cautionary tale. In Victoria and New South Wales support was up by only a little over 1 percentage point and in Western Australia down by 5.7 percentage points; the one candidate in South Australia and those in Tasmania contesting four of the five available seats polled badly. Only in Queensland (an increase of 3.1 percentage points) and in the Northern Territory (4.6 percentage points), where the two seats are contested in a straight fight between Labor and the Country party, was there just cause for elation.

Overall, the results made clear that the strength of the Country party at the national level is drawn almost exclusively from three of the six states, New South Wales, Queensland, and Victoria. The marginally greater success it has achieved in the past in state elections can be attributed to the marked differences between politics at the national and state levels. In the state electoral systems, greater use is made of gerrymandering and greater weight given to rural areas; from time to time both of these practices have been of considerable assistance to the Country party in maintaining and increasing its representation in the state legislatures.[23]

---

[22] Of the four Queensland seats—Capricornia, Dawson, Leichhardt, and Wide Bay—won by the Country party from Labor since 1974, only one, Leichhardt, has a history of continuous representation by a Labor member (since 1951). Of the others, Capricornia was held by the Liberal party from 1949 to 1961 before passing to the ALP; Dawson was held by the Country party from 1949 to 1966 when it was won by Labor at a by-election and subsequently retained; Wide Bay returned a Country party member from 1949 to 1961 before it went to Labor.

[23] See Colin A. Hughes, "Measures of Malapportionment," *A Handbook of Australian Government and Politics 1965-1974* (Canberra: Australian National University Press, forthcoming), appendix I, pp. 136-43.

Conclusion

In forming his ministry the Liberal prime minister, Malcolm Fraser, did not exclude the Country party, though allegedly he was under strong pressure from within his own party to do so. (Since the Liberals held only twenty-seven out of the sixty-four Senate seats, this was a realistic decision.) Instead, the usual arrangements for determining the Country party's share in a coalition government held good: Anthony put forward the names of the selected Country party members (subject, as is normal procedure, to a prime ministerial veto, which was not invoked) and chose his own portfolio.

Six out of the twenty-four ministerial positions were given to Country party members, three of them in an inner cabinet of twelve.[24] In this respect the party did very well. But of far greater relevance than numbers to its own position within the coalition were the actual portfolios assigned to party members. As minister for national resources and overseas trade, Anthony will clearly be the most powerful person in the government after the prime minister. The key ministries from the point of view of rural interests—primary industry, transport, and Northern Territory—will also be Country party fiefs. Together they have the potential to give the party a base of considerable power and influence within the new government. However, the loss of secondary industry and interior to the Liberals may be of greater long-term political significance. Under McEwen, the department of secondary industry had been used for many years as an economic power base for his party within the coalition. The removal of the department of the interior from Country party hands will also diminish appreciably its influence over future electoral redistribution—a matter vital to the party's interests.

It is still too early in the life of the government for exact predictions as to the short-term future of the Country party within the coalition or, in the longer view, as to its future as a viable, independent political party in the country at large. The loss of the most effective bargaining weapon—the threat to walk out of the coalition—may well be offset by the close affinity between Fraser and Anthony: in the short time the government has been in office there have already been signs that if the prime minister takes advice from anyone it is from Anthony and the deputy Country party leader, Ian Sinclair. Much will hinge on whether the Liberals keep Labor's Commonwealth

---

[24] This gave the Country party a 25 percent representation in both cabinet and ministry, 18 percent of the seats in the House of Representatives (25 percent of the combined total of Liberal and Country party seats), and 11 percent of the national vote.

Electoral Bill (No. 2, 1973) on the statute books, for 1976 is a census year and an electoral redistribution should normally follow; under the present electoral law, this would write some Country party seats off the electoral map. The party will need to survive this without any appreciable attrition in strength in its heartland, the three eastern states.

Nevertheless, on the credit side, it must be assumed that in future elections the pendulum will swing back, however marginally, to Labor, and when it does more Liberal than Country party seats are likely to be lost. The coalition's ability to come to grips quickly with the problems of inflation and unemployment will be of importance here, though the total disarray of the Labor party at the time of writing seems to indicate a slow recovery for Labor and a lengthy period of electoral supremacy for the coalition.

The Country party has its problems, indeed, some of which have been touched on in this study. To date, its campaign to extend its electoral support beyond the rural population has borne little fruit at the national level except in Queensland. There the state branch believes that the party as a whole would do well to adopt the Queensland organization's name (National party of Australia) and more of its methods and strategy in the quest to extend Country party representation in the national Parliament. Certainly the party might suffer in the long term if its return to office halted or slowed down the self-reappraisal it was undergoing while in opposition. Other serious questions to which it must find answers have arisen as a consequence of its relative success in breaking out of its historic mold to become a political power broker for the mining and oil exploration industries and some sections of business, a role that Anthony's present ministerial posts only serve to emphasize. As spokesman for these interests, Anthony will need to persuade Fraser and the Liberals to formulate policies on tariffs, foreign investment in Australia, and so on, which will be more palatable to his backers than were those of the Labor government.

But for all that, the Country party is still in comparatively good health. Luck, the personalities of some of its leaders, and excellent organizational management and initiative in some areas have given it a new lease on life. Opportunistic and clear-sighted where its own interests are at stake, it will no doubt stand, well into the future, ready and able to exploit to its own advantage any changes that may develop in the existing party and political systems.

6

THE ROLE OF
THE MINOR PARTIES

Paul Reynolds

Minor-Party Formation

There are a number of ways in which a minor party can be formed and thereby become a participant in an established political system. First, it may originate as the offshoot of another, usually major, party, invariably as a result of a split in the ranks of the parent party. A section of the older party becomes alienated from the main body of that party, moves outside its structures, and founds a new group, which, however, fails to attract enough support to allow it either to replace the original party or to threaten its major-party status. The two contemporary examples in Australia of this development are the formation of the Democratic Labor party (DLP), which split from the Australian Labor party over the issues of communism, defense, foreign policy, state aid, and related matters in the middle 1950s,[1] and the Liberal Movement (LM), which broke with the Liberal party branch in the state of South Australia in the late 1960s over electoral reform and matters internal to the branch's structure.[2] In 1975 the LM contested Senate elections outside South Australia for the first time, nominating candidates in Victoria, New South Wales, and Queensland.

---

[1] For the formation of the DLP, see R. S. Murray, *The Split: Australian Labor in the Fifties* (Melbourne: Cheshire, 1970); D. W. Rawson, *Australia Votes: The 1958 Federal Election* (Melbourne: Melbourne University Press, 1961); P. L. Reynolds, *The Democratic Labor Party* (Brisbane: The Jacaranda Press, 1974); K. Tennant, *Evatt: Politics and Justice* (Sydney: Angus and Robertson, 1970); T. Truman, *Catholic Action and Politics* (Melbourne: Georgian House, 1959). For one participant's view, see B. A. Santamaria, " 'The Movement' 1941-1960: An Outline," in H. Mayer, ed., *Catholics and the Free Society* (Melbourne: Cheshire, 1960), and Santamaria, " 'The Split': Review Article," *Australian Quarterly*, vol. 43, no. 2 (June 1971).

[2] See Steele Hall, *A Liberal Awakening: The LM Story* (Adelaide: Leabrook South Australia Investigator Press, 1973).

Second, a minor party may be the political embodiment of the aspirations and/or grievances of a limited section of the society. Sectional parties are, by their very nature, unlikely to encompass sufficient interests and, therefore, supporters in the wider society and thus rarely become major parties in their own right. They can usually share political power only to the extent that they become allies of, or make themselves indispensable to, a major party. The National Country party is Australia's example of this species.[3]

A third variant is the founding of a party to express an ideological position which has not been accorded sufficient recognition by an existing party. Frequently this ideological viewpoint is somewhat apocalyptic, and often it seeks a radical alteration in the existing social order. This country's three Communist parties [4] could loosely be held to belong to this type, as could the newly formed right-wing Workers' party (WP), which espouses a return to laissez-faire capitalism and has, as its first objective, "to offer a practical alternative to socialism as practised and preached by the Labor and Australia Parties and as practised by the Liberal and Country Parties." [5]

The fourth way a minor party can be formed is through a combination of the first and second. A split can develop in the ranks of a major party over a policy plank which embodies a fundamental issue of principle. This division may then broaden into a movement catering to a section of the electorate that has felt generally estranged from the existing political processes. The early leadership of the Australia party (AP) broke with the Liberals in 1966 over the latter's Vietnam War policy, but subsequently became a focal point for middle-class radicals who were concerned about the government's inaction in the general area of "value politics"—specifically, conservation, legal reform in sex-related areas, civil liberties, race relations, education, and general quality-of-life matters.[6]

Pressure groups may utilize the electoral and political processes in order to field candidates and draw attention to their particular causes. Within a system of preferential voting, their aim is often

---

[3] This is called the National party in Queensland. Prior to 1975, it was known simply as the Country party. For details on the names by which this party is known, see chapter 5, footnote 1.

[4] The Communist party of Australia (CPA), the Communist party of Australia (Marxist-Leninist) (CPA [M-L]), and the Socialist party of Australia (SPA). The first is generally Titoist, the second Maoist, and the third Moscow-oriented. This chapter will not deal with the Communist parties since their electoral impact is minimal and they represent a special type of minor party compared to those which are non-Communist.

[5] Workers Party, Platform and Constitution (Sydney: Workers' Party, n.d. [1974]).

[6] See T. Blackshield, "The Australia Party," Current Affairs Bulletin, July 1, 1972.

to assist a preferred major-party candidate and hurt a nonfavored opponent. Thus the Council for the Defence of Government Schools (DOGS), which opposes state aid to private schools, participated in the federal elections of 1969, 1972, and 1974 in Victoria, while the United Tasmania Group (UTG), a conservation body, has fought recent state and federal elections in that state. Finally, a small party may be the remnant of a major party that has gradually declined in support and status. Australia has no examples of this type of minor-party formation, unlike, for example, the United Kingdom with its Liberal party.

Minor-Party Survival

Historically, Australia's federal experience with minor parties has been relatively slight since the emergence of the modern two-party system in 1910. Apart from the Lang Labor party, which lingered in New South Wales from the mid-1930s into the early 1940s, and the Communist party of Australia, formed in the early 1920s, it is difficult to cite any important examples. The society's current experience with such parties, then, dates from the upheavals of 1955–57 within the ALP, which led to the creation of the DLP; the less dramatic falterings of the Liberals in the mid-1960s, which produced the AP; a fight in the most conservative state branch of the Liberal party in the late 1960s, which generated the LM; and the anxieties and trepidations of a number of right-wing business and professional men at the advent of the first Labor government in twenty-three years, which produced the WP. According to conventional political wisdom, in 1975 Australia had two minor parties of the center-left (the LM and the AP) and two of the right (the WP and the DLP).

A number of important factors appear to sustain minor parties once they have emerged as separate political identities. These variables can assist in prolonging the existence of minor parties despite the limited political and electoral success they usually enjoy. In the context of current Australian politics, the most important of these seem to be the relative cohesiveness of an identifiable base of support, the nature of the electoral system, and the party's success in aligning itself with any of the major parties.

To achieve any degree of permanence, a small party must appeal to a definite class, group, or section of the electorate. A splinter party has a potentially easier task in this regard than does an entirely new party; the latter, if its appeal is based on the special vision of a few individuals, must piece together its electoral support from scratch.

The position of the splinter party is further enhanced if the split has run wide and deep in the ranks of the parent organization. Both the DLP and the LM are ready examples in this regard. The former, especially in Victoria where the ALP split was greatest, gained 12 to 15 percent of the vote in its early days. In the fourteen years and six House of Representatives elections between 1955 and 1969, the DLP's vote in Victoria fluctuated between 10.8 percent and 15.8 percent. The slide in its support occurred after 1972, when it polled 8.4 percent; thereafter the DLP vote fell away to 5.2 percent in 1974 and 4.8 percent in 1975. The LM in South Australia contested federal (but not state) elections for the first time in 1974, winning 8.2 percent, but falling to 6.5 percent in 1975.

The DLP in Victoria and, to a lesser extent, in Queensland appealed to upper-working-class and lower-middle-class Roman Catholics who were pious and orthodox, and regular in their attendance at mass. They had been socialized at the hands of church agencies, such as parochial primary and high schools, and were securely locked into the social network which revolved around the local church and its agencies.[7] Owing to the pattern of Australian colonization and settlement, the majority of Catholics were Irish immigrants who, until the mid-twentieth century, were disproportionately concentrated in the working class. They had given their allegiance to the ALP when it was formed in the 1890s and had, for the most part, continued to support Labor, despite the relative upward social mobility they enjoyed following the depression and World War II.

The Labor split of the mid-1950s, then, can be attributed partly to the rising socioeconomic expectations of this group, partly to the factionalism which has been endemic in state ALP machines, and partly to a policy dispute over the stance the party should adopt in response to rising Communist strength in the union movement and the emergence of Communist governments and movements in Asia. This dispute had strong ideological and sectarian overtones, with those who left the ALP being, in most cases, prominent Catholic Labor parliamentary and machine politicians. Together with their ideological mentor, B. A. Santamaria,[8] they could appeal to voters who were un-

---

[7] A survey of 322 DLP voters in Melbourne in 1972 reported that 77.6 percent were Roman Catholics and 63.7 percent had attended church within the preceding two weeks. See P. L. Reynolds, *Minority Party Support: A Study of the D.L.P. Vote in Melbourne, 1970-1972* (unpublished Ph.D. dissertation, University of Melbourne, 1976). Also H. Mol, *Religion in Australia* (Melbourne: Nelson, 1972), pp. 293-300.

[8] Santamaria is president of the National Civic Council, an organization of Catholic laymen which seeks to combat communism in the Australian trade union movement and propagate an anti-Communist foreign policy.

easy about supporting a Labor party that possessed a strong and vocal left wing. The misgivings of such voters were reinforced by socio-economic factors which predisposed them to support an alternative non-Labor party. The DLP was a way of resolving this dilemma, and with consummate political skill the party kept its constituency together until the 1970s. Thereafter its support base fragmented in the wake of increased political, social, and religious pluralism within the Catholic subculture engendered by developments such as the liberal reforms adopted by Vatican II, further upward social mobility, and the decline of anticommunism as a viable basis for a political program and style.

The Liberal Movement similarly had a relatively cohesive clientele in South Australia. The movement was established by Steele Hall, an ex-leader of the Liberal Country League (LCL)—that is, the South Australian branch of the Liberal party—who had also served as state premier from 1968 to 1970.[9] As premier of South Australia, Hall had fought for internal party reform against the LCL's entrenched right wing, which had as its power base the state upper house, the Legislative Council. The result of this split was the emergence of the LM as a progressive, largely urban-based, nonsocialist reform party, in contrast with the LCL which remained dominated by its traditional alliance of big-business urban and affluent rural-grazier interests.[10] The LM sought to supplant the LCL as the major non-Labor party in Adelaide and its hinterland. The strength of this appeal was demonstrated by the 1974 election results, with 82.8 percent of the LM vote coming from Adelaide seats where 70 percent of the state's total voting population was concentrated. In the 1975 election, 42.9 percent of the LM's national vote came from Adelaide.

The task of consolidating a permanent constituency was more difficult for the AP and the WP. The former was founded largely by Sydney business and professional people who opposed the Vietnam War but who felt unable to join or identify with the ALP. Thus, the party became dependent upon middle-class radicals, especially in the big cities of Sydney and Melbourne. Like the British Liberal party, the AP performed best when discontent with the major conservative party was greatest, that is, in the House of Representatives elections of 1969 and 1972 and in the Senate election of 1970. With the advent of the Labor government and the resurgence of the Liberals

---

[9] Hall was elected to the Senate in 1974 and reelected in 1975.

[10] For the period immediately prior to the South Australian Liberal party split, see N. Blewett and D. Jaensch, *Playford to Dunstan: The Politics of Transition* (Melbourne: Cheshire, 1971).

in 1974 and 1975, the number of anti-Liberal protest voters shrank and the AP's support ebbed. Accordingly, the party was driven back to the small core of non-Labor middle-class progressives, a base scarcely large enough to be viable.

The Workers' party experienced difficulties similar to those of the AP. The WP was formed out of hostility to the Whitlam government's presumed socialism and was financially supported by the Western Australian mining magnate Lang Hancock, previously the major backer of a Western Australian secessionist party. It advocated minimal taxation and minimal government intervention in the economy and national life, doing so at a time of increasing electoral polarization between the major Labor and anti-Labor forces. Hence the support it might have achieved by-passed it. By the end of 1974 an atmosphere of general suspicion and distrust of the competence and style of the Labor government prevailed, particularly among middle-class voters, but the paramount concern of this section of the electorate was the desire to replace the ALP with another L-NCP government. Middle-class voters saw little point in wasting their votes on a new and untried minority right-wing party.

A small party's life span is frequently affected by the society's electoral system. Australia has a system of preferential voting in single-member electorates for the House of Representatives and one of preferential voting coupled with proportional representation on a statewide basis for the Senate. The small party, then, can aim to maximize its first-preference vote, and, if no overall majority is produced by the first count, have its second-preference votes allocated to major-party candidates in order to obtain the requisite majority. The DLP pioneered the exploitation of this system by tightly disciplining its second preferences and allocating these to Liberal or National Country party candidates in a bid to deny office to the ALP as long as Labor remained, in DLP eyes, tainted by left-wing socialism. In most cases, about 85 percent of DLP voters followed their party's instructions,[11] with the result that in close elections, such as those of 1961 and 1969, the DLP was instrumental in denying Labor office, despite the latter's gaining a plurality of the first-preference vote.[12]

The DLP, then, provided a lead for other parties in terms of electoral strategy, a lead which, ironically, was adopted by those

[11] For an analysis of DLP preference allocation, see M. Mackerras, *Australian General Elections* (Sydney: Angus and Robertson, 1972), pp. 245-51.

[12] In 1961 the national voting figures were: ALP, 47.9 percent; LCP, 42.1 percent; DLP, 8.7 percent; other, 1.3 percent. In 1969: ALP, 47.0 percent; LCP 43.4 percent; DLP, 6.0 percent; AP, 0.9 percent; other, 2.8 percent.

opposed to the DLP and to its major-party ally. The AP and the Council for the Defence of Government Schools both directed their second preferences to the ALP in 1969 and 1972 in a bid to defeat the coalition government. The AP did so again in 1974, with such success that one scholar observed:

> If the Australia Party "how-to-vote" cards had reversed preferences Labor would not have won four seats, Cook and Eden-Monaro in New South Wales and Diamond Valley and Isaacs in Victoria. The Australia Party can, therefore, fairly claim to have swung the election in Labor's favour. Indeed Mr. Whitlam owes both his 1972 and 1974 victories to Australia Party preferences.[13]

If the DLP had been responsible for keeping Labor from office in 1961 and 1969, its minor-party rival had reversed the position for 1972 and 1974. In this respect, small parties can be held to have reached the zenith of their electoral influence in the elections immediately preceding 1975.

This analysis leads to the third factor of importance for the longevity of small parties, namely, the ability to forge alliances with majority parties. Such an alliance is always a matter of mutual convenience and rests on three factors: first, the minor party feels intense antipathy to one of the main parties; second, it directs the vote preferences of its supporters to the other major party; and third, it expects its ally to enact or maintain certain policies which it sees as crucial. The exception has been the LM, with its desire to replace the LCL as South Australia's major non-Labor party. Until it could achieve its goal, it sought to demonstrate its basic anti-Labor credentials by directing preferences to the Liberals on the assumption that even an "unregenerate" LCL is preferable to a "socialist" ALP.[14]

1975: A Watershed

In the light of these developments, the 1975 election was something of a watershed for the minor parties. After 1955, the electoral system had settled into a period of stability. Liberal-Country party govern-

---

[13] M. Mackerras, "City vs. Country: An Analysis of the 1974 Election Results," *Politics*, vol. 9, no. 2 (November 1974), pp. 198-99.

[14] In 1976, in response to Liberal party overtures, the majority of LM members, led by Senator Hall, voted, at a special conference in Adelaide, to rejoin the South Australian Liberal party. However, a minority, led by the former deputy leader of the LM, Robin Millhouse, decided not to participate in this merger and to keep the LM in existence as a separate party.

ments had periodically been reelected with the help of DLP second preferences. In the late 1960s the AP had emerged, gaining 0.9 percent in 1969, 2.4 percent in 1972, and 2.3 percent in 1974. The advent of a Labor government in 1972 had altered the political status quo in a number of ways, not least for minor parties. The DLP had finally lost its raison d'être when the ALP was elected without first undergoing the reconstruction favored by the DLP. The AP had helped Labor to power and thus had won an important moral victory over the DLP, despite being outpolled by the latter by a margin of three percentage points.[15]

The DLP still held the balance of power in the Senate, a legacy of the politics of the 1960s, but this advantage was wiped out in the 1974 double-dissolution election when the four remaining DLP senators failed to be reelected. The LM leader, Hall, together with an independent, held the balance of power in the Senate after 1974, the LM then being the only minor party to be represented in the federal Parliament. The 1974 election had dealt the DLP a mortal blow. The party was bereft of funds, and the alliance with the L-NCP coalition had collapsed amid a welter of recrimination over the joint-ticket issue, the upshot of which was that the DLP ran candidates for the House of Representatives only in Victoria. Thus, its impact on Australian national politics had abruptly ended. The 1975 election was basically a rerun of 1974: again the party limited its House of Representatives candidates to Victoria; again its Senate teams in Victoria and Queensland, the two states where it had previously enjoyed its greatest electoral success, were led by prominent ex-senators; [16] again its vote decreased in all states.

The AP's experience was similar. Its vote was static between 1972 and 1974 but fell away in 1975 to a mere 0.4 percent of the total national vote for the House and 0.5 percent for the Senate. The AP's best showings in individual races were 2.3 percent for the Northern Territory's House seat and 2.0 percent for the Northern Territory's Senate vacancies. Except in Victoria, where the AP polled 1 percent of the vote, its support in the House elections fell below 1 percent in every state. Like the DLP, the AP had been swamped by the movement of votes between the major parties.

In the preelection period the LM seemed to be in a better position than the other smaller parties. A number of Liberals resigned from

---

[15] In New South Wales, the DLP's weakest state but the AP's strongest one, the result was: DLP, 3.5 percent; AP, 3.3 percent.

[16] The two DLP candidates for the Senate in 1975 were Frank McManus in Victoria and Condon Byrne in Queensland.

Table 6-1

DLP'S SHARE OF SENATE VOTE, BY STATE, 1974 AND 1975

(in percentages)

State	1974	1975
New South Wales	2.9	1.7
Victoria	6.4	5.9
Queensland	4.0	2.5
South Australia	0.9	0.1
Western Australia	—	0.5
Tasmania	0.8	—

Source: Compiled from election night returns, *Australian*, December 15, 1975.

their party in public protest against the way the election had been forced. This was the prelude to the LM's mounting Senate teams outside its home state for the first time in an attempt to capture an anti-Liberal backlash which, it was hoped, would reelect Hall, gain him a couple of colleagues, and again give the LM the balance of power in the Senate. These hopes were dashed, however, as the tide moved strongly in favor of the coalition and the predicted backlash failed to eventuate. Hall's vote declined in South Australia by 1.7 percentage points, from 8.2 percent to 6.5 percent, so that he won his seat only with the help of ALP preferences. In no other state did the LM poll above 1 percent.

The WP also mounted a determined effort to make a national impression in this, its first federal, election. Some months before the general election, after obtaining 17 percent in a state by-election, it had high hopes of winning a rural seat in Western Australia. However, it soon learned that a party's national performance cannot be predicted on the basis of its performance in such contests. All of the WP candidates lost their deposits and in the five states where the WP fielded Senate teams they gained only derisory support. The WP vote was: Queensland, 2.1 percent; Western Australia, 1.2 percent; New South Wales, 1.1 percent; South Australia, 0.6 percent; and Tasmania, 0.4 percent.

While none of the four parties could have hoped to supplant either of the major parties in the short term, all attempted to capitalize on the heightened interest in politics which attended the 1975 election. All hoped for some parliamentary representation, usually in the Senate, in order to enhance their status, demonstrate their political relevance,

Table 6-2

MINOR PARTIES' SHARE OF SENATE VOTE, BY STATE, 1975

(in percentages)

State	Party			
	DLP	AP	LM	WP
New South Wales	1.7	0.4	0.2	1.1
Victoria	5.9	0.2	0.8	—
Queensland	2.5	0.2	0.4	2.1
South Australia	0.1	—	6.5	0.6
Western Australia	0.5	0.3	0.9	1.2
Tasmania[a]	—	—	—	0.4
Northern Territory	—	2.0	—	—

[a] An independent, Brian Harradine, who had been expelled from the ALP prior to the election, stood and gained 13.2 percent of the vote in Tasmania, thus making him the only independent in the new Parliament.

Source: Compiled from election night returns, *Australian*, December 15, 1975.

and acquire a national platform from which to present their own brand and style of politics. They competed in vain; all were overwhelmed by the polarization of political attitudes and votes which characterized the 1975 election. This polarization had begun with the 1974 election, when the Labor vote held but the coalition made heavy inroads in the DLP and AP vote. In 1975 there was a 6.5 percentage point swing against the ALP, a 7.3 percentage point swing to the coalition, and a drop of 1.0 percentage point in the combined minor-party vote. For the Senate, Labor fell by 6.4 percentage points and the minor parties, collectively, by 1.4 percentage points, while the coalition rose by 7.9 percentage points.

Electorally, small parties perform best under two circumstances. First, if there is a swing against both major parties, the minor ones will profit accordingly; this occurred in the 1958 House and 1967 and 1970 Senate elections. Second, if there is a swing against one major party which is not monopolized by the other main alternative, minor parties can again profit. In both instances, the small parties' limited electoral bases will be augmented by disaffected or protest voters. Neither of these situations, however, has arisen in Australian politics in the last few years. In 1966 all minor parties and independents together polled 10.0 percent of the total valid vote. In 1969 this fell to 9.7 percent in the face of a 7 percentage point swing to Labor. In 1972 the non-major-party share of the vote declined to 8.9 percent, in 1974 to 4.9 percent, and in 1975 to 4.0 percent. The 1974 election accentuated the consolidation of the national vote behind the large parties, and this development was confirmed in 1975.

By the mid-1970s the Australian political system had largely reverted to the position it had been in prior to 1955. The advent of the DLP had heralded a period of minor-party activity, augmented some ten years later by splits among Liberal voters that produced the AP and the LM. The WP, whose formation was prompted by the election of a Labor government, came into being at a most unpropitious time, when the erosion of small-party support was already well advanced. Rather than reversing this process, the 1975 election confirmed how tenuous is the small parties' hold on life when the electorate is faced with a significant choice between the major parties.

7

THE MEDIA AND THE ELECTIONS

C. J. Lloyd

The constitutional crisis and the general election of 1975 singed many of Australia's public institutions. Inevitably the mass media were badly scorched.[1]

It was an election in which media bias was elevated into a major theme. Alleged bias sparked the first strike in Australian history by journalists protesting the manner in which political news was presented in their papers. Charges of bias were leveled against the Australian Broadcasting Commission (ABC) and a call was made for the appointment of a moderator to vet its political coverage. Media bias is not, of course, a revolutionary concept in the conduct of elections. Rarely, however, have charges of bias been pressed with such vehemence and venom as in the embittered political context of Australia in 1975.

The campaign of 1975 changed the conventional rules of the game in other ways. It saw a marked diminution in the influence on coverage of the national campaign of the National Press Gallery based in Canberra. Careful media management of the campaign of then caretaker Prime Minister Malcolm Fraser opened the way for new means of dampening the effectiveness of the media in probing party politics and policies during election campaigns. Election advertising, both paid and unpaid, revealed new dimensions of skill and resourcefulness. The aftermath of the election produced a clamor for

---

[1] Accounts of the 1975 elections and the constitutional crisis that preceded it are given in: Laurie Oakes, *Crash Through or Crash: The Unmaking of a Prime Minister* (Melbourne: Drummond, 1976); Paul Kelly, *The Unmaking of Gough* (Sydney: Angus and Robertson, 1976); Clem Lloyd and Andrew Clark, *Kerr's King Hit!* (Sydney: Cassell, 1976).

media reform and an anguished reassessment among sections of the media. These are the main themes taken up in this chapter.[2]

The Australian Mass Media

Structure. There is no convenient model for defining Australia's sprawling and complex mass media structure. The following description divides it roughly into six groups and lists the main components of each.

The Melbourne Herald group. This far-flung empire dominates Australia's press and much of its electronic media outside of Sydney (the capital of New South Wales). It controls more than 90 percent of newspaper circulation in three of the six state capitals—Brisbane (Queensland), Perth (Western Australia), and Hobart (Tasmania). In Melbourne (Victoria) it controls more than 80 percent of circulation and in Adelaide (South Australia) more than 55 percent.[3] In its traditional base of Melbourne, the group publishes the nation's top-selling daily, the *Sun News Pictorial* (morning), and its most substantial evening paper, the *Herald*. In partnership with David Syme & Co., it has a 50 percent interest in the *Sunday Press*, a weekly of modest circulation.

Outside of Melbourne, the group controls Brisbane's two dailies, the *Courier Mail* (morning) and the *Telegraph* (evening), and the *Sunday Mail*. In Perth, the Melbourne *Herald* group controls both

[2] The best work on the Australian press is Henry Mayer, *The Press in Australia*, rev. ed. (Melbourne: Lansdown, 1968). The annual summer schools of professional journalism conducted by the Australian National University, Canberra, have yielded some useful material, particularly the papers collected in *The Social Responsibilities of Journalism*, Sixth Summer School of Professional Journalism, ANU, Canberra, 1970. The many gaps in studies of the Australian media are being filled only slowly. Valuable works include: J. S. Western and C. A. Hughes, *The Mass Media in Australia: Use and Evaluation* (St. Lucia: Queensland University Press, 1971); A. F. Davies, "Mass Communication," in A. F. Davies and S. Encel, eds., *Australian Society: A Sociological Introduction*, 2nd ed. (Melbourne: Cheshire, 1970), chap. 18. A more venerable treatment of the Australian press by an American academic is W. Sprague Holden, *Australia Goes to Press* (Melbourne: Melbourne University Press, 1961). There is no definitive study of Australian television, radio, the Australian Broadcasting Commission (ABC), or Australian advertising. The best recent symposium covering the broad span of the Australian media is G. Major, ed., *Mass Media in Australia* (Sydney: Hodder & Stoughton, 1976), published for the Australian Institute of Political Science.

[3] A useful breakdown of press statistics is given in: Henry Mayer and Sara Pantzer, *Australia's Press: Control, Circulation, Readership*, 1974, monograph published by the Department of Government and Public Administration, Sydney University.

daily papers, the *West Australian* (morning) and the *Daily News* (evening). In the state of Tasmania, the group controls the *Mercury* (morning), Hobart's only daily and the island's most widely circulating daily. Other printing interests include papers in Papua New Guinea, interests in provincial papers, news agencies, and substantial holdings in newsprint production.

In the electronic media, the group either controls or holds substantial interests in television stations in Melbourne, Brisbane, Hobart, and Adelaide. It maintains diverse interests in a number of radio stations.

The John Fairfax group. This is the oldest media organization in Australia, with origins going back to colonial New South Wales. Its control has remained in the hands of successive generations of the Fairfax family. The group's flagship is the venerable *Sydney Morning Herald,* described by Whitlam during the election campaign as a dynastic indulgence read only by members of the Fairfax family. It also controls the *Canberra Times,* the national capital's only daily, the *Sun,* a Sydney evening paper, the weekly *Sun Herald* with the largest circulation of any single Australian paper, another weekly, the *National Times,* and the *Australian Financial Review,* the nation's only financial daily. In recent years Fairfax has acquired a controlling interest in the Melbourne *Age,* formerly owned by another famous family company, David Syme & Co., which still retains a major interest in the *Age.* The Fairfax group prints a number of magazines, controls television stations in Sydney, Brisbane, and Canberra, and has a substantial interest in a major radio network.

The Murdoch group. This group originated in Adelaide where it still publishes the *News,* an evening daily, and shares a 50 percent interest with the Melbourne *Herald* group in the *Sunday Mail.* These Adelaide origins are preserved in the company name of the group's newspapers, News Ltd. The group's founder, K. R. (Rupert) Murdoch, moved into Sydney in the early 1960s, buying the *Daily Mirror* (evening) and the *Sunday Mirror.* In 1964 he started Australia's first national daily, the *Australian,* published initially in Canberra but now in Sydney.

In 1972 Murdoch acquired two other Sydney newspapers, the *Daily Telegraph* (morning) and the *Sunday Telegraph,* which now incorporates the *Sunday Australian,* founded in an abortive attempt to produce a quality weekly. Murdoch also publishes Sunday newspapers in Brisbane and Perth and the weekly, *Truth,* in Melbourne. His group prints a number of magazines and publishes important provincial papers such as the *Northern Territory News* in Darwin. The group has television stations in Adelaide and the NSW provincial cities of Wollongong and Newcastle. It maintains some radio interests and produces a significant share of Sydney's suburban newspapers. It has lesser suburban newspaper interests in Melbourne.

Murdoch has achieved some international standing as a media magnate with his successful incursion into London (*Sun, News of the World*, London Television). He is now engaged in a similar attempt to penetrate the American media through the *National Star*.[4]

The Packer group. This is a remnant of the Sydney empire of Sir Frank Packer who sold his two newspapers, the *Daily Telegraph* and the *Sunday Telegraph*, to the Murdoch group two years before his death in 1974. Sir Frank was a colorful and idiosyncratic newspaper nabob who won wide publicity in the United States for an unsuccessful bid to capture the famous yachting trophy, the America's Cup.[5] The Packer press was virulently anti-Labor; in the view of one critic the *Daily Telegraph* was operated as a political instrument by Sir Frank Packer in a brutish and unapologetic way.[6] Sir Frank's son, Kerry Packer, controls the group's remaining interests: television stations in Sydney and Melbourne, radio stations, provincial newspapers, and an influential group of magazines, including the *Australian Women's Weekly*, Australia's top-circulation magazine, and the weekly *Bulletin*. The Packer group and the Fairfax group have also collaborated to produce suburban newspapers in Sydney.

The Australian Broadcasting Commission. The ABC is a statutory authority funded by the Australian government, similar in many ways to the British Broadcasting Corporation. It controls 84 of Australia's 202 radio stations and 84 of its 132 television outlets. In particular, the ABC provides television services through repeater and translator stations to the remote and scantly populated parts of the continent. In the capital cities, it is outgunned by the ratings-conscious commercial stations.

Others. The remaining media interests and outlets cannot be classified in any intelligible way. Of some political significance is the

---

[4] See Simon Regan, *Rupert Murdoch: A Business Biography* (London: Angus & Robertson, 1976). Since this chapter was written, Murdoch has purchased the *New York Post* and *New York Magazine*.

[5] See R. Whitington, *Sir Frank: The Frank Packer Story* (Melbourne: Cassell, 1971).

[6] Max Walsh, "Case Study No. 1: Bias in News Reporting," in Major, ed., *Mass Media in Australia*, p. 98.

group of thirty-three provincial dailies with a total circulation of about 500,000. The remainder of Australia's rural and provincial press is weekly or biweekly; its political significance is meager. There is a small group of independent weekly papers—the *Observer* in Melbourne, the *Nation Review* in Sydney and Melbourne, and the *Independent* in Perth. Apart from the ABC and the television stations run by the Melbourne *Herald*, Fairfax, Murdoch, and Packer groups, other television stations operate in Brisbane, Sydney, Melbourne, and Adelaide under the direction of interests without strong traditional links with the media. The most important is the Ansett Transport group, which controls television stations in Melbourne and Brisbane.

Characteristics of the Media System. From this quick sketch of the media structure, a number of broad characteristics of the media system emerge. The dynastic character of media control is obvious, a quality reflected in a strong attachment to conservative politics. The traditional newspaper families—Fairfax, Murdoch, Packer—still dominate much of the Australian media. Even the Melbourne *Herald* group, which has no overtly dynastic character, was founded by Sir Keith Murdoch, Rupert Murdoch's father.

The concentration of media control is also obvious. Three groups control all of Australia's metropolitan daily newspapers. Four groups control most of the metropolitan television stations, a large slice of the radio stations, most suburban newspapers, and an important proportion of the provincial papers.

Most of the commercial electronic media are bland and lacking in character; there is a numbing uniformity about this sector of the Australian media. Despite the high degree of concentration, however, the Australian press has not lacked diversity or a willingness to experiment. Recent newspaper history is littered with the remains of brave ventures that failed. It has also produced a handful of new publications that have survived and flourished as quality papers. The *Australian*, the *Australian Financial Review*, and the *National Times* are the most notable examples from the past twenty years.

Generally, the media have been conservative in management techniques and technology. A former newspaper editor has made some strong criticisms of the management side of the media:

> Let the media try to look to their ancient management structures and bring them into the last quarter of the 20th century. The Australian newspaper is one of the few remaining vestiges of feudalism left in the modern world. It has a straight-line hierarchy in which everyone a little higher up

the line sits on someone lower down the line, regardless of merit, ability or enthusiasm.[7]

Australian newspapers have been slow in adopting new technology because of the problems of redundancy it creates; as in the United Kingdom, the trade unions have plenty of muscle. The electronic media have discouraged technological experimentation and innovation because of the profitability of the status quo. The first tentative signs of greater access to the air waves and the development of social experiments in media use through innovations such as cable television are only now starting to appear.

The rudiments of a national medium exist in the radio and television outlets of the ABC and in the publication on a national basis of two daily papers, the *Australian* and the *Australian Financial Review*. This is a notable achievement for Australia's small population, considering the immense distances and technical problems of production and distribution which have been overcome, but it should not be overstated. Both national newspapers have relatively small circulations. The ABC commands a mass audience only where there is no alternative outlet. The basic character of the Australian media is still overwhelmingly parochial, with local newspapers and electronic media outlets still dominant.

Political Campaigning and the Media. Compared with campaigns in countries like Canada, the United States, and even Britain, Australian election campaigns are relatively short. Usually the official campaign spans no more than three weeks, and in 1975 even less—nineteen days for Whitlam and sixteen for Fraser. The campaigns usually begin with some form of ritualized set piece. The party leaders visit each of the six states and the two territories at least once.

Coordinating the party leaders' schedules to get the maximum political benefit out of a tight campaign is an immensely complex art. There is no room for mistakes; a wasted day cannot be retrieved because of Australia's difficult logistical problems. Past mistakes have geared the campaign organizers to plan schedules that allow their leaders to visit as many strategic electorates as possible while still ensuring maximum exposure in the crucial metropolitan media. There are three major objectives to be reconciled: covering all the states and territories of a huge continent in a brief campaign, getting to the key electorates which decide the result, and attracting as much media attention as possible.

[7] Peter Robinson, "The Media and Australian Politics," in Major, ed., *Mass Media in Australia*, p. 14.

The national campaigns of the party leaders have been the traditional preserve of the Federal Parliamentary Press Gallery, based in Canberra. The organization of the Canberra press gallery is broadly the same as that of national press galleries in the United States, Canada, and the United Kingdom. Newspapers, television networks, and radio stations are represented in the gallery, which houses more than 100 journalists in cramped quarters above the chambers in Canberra's antiquated and inadequate Parliament House. The physical dimensions of the Parliament building bring media representatives into a closer relationship with politicians than often exists in bigger or more closely regulated parliaments. The peculiar flavor of Canberra's Parliament House and the relationships it breeds have been described by Whitlam:

> It's true that in our Parliament House, not the least because of its physical characteristics—the extraordinary range of functions it is required to meet, its very inadequate facilities, its relative isolation within Canberra and the relative isolation of Canberra itself, the enforced intimacy which such a situation creates—it's true that all these factors create a complex and not always healthy relationship between the press and politicians. Yet those very circumstances provide certain guarantees. The propinquity and ubiquity of journalists; the almost total lack of privacy; the enforced intimacy between us; all these do, perhaps, in a rather perverse way, provide certain safeguards against gross misconduct and impropriety.[8]

Press gallery journalists travel extensively with party leaders and ministers within Australia and on official overseas visits with the prime minister, as well as on occasion with senior ministers. This reinforces the close links that often build up between politicians and the Canberra press gallery. The Canberra press gallery journalists regard themselves as the elite of political journalists and insist on their prerogatives. One of these is the important right to cover national election campaigns and to travel with political leaders.

The itineraries of party leaders during election campaigns are designed to exploit as wide a range of local media outlets as possible. All of the mass audience outlets—radio phone-in shows, radio and television current affairs programs, television personality programs, top-circulation newspapers and magazines—are based in the six cap-

[8] E. G. Whitlam, Address to the Melbourne Press Club, November 10, 1975. Transcripts of speeches and media appearances have been obtained from a variety of sources. Only page references from official transcripts are cited.

ital cities. Press conferences are also arranged with the local media at each point of call. These conferences are attended by press gallery representatives traveling with the leaders, but preference is usually given to local media representatives. The daily schedule of each leader is usually devised to allow for extensive travel time, a limited number of electronic media appearances designed to give maximum exposure, a press conference, a media event which has both relevance to the campaign and substantial news value, and one or more public meetings. Australian election campaigns make heavy demands on the stamina and resilience of the participants.

An important trend in recent election campaigns has been the growth of press club functions attended by leaders. These are regarded as excellent forums, coupling a public address of media interest with a subsequent press conference which can either reinforce the news value of the speech or open up other lines of media interest. In recent campaigns, both leaders have made a National Press Club luncheon in Canberra, towards the end of the campaign period, the climax of their campaigns. The speeches delivered at these events and the questions asked by journalists are usually reported very fully by the press, and electronic media coverage is maximized at the national level.

The Buildup to the 1975 Campaign

It is doubtful whether there has ever been a greater news year in Australia's political history than 1975. The press in particular was deeply involved in the sequence of events that sparked the election and ultimately toppled the Whitlam government. This participation took the form of investigative journalism. Crucial political events such as the dismissals of Deputy Prime Minister Jim Cairns and Minister for Minerals and Energy Rex Connor were triggered by newspaper investigations and revelations. Media involvement also took a less direct form in the intensive reporting of every facet of the Whitlam government's performance in a year of extreme pressure. Rarely has a government been subjected to such relentless scrutiny by the media.

It was a year which produced a united front of editorial opinion against the Whitlam government. Australia's newspapers have invariably been extremely conservative in their politics. Support for the Australian Labor party has been very rare indeed. The Fairfax group supported Labor in 1961, the only breach in an otherwise impeccable record of support for the conservative coalition. The

Murdoch press supported Labor in 1963, at the same time supporting the Country party element of the coalition government and strongly opposing the Liberal party majority. This difficult piece of political legerdemain—supporting an opposition and part of a government against the rest of the government—was not repeated. In the two subsequent elections Murdoch supported the coalition.

The solid front against Labor began to wilt after the 1969 elections which Labor came within an ace of winning. The coalition government, which had held office since 1949, was running out of steam. The Liberal prime ministers who succeeded the legendary Sir Robert Menzies had lacked distinction. Labor under Whitlam had emerged, relatively united, with a new set of coherent and attractive policies. Plainly the era of Liberal-Country party domination was running out.

These factors drew Murdoch to the Labor camp. In addition, the *Australian*, which Murdoch had launched as a national newspaper in 1964, had won considerable support as a progressive newspaper tinged with radicalism. Murdoch had also purchased two Sydney newspapers from Sir Frank Packer. This was a double bonus for Labor: it removed the harmful impact of the Packer press, which had been remorseless in its opposition to Labor, and it brought Murdoch to the support of Labor with a string of daily newspapers. Murdoch also made a substantial contribution to the Labor party's campaign funds. Supported by the influential Melbourne paper, the *Age*, Labor entered the 1972 election campaign with a considerable volume of media backing, and this it had lacked in all previous elections. Murdoch later explained his support for Labor in 1972 in this way:

> I had great hopes for the Labor Party, for Mr. Whitlam. I still believe it was the right thing to have a change. We'd had too long under one party rule and whatever Mr. Whitlam says now the fact was that I was close to him at the time, certainly fairly friendly with him and I felt that he was going to lead Australia into a new and worthwhile period.[9]

But the rapport between Whitlam and Murdoch soon faded. Although Murdoch quickly became disillusioned with the Labor government, he did not become immediately hostile. When Labor was forced to the polls early in 1974 the Murdoch group gave rather tepid support to the coalition opposition, which narrowly lost the election. By the end of the year Murdoch's antipathy to the Whitlam

---

[9] "A Current Affair," Channel Nine network, December 5, 1975. Interviewer, Michael Schildberger.

government had hardened into vehement opposition, and this was reflected in the ferocious anti-Labor tone of his papers during 1975.

The growing rift and ultimate animosity between Whitlam and Murdoch has not been satisfactorily explained. Whitlam publicly attributed it to his government's refusal to approve a major mining venture in which Murdoch had an interest. He expressed this interpretation of Murdoch's motivation quite strongly during the election campaign:

> I believe the clue to Mr. Murdoch's attitude and the attitude which is expressed by the *Australian*—which I think mightn't be published for very many more weeks—and by the Sydney *Mirror* and the Adelaide *News* and some of the publications which bear the name *Truth*, the clue is that Mr. Murdoch has an interest in some bauxite deposits near Perth [Western Australia], and he wanted to develop those deposits in association with Reynolds, one of the great multi-national aluminium companies . . . and the proposition was not one that we could approve. . . . Now Mr. Murdoch wasn't pleased. But we were right and it is just as well that the public, I believe, should know what may be behind his vindictive campaign against the Labor Party in this election, why he's turned against us.[10]

Murdoch emphatically denied this contention:

> Well if Mr. Whitlam wants to get under the gutter now that's his business . . . a consortium did apply to the Government for permission to put up a refinery. A consortium in which we had a minute share, but never mind, it did go ahead with that application to the Government. Now the reason it went ahead, and the timing of that was that we were asked by Mr. Whitlam's own advisers to do it at that time and that he would see that it went ahead because he wanted some major capital projects to talk about . . . and the fact that he didn't get it through Cabinet is another matter.[11]

It was also widely reported in a series of press stories that Murdoch had sought the post of Australian High Commissioner to London from the Whitlam government.[12] Neither Whitlam nor Murdoch

---

[10] E. G. Whitlam, Press Club Lunch, Brisbane, December 4, 1975.

[11] "A Current Affair," December 5, Channel Nine. Interviewer, Mike Schildberger.

[12] "High Commissioner" is the diplomatic designation of an ambassador appointed by one British Commonwealth country to another British Commonwealth country.

made any public comment on these stories, although it was generally believed in Canberra that they came from sources close to Whitlam.

These vicious exchanges between a former prime minister and a media tycoon encapsulate the extraordinary bitterness of the relationship between the Murdoch group and the Labor party during the campaign. One of Whitlam's attacks on Murdoch was so derogatory in its physical description that it had to be deleted from a current affairs program.[13] The attitude of the Murdoch newspapers was implacably hostile. It was remarkable enough that such a personal duel should be fought between a political leader and a media proprietor during an election campaign. Even more remarkable was the eruption of a major industrial dispute involving Murdoch's journalists over the coverage of political news in the Murdoch press. For the first time in Australian newspaper history journalists went on strike in December 1975 over the handling of politics in the papers on which they worked. It is doubtful whether there has been any comparable experience in the electoral history of any country.

Bias and the Journalists' Strike

Australian journalists are organized industrially in a federal trade union, the Australian Journalists' Association (AJA). The union's broad structure parallels that of many federal organizations in Australia: the basic unit is the state branch, with each branch represented in a federal council which meets at regular intervals. The federal secretary is the principal executive officer of the union. At the branch level, the main functional body is the branch committee, serviced by a secretary who conducts the day-to-day administration of the union. Apart from the branch committee, some of the major media organizations have AJA house committees representing the journalists who work for them.

The AJA has never been a strongly radical union. There have been occasional strikes of journalists, usually over pay and conditions. It would have been anathema even a few years ago for journalists to contemplate strike action over the policies of their proprietors. Older members of the profession on many papers retain a conservative approach to newspaper policy and practice. In the past few years, however, another generation of journalists has emerged, and it is prepared to criticize the organization and policies of those

[13] "This Day Tonight," ABC public affairs television program, December 9, 1975.

who control the media. This skepticism about conventional newspaper practice has centered on a magazine, the *New Journalist*, which has sponsored serious scrutiny and reassessment of the Australian media.[14] The emergence of a more skeptical approach to the media among many of its employees was an important factor in the industrial turbulence which culminated in the strike of News Ltd. journalists. The focal point of this restiveness was the Sydney offices of News Ltd. where five of the Murdoch group's newspapers are produced: the *Australian*, the *Daily Telegraph*, the *Daily Mirror*, the *Sunday Mirror*, and the *Sunday Telegraph*.

The Grievances. The strike of journalists employed by News Ltd. was the climax of a period during which a substantial part of the AJA membership had become increasingly uneasy about their papers' editorial policies. It followed the adoption of a hard-line antigovernment stance by all of the Murdoch papers throughout 1975. Murdoch's right to change the line of his political support was unquestioned. Many journalists, however, felt strongly that editorial policy had spilled over to produce a blatant bias in the selection and treatment of news.

Even before Sir John Kerr's dismissal of the Whitlam government, resentment over editorial policy had grown on the *Australian* and the *Telegraph*. This was expressed in a letter sent by three News Ltd. journalists, who were also union officials and members of the News Ltd. House Committee, to Rupert Murdoch. The letter read in part:

> We would not be loyal to you if we failed to say that, among the influential Australians with whom we come into daily contact—including and especially the intelligent income earners it is the paper's policy to attract—the *Australian* has become a laughing stock. Reporters who were once greeted with respect when they mentioned the *Australian* have had to face derisive harangues before they can get down to the job at hand. It is not so much the policy itself but the blind, biased, tunnel-visioned, ad hoc, logically-confused and relentless way in which so many people are now conceiving it to be carried out, both in the editorial and news columns.[15]

---

[14] Published in Sydney. The *New Journalist*, no. 21, December 1975-January 1976, contains valuable material on the media and the 1975 election campaign. See also issue no. 11 on the Federal Parliamentary Press Gallery.

[15] Officers of the AJA News Ltd. House Committee to K. R. Murdoch, dated October 28, 1975, dispatched November 2, 1975.

In short, the journalists did not challenge Murdoch's right to set the political guidelines for his papers. They objected to the way in which these guidelines were applied by his executives on his behalf. The letter continued:

> We can be loyal to the *Australian,* no matter how much its style, thrust and readership changes, as long as it retains the traditions, principles and integrity of a responsible newspaper. We cannot be loyal to a propaganda sheet. Indeed, we cannot imagine that you would want on your staff journalists whose professional standards were so low. . . . We cannot be loyal to those traditions [of journalism] or to ourselves, if we accept the deliberate or careless slanting of headlines, seemingly-blatant imbalance in news presentation, political censorship and on occasion distortion of copy from senior, specialist journalists, the political management of news and features, the stifling of dissident and even unpalatably impartial opinion in the paper's columns. All these things have happened to greater or lesser degree in recent months, and the tragedy is that because of this more are mistakenly imputed, by people both inside and outside the paper. . . . We make no case for a dull paper, a bleeding hearts paper, a worker-controlled paper. Our catch-word is simply: integrity.[16]

The letter concluded with an acknowledgment of Murdoch's loyalty to the paper and its staff and affirmed that this had kept the *Australian* going through bad times. It sought a conference with Murdoch and his senior officers as soon as possible to discuss the issues raised.

This emotional *cri de coeur* was dispatched to Murdoch on November 2. When he had not responded by November 12—a day after the dismissal of the government—another letter was sent on behalf of the seventy-five journalists who had supported the initial letter. The AJA leadership at News Ltd. had been asked to distribute a bulletin on behalf of these members and a response was sought from Murdoch before it was distributed. Murdoch replied tersely on the same day, saying that the intention to distribute a bulletin had made impossible any dialogue: "If you insist on providing ammunition for our competitors and enemies who are intent on destroying all our livelihoods, then go ahead."[17] The union leadership re-

---

16 Ibid.

17 K. R. Murdoch to officers of News Ltd. House Committee, November 12, 1975.

sponded with a conciliatory reply and Murdoch answered in a more amenable vein:

> Thank you for your reassuring answer to my note of November 13 in which I only said that dialogue was impossible in view of your threat to post a public bulletin. We seem to be all agreed in working for the best interest of the newspaper and above all its integrity, especially through factual and objective reporting.[18]

A special meeting of the AJA membership was called for November 17 to discuss the exchange of letters with Murdoch. It was stressed that the meeting was unofficial and not a stopwork meeting, but the attendance of all staff who could attend was sought. The meeting hammered out guidelines for the conduct of News Ltd. journalists—in particular, the *Australian* journalists—in the electoral campaign, then only a week away. It was resolved that the campaign should be reported according to the highest professional standards of integrity. The journalist's duties according to the AJA Code of Ethics were stated:

> —To report and interpret the news with scrupulous honesty.
> —Not to suppress essential facts and not to distort the truth by omission or wrong or improper emphasis.
> —Always to maintain through his conduct, full public confidence in the integrity and dignity of a journalist's calling.[19]

The resolution went on to sound a cautionary note:

> We will resist and react to any instances in which, deliberately or inadvertently, management or editorial executive decisions could give readers of our work the impression of undue bias or imbalance. We will react similarly to published work, whether in reporting or production, not performed by ourselves. However we will not object to, nor will we obstruct, the proprietor's right to express his views on all issues in the leading [editorial page] articles. Those of us involved in interpretative reporting or commentary will express our views honestly and fairly but also fearlessly, and we will expect these qualities to be respected by man-

---

[18] Murdoch to News Ltd. House Committee, November 17, 1975.

[19] The AJA Code of Ethics is registered under the Conciliation and Arbitration Act which regulates the activity of national trade unions in Australia. It is disseminated regularly to all Australian journalists. The code is enforced by ethics committees in each state branch.

agement and therefore published whenever normal circumstances permit.[20]

The meeting agreed to elect a panel of four staff members to liaise with the management on breaches of these principles and called on the management to reaffirm them. It concluded with a rededication to the ideal of making the *Australian* one of the country's great newspapers.

Mounting Tensions. With resentment and uneasiness about editorial policy festering among News Ltd. journalists, there was little chance that the tensions and strains of an election campaign would pass without a major convulsion. It came surprisingly late in the campaign. Direct confrontation was avoided in the early phases. The editorial management did not issue specific instructions to journalists about coverage of the campaign. Friction arose mainly over the preparation of copy for publication and its ultimate presentation in the papers. The cockpits were the subeditors' tables of the *Australian* and the *Daily Telegraph* where copy was prepared for the printers and the page layouts compiled. Many journalists working in these areas felt that Murdoch's support for the Fraser coalition had been interpreted with excessive zeal by editorial executives. They particularly resented the fact that political stories were being handled by staff members who were exempt from AJA membership. All sensitive political material, it was felt, was being handled by the "backbench," the senior subeditors and production staff who were not AJA members, while most of the AJA subeditors were underoccupied.

Examples of alleged bias and unfair treatment of the Labor party on all of the Murdoch papers multiplied in this atmosphere. AJA members built up dossiers of alleged breaches of the principles endorsed by the journalists before the opening of the campaign: the "spiking" (discarding) of stories about the Labor party, the changing of headlines, the use of misleading headlines written by nonunion members, and the direction of reporters to report in a certain way. Some of these alleged cases of bias were susceptible to two interpretations. Undoubtedly, some were also the result of technical limitations: because of its national distribution the *Australian* has early deadlines for production schedules, a problem which was accentuated by the demands of an election campaign. Others were the result of ignorance and incompetence. There were, however, sufficient examples of questionable treatment of copy to lend credence to staff fears about the

---

[20] Copy of resolution supplied by News Ltd. House Committee.

misuse of news pages for political purposes. These fanned the flames of rumor in the offices and corridors of the Murdoch papers and in the bars where News Ltd. journalists drank.

One of the most quoted examples was a story on unemployment figures. The rapid growth of unemployment in Australia from the end of 1974 had been a major news story throughout the following year. The figures for the registered unemployed issued each month were one of the major indicators of the performance of the Whitlam government in economic management. They always made an important news story. The brief prepared by AJA officials listing examples of alleged bias at News Ltd. reads as follows:

> Friday—December 5. Another scoop. Unemployment up 18,368 to 4.5 percent in the *Australian*. The *Age* and *Canberra Times* and other papers all reported unemployment was down 24,000 based on the key figure of seasonally adjusted unemployment rather than the registered unemployment [raw] figure. The figures released at 10:30 p.m. by the Liberal Party by telex were described by the editor as too confusing for him to understand. Efforts to reach the economic writer in Canberra were unsuccessful and so the editor was left to figure it out. He ignored the advice of the night news editor and assistant editor that the key figure was the seasonally adjusted one. He refused to look at the library files to see how the jobless figures were handled previously. The story was taken away from the night news editor whose job it would normally be to write or assign the story to be written by a reporter.[21]

Whatever the reason, the result was a sensational story in the *Australian*, very damaging to Labor because it demonstrated that unemployment was still rising. In real terms there had been a fall in unemployment.

Another notorious case was a change in the editorial treatment of a front-page story between successive editions of the *Daily Mirror* on November 26, 1975. The late final edition of the paper carried a story on Labor housing policy bylined by a staff writer who was traveling with Whitlam. Under the headline "Gough's Promise— Cheap Rents," the introductory paragraphs of the story read:

> A Labor Government will introduce a scheme to provide cheap rental housing for low income earners if it is re-elected next month. The Labor leader, Mr. Whitlam, is

---

[21] Running report on alleged bias prepared by members of the News Ltd. House Committee.

promising to use the Australian Housing Corporation to provide money for co-operatives to make the cheap rent available.[22]

In the late final extra edition of the paper, the headline was changed to "Gough Panics—Cheap Rents" and the reporter's byline was dropped. The introductory paragraphs of the story were rewritten to read:

> The Labor leader, Mr. Whitlam, will today promise a scheme to lower rents in an attempt to trump a Liberal promise to help home buyers. Mr. Whitlam's panic move towards making promises rather than relying on his record came after he read a pirated copy of the Liberal election policy speech.[23]

The story went on to suggest in strong terms that Whitlam had used an embargoed copy of the Liberal policy speech to preempt Liberal policy. A straight news story with favorable implications for the Labor party thus had been rewritten to become extremely damaging for the Labor party.

The Strike and Management's Response. Tensions on the News Ltd. papers over campaign coverage were vented in strong moves for industrial action over the weekend of December 6-7, a week before the elections. Opinion in favor of industrial action was fanned by the publication of strong anti-Labor editorials in the two Murdoch Sunday papers, the *Sunday Mirror* and the *Sunday Telegraph*. A petition was immediately circulated among the AJA membership, which read in part:

> We, the undersigned financial members of the Australian Journalists Association, request an emergency meeting this afternoon, Monday December 8, to consider what action should be taken by employees of News Ltd. to protest repeated and continuing bias in the reporting and presentation of political stories during the election campaign.[24]

It was signed by fifty-five members. The branch committee of the union agreed to accept the call for a meeting, and more than 100 member journalists—mostly members of the staff of the *Australian*

---

[22] Sydney *Daily Mirror*, November 26, 1976, late final edition, p. 1.

[23] Sydney *Daily Mirror*, late final extra edition, p. 1.

[24] Petition signed by News Ltd. journalists, conveyed to AJA officers on December 8, 1975.

and the *Daily Telegraph*—attended a meeting late in the afternoon of December 8.

A strike motion was carried overwhelmingly for the five Murdoch papers. This created friction when the staff of the *Daily Mirror* arrived for work on the following morning. There were complaints that insufficient notice had been given to News Ltd.'s 400 journalists working for papers other than the *Australian* and the *Daily Telegraph*. Despite some restiveness about the decision, the strike action was not challenged by elements of the union membership from the other three papers.

A statement issued by the NSW branch of the AJA after the strike meeting set out the attitude of the striking journalists at some length. It read in part:

> The AJA members of News Ltd. are acting in defence of the principles of fair and honest journalism. They are concerned not with the proprietor's right to express his views in editorials but against a very deliberate and blatant bias in the presentation of news. The AJA members believe this bias has become so obvious to readers that they could well believe that we are in part responsible for it. We have therefore felt it necessary to dissociate ourselves entirely from the desecration of the traditional and historic ethics of journalism, which we expect of ourselves and of our employers, and which we sincerely believe that readers expect of both of us. . . . The AJA Code of Ethics forbids that we deliberately slant the news and we have followed this code. Our members have not "managed" the news by omitting some stories and distorting others through headlines or opening words. Of course AJA members have political opinions. But we have not before, and do not now, seek to impose these views any more than we desire to deprive Mr. Murdoch of his. Our action is unprecedented in Sydney journalism only because the circumstances are unprecedented. . . . Freedom of the Press is not a right owned by publishers nor by journalists. It is a right that belongs to the people of Australia, a right to know all the facts and viewpoints so that the people can make intelligent judgments on the political, social and personal issues which affect their lives.[25]

The management's attitude to the strike was stated plainly by the group editorial manager, Brian Hogben, in comments to other media representatives in Sydney:

---

[25] Bulletin issued by the New South Wales District of the AJA, December 9, 1975.

It's not been so much a question of putting bias into the paper, it's been a question of putting bias out of the paper and I think this is what has annoyed a lot of people on the *Australian*. Now to an extent these are young staff, enthusiastic about the promises of the Labor Government, very definitely pro-Labor. . . . Now that is their right, nobody denies them, nobody criticises their feeling that way but in the course of doing this they have taken anything that's slightly critical of the Labor Government to be a distortion of the news. They cannot believe that the Labor Government did anything wrong and conversely they have seemed to have been unable to believe that the other parties were capable of doing anything right.[26]

Certainly the radicalism of part of the staff was a factor in the strike. Many of the staff of the *Australian* remembered the days of a more liberal editorial policy. Inevitably, problems of adjustment were caused by the abrupt switch to conservative policies and a virulent anti-Labor line. It would not be correct, however, to categorize all of the protesters and strikers as a radical minority among the News Ltd. journalists. In particular, the complaints of bias were strongly pressed by older members of the subeditorial tables of both the *Australian* and the *Daily Telegraph*, traditionally a strongly conservative element of newspaper journalists. The protesters represented all political parties; they were not all committed Labor party voters.

Under the procedures prescribed by Australian industrial law, the contending parties—the AJA and News Ltd.—appeared before the Arbitration Commission on the following morning. Justice Staples directed that the striking journalists should return to work and that Murdoch should meet a delegation from the union to discuss the charges of bias in the company papers. A meeting of journalists later that day endorsed the court direction to return to work, and the strike ended, despite some attempts to maintain it until the following morning.

The meeting between the journalists and Murdoch was held on the following day (December 10). The AJA House Committee of News Ltd. and the federal secretary of the AJA, Syd Crosland, represented the union; Murdoch was supported by the chairman of News Ltd., Ken May, and the group editorial manager, Brian Hogben. The journalists found Murdoch in a truculent mood. He struck hard at members of the delegation, accusing them of disloyalty, castigating in

---

26 "AM," ABC radio public affairs program, December 9, 1975.

particular a senior reporter to whom Murdoch claimed he had given professional preferment and personal assistance. The delegation presented a number of cases of alleged bias. They found that Murdoch was prepared to concede nothing on the bias issue. Hogben countered with a file of incidents designed to show alleged mistakes and incompetence by News Ltd. journalists. In some cases these had earned the Murdoch papers libel writs, but the management had not made reprisals.

The union delegation persisted with their charges that editorial policy had permeated the news columns of the paper. This was denied by Murdoch, who agreed that the group's policy was strong support for Fraser. He agreed also that News Ltd. executives were bound by the principles stated in the AJA Code of Ethics. After further desultory discussion, the meeting ended in an impasse. Both sides agreed to a three-paragraph communiqué which set out the substantive conclusions of the meeting:

> —Mr. Murdoch looks for fair and accurate reporting from all members of the staff.
> —Mr. Murdoch has always expected, and he reiterates that he will continue to expect, that all staff, including executives, should act in accordance with the clauses of the AJA's Code of Ethics.
> —The House Committee, while recognising management's rights, may take up with Mr. Murdoch, Mr. May or in their absence, the Editorial Manager, matters which it regards as bias in the company's newspapers.[27]

On December 11, Hogben supplied the House Committee with a management report on allegations of bias in the *Australian* made by one of the paper's reporters, Bruce Stannard. Stannard had been assigned to cover segments of both the Fraser and Whitlam campaigns. He lodged a series of eleven complaints of alleged bias in the handling of the *Australian*'s campaign coverage. Two samples of these complaints and the management's response follow:

> COMPLAINT: That the news editor of the *Australian*, Mr. Brian Boswell, told Mr. Stannard: "Don't knock Fraser," thereby meaning that Mr. Stannard was to write nothing that was not favourable to Fraser.
> COMMENT: Mr. Stannard repeats that Mr. Boswell said this to him. Mr. Boswell denies the charge categorically and

---

[27] Circular issued to AJA membership of News Ltd. after meeting between K. R. Murdoch and officers of the News Ltd. House Committee.

has offered to depose to this effect in the form of a statutory declaration.

COMPLAINT: That the editor of the *Australian*, Mr. Les Hollings, told Mr. Stannard of his election coverage: "Keep your feet on the ground. Don't get carried away," conveying to Mr. Stannard the impression that Mr. Hollings wanted him to cover Mr. Whitlam in a lukewarm fashion.

COMMENT: This seems to be a perfectly valid remark for any editor to make to any journalist. Mr. Hollings says it was only an extension of his original instruction to Mr. Stannard about covering the election campaign, which was to write straight down the middle.[28]

Another complaint by Stannard referred to a report in the *Australian* that Whitlam had drunk six cans of beer followed by three glasses of ouzo at the Darwin Greek Club. Whitlam had strongly condemned this story. It had aroused his ire, and it had startled journalists familiar with Whitlam's extreme temperateness, particularly during election campaigns. Stannard claimed that he personally knew that Whitlam had drunk nothing stronger than mineral water in Darwin. The official comment is worth quoting in full for the insights it provides into Australian society and Australian election campaigning:

COMMENT: The drinks story was filed by Pat Cusick of the *Northern Territory News*. Editorial executives had no reason to doubt its veracity, particularly in view of predominantly pro-Labor politics of Darwin journalists. Executives say they saw nothing derogatory in the copy. In any event, a Darwinite would almost certainly consider such a story favorable to any man because it would show that he could hold his liquor like a Territorian.[29]

The frontier is still very much a part of Australian election campaigning. The report concluded with some interesting general comments about News Ltd. coverage of the election campaign:

Editorial executives say it is possible that some stories filed by Mr. Stannard and, indeed, other reporters may have been spiked because, although filed in time for normal deadlines, they were too late to meet advanced deadlines in operation for a limited period of the campaign. Executives recall rebuking Mr. Stannard for not filing one Fraser story which

---

[28] Report on allegations of bias in the *Australian*, Brian Hogben, group editorial manager, News Ltd., December 11, 1975.
[29] Ibid.

made the lead-out in the *Sydney Morning Herald* and a page lead in the *Argus*.[30] This story was an attack on the Hayden tax plan which revealed that it was not as beneficial as taxpayers claimed. It should be noted that today's issue of the *Australian* gave scant coverage to the mobbing of Mr. and Mrs. Fraser last night although the *Sydney Morning Herald* led Page One with it. The *Australian*'s handling of the story was a decision by editorial executives.[31]

The claim that the *Australian* had deliberately played down a sensational story favorable to Fraser was denied by News Ltd. journalists, who claimed that the *Australian* had missed the story because its reporter had been inside the hall when the crowd had mobbed Mr. and Mrs. Fraser outside. Fraser had been struck on the back by a beer can during the melee.

Reaction to the Strike. Industrial action over alleged bias was confined to the Murdoch group. There was some restiveness among journalists on other papers, but judicious management by newspaper executives prevented any flareups. On November 12, the day after the dismissal of the Whitlam government, the executive director of the Fairfax papers, D. N. Bowman, issued a memo to all staff setting out the group's approach to election coverage:

> The tradition and policy of our paper is to try to be as even handed as is humanly possible in reporting election campaigns. Any championing of causes is for leader columns only. . . . We cannot hope to achieve always a balance in what we publish in any one day, in space, content or display—events don't occur as conveniently as that. But over a period we can and must. We want to inform readers of what both sides are saying, doing, thinking and planning, and how they are behaving, and we want a consistently rigorous approach. . . . Our intention, then, is to be informative, fair, professional. We will not satisfy everyone, but it is the only policy for us to pursue.[32]

The general fairness of the Fairfax papers in applying these principles to its news pages was acknowledged by Whitlam late in the campaign. The AJA House Committee of the Fairfax papers issued a statement supporting the stand of the News Ltd. journalists against "bias and dishonesty" in their papers:

---

[30] The author seems to mean the Melbourne *Age*. The *Argus*, a famous Melbourne morning daily, has been defunct for twenty years.

[31] Allegations of bias in the *Australian*, Brian Hogben, December 11, 1975.

[32] John Fairfax & Sons, internal memorandum, D. Bowman, executive editor, to all staff, November 12, 1975.

The Fairfax House Committee believes that journalists have a duty to their readers which transcends their duty to their bosses. The committee believes that journalists have a responsibility to try to ensure that their newspapers are balanced and accurate in their news coverage.[33]

The ramifications of the strike spread beyond Sydney. Murdoch group journalists employed in Brisbane, Canberra, and Melbourne joined the strike. The journalists of the Melbourne *Truth*, a sensational weekly with little political identification, issued a fiery statement asserting that news should be free and untainted and should not reflect the views of the management of a newspaper.[34] In Adelaide, News Ltd. journalists held a meeting and decided to insert an advertisement in their paper dissociating themselves from any bias that might appear.

Reaction to News Ltd.'s political coverage was not confined to journalists. There was considerable unrest among members of the Printing and Kindred Industries Union (PKIU) employed at News Ltd. This sparked a number of disputes but no major strike. One clash was resolved by the management's agreeing to publish in full a letter from the News Ltd. chapel of the union to Murdoch. This took Murdoch to task for having stated on television that it was in the interests of all his employees for the Labor government to be defeated. His printing staff rejected this solicitude on their behalf and affirmed their active financial support for the twice-elected Labor government:

> We were requesting that you take these opinions into account when setting editorial policy as we believed that the tone of these had been getting so dangerously provocative of late as to cause our members concern with their conscience when instructed to handle the material.[35]

The letter poignantly recalled happier days, citing Murdoch's erstwhile support for the Labor party and the considerable respect he had once enjoyed among his workers:

> Trade unionists have always had to contend with what they consider to be a hostile press. However, your own employees and an enormous number of people outside all felt over

[33] Press statement, AJA House Committee, John Fairfax & Sons, issued by the chairman, David Dale, December 9, 1975.

[34] Resolution passed by AJA members of Melbourne *Truth*. Supplied by News Ltd. House Committee.

[35] *Australian*, December 9, 1975, p. 3.

the years that you were in fact a fair dinkum person [36] and gave a fair go to all. This was crystallised in 1972 when you again set yourself against standard practice. However, now it seems that to those people that what you have done is best described in the language of the trade unionists: you appear to have left high and dry those people.[37]

Advertisements condemning bias were placed by the PKIU in other Murdoch papers. Workers at Cumberland Press, a Murdoch subsidiary producing Sydney suburban papers, took up a collection to finance an advertisement rebutting contentions made in strongly anti-Labor editorials.

The Murdoch group was under constant threat of wider trade union retaliation. On November 14 demonstrating unionists and students had rushed the Murdoch offices in Sydney and disrupted delivery trucks handling editions of the *Daily Mirror*. Papers had been strewn on the street and set on fire. One union official and a well-known union militant in Sydney, R. Pringle, had told the crowd of 600: "Murdoch has got between now and Saturday night to improve his rotten papers. If they haven't improved by then, we'll stop the *Sunday Mirror* and *Sunday Telegraph* from getting out." [38] Despite such rhetoric, wider industrial action against News Ltd. did not materialize. An effort was made to ban the handling of newsprint for the Murdoch-owned *Sunday Times* in Perth, but this was an isolated instance.

Rupert Murdoch's father, Sir Keith Murdoch, in 1929 issued a memo to the staff of one of his papers about political bias:

> Concerning the second [edition] we dropped again into a "Dish Labor" attitude. It must be realised that we are not a Nationalist organ. Scores of thousands of our readers are being encouraged to regard us as biased and to discount all our own political articles.[39]

Sir Keith Murdoch's record in keeping the "dish Labor" tone out of his papers was less than perfect, but he expressed a cardinal principle given frequent lip service by media proprietors: political impartiality in the news pages. It is a principle which his embattled son forty-six years later found impossible to reconcile with his own enthusiastic

---

[36] Australian argot for a fair dealer.

[37] *Australian*, December 9, 1975, p. 3.

[38] *Sydney Morning Herald*, November 14, 1975, p. 8.

[39] Manuscript papers of Sir Keith Murdoch. Folder 54, Managing Editor's notes, April 1, 1929, Australian National Library, Canberra.

"dish Labor" attitudes. There is some evidence that the strong anti-Labor tone of the Murdoch papers went rather further than Murdoch intended. He acknowledged this in one instance, as the following extract from a television program shows:

> SCHILDBERGER: What about a headline like "Fraser Accuses, Gough Guilty" which was after the Frank Stewart phone call to the Governor-General.[40] That particular report of Alan Reid's. Is that a fair headline?
>
> MR. MURDOCH: I'm glad you raised that because I complained about it myself and thought that it was going too far, that the emphasis should have been on the Governor-General refusing to comment.
>
> SCHILDBERGER: When you say you complained, did you complain to your own editor?
>
> MR. MURDOCH: Yes.
>
> SCHILDBERGER: Do you do that frequently? About possible bias?
>
> MR. MURDOCH: If I think I detect bias I always complain.
>
> SCHILDBERGER: You don't smile sometimes when you think they might be doing the right thing by you?
>
> MR. MURDOCH: Not at all. It's not a question of doing the right thing by me. They must do the right thing by the profession, by the public. Most important by their readers who part with their ten or twelve cents or whatever and expect to find out what's been going on in Australia that day.[41]

If Murdoch rarely detected bias in his own papers, a substantial part of his reporting and printing staffs had no doubt that bias was tainting them. Enough of the News Ltd. journalists felt sufficiently strongly about it to resort to unprecedented industrial action. There was an unbridgeable gulf between what Murdoch saw as the proper reporting of an election campaign and his staff's conception of the same function.

---

[40] During the election campaign, a political writer for the *Bulletin*, Alan Reid, reported that Frank Stewart, a minister in the Whitlam government, had contacted the governor general, Sir John Kerr, to complain about certain aspects of the dismissal of R. F. X. Connor, the minister for minerals and energy in the Whitlam government. This was widely publicized and prompted a denial from Stewart. The story was followed up in a sensational front-page story by the Sydney *Daily Mirror* on December 3, 1975. This is the story referred to in the extract.

[41] "A Current Affair," Channel Nine network, December 5, 1975. Interviewer, Michael Schildberger.

The ABC and Political Bias. The Australian Broadcasting Commission was the other focal figure in the controversy over political bias during the election campaign. The ABC is inherently conservative in the programs it disseminates throughout Australia. Indeed, it is the only media institution in Australia that, in its programming, gives full play to traditional values. Most of the ABC's radio programs are devoted to rural broadcasts, religious services and discourses, classical music, sports, and a wide variety of information services. In recent years this overwhelming preponderance of conventional programming based on traditional values has been partly offset by a tincture of radicalism. A handful of new current affairs programs have covered social issues in a way which has offended sections of the national audience. The ABC also moved into popular culture with the Sydney radio station 2JJ, which broadcast an irreverent blend of hard rock, satire, and social criticism. But these ventures have encroached only marginally on the conventionalism of ABC programming.

This has not prevented persistent attacks on the ABC for political bias. The coalition parties which won the election have long been convinced that the ABC is strongly slanted toward the Labor party. This charge has been leveled at the regular ABC news bulletins on radio and television, which are for the most part as bland and innocuous as the newscasts on commercial television. Frequent surveys of ABC news and public affairs programs have failed to detect any measurable bias. An ABC analysis of its news programs between November 12 (the day after the Whitlam government was dismissed) and December 10 (the last day on which election material could be broadcast) [42] disclosed the following result:

Labor stories	6,550 lines
Liberal stories	5,991 lines
Country party stories	660 lines

(An experienced ABC announcer usually reads fourteen standard lines in a minute.) This gave the coalition parties a total of 101 lines, or about 7 minutes' news time, more than Labor.[43] Surveys of public affairs programs in the crucial month of October, when both sides resorted heavily to the electronic media to advance their cases, showed

---

[42] Under Commonwealth legislation radio and television stations cannot broadcast any election material from midnight on the Wednesday before polling day until after the polls close. This ban applies both to paid election advertising and to news reports on the election. In the 1975 elections the blackout was imposed from midnight on December 10 until after the polls closed on the evening of December 13. There is no rational justification for this blackout, which does not apply to either paid advertisements or news reporting in the printed media.

[43] *New Journalist*, no. 21, December 1975-January 1976, p. 8.

that television programs had given 349 minutes to coalition spokes-men and 267 minutes to Labor spokesmen. Radio public affairs pro-grams showed a similar pattern, with the coalition parties getting 88 minutes and the Labor party 66 minutes.[44] The imbalance became so apparent that the host of one key ABC public affairs program, "This Day Tonight," had to explain it to his audience:

> Well over the past couple of weeks the ABC has been cop-ping it a bit from both sides over so-called bias and I can tell you that "This Day Tonight" has been getting a large number of calls saying that we are giving more time to Mr. Fraser than to Mr. Whitlam or to the [Labor] Govern-ment. It's true. It's a little bit ironic when you consider that the ABC is being criticised at the same time in Parlia-ment for being biased in favour of the [Labor] Govern-ment. Well, Mr. Fraser is on again tonight but we would like to say first by way of explanation that we have been hoping to talk to the Prime Minister [Mr. Whitlam] on the program but his schedule has been a bit too busy today. However, we hope to balance things up before long.[45]

In the absence of any agreed means of measuring bias, com-plaints about political bias in the mass media are usually based on indeterminate factors such as the interviewer's intonation, his relative aggressiveness, the line of questioning, the relative emphasis allotted to party spokesmen in debates or panel discussions, or the com-plainant's own estimate of the political history and voting patterns of the interviewer. These intangibles can be applied, of course, just as strongly to electronic media owned by commercial interests as they can to public broadcasting. Many Labor politicians were just as convinced that they received biased and unfair treatment from commercial interviewers and commercial current affairs programs as coalition spokesmen were certain of the ABC's partiality to Labor.

The coalition's hostility to the ABC was asserted very soon after it was installed as caretaker government on November 11. The care-taker postmaster general and transport minister, Peter Nixon, had been a consistent critic of alleged political bias on ABC current affairs programs. On November 12, he strongly attacked ABC coverage of the constitutional crisis and called for a moderator, preferably a judge, to be appointed to ensure a balance of time and content on ABC news and current affairs programs during the election campaign:

---

[44] *Sydney Morning Herald*, November 17, 1975, p. 2.
[45] "This Day Tonight," ABC public affairs television program, November 6, 1975, host, Iain Finlay.

197

When there is something critical occurring here in Canberra as on the last two occasions, take the sacking of the Prime Minister, that's the first one, and go back a couple of weeks to the day the Senate decided to stop Supply. It's my view that on those occasions, and I've got the figures to back it up that in the first few presentations of programs—not the news so much as the current affairs programs—that the public were almost snowed by a number of pro-Labor speakers. . . . Let's have fairness in the ABC. The ABC will be doing itself a great justice if they produce a moderator who will make sure there is a lack of bias and a fair go on the ABC.[46]

This is a fair sample of the criticism heaped on the ABC by coalition spokesmen. The ABC rejected the argument for a moderator of its political content and insisted that balance had been maintained in news and current affairs programs over a period. The appointment of a moderator for the campaign was not pressed by the caretaker government, despite its being advocated by a senior minister. During the campaign there were occasional clashes between ABC interviewers and coalition spokesmen, most notably Fraser. On one occasion Fraser rebuked on camera a television reporter for a summary of political events he had given on the same program the night before: "If Mr. Whitlam had been speaking for four or five minutes on 'This Day Tonight' I really don't believe he could have argued his case better and I'm sure you really did not mean to do that." [47] Fraser was involved in another incident with the same reporter, Richard Carleton, during the recording of an interview for the ABC current affairs program, "This Day Tonight." The interview was abruptly broken off after Fraser accused Carleton of having expressed Labor sympathies to members of the crowd at an election rally. It was not televised.[48]

The Media and the Campaign

The Press Gallery. The National Press Gallery were under fire from Fraser and his caretaker government virtually from the moment of their taking office on November 11. Fraser strongly criticized the prevailing reporting patterns of the Canberra gallery:

---

[46] "A Current Affair," Channel Nine network, November 13, 1976. Debate between Peter Nixon and Marius Webb, a member of the Australian Broadcasting Commission.

[47] "This Day Tonight," ABC public affairs television program, November 4, 1975.

[48] *Sydney Morning Herald*, December 11, 1975, p. 1.

I think some of the reporting has very much favoured the [Labor] Government, I believe that. And at the same time it needs to be noted that some members of the gallery had been wearing Labor Party badges—now whether they were doing it for fun or whether because it exhibited a conviction or not, I'm not too sure. But I would also hope that the great majority of the Press Gallery will see their duty to their journals, to Australians, to report events, to report what occurs, to report what people say. If I've got a criticism of the gallery it's that there isn't enough straight reporting, too much interpreting. And very often you get the interpretation and the reader can't find anywhere what the facts are that are being interpreted. And this is a change in journalism over the last twenty years, maybe because TV gets in quicker with the factual news in some instances, but I would like to see—this might be a vain hope, in the media—here are the facts, here are the comments, and have them plainly branded as being separate.[49]

Certainly the Canberra gallery took pride in the interpretative reporting standards it had built up. The mechanical processing of parliamentary debates and ministerial handouts had been supplanted by interpretative reporting, occasionally erratic and incompetent but often of high quality. The gallery had also earned the marked hostility of the Liberal party in particular for its aggressive coverage of the 1974 campaign. The coalition leader in 1974, B. M. Snedden, had been subjected to sustained and coordinated questioning by journalists covering his campaign. Snedden had stood up to this questioning reasonably well, but there were occasional inconsistencies in his exposition of policy and these were exploited to his party's detriment. Press gallery journalists had also been able to expose differences between the leaders of the two coalition parties, Snedden and J. D. Anthony, over policy issues.

Journalists covering the 1975 elections found no such opportunities for penetrating campaign coverage. They were subjected to pressures which inhibited their traditional supremacy in the reporting and interpretation of the national campaign. First, there were pressures from editorial management. It was widely believed among journalists that Fraser was in constant touch with the senior echelons of media management, particularly the newspaper proprietors, during the constitutional crisis and subsequent election campaign. When asked about specific instances, Fraser denied having consulted with

---

[49] "This Day Tonight," ABC public affairs television program, November 12, 1975.

newspaper managements, but this did not quell the widespread suspicion of collusion. Journalists covering the two party leaders were not given specific directions from their editors on how they should do their job, except in the disputed instance mentioned earlier involving Bruce Stannard, but many were unhappy about the way their editors treated the copy they handed in.

National Press Gallery journalists encountered difficulty in getting their stories used, particularly interpretative articles and general political features. The distinction between the 1975 campaign and earlier campaigns was most marked in the Melbourne *Sun*, a paper which in previous elections had insisted on a constant diet of short campaign features. In the 1975 elections, its national correspondents were aware that these features would not be required. Instead, the *Sun* ran only a fraction of its usual quota of political features and these were provided by Melbourne-based correspondents away from the campaign trail. Correspondents traveling with the two leaders found difficulty in getting their material used. Even the *Age*, which had always run a wide range of political columns giving force to the admirable principle of fairness through diversity, clamped down hard on the number and variety of its columns. In particular, it gave very little space to interpretative comment by the principal political correspondent and the Canberra-based economics correspondent who had dominated the *Age*'s coverage of the 1974 election campaign. The same difficulties were encountered in lesser degree by other correspondents and a great many newspapers drew a substantial part of their coverage from the resources of their head office rather than from the national correspondents working on the campaigns.

More direct pressure was applied to the correspondents covering Fraser's campaign. All formal contacts between Fraser and the media covering the coalition campaign were tightly managed by his staff in a way that left the journalists little opportunity to analyze coalition policies in any depth. This new approach adopted by the planners of the Liberal campaign was principally a result of the success with which the media had grilled Fraser's predecessor in the 1974 campaign. Fraser held fewer press conferences than Snedden had, and he carefully controlled their coverage by the media. The electronic media and newspaper journalists were invited to separate conferences; press journalists could attend the electronic media conferences but could not ask questions, and the electronic media could neither film nor record the press conferences. This separation was justified on the technically correct grounds that each television station or radio outlet usually insisted on its own separate interview anyway. In the past the television cameras had covered not only the special television appearances but also the general press conferences, where they were able to obtain vivid footage of aggressive journalists in the full cry of coordinated questioning of a political leader. These open conferences had been damaging to Snedden. By separating the media and prescribing rigid guidelines for media and press conference formats, Fraser's media advisers were able to ensure that the electronic media did not have the best of both worlds. They were allotted their own exclusive encounter with Fraser but missed the more newsworthy confrontations with the press. When asked at a press conference why he would not allow television coverage, Fraser replied: "I just think it's better doing it separately, that's all."[50]

Press opportunities to question Fraser were limited in other ways. The convention of giving local journalists first cut of the cake was firmly enforced. At one conference a substantial portion of the scheduled time was given over to a rather fatuous group of ethnic media representatives, including one windy spokesman for the Baltic States who was not a journalist. And even when the press gallery got a clear sight on Fraser, they found an elusive quarry. Installed as caretaker prime minister and well on top in the campaign he had no reason to enter into a risky dialogue with journalists over the details of his policies. Difficult questions he evaded or ignored. With the traditional rhythm of press conferences disrupted by the guidelines described above, there was little chance for journalists to build up the coordinated questioning which had proved so successful on previous occasions. Fraser also revealed a talent for needling responses which riled the questioners and deterred productive supplementary questioning. With a campaign of only just over a fortnight to coast through to easy victory, Fraser had little difficulty in deflecting press questioning and completing the campaign unscarred by media barbs.

Journalists covering Whitlam's campaign encountered other frustrations. Whitlam was willing enough to talk and answer questions from any source. The rapport he had built up with National Press Gallery journalists during his years as opposition leader and prime minister was sustained. But his campaign did not generate enough of the basic currency of the media—hard news. Campaigning without new policies and on constitutional issues whose immediacy and political relevance declined a little further each day, Whitlam lacked news value. Ironically, the few news-making initiatives taken by Whitlam were his fierce attacks on the media whom he claimed had

---

[50] Press conference by Malcolm Fraser, caretaker prime minister, December 5, 1975.

"ganged up" against him: "I think the public have now realised that the newspapers—the three people who run all the daily papers in Australia—have made such a welter of it in their vendetta against Labor that it will be counter productive." [51] Whitlam also championed the correspondents traveling with him who could not get their stories published, though his support is unlikely to have advanced their cause. Repeatedly he excoriated the press proprietors, principally Murdoch but also the venerable Sir Warwick Fairfax, head of the Fairfax group, whom he described as "desiccated and doddery." [52] Such remarks provided great theater, but in a campaign that hinged on one issue and offered no new policies, they were not a substitute for hard news.

Patterns of Media Coverage. In terms of media interest, the election campaign of 1975 was anticlimactic. After a year filled with events of unsurpassed news value and culminating in the unprecedented dismissal of a government, the twenty days of the campaign itself were relatively lackluster. In many ways the campaign was a mechanical exercise. Once the first polls had been released and assessed, the result was never in doubt. The campaign was dull and so was the news coverage.

The last really hard news stories before the election had concerned three letter bombs sent in the week before the official campaign began to the governor general, the prime minister, and the premier of Queensland. The first two bombs had been intercepted, but the third had exploded in a mail room, severely injuring two men. The campaign, by contrast, was surprisingly free of violent incident despite the highly charged atmosphere of the previous weeks. Fraser and Whitlam were mobbed and jostled by partisan crowds, and Fraser was struck in the back by a beer can in one melee late in the campaign. This was reported with varying degrees of sensationalism and indignation. For the most part it was a low-voltage campaign lacking in conventional news value.

In such a muted atmosphere, the public opinion polls were the big stories of the campaign. The announcement of each successive poll produced a wave of stories predicting an overwhelming victory for the coalition and the annihilation of Labor. The polls were commissioned by media groups. Each of the pollsters got in at least two samplings of the electorate in the month before election day. Media

---

[51] "This Week," current affairs television program, Channel Seven, Melbourne, December 8, 1975.
[52] "This Day Tonight," ABC public affairs television program, December 9, 1975.

202

outlets had no qualms about pirating the poll results of rivals. This produced a crescendo of public opinion poll stories often headlined and written in a sensational way to the detriment of Labor: "Polls tip a big win by coalition," "Libs grip tightens—Sydney poll latest," "Last poll points to big Fraser majority," "Libs in lead—by 13 pc— Poll gives 39-seat majority."

The reporting of the polls had a shattering impact on the Labor campaign and on the morale of Labor supporters. Attempts were made to discount the accuracy of the polls and play down the battering that the poll stories were giving to Labor's prospects. Whitlam commented, "The public opinion polls are all commissioned by one or other of the three organisations that run all the daily papers in Australia. And they have used the public opinion polls to psych the Australian public into thinking that we're going to be beaten." [53] Undoubtedly the polls played a part in consolidating the support for the coalition, but it is impossible to assess to what extent they "psyched" the electorate. As the dominant news story of the campaign, the polls reinforced the impression that the coalition would win an overwhelming victory. As in the preceding two elections, the polls proved to be extremely accurate. Just as the Labor party had benefited from the favorable climate created by the polls in 1972 and 1974, it suffered quite drastically when the samples detected the strong drift to the coalition in 1975. The media, meanwhile, had the dual satisfaction of commissioning the polls and then exploiting them as the big news stories of the campaign.

Radio and television had enjoyed an embarrassment of riches through all the crises of 1975. Current affairs programs had repeatedly broken news stories throughout the year, and during the final decisive month before Whitlam was sacked both leaders appeared frequently on the main television current affairs programs—"A Current Affair," "The Willesee Show," "State of the Nation," "Four Corners," "This Day Tonight," and "Nationwide." These media appearances continued on a diminished scale during the campaign when opportunities were more restricted because of the campaign commitments of both leaders. Attempts were made to bring Fraser and Whitlam together in a television confrontation. The Labor party campaign organizers made strenuous efforts to set up a media debate between the two leaders using David Frost as a mediator but these fell through. [54]

---

[53] E. G. Whitlam, National Press Club Lunch, Canberra, December 11, 1975.
[54] Melbourne *Age*, December 6, 1975.

The most thorough and innovative coverage by the electronic media came from the ABC whose current affairs radio programs, "AM" and "PM," had provided a consistently high level of political coverage throughout 1975.[55] These programs maintained their standards during the campaign and were reinforced by a number of other programs which made an effort to dig into policy issues, a rarity in the media coverage of 1975. The most notable was a special series, "The Policy Makers," which exposed spokesmen from both parties to questions by a staff interviewer and to phone-in questions from listeners. A regular program, "New Society," was used to put opposing spokesmen into an extended debate on social issues such as welfare, health, and urban affairs. The commercial media also made some attempts at innovation, most notably with a program prepared by Sydney television Channel Ten called "The Alternatives." It made a worthy attempt to show something of the human quirks and qualities of Fraser and Whitlam in relatively relaxed interviews. This partly compensated for the absence of the Frost interviews which had dominated commercial electronic media coverage in the previous two elections.

Advertising and the Election. To international observers, one of the striking features of an Australian election campaign is the immense volume of paid media advertising. Enormously expensive advertising campaigns are prepared and funded by both sides. This generates elaborate and often extremely skillful national campaigns on the electronic media and a remarkable range of printed material of varying quality. The ABC also makes available to the political parties a reasonable amount of free air time on television and radio.

The paid advertising of the political parties can be grouped broadly into five categories: (1) national campaign advertising, (2) state and local campaign advertising, (3) machinery advertising, (4) advertisements involving third-party endorsement, and (5) response advertising.

The national campaign is conducted primarily on the main commercial television outlets in prime viewing time. The main thrust of the television advertising is often supported by thematically linked press and radio advertising. The Labor party brought this sort of package to the forefront of Australian electioneering with the innovatory campaign that helped it win the 1972 elections. The Liberal party perfected the style with a minutely organized and superbly mounted national campaign in 1975. The campaign hinged on an

---

[55] "AM" is broadcast for half an hour at 8:00 each morning from Monday to Friday. "PM" is broadcast for twenty-five minutes each evening at 6:05.

elaborately produced television advertisement that was devoted to the theme "Turn on the Lights, Australia" and featured a pop song belted out in plangent style by Rennee Geyer, Australia's leading woman pop singer. These themes were carried over into packages of radio advertisements and into press ads which contrasted Fraser and his colleagues with the battle-scarred Labor ministry; another television ad used still pictures and news headlines to set out Labor's record in an extremely unflattering way.

Labor's national campaign was much more fragmented. Caught badly off guard by the calling of the election, the party did well to mount any sort of effective national television campaign. Although its individual ads were of good quality and showed some imagination, they did not meld into a thematically consistent national campaign. The party's press advertising took a different tack from its television and radio ads, attempting to set out in some detail inconsistencies in Fraser's public record. Labor supporters criticized this line of advertising as too long-winded. Overall, Labor's campaign was outshone by the resources and expertise of the Liberal party campaign.

In state and local campaigns, issues of restricted regional application mingle with the grassroots campaigns of the local candidates. The lack of new policy constrained this sort of campaigning in 1975 and threw most of the emphasis onto the national campaign, although there were some interesting deviations. The four coalition state premiers participated in a strong campaign designed to put their local support behind Fraser. Liberal party advertising played up Fraser's links with state politicians, particularly the popular premier of Victoria, Dick Hamer, who was featured in broadsheet-size advertisements with Fraser and his wife. A more direct intervention in support of Fraser came from the Queensland premier, Joannes Bjelke-Petersen, who utilized a regular ad, "The Premier Reports," ostensibly paid for by the Queensland government as a report on its activities, to launch a blistering attack on Labor:

> Before you vote on December 13, ask yourself—Will my son or daughter get a job when he or she leaves school next year under a Labor Government?
>
> Is my nation safe, with the weakest defences in its history, its traditional allies insulted and every Communist nation around the world welcomed with open arms?
>
> Are my religious beliefs safe, with a Labor Government that contains so many self-professed atheists and a Government with so many Communist friends in its high places? [56]

---

[56] Brisbane *Courier Mail*, November 27, 1975.

This sort of jugular attack was published under the state coat of arms and presumably financed out of the public till. Labor's protests were brushed aside and the party had to resort to paid advertisements to refute it.

In general, advertising at the state and local level was more professional than it had been in previous campaigns. Crude cartooning and the lavish use of red to link the Labor party with communism were used only in a handful of coalition advertisements. Some of the state advertising sponsored by the Labor party focused on basic issues such as medical care and state taxes more effectively than the national campaign, which was confined mainly to the constitutional issue.

The nature of Australian electioneering makes necessary a substantial amount of "machinery" advertising. The problem is not to get the voters to the polls—compulsory voting ensures a high turnout—but to see that they vote correctly once they get there. With voting requirements that are complex in comparison with those in other countries, it is of prime importance to the political parties that lists of their candidates ranked in the proper order be disseminated as widely as possible. This information is distributed at polling places in the form of "how-to-vote" cards. Such "point-of-sale" material is reinforced by frequent repetition in press advertising which reaches a crescendo in the final days of the campaign. The Australian Electoral Office, which controls the ballot, also distributes a considerable amount of technical information as paid advertising.

Advertising in the form of third-party endorsements has developed over the last three election campaigns. Usually this takes the form of a list of names following a political slogan and a brief statement of principles in support of a political party. This sort of advertising was taken to extraordinary lengths by the Labor party during the 1975 campaign, with such banners as "Librarians for Labor," "Democracy in danger—a statement by 1,650 Australian academics," "The Australian Government Lawyers' Association," or "Clergy and laity concerned about democracy" followed by long columns of names. The coalition parties used this technique only a few times. Undoubtedly, it provides a vent for political frustrations and an outlet for modest political activity, but it is questionable whether it has much persuasive effect, even as a signal to professional and community groups.

The final category of advertising consists of responses to the election propaganda of the other side, including its advertisements. This was employed rather sparingly in 1975, mainly by the embattled

Labor party in an attempt to correct the perceived distortion of its policies, particularly its budget promise to provide tax rebates from January 1, 1976.

Apart from paid advertising, the ABC provided two and one-quarter hours of free television time and two and one-half hours of free radio time for each of the major political alignments, the Labor party and the coalition. Labor directed a substantial part of its time to telecasting the speech with which Whitlam opened his campaign (thirty minutes) and the candlelight vigil outside Parliament House that closed it (thirty minutes). Both set pieces were effectively produced, particularly the Whitlam telecast, which used careful camera work to emphasize the Labor leader's imposing figure and the frantic enthusiasm of his audience. The telecast may even have been too effective; there was some feeling among Labor officials that this demonstration of the "Fuhrerprinzip" cost Labor electoral support.

The remainder of Labor's television and radio time was used in an imaginative way to avoid the traditional "talking head" approach to election programs. The use of current affairs techniques similar to those adopted in ABC programs often made it difficult to distinguish the unpaid ads from regular programs. According to Labor's federal secretary, David Combe, the ABC received hundreds of complaints that it was broadcasting programs slanted towards the Labor party. Ironically, this sort of exploitation of ABC free time may have reinforced the impression of ABC bias held by many listeners. The coalition made more conventional use of its free time, relying on traditional campaign speeches and some rather awkward audience questioning of Fraser. The bulk of the creative resources of the coalition went into paid advertising.

Surprisingly enough, the paid media campaign was also marked by accusations of bias by the Labor party. These were stated in strong terms by the party's federal secretary and national campaign director, David Combe:

> In the almost eleven years during which I have been professionally employed in politics, I have never known anything to approximate the vicious manner in which the ALP was subjected to discrimination in respect of paid media during the recent election campaign.[57]

Combe outlined in some detail nine examples of what he claimed was discrimination against Labor campaign material. These ranged from

---

[57] David Combe, national secretary of the Australian Labor party, address to National Conference of Young Labor, January 25, 1976, pp. 12-13 of official text.

quibbles over the interpretation of regulations under federal statutes governing elections to the charge that certain material had been rejected because of its technical shortcomings or the seemingly excessive sensitivity of the media managers to the risks of libel. In some cases there had been considerable delays in getting advertising material onto the air. The coalition parties may have experienced similar frustrations, but if so they did not complain of them publicly.[58]

Some Final Thoughts

In political terms the 1975 election was the anticlimax to a highly eventful year. For the media, the campaign brought no such letdown. The coverage, if not the substance, of the campaign was the most turbulent and emotional in Australia's political history.

In retrospect, the campaign produced an agonizing reappraisal by sections of the media. In particular, Ranald Macdonald, the chairman of the Australian Newspapers Council and managing director of David Syme & Co. (publishers of the *Age*), made some strong criticisms of media performance:

> Our credibility is at an all-time low. In the months leading up to the last federal election, the Labor Party didn't have a fair go. Media fell down in not providing enough variety in news and opinion. They also were not effective in eliciting from the current Prime Minister [Mr. Fraser] enough about his program; he was able to go through the election campaign without promising very much. . . . There should have been a representative cross-section of commentators and more objective journalism. . . . The economy became the main election issue apart from the Kerr sacking. All *Age* commentators wrote on that. We didn't cover many other issues such as the Aboriginal situation, defence, urban affairs or decentralisation. Editorially we listed Whitlam's achievements (and there were many). Perhaps it can be said that some other papers did not acknowledge his successes.[59]

This remarkable mea culpa from a newspaper proprietor provided little solace to the defeated Labor party.[60] It suggests the justice

---

[58] Accounts of campaign strategy are given in Oakes, *Crash Through or Crash*, chapters 13 and 15; Lloyd and Clark, *Kerr's King Hit!* chapters 25 and 26.

[59] *The Journalist*, published by the AJA, April 1976, p. 3.

[60] The Labor party had been extremely chagrined by the harsh opposition of the Melbourne *Age* which had supported Labor in 1972 and had opposed it in mild terms in 1974.

of the criticism leveled at the press in particular during the election campaign. It seems likely that Macdonald's assessment expedited the formation of a Press Council, sponsored by the Australian Newspapers Council, to give some sort of scrutiny to newspaper practice and to publicize abuses. The newspaper owners had rejected an earlier move by the Labor government to establish such a watchdog council. Unfortunately, the ambit of the new council does not include the important Fairfax newspapers, which are not members of the Australian Newspapers Council.

The general lack of confidence in press coverage of politics was reflected in a public opinion poll published in April which indicated that only 31 percent of Australians trusted press political coverage while 59 percent distrusted it.[61] A similar poll showed that 67 percent trusted the ABC's television coverage of politics, while only 13 percent distrusted it.[62]

From Rupert Murdoch, the election post-mortems brought no signs of remorse. His group issued a history of 1975 in the form of an elaborate brochure, juxtaposing the front pages of the *Australian* throughout the year with editorials chosen to "show the consistent policy followed by Australia's only national newspaper during this turbulent period of our history."[63] In all of the controversy over political bias and the resort to direct action by a significant part of his labor force, Murdoch did not budge an inch from the opposition to "free communication" and "the new journalism" he had expressed earlier:

> I'm against these people, not because of their ideas, some of which are good and humane—but because they threaten the basic fabric of the press. If they got the control they seek, and turned newspapers into propaganda sheets these papers would cease to exist. The public does not want to read propaganda. It wants to read objective news and informed comment.[64]

Whatever his journalists might have thought, there was no doubt in Murdoch's mind that during 1975 his readers had been presented with objective news and informed comment.

---

[61] *Age* Polls, published in the Melbourne *Age*, April 23, 1976.

[62] Ibid., April 24, 1976.

[63] "History in the Making," a record of news and opinions from Australia's national newspaper, the *Australian*.

[64] ABC Science Programs Unit, *New Society*, no. 55, February 18, 1975. ABC transcript, p. 12.

8

OPINION POLLING AND THE ELECTIONS

Terence W. Beed

During the unique period of Australian political history that coincided with Labor's term of office from 1972 to 1975, public opinion polling in the mass media proliferated beyond the bounds of a single organization and a strongly competitive multiorganization structure grew up. The information generated by this new opinion measurement apparatus has afforded Australians insights not previously available into public reactions to the government, parliamentary leaders, and political issues. Before accounting for the events which preceded the 1975 election and the performance of the opinion polls, it is useful to discuss the background of opinion polling in Australia and the conditions under which survey work is conducted there.

A Concentrated Press and a Concentrated Population

From 1941 to 1971 Australia was served by only one public opinion polling company. In other Western countries during the same period, commercially backed polling organizations proliferated at the behest of competing publishers, but in Australia, only one publishing group (the largest) sponsored opinion polling, while its competitors stayed out of this specialized field of newsmaking. In 1971 this changed, and by 1975 Australia's three major publishing groups were sponsoring polls conducted regularly by four polling organizations. The new pollsters have maintained the record of their predecessor—no wrong final election forecasts have yet been issued—but in the past five years poll findings have disagreed and the corporate structures of the polling firms have been unsettled.

In 1941 Australia's largest media organization, the Melbourne *Herald* group, registered the Gallup name for use in the publication of opinion polls. At the time it was thought that widely publicized poll findings concerning public morale in wartime Australia would be useful for both politicians and the public. The person responsible for the Melbourne *Herald*'s Gallup Polls was an employee named Roy Morgan, who in later years left the company and established the Roy Morgan Research Centre, a market research agency independent of the *Herald*. Ownership of the name Gallup Poll remained in the hands of the *Herald*. This is important to some developments subsequent to 1972 in which Australia became the only country in the world with two Gallup Polls run by rival companies.

Before 1972 results of the poll run by Morgan were also published by a different media group based in Sydney—John Fairfax & Sons Limited—under an interstate agreement with the *Herald*. This meant that the same set of results was disseminated to daily and weekend newspaper readers in all Australian capital cities. The Melbourne *Herald* and the Fairfax groups between them ran newspapers in all of the capitals, accounting for the lion's share (74 percent) of the combined circulations of Australian metropolitan newspapers.

Several interest groups were not satisfied that a single polling organization was adequate in a modern democracy. This was especially true of nonconservative politicians and the smaller newspaper publishers outside of the *Herald*-Fairfax empires. Following the 1969 federal elections, Labor politicians and officials were concerned that the Gallup Poll preelection forecasts might not have reflected the true state of their party's public support. Not coincidentally, Rupert Murdoch received proposals from American and British pollsters to establish an alternative polling organization in Australia.

Murdoch's group, News Ltd., was at the time the fastest growing publisher outside of the *Herald* and Fairfax groups and had a more comprehensive national operation than its smaller counterparts, in particular than Consolidated Press Ltd., which then published the *Daily Telegraph* and *Sunday Telegraph* in Sydney and the national weekly, the *Bulletin*. News Ltd., therefore, could circulate polls more widely than any other publisher through a collection of newspapers in each state of Australia that represented 24 percent of the national metropolitan circulation of daily newspapers and 54 percent of weekly and weekend newspaper circulation.

Murdoch received proposals from Marplan, Louis Harris, and the British National Opinion Polls (NOP) organization. In 1970 he decided upon the format of a joint polling and market research venture between News Ltd. itself and NOP, to be known as Australian Nationwide Opinion Polls (ANOP). From the outset, this was to be a true competitor of the Gallup Poll, surveying public opinion on a national scale in all capital cities, provincial centers, and rural areas. Operations commenced early in 1971.

Also in 1971, the *Age* of Melbourne concluded an agreement with Australian Sales Research Bureau (ASRB), a member of the British P.E. Consulting Group, to regularly conduct opinion polls in Melbourne and Sydney. In strict terms, the ASRB poll was not an alternative to the Gallup Poll since it did not provide repetitive sampling from the national population. On occasion, however, ASRB did sample from populations outside Sydney and Melbourne, in selected "marginal" electorates where only a small shift in voter support could mean a change of hands from the government to the opposition. ASRB polls were published simultaneously in the *Age*, the *Sydney Morning Herald*, and the *Canberra Times*, all of which were controlled by Fairfax but which had a considerable degree of de facto autonomy.

With these changes in polling resources by 1971, the stage was set for Australia's first competitive monitoring of public opinion in the lead-up to the December 1972 federal election. The polls were contradictory. For most of 1972, ANOP and Gallup disagreed about the likely winner of an election: ANOP forecast a Labor victory consistently from March right up to the election in December, while Gallup forecast a Liberal-Country party coalition victory until November. At one stage (July 1972) Gallup showed a gap of five percentage points between the two parties, while ANOP showed a sixteen percentage point gap.[1] The ASRB polls in the same period, although not as geographically extensive in sample coverage, tended to confirm the ANOP findings.

In the period from the 1972 to the 1975 federal elections, more changes took place in the structure of the opinion polling organizations. Early in 1973 the Melbourne *Herald* group terminated its longstanding agreement with the Roy Morgan Research Centre for undisclosed reasons and appointed the Sydney-based media survey firm, McNair Anderson Associates, to operate the Gallup Poll, referred to in this chapter as the McNair Gallup Poll.[2] Later Morgan

---

[1] For an account of ANOP's study of public opinion trends prior to the 1972 federal election see, Terence W. Beed, "Monitoring Trends in Australian Public Opinion, 1971-72," in Henry Mayer, ed., *Labor to Power* (Sydney: Angus and Robertson, 1973), pp. 252-258. The author is indebted to Professor Mayer for his comments on an earlier draft of this chapter.

[2] There was an immediate (and as yet unresolved) legal dispute by Morgan over McNair Anderson's right to use the Gallup name. The current position is that

reached an agreement to publish the Morgan Gallup Poll in the national weekly newsmagazine, the *Bulletin*, owned by Consolidated Press. The only outlet for the Morgan Gallup Poll, the *Bulletin* has a national circulation of 60,700.

In late 1974, ANOP became completely independent under the ownership of its employees and ceased publishing its polls in the News Ltd. press. Instead, ANOP polls were later published jointly by the Australian Broadcasting Commission and the *National Times*, a weekly national newspaper with a circulation of 105,905, owned by the Fairfax group. Also late in 1974, ASRB was taken over by Morgan. This takeover did not, however, net Morgan the ASRB poll. Former employees of ASRB reconstituted the poll under the management of Irving Saulwick, previously chairman of ASRB, and continued their relationship with the *Age* and the *Sydney Morning Herald*. In the discussion of the 1975 election this poll is referred to as the Saulwick *Age* Poll.

During the 1975 election campaign a new but short-lived relationship was struck up between Morgan and News Ltd. Part of the Consolidated Press empire was also involved, the Channel Nine Network. Late in the campaign, Morgan Gallup Polls commissioned by Consolidated Press were published in the *Bulletin* several days after they had been headlined in News Ltd.'s evening *Daily Mirror* in Sydney, and on the same evenings they were presented on the Nine Network program "A Current Affair." Clearly, the weekly *Bulletin* was not a timely enough medium for up-to-the-minute poll releases. But this arrangement increased the ire of Labor politicians already incensed by the anti-Labor stance of News Ltd. The federal secretary of the ALP said that these arrangements suggested "clear collusion between the management of the Packer [Consolidated Press] and Murdoch empires, a collusion which in view of the already existing concentration of media in few hands is a source of considerable worry." [3]

There are now four public opinion polls which can be considered active in Australia (see Table 8-1). The period since 1972 is the

McNair Anderson issues press releases entitled Australian Public Opinion Polls (The Gallup Method) incorporating the words Gallup Poll in a logotype. Morgan issues press releases entitled Morgan Gallup Poll with the footnote, "Morgan Gallup Poll conducted by the only Australian member of the Gallup International Research Institutes Inc. No other public opinion poll taken in Australia has this qualification."

[3] Transcript of an unpublished address by David Combe, national secretary of the ALP, to a public meeting organized by the Media Action Group, Melbourne, April 23, 1976.

complete antithesis of the monopolistic phase that spanned the previous thirty years. The four publishing groups which between them control Australia's metropolitan and national press have played an important role in this metamorphosis. By 1973 each of them was served by at least one opinion poll. To this has been added no small measure of competitive turmoil among the pollsters themselves, involving changes in contractual allegiances and management structures. From the turmoil have emerged a diversity of polling approaches and results and great innovations in the style of their editorial presentation. As a result Australians now have at their disposal a much richer information source than they had before 1972.

Australia has not been without its share of academic opinion polling efforts, although none of these has ventured into the area of forecasting the outcome of elections on a national scale. In fact, only one academic survey has used a national sample (N = 2,054) to measure public opinion about Australia's political climate.[4] While this may be a reflection of the relatively small number of Australian academics with an orientation to this type of survey research, it also reflects the relatively high costs of studying national samples of the Australian population: the fieldwork budget alone for a modest interview with a national sample of 2,000 respondents would exceed $20,000, a sum not easily commanded by Australian social scientists.

Australia's distribution of population and its peculiar electoral geography pose significant operating constraints for the opinion pollster. Vast distances separate the six state capital cities in which the bulk (61 percent) of the population lives. The balance of the

---

[4] The data gathered in this survey are held by the Inter-University Consortium for Political and Social Research, University of Michigan, Ann Arbor. Don Aitkin, Michael Kahan, and Donald E. Stokes, *Australian National Political Attitudes, 1967* (ICPSR #7282). The methods used in the survey are described in Don Aitkin and Michael Kahan, *Drawing a Sample of the Australian Electorate* (Canberra: ANU Press, 1968); some results are reported in Don Aitkin and Michael Kahan, "Class Politics in the New World," in Richard Rose, ed., *Comparative Electoral Behavior* (N. Y.: Free Press, 1974), pp. 437-80, which also contains useful reference to the dearth of Australian surveys by political scientists. A more elaborate treatment of Aitkin & Kahan's 1967 study can be found in Don Aitkin, *Stability and Change in Australian Politics* (Canberra: ANU Press, 1976). Aitkin is also a regular correspondent of the *National Times* where he has published many articles on Australian opinion polls and has contributed to an increased public awareness of the practice of opinion polling. Useful references to opinion poll and market research agency surveys are contained in Henry Mayer, Margaret Bettison, and Judy Keene, *ARGAP: A Research Guide to Australian Politics and Cognate Subjects* (Melbourne: Cheshire, 1976), pp. 107 and 113-15. Other Australian academic surveys are reviewed in Cora V. Baldock and Jim Lally, *Sociology in Australia and New Zealand* (Westport: Greenwood Press, 1974).

Table 8-1

OPINION POLL ORGANIZATIONS OPERATING IN AUSTRALIA, 1975

Name of Poll	Year Began Political Polling	Operating Company and Location of Main Office	Publications Served			
			Name	Type	Circulation Area	Circulation September 1975
Morgan Gallup Poll	1941	Roy Morgan Research Centre Pty. Ltd., Melbourne	*Bulletin*	Weekly newsmagazine	National	60,700
Australian Public Opinion Polls[a] (The Gallup Method)	1973	McNair Anderson & Associates Pty. Ltd., Sydney	*Herald*	Evening newspaper	Melbourne	457,509
			Sun	Morning newspaper	Melbourne	627,236
			Sun	Evening newspaper	Sydney	340,434
			Sun-Herald	Sunday newspaper	Sydney	638,654
			Courier-Mail	Morning newspaper	Brisbane	265,990
			Advertiser	Morning newspaper	Adelaide	234,330
			Daily News	Evening newspaper	Perth	120,087
			Mercury	Morning newspaper	Hobart	55,859

Australian Nationwide Opinion Poll (ANOP)	1971	ANOP, Sydney	*National Times*	Weekend newspaper	National	105,905
Age Poll or Herald Survey[b]	1971	Irving Saulwick & Associates, Melbourne	*Age*	Morning newspaper	Melbourne	221,811
			Sydney Morning Herald	Morning newspaper	Sydney	267,303

[a] Referred to in this chapter as McNair Gallup.

[b] Referred to in this chapter as ASRB up to 1974, Saulwick *Age* Poll after 1974.

Source: Author's compilation. For circulation data: Audit Bureau of Circulations; Publishers' Statements and Publishers' Claims.

population is largely scattered along the comparatively well-watered and temperate coast or the near-coastal inland of the east, southeast, and southwest of the continent (see Figure 8-1). However, there has been a tendency for rural dwellers to be overrepresented in the House of Representatives, although this is decreasing.[5] This makes the inclusion of rural respondents in the sampling frame of critical importance. Accordingly the survey researcher must effect an appropriate cost-benefit solution to the problem of sampling from electorates in a half-dozen capital cities, some of which are thousands of miles apart, and from rural electorates, some of which are thousands of square miles in size. The implementation of fieldwork is a very decentralized affair involving high overhead outlays in the set-up phase and high on-going transport and field force maintenance costs.

The problems posed by Australia's geography heighten the economic barrier against entry into the polling game and underline the sheer necessity of adequate contractual funding for the profitable operation of polls. A company that wished to establish a repetitive opinion poll in today's economic climate would be faced with an initial outlay of at least $50,000 and continuing costs of at least half this amount per survey. The expenses for an interstate trip by a field manager to all capitals and some rural centers over a two-week period could easily amount to $2,000 in fares and accommodation alone. Australian opinion polls are only viable if structured as omnibus survey research vehicles, in which questions about voting intentions are intermingled with questions of a social, economic, or marketing nature. Funding for the political questions comes from the contracts with the publishers, and further funds for each survey come from contracts with a collection of clients who share the objective of surveying a general purpose sample of the national population. In this, the operational context of opinion polls in Australia is comparable to those in the United States, Great Britain, and other Western economies.

The Record of Australian Opinion Polls

Throughout their history Australian opinion polls have provided regular measures of the public's voting intentions and its knowledge and attitudes about a wide variety of societal issues. Since 1971 the studies of societal issues have proliferated.

---

[5] Joan Rydon, "The Electoral System," in Henry Mayer and Helen Nelson, eds., *Australian Politics: A Fourth Reader* (Melbourne: Cheshire, 1976), pp. 402-14.

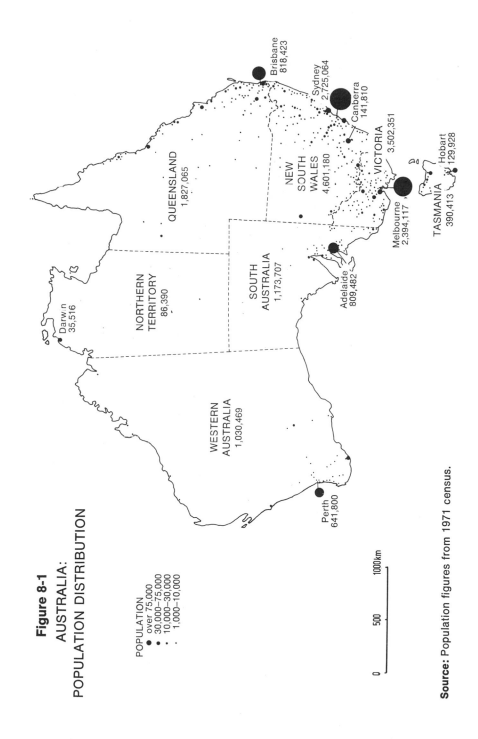

Figure 8-1
AUSTRALIA:
POPULATION DISTRIBUTION

POPULATION
● over 75,000
● 30,000–75,000
∶ 10,000–30,000
· 1,000–10,000

0   500   1000km

Source: Population figures from 1971 census.

QUEENSLAND
1,827,065

NORTHERN
TERRITORY
86,390

SOUTH
AUSTRALIA
1,173,707

WESTERN
AUSTRALIA
1,030,469

NEW
SOUTH
WALES
4,601,180

VICTORIA
3,502,351

TASMANIA
390,413

Brisbane
818,423

Sydney
2,725,064

Canberra
141,810

Hobart
129,928

Melbourne
2,394,117

Adelaide
809,482

Perth
641,800

Darwin
35,516

219

Election Forecasting. Unlike opinion polls in the United States and Great Britain, Australian polls to 1975 have never failed to produce a final forecast in line with the result of the federal election itself.[6] As Table 8-2 shows, the forecasts for each party's share of the vote in House of Representatives elections since 1958 have been mostly within three percentage points of the actual outcome, a figure which can be regarded as within the tolerance of sampling error.[7] Only on one occasion has there been a forecast error exceeding this, when the forecast for the Liberal-Country party coalition exceeded the actual vote by five percentage points (Gallup, 1961 election). On another occasion there were no errors in the forecast (Morgan Gallup, 1974).

Another aspect of Australian opinion polling accuracy is shown by Table 8-3, which analyzes the errors in the Morgan Gallup Poll predictions of gaps between the major parties for the same series of elections. Errors have been greatest in cases of L-NCP election wins and least where elections have been won by the ALP. It is possible that this is just a chance occurrence, but the fact that the effect is confined to Morgan Gallup Polls, as shown by Table 8-4, suggests that some other systematic effect may have been at work. In the absence of any published survey performance data it is impossible to determine whether this effect resides in the Morgan Gallup sample design or in some other area of the survey procedure.

In accounting for the enviable record of Australian opinion polls one might be tempted to conclude that the Australian system of polling is in some way better than the systems used in the United States and Great Britain. This is unwarranted: the methods employed by Australian polls are derivative and essentially similar to those used elsewhere (see Table 8-5). Two of the polls use the electoral rolls as a sampling frame (ANOP) or as a source of randomly selected starting points (Morgan Gallup). The others use a clustered area probability design based on the occupied dwellings frame of the 1971 Australian

---

[6] For a critical discussion of the accuracy of Australian opinion polls up to the 1972 federal elections, see David Butler, *The Canberra Model* (Melbourne: Cheshire, 1973), pp. 105-14.

[7] Forecasts of the outcome of Senate elections have also proved reliable, although to date these have only been issued by Morgan Gallup and McNair Gallup. Since government is won or lost in the House of Representatives, not much interest has been shown by the public or by political scientists in forecasts of Senate election results. In contrast, forecasts of the outcome of referenda in Australia have been remarkably inaccurate, a fact that reflects the problems of predicting the proportion of voters who will abandon party lines when asked to vote in a referendum. The choice of 1958 as a base year for the comparison of poll results in Table 8-2 is a matter of convenience. Prior to 1958, the Gallup Poll correctly forecast the winner of each election.

Table 8-2

ELECTION RESULTS AND OPINION POLL FORECASTS, HOUSE ELECTIONS, 1958–1975

Election	Winning Party	Vote and Forecast Error			
		L-NCP	ALP	DLP	Other
1958					
Actual Result	*L-NCP*	*47*	*43*	*9*	*1*
Gallup	L-NCP	−1	+3	−2	0
1961					
Actual Result	*L-NCP*	*42*	*48*	*9*	*1*
Gallup	L-NCP	+5	−1	−3	−1
1963					
Actual Result	*L-NCP*	*46*	*46*	*7*	*1*
Gallup	L-NCP	−2	+3	−1	0
1966					
Actual Result	*L-NCP*	*50*	*40*	*7*	*3*
Gallup	L-NCP	+2	−3	+2	−1
1969					
Actual Result	*L-NCP*	*43*	*47*	*6*	*4*
Gallup	L-NCP	+1	−1	+1	−1
1972					
Actual Result	*ALP*	*41*	*50*	*5*	*4*
Gallup	ALP	+1	0	0	−1
ANOP	ALP	+2	−1	0	−1
ASRB [a]	ALP	+0.4	+0.3	0	−0.7
1974					
Actual Result	*ALP*	*46*	*49*	*1*	*4*
Morgan Gallup	ALP	0	0	0	0
McNair Gallup	ALP	−3	+3	0	0
ANOP	ALP	−2	+2	0	0
ASRB [a]	ALP	−2.9	+2.3	+1.6	−1
1975					
Actual Result	*L-NCP*	*53*	*43*	*1*	*3*
Morgan Gallup	L-NCP	+2	−2	+1	−1
McNair Gallup	L-NCP	−1	−1	0	+2
ANOP [b]	L-NCP	−1	0	0	+1
Saulwick	L-NCP	0	−3	+1	+2

Note: Actual election results, in italics, are given in percentages of total valid vote. Forecast errors are given in percentage points. Except where specified, polls are based on national survey samples. Other parties include the Australia party, the Workers party, and independent candidates.

[a] Based on a survey sample of voters in twenty-five marginal electorates.

[b] Based on a survey sample of voters in capital cities only.

Source: Press releases by Morgan Gallup Poll, 1958-75, McNair Gallup Poll, 1973-75, ANOP, 1973-75, and *Age Poll Reprint Series,* 1973-75.

Table 8-3

FORECAST ERRORS BY MORGAN GALLUP POLL, HOUSE ELECTIONS, 1958–1975

(in percentage points)

Gap Between L-NCP and ALP	Election							
	1958	1961	1963	1966	1969	1972	1974	1975
Actual gap	4	6	0	10	4	9	3	10
Forecast gap	0	0	5	15	0	8	3	14
Error	4	6	5	5	4	1	0	4
Winning party	L-NCP	L-NCP	L-NCP	L-NCP	L-NCP	ALP	ALP	L-NCP

Source: Calculated from press releases by Morgan Gallup Poll, 1958-75.

Table 8-4

FORECAST ERRORS BY OTHER OPINION POLLS, HOUSE ELECTIONS, 1972–1975

(in percentage points)

Gap Between L-NCP and ALP	Election		
	1972	1974	1975
Actual gap	9	3	10
Forecast gap			
ANOP	6	7	9
ASRB/Saulwick	10	8	13
McNair Gallup	—	9	10
Error			
ANOP	3	4	1
ASRB/Saulwick	1	5	3
McNair Gallup	—	6	0
Average error	2	5	1.3
Winning party	ALP	ALP	L-NCP

Source: Calculated from press releases by ANOP, 1973-75, McNair Gallup Poll, 1973-75, and *Age Poll Reprint Series,* 1973-75.

Table 8-5

SURVEY METHODS USED BY AUSTRALIAN OPIONION POLLS

Survey Characteristic	Opinion Poll			
	Morgan Gallup	McNair Gallup	ANOP	Saulwick Age Poll
Sampling frame	Electoral roll	1971 census: occupied dwellings	Electoral roll	1971 census: occupied dwellings
Sample size (approximate)	2,200	2,200	2,000	2,500
Respondent selection	Random selection of approximately 220 electors' addresses in all electorates; field selection of neighboring electors to yield total cluster of 10	Random area selection of clusters of 10 dwellings in Census Collector Districts distributed in all electorates of each state	Prestratified random selection of 2,000 unclustered electors' addresses in sample of electorates and electoral subdivisions in each state	Random selection of clusters of 3 dwellings in Census Collector Districts in all electorates of each state
Collection of voting-intention data	Simulated ballot box	Simulated ballot box	Face-to-face questioning using precoded questionnaire	Face-to-face questioning using precoded questionnaire

Source: For ANOP, *Australian Public Opinion Newsletter*, vol. 1, no. 1 (November 1971); for other polls, author's inquiries, unofficial handouts.

Census. Within these procedures, there are certain important differences: ANOP, in contrast to Morgan Gallup, uses an unclustered and intricately stratified design, selecting respondents who are enrolled voters from a sample of the electorates and electoral subdivisions within electorates. Since early in 1975 the Saulwick *Age* Poll has been drawing respondents from Census Collector Districts in all of the electorates in each state of Australia and has interviewed in clusters of three dwellings, with a random selection of electors in dwellings. McNair Gallup selects respondents in clusters of ten from Census Collector Districts in all electorates of each state but there is no random selection of electors in dwellings. Sample sizes for all of the polls are fairly similar and two of them (Morgan and McNair Gallup) use the simulated ballot box technique for gathering voting intention data.

Regrettably, no systematic research has been conducted into the efficacy of these methods and it is not possible to conclude that the apparent technical differences make one more reliable than the others. This information is sorely needed; its absence hinders academic discussion of poll findings. The period since 1971 has brought forth greater frankness and openness about methods on the part of some of the new pollsters, but there is still a serious need for a critical overview.

It is more likely that the Australian opinion polling record owes much to the existence of compulsory voting in Australia. Opinion pollsters, particularly those in the United States and Great Britain, have a hard enough time estimating voter turnout, let alone voting intentions, and therefore have to cope with two error factors rather than the single one confronting pollsters in Australia. Compulsory voting means that a fairly constant 95 percent of eligible voters cast votes from one election to another—and that the vagaries of weather and the so-called lulling of support for parties performing well in campaigns do not have an impact on turnout.

Compulsory voting however, has not bred an air of complacency among Australian pollsters and many of the lessons learned by British polls in the 1970 and 1974 general election debacles have been put to good use in Australia. There is a healthy respect for elector volatility among Australian pollsters, and during the 1972 election campaign several attempts were made to monitor the intentions of undecided and "swinging voters" (that is, people who do not vote for the same party from one election to the next). These voters were subsampled from the full sample interviewed a week or two prior to the election and were reinterviewed until election eve. These procedures were used by ANOP in 1972, ASRB in 1974, and by the McNair Gallup Poll and Saulwick *Age* Poll in 1975.

Much original research has been conducted into swinging voters in Australia by polling organizations and academics alike. For political scientists, the behavior of swinging voters has been a serious field of empirical research, unlike the behavior of the national voting population as a whole. There is evidence to suggest that the proportion of voters who claim to have altered their party preference since the previous federal election increased by six percentage points in a twelve-year period (1961–72), from 10.8 percent to 17 percent.[8] Immediately after the 1972 election, another study concentrated on measuring the extent of swing among L-NCP voters whose intentions had been measured just prior to the election.[9] It was found that 84 percent of the preelection sample who intended to vote for the L-NCP coalition, had in fact voted L-NCP, leaving 16 percent whose intentions had changed. One-half of these voters were found to have voted ALP. In 1974 and 1975, further postelection studies of swinging voters were conducted in Melbourne. Academic researchers reinterviewed a subsample of the ASRB and Saulwick *Age* Poll preelection samples. Also, in 1972, 1974, and 1975 McNair Gallup conducted surveys at voting booths in some marginal electorates of Sydney on election day before the outcome was known. These studies are considered in more detail later in this chapter.

If compulsory voting has been something of a blessing for the Australian pollster, preferential voting has not, particularly in the elections of the 1960s when the minor parties accounted for a much larger share of the total vote than they do now. The pollster's problems are compounded when the winner of an election is not the candidate who had the most first-preference votes but instead one whose majority depended upon the allocation of voters' second (or higher-order) preferences after the first count.

Until 1972, the most important minor party was the Democratic Labor party (DLP), and errors in its forecast share of the vote have led to hazardous situations for the pollster. As Table 8-2 shows, the 1961 election forecast by the Gallup Poll, although on the right side, was a long way from the actual result, underestimating the DLP vote by as much as one-third. It is clear that the DLP's role in returning the L-NCP to power that year was greatly understated, despite

<hr>

[8] David Kemp, "Swingers and Stayers: The Australian Swinging Voter 1961-72," in Mayer, ed., *Labor to Power*, pp. 281-92.

[9] Rodney Cameron, "Swingers: Undecided Mavericks v. Conformist Switchers," in Mayer, ed., *Labor to Power*, pp. 275-80.

the fact that most DLP preferences were directed to the L-NCP. In effect, Gallup concluded in 1961 that the national vote would divide evenly between the L-NCP and ALP and that DLP preferences would simply ensure success for the L-NCP. In fact, however, it can be seen that the DLP had a much larger role to play. The L-NCP finished six percentage points behind the ALP in share of the total vote and became almost desperately dependent upon DLP preferences to retain office. Today the DLP is all but a spent force in Australian politics and has largely amalgamated itself with the Liberal-National Country party coalition, but an important few percent of the vote remain in the hands of other minor parties. The allegiances of these parties have proved to be less predictable than those of the DLP when it comes to marking preferential ballots. In any future neck-and-neck contests between the major parties, accuracy in forecasting the minor parties' share of the vote can be expected to be crucial for pollsters.

Opinion Polls, Social Issues, and Political Campaigning. The year 1971 heralded the change from a monopolistic to a competitive structure in Australian polling and provided alternative measures of voting intentions. It also ushered in a new approach towards polls on social issues.[10] Politicians and the public alike have been given a veritable feast of survey results ranging from studies of the perceived personality attributes of political leaders to comprehensive analyses of the permissive society in Australia. Not only the scope of the data themselves, but also their presentation by the media (especially the papers and stations that have recently begun sponsoring polls themselves) has been lavish. In addition to the traditional front-page news leads based on poll results just before elections, readers and viewers have been treated to more and more opinion-poll-based feature articles or series of articles since 1971. As the introduction to the *Age Poll Reprint Series,* widely distributed to schools, remarks:

> In these articles, we continue to study, in some depth, the social and political attitudes and beliefs of people in our community.
> We believe that this type of investigation is an important task.
> Over the past ten years Australia has changed in many ways. The attitudes and needs of those who live in Australia may also have changed.

---

[10] For a comprehensive analysis of the content of polls prior to 1971, see Murray Goot, *Policies and Partisans, Australian Electoral Opinion 1942 to 1968,* Occasional Monograph No. 1, Department of Government, University of Sydney, 1969.

People who are concerned with education will, perhaps, have a special interest in the interaction of community attitudes and change.

The information gleaned by Age Poll can be used for teaching purposes and, more generally, as a stimulus to discussion about the attitudes the community holds and the implication for community planning of such attitudes.

We would also be happy to receive suggestions from educationists and students about subjects which might be studied in future Age Polls.[11]

This is perhaps the only statement made by an Australian publishing organization about the need for and use of opinion poll data in the mass media. Nevertheless, it reflects the sentiments of many journalists who have abandoned the factual reporting of polls between elections in favor of a more considered, lively, and extensive treatment of polls covering social and political issues alike.

Not surprisingly, the wide publicity given to opinion poll findings in recent years has whetted the political parties' appetites for private polls of their own. The planning of election campaigns and policy platforms has become increasingly dependent upon opinion survey research as a decision-making prop. In the middle to late 1960s, there was evidence among the major parties of an increasing orientation towards private data collection, and the ALP's bid for power in 1969 was assisted by a study of selected electorates that the party commissioned from Marplan. This was a very close election and the Marplan exercise led to a growing faith in the survey research approach. The ALP's successful election campaign in 1972 turned into an object lesson in survey-based marketing and advertising without precedent among any of Australia's political parties. The methodologies created in the eighteen months of campaigning prior to December 1972 set the stage for future election campaigning by the ALP at the state as well as the federal level. The surveys were used to identify salient political, social, and economic issues and their platform applications; to study the image of Whitlam and his wife and other key figures; to test the effectiveness of advertising as a means of communication; to test alternative slogans and even alternative names for the party. Indeed, as one observer has remarked, almost nothing in the course of the campaign was consciously left to chance.[12]

---

[11] *Reprints of the Fifteenth Series of Articles from the Age Poll*, Melbourne *Age*, April-May 1975.

[12] Vicky Braund, "Timely Vibrations: Labor's Marketing Campaign," in Mayer, ed., *Labor to Power*, pp. 18-28.

The 1974 and 1975 campaigns were far more truncated than that of 1972. They were snap elections with campaign periods lasting only a matter of weeks. Nevertheless, important research initiatives were taken by the ALP and there is little doubt that the survey approach has retained its position in the value systems of the party hierarchy, despite the ALP's eventual loss in 1975.[13]

The Liberal party did not match the ALP's preelection survey research and marketing preparations in 1972. Its partner, the Country party, did, however, lean towards surveys in 1972 but at a much later stage than the ALP.[14] In addition to conducting research among electors, the Country party introduced a program of surveys of its branch members in all states, designed among other things to foster a greater sense of participation by members in the party's policy-making processes.

During 1975 there was evidence of an increasing orientation in the Liberal party towards specially commissioned surveys of the electorate, to be used especially in planning the party's platforms. Surveys were conducted on behalf of the party in various states and in certain key electorates and the results circulated widely among party members.[15] On election eve the results of one of these so-called secret polls were published in a front-page headline in the Sydney Fairfax newspaper the *Sun*. The lead story claimed that this survey had revealed an eleven percentage point swing in Sydney towards the Liberals and that "the result was so dramatically their way the Liberals have kept details secret." The story further claimed that the Liberals "were afraid that over-confidence could cost them support in the last vital hours to the poll" to be held the following day.

Although it is difficult to quantify the extent of the use of opinion poll data by the political parties, there can be no doubt that the survey approach has become increasingly important in the marketing and advertising mix of the Australian political parties during election campaigns. The 1972 ALP campaign set the pace for this transition.

[13] The transcript of an address to the National Conference of Australian Young Labor by David Combe, national secretary of the ALP, in January 1976, contains excerpts from a memorandum to Whitlam by the head of the ALP's market research agency which gave him a research-based assessment of the ALP's slim chances of winning an election in the brief campaigning period available following the government's dismissal. (David Combe, Address to National Conference of Australian Young Labor, Women's College, University of Sydney, January 25, 1976, unpublished transcript.)

[14] Peter Warrick, "The Country Party's Campaign," in Mayer, ed., *Labor to Power*, pp. 62-64.

[15] See for example, *Current Issue Note of the Liberal Party Federal Secretariat*, no. 22, Canberra, August 5, 1975.

Future election campaigns will be heavily dependent on the findings of survey researchers.

Apart from serving the needs of the parties, the opinion research approach has also come to serve the needs of incumbent politicians and government officials. Opinion surveys have helped gauge areas of need in social and economic welfare planning and in monitoring community reaction to proposed legislative programs. In the period of Labor government, the Australian Bureau of Statistics found it necessary to place a new emphasis on sample surveys of the population to gather data on topics ranging from the proposed change of Australia's national anthem to household expenditure, crime victimization, and poverty in the community. Likewise private survey contractors were appointed by the Labor government to examine community reactions to the introduction of a universal national health insurance scheme (Medibank), regional tourism planning schemes, changes in the educational system, and the future planning of the postal system, to name a few areas of investigation.[16]

The 1975 Election

Overview of Public Opinion, 1974–75. In studying the 1975 election it is necessary to consider public opinion trends from the 1974 election on. Many of the events which culminated in the dismissal and later defeat of the Labor government had their roots in this period. Bitter infighting that involved the Labor leader and senior parliamentary members led to changes in the power structure within the ALP; the opposition regrouped under a new leader and pursued an uncompromising bid for power; the Senate's functions and power structure changed; and the long-dormant powers of the Australian governor general were awakened and exercised.[17]

Between the 1974 and 1975 elections over fifty soundings of public opinion were taken by the two Gallup Polls and at least a

---

[16] A pacesetter for many opinion research initiatives and later policy making by the Labor government was the work of the Institute of Applied Economic and Social Research, University of Melbourne, in its program of research into poverty. Much of its early work is described in Ronald F. Henderson, Alison Harcourt, and R. J. A. Harper, *People in Poverty: A Melbourne Survey* (Melbourne: Cheshire, 1970). A technical document was later produced as a model for future poverty surveys in Australia: Ronald F. Henderson, Alison Harcourt, R. J. A. Harper, and Sheila Shaver, *The Melbourne Poverty Survey: Further Notes on Methods and Results*, Technical Paper No. 3, Institute of Applied Economic and Social Research, University of Melbourne, 1972.

[17] A useful appreciation of these events is given in John Edwards, "Labor's Record, 1972-75," in Mayer and Nelson, eds., *Australian Politics*, pp. 530-38.

dozen more by the Saulwick *Age* Poll and ANOP. Figure 8-2 has been constructed on the basis of the measures made by both Gallup Polls. It provides an overview of voting intentions during the period.

The 1974 election, eighteen months after Labor's victory in 1972, was brought about by the Senate's blocking of several important social reform bills submitted by the House of Representatives. Having won the 1974 election with a reduced majority, the Labor government enjoyed a brief honeymoon period but rapidly lost its advantage in public support; later in 1974 it trailed the opposition by a margin of about seventeen percentage points. In the first four months of 1975, however, this margin narrowed considerably, with the Morgan Gallup Poll claiming a momentary return of the government's ascendancy over the opposition. Thereafter began the government's "horror period," [18] which lasted through most of 1975, in which the opposition enjoyed substantial leads, sometimes as high as twenty percentage points. This gap only diminished at the time of the government's dismissal early in November. As the election campaign proceeded, the opposition consolidated a lead of over ten percentage points, which it sustained in the election itself.

From this overview, three distinct phases can be identified: the period early in 1975 when the government was staging a comeback in public support after its weaker showing in 1974, the horror period from April to November, and the campaign period of November and December.

How was public opinion measured by the pollsters, and do differences in method account for some of the differences in the findings presented in Figure 8-2? In 1974–75, the Morgan Gallup Poll published half as many polls more than did McNair Gallup. Some of these polls were taken simultaneously or in rapid succession, allowing analysts to make direct comparisons of their findings. Polls taken at different times, of course, cannot be compared since the impact of specific events may be reflected in one poll and not the other.

There is a more serious difference between the methods of data collection employed by the two polls and this should be borne in mind when studying the trends in public opinion depicted by Figure 8-2. The phraseology of the question used by the two polls to elicit voting intentions differed. In addition, one of the polls changed its phraseology four times in 1974–75. The McNair Gallup Poll used the same question throughout the period under review: "If a Federal election were being held today, which party would receive your first prefer-

---

[18] The term "horror period" was coined by Don Aitkin in his, "A Glance Back at the Polls since Fraser's Rise to Power," *National Times*, May 31, 1976, p. 15.

Figure 8-2

McNAIR AND MORGAN FINDINGS ON VOTING INTENTIONS, MAY 1974–DECEMBER 1975

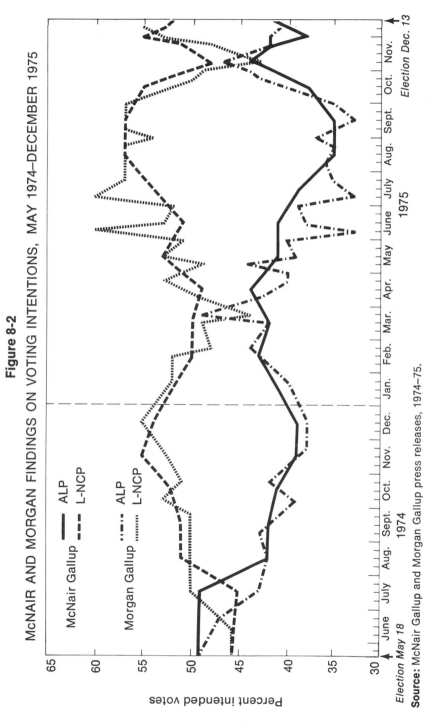

Source: McNair Gallup and Morgan Gallup press releases, 1974–75.

231

ence?" The Morgan Gallup Poll used four different questions during the 1974–75 period. The first, used until late in 1974, was similar to the McNair Gallup question: (1) "Supposing that an election were being held today, which party would receive your first preference (if you had a vote)." In December 1974, this question was dropped and another substituted: (2) "Supposing the Federal Opposition forced an election soon, which party would receive your first preference (if you had a vote)?" In late October 1975, before the dismissal of the Labor government on November 11, the preceding question was dropped in favor of: (3) "As you know, there may soon be elections for the House of Representatives and the Senate. Firstly, we would like your opinion on an election for the House of Representatives—If an election for the House of Representatives were being held today, which party would receive your first preference?" Finally, after November 11, this question was modified to read: (4) "As you know, there will soon be elections for the House of Representatives and the Senate. Firstly we would like your opinion on an election for the House of Representatives. If an election for the House of Representatives were being held today, which party would receive your first preference?"

Clearly, the second and third Morgan Gallup questions were not as emotionally detached as the standard question used by McNair Gallup. Furthermore, careful examination of Figure 8-2 shows that Morgan Gallup tended to yield consistently lower readings for ALP support and about the same general reading for L-NCP support compared with McNair Gallup, most noticeably in the period when the "election forcing" question was used, from December 1974 until August 1975. On six occasions from February to November 1975 the two polls were in the field at the same time. On two of these occasions Morgan Gallup produced ALP voting-intention levels identical to those produced by McNair Gallup. All four of Morgan's remaining polls showed the ALP below the level found by McNair by from one to three percentage points (mean: −2 percentage points). For L-NCP voting intentions there were again two instances of agreement by the polls. Of the remaining four polls, two of Morgan's were above McNair's by two percentage points and two were below by one percentage point (mean: +0.5 percentage points). Strangely, the question did not yield a higher incidence of "don't know" responses than the more neutral question first used by Morgan.

In this author's view the use of the words "forced" and "soon" in the second Morgan Gallup question was likely to bring forth an approval-disapproval set in the respondent's decision about which party he or she might vote for in a hypothetical election "today."

Given its commitment to this type of questioning Morgan Gallup should have posed an additional obverse question to explore voting intentions on the condition that the federal opposition did *not* force an election soon.

Evidence of the approval-disapproval set comes from a question asked in the Saulwick *Age* Poll of May, the McNair Gallup Poll of October, and the ANOP capital cities poll of November. Sixty-five percent of those questioned by Saulwick claimed they would "not welcome" an election before the end of the year, 31 percent said they would welcome it, and only 4 percent were undecided. In October McNair found that 55 percent said there should not be an "early Federal Election" and 42 percent felt there should. Early in November, on the eve of the government's dismissal, ANOP found that 58 percent did not favor an early election, while 39 percent were in favor. This was an issue on which electors had clear ideas; moreover the antielection bias among ALP supporters was very much stronger than the proelection bias among L-NCP voters.

The question used just prior to the Senate stalemate seems even less adequate as an unbiased gauge of voting intentions. It might be argued by the designers of such a question that, with the Senate at the time continually deferring passage of the government's vital money supply bills, an election was inevitable. This argument is specious: there were several other possibilities surrounding the deferral period, including a backdown on deferral by opposition senators and even intervention on the side of the government by the governor general. The point is that alternatives such as these were not posed in the questioning of poll respondents, nor was the change in questioning strategy made clear in any of the press reports of the Morgan Gallup Poll carried by the *Bulletin* at the time. For example, in the October 11 issue of the *Bulletin*, one month before the government's dismissal, it was reported:

> Of 2,219 men and women interviewed, 57 percent said they would vote for the Liberal-NCP coalition at the next election. 35 percent said they would vote ALP, 3 percent for the Australia Party, 2 percent for the DLP and 3 percent for other groupings. 5 percent had not decided which way they would vote.

This report carries no reference to the question actually used in the field collection of data and fails to deal correctly with those persons interviewed who were undecided about their voting intentions. To be entirely faithful, the report should have read:

233

Of 2,219 men and women interviewed, 1,907 were voters. 5 percent of these voters had not decided which way they would vote. Of the remaining, 57 percent said they would vote for the Liberal-NCP coalition on the condition that the coalition forced an election soon. 35 percent said they would vote for the ALP, 3 percent for the Australia party, 2 percent for the DLP, and 3 percent for other groupings.

Against this background, it is interesting to note that the former prime minister, Gough Whitlam, attacked the veracity of the Morgan Gallup Polls published during the 1975 election campaign on grounds other than those discussed above.[19] This moved the *Bulletin* to publish on December 13, 1975 a special editorial entitled, "Mr. Whitlam and the Bulletin":

> The Bulletin ran foul of the former Prime Minister Gough Whitlam on two fronts last week. Whitlam implied that the Morgan Gallup Polls were rigged and that Alan Reid's report of the loans affair was false.
> The Morgan Gallup Poll is purchased by the Bulletin under a contract arrangement with the Roy Morgan Research Centre. The Bulletin has no financial or any other interest in that company. It has no influence over how polls are carried out. The Managing Director, Gary Morgan, has announced that he is taking legal action against Whitlam over his allegations so further discussion of the subject is sub judice.

True, no survey is immune from bias and there is little need to elaborate here on the opportunities for bias in survey research generally. Apart from any bias in their design, opinion poll findings can be distorted by biases in their reporting by the news media, and in the 1975 election campaign in Australia there were instances of both problems' affecting all of the polls. It is regrettable that Australian opinion pollsters have never met to discuss problems such as bias minimization, standards of reporting, and codes of professional practice. There is no Association for Public Opinion Research or any National Council on Public Polls, as there is in the United States, which might otherwise serve the interests of the pollsters and survey researchers alike and help maintain standards of objective enquiry.

---

[19] Whitlam's attack was later made more general. The *Age*, December 11, 1975, quoted Whitlam as saying, in a press conference at the National Press Club in Canberra on December 10, 1975, ". . . the public opinion polls are all commissioned by one or other of the three organizations that run all the daily papers in Australia. And they have used the public opinion polls to psych the Australian public into thinking that we're going to be beaten."

Up to 1974 the universities had shown only an intermittent and marginal interest in survey methodology and ethics. With the setting up of survey research centers at the Australian National University and the University of Sydney, one may hope that academics will show a new and stronger interest in these matters.

Events and Issues during Early 1975. In the wake of the 1974 election win by the Labor government, Labor's ascendancy in public support lasted only briefly: according to Morgan Gallup the tables had turned against Labor by mid-June; according to McNair Gallup the reversal in support came some weeks later in July and August. Curiously, by mid-July 1974 the two Gallup Polls were showing opposite trends (Figure 8-2), with the government in the lead in the McNair Gallup and the opposition ahead in the Morgan Gallup.

The opposition lead shown by Morgan Gallup may be attributable to the first of the Labor party's restructurings of its power hierarchy when the deputy prime minister, Lance Barnard, was replaced by Jim Cairns early in June, although according to McNair Gallup during July the bulk of its poll respondents preferred Cairns over Barnard (47 percent to 35 percent) and approved of the way in which he was handling his job as deputy prime minister.

By August 1974, the opposition had enough support to win an election and the government's position was deteriorating rapidly. The gap reached a maximum of about sixteen percentage points by the end of the year. During this period, nationwide oil, fuel, and transport strikes had a serious impact; there was considerable public concern about both inflation and unemployment; the prime minister, deputy prime minister, and treasurer incurred some public displeasure over their simultaneous overseas trips (in particular the prime minister's five-week excursion late in the year); and a "mini-budget" following the main August Budget was introduced early in November as a special measure to arrest inflation. The treasurer, Frank Crean, was sacked by Whitlam late in November and the treasurer's portfolio was added to that of Deputy Prime Minister Cairns.

This period can be seen as one in which the "competence to govern" theme was established by the opposition and used against the government. It was to become one of the main planks in the opposition's campaign platform in 1975. This was also a period in which serious problems of leadership began to emerge in the opposition ranks, and on the strength of this, public support for the government revived briefly during the early part of 1975 while support for the opposition slumped.

By this time, the two Gallup Polls were again at odds in their picture of public opinion. Late in March 1975, about the time when opposition leader Bill Snedden was ousted and replaced by Malcolm Fraser, Morgan Gallup showed the government in an election-winning position with the support of 49 percent of the sample to the opposition's 44 percent. McNair Gallup may have "missed" this temporary revival because their voting-intention polls were taken in early March and early April. By early April, both McNair and Morgan Gallup were in agreement, with the opposition commanding 49 percent of intended votes and the government 43 percent (Morgan) or 44 percent (McNair).[20]

Consideration of the relative standing of the prime minister and opposition leader during late 1974 and early 1975 provides an important clue to the eventual leadership and party hierarchy reshuffle carried out by the opposition late in March 1975. Figure 8-3 shows that between May 1974 and March 1975, the approval rating of opposition leader Bill Snedden slipped from around 40 percent to just over 30 percent. The important feature of this slide, however, is that it was not downhill all the way. Between October and December 1974, Snedden's rating improved while Whitlam's standing was deteriorating in the midst of the general loss of support for the government.

The important point about Snedden's recovery is that he failed to sustain it into the New Year, and by March 1975 his approval ratings had dropped by nine percentage points to an all-time low of 31 percent. In the same period Whitlam recovered as support for his government strengthened, despite some further controversies surrounding the Labor party power structure, including Cairns's appointment of Junie Morosi in January as his private secretary, the resignation of Labor's speaker of the House of Representatives, Jim Cope, in February, and continuing public gloom over the state of the economy.

A comparison of Figures 8-2 and 8-3 shows that the deterioration of Snedden's approval ratings and of public support for the opposition were linked in the period from December 1974 to March 1975. These trends, coupled with growing criticism in the media of Snedden's leadership qualities and his censure by the government in the House

---

[20] The Saulwick poll published in the *Age* and the *Sydney Morning Herald* early in April disagreed with this. It revealed a government lead over the opposition of three percentage points in the capital cities only. This is in marked contrast to the five to six percentage point lead of the opposition over the government shown in the national samples of McNair and Morgan Gallup at about the same time. This difference may in part be explained by the sample differences of the McNair and Morgan Gallup Polls, but gaps between voting intention results for capital city samples and national samples are rarely of this size.

Figure 8-3

McNAIR GALLUP APPROVAL RATINGS FOR WHITLAM, SNEDDEN, AND FRASER, 1974–75

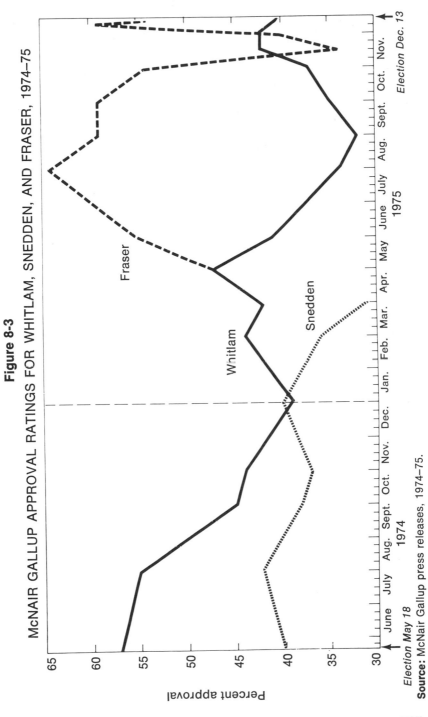

Source: McNair Gallup press releases, 1974–75.

237

of Representatives,[21] paved the way for Malcolm Fraser's swift and successful bid for the opposition leadership together with a fundamental restructuring of the Liberal party power structure. This move set the stage for the coalition's election win in December 1975 and ushered in the Labor government's horror period.

Labor's Horror Period. Studded by a series of leadership incidents, scandals and growing controversy over the role of the press, especially the Murdoch papers, Labor's horror period, from April to November 1975, unfolded against a background of growing public concern about the Australian economy. The period culminated during October in the Senate's blocking of the government's August budget bills and in the dismissal of the government by the governor general early in November. Malcolm Fraser's subsequent winning campaign revolved around the issue of Labor's "competence to govern." This was a combination of trenchant criticism of the government's alleged mishandling of the economy, particularly the problems of inflation and unemployment, and criticism of the behavior of the power elite of the parliamentary Labor party.

That the competence issue was fertile ground for the opposition's electioneering can be seen from analyses of public perceptions of the economy. In Table 8-6 a general view of increasing public pessimism about the economy has been constructed from the ASRB and Saulwick *Age* Polls from April 1974 to September 1975, just prior to the Senate's blocking of supply bills. Over this period, there was a sharp increase in the combined "poor" and "very poor" ratings, reaching a peak (52 percent) in November and December 1974, and a matching trough in the "very good" and "good" ratings, which reached their lowest ebb then and again in September 1975 (14 percent).

A second view of the public's feelings about the economy is derived from a comparison of the data collected by McNair Gallup during March and September 1975 shown in Table 8-7. Respondents were asked whether they thought certain economic indicators including inflation, unemployment, and the number of strikes and industrial disputes were improving or deteriorating. A comparison of the two sets of results for all respondents, irrespective of voting intention, showed a strong conviction that inflation and unemployment were increasing, as were the number of strikes and the level of interest rates. In March the margin between those who felt company profits

---

[21] In the week of March 3-7, 1975, Snedden led an abortive censure motion against Whitlam in the wake of Jim Cope's resignation. Snedden was in turn counterattacked and censured by the government.

Table 8-6

RESPONSES TO ASRB/SAULWICK *AGE* POLL QUESTION:

"Would you say that economic conditions in Australia
are very good, good, fair, poor or very poor?"

| | Response (in percentages) | | | |
| | Very Good | | Poor or | Don't |
Date of Poll	or Good	Fair	Very Poor	know
1974				
April	41	41	19	—
July	25	41	33	1
August	28	43	27	2
September	15	35	49	1
October	23	47	29	1
November	13	35	51	2
December	13	35	52	1
1975				
April	20	45	35	—
June	18	40	42	—
September	14	45	39	2
				(N = 2,000)

Source: *Age Poll Reprint Series*, 1974-75.

were declining and those who felt they were increasing was only two percentage points; by September, the gap had widened to sixteen percentage points, with the majority (51 percent) believing that a decline had set in.

There were some important but expected differences in opinion about these indicators as between intending ALP and L-NCP voters. On the issues of inflation and unemployment during September, for every intending L-NCP voter who believed inflation was declining (9 percent) there were three intending ALP voters with the same belief (27 percent). This pattern was repeated for unemployment. Regarding company profits, for every intending ALP voter who believed they were declining (33 percent), there were nearly two intending L-NCP voters with this belief (62 percent).

Table 8-7

RESPONSES TO McNAIR GALLUP QUESTION:

"Over the *next few months,* do you expect that we will have a declining or increasing rate of inflation / rate of unemployment / number of strikes and industrial disputes / shortage of goods / interest rates / and company profits and dividends?"

	Response (in percentages)	
Question Area	March 1975	September 1975
Inflation		
Declining	32	16
Increasing	62	78
Stable	3	2
Don't know	3	4
Unemployment		
Declining	40	16
Increasing	54	79
Stable	2	2
Don't know	4	3
Strikes and industrial disputes		
Declining	32	20
Increasing	58	72
Stable	4	3
Don't know	6	5
Shortage of goods		
Declining	39	32
Increasing	52	55
Stable	3	4
Don't know	6	9
Interest rates		
Declining	52	30
Increasing	35	53
Stable	5	5
Don't know	8	12
Company profits and dividends		
Declining	44	51
Increasing	42	35
Stable	2	2
Don't know	12	12
	(N = 1,989)	(N = 1,997)

Source: McNair Gallup Poll Press Release, September 25, 1975.

Despite these differences in opinion between government and opposition supporters, the outstanding feature was that the majority of intending ALP voters themselves were convinced of a deterioration in all of the indicators except company profits. In the midst of this wide and growing concern about the economy, the rapid succession of incidents affecting the government's power hierarchy was a formula for the massive deterioration in its public support experienced in the period June to September.[22] The "loans affair" was probably the most significant factor behind the government's poor performance in this period, but it was far from the only one. In late May and early June, just when Deputy Prime Minister Cairns was being identified with attempts by senior cabinet ministers to authorize the raising of a huge petrodollar loan outside of the federal statutory loan-raising procedures and the payment of a hefty commission to brokers, it was also revealed that Cairns's stepson Phillip was engaged in a questionable multimillion dollar business venture while a member of his personal staff. At about the same time, a cabinet reshuffle took place. When Clyde Cameron, the high-ranking minister for labor, refused to accept his demotion there ensued an embarrassing public debacle between Cameron and the prime minister. The Bass by-election, prompted when the defense minister (and former deputy prime minister), Lance Barnard, resigned from Parliament to accept an ambassadorial post in Sweden, gave the L-NCP a sweeping victory over the Labor candidate on June 28.

By late June, controversy over the loans affair and Phillip Cairns's business dealings had reached new heights and this led to the sacking of Cairns as deputy prime minister on July 2. Events moved so quickly in this period that only an opinion poll which was actively interviewing every weekend could cope with measuring the precise impact of each new development. This may explain the sharp upward trend in support for the opposition and the collapse of support for the government during the first week of July, when the Morgan Gallup Poll reported an opposition lead over the government of twenty-seven percentage points in voting intentions (Figure 8-2). In mid-July, Morgan Gallup produced an assessment of public attitudes to the loans affair and to the dismissal of Cairns: while 21 percent of those interviewed were undecided about the government's handling of overseas loan raising, 67 percent disapproved and only 12 percent approved. This sentiment did not, however, carry over to the dismissal of Cairns: in the same poll, 46 percent of respondents said

---

22 For a fuller account of the events mentioned here, see the chapter by Patrick Weller and R. F. I. Smith in this volume, pp. 68-73.

Whitlam had been wrong to sack Cairns, 37 percent said he had been right, and 17 percent were undecided. A McNair Gallup Poll taken about a week after Cairns's dismissal showed that 46 percent disapproved of the way in which Cairns had been handling his job as deputy prime minister while 39 percent approved. The issue of the propriety of the sacking was clearly not synonymous in the public mind with the way in which Cairns had been handling his job.

The public was perhaps in some doubt about the culpability of Cairns, especially after other senior cabinet ministers were implicated in the loans affair. Rex Connor, minister for minerals and energy, was becoming a central figure in the controversy, and at the same time Whitlam's leadership approval ratings were plummeting to his 1975 McNair Gallup low of 32 percent during late July and early August. The bare survival of the Labor government in the state of South Australia during the state elections of July 12 dampened the government's hopes of a reprieve from the downward course of its public support.

The government's losses in this period very quickly became the opposition's gains, and the approval ratings of the opposition leaders, which had been sinking before December 1974, swung upwards to the unprecedented height of 64 percent by early July (Figure 8-3). On his election to the party leadership earlier in the year Fraser had stated that he would not force a double dissolution of the House and Senate unless "extraordinary and reprehensible" circumstances demanded it. In the prevailing climate of public opinion during July and August, the media particularly were clamoring for a definition of these terms and began speculating about when and how they might apply. Although the speculation was ended on October 15, when Fraser opted for blocking the passage of the supply bills through the Senate, several other developments affected the standing of the government, the opposition, and the leaders. The government's Budget was introduced by the new treasurer, Bill Hayden, at a time when Whitlam's popularity was at an all-time low and at about the time when the level of unemployment had reached a new peak of 5 percent of the work force. With Cairns on the backbench, Rex Connor became the principal figure in the loans affair. Prior to the budget session of Parliament, Connor had gone on record about the intended use of the loan money to "buy back the farm" and secure a higher Australian equity in the extraction of natural resources dominated by "multinational" corporations.

The Morgan Gallup Poll took this opportunity to pose the following question in its poll from August 9 to 16:

Next about Mr. Connor, the Minister for Minerals and Energy who wants to borrow a thousand million dollars a year from foreigners, and spend it on energy projects and buying out foreign interests in Australian mineral projects. Do you favour—or oppose—Australia borrowing a thousand million dollars a year from foreigners to do that?

The results showed 58 percent opposed, 27 percent in favor, and 15 percent undecided. But because the question itself supplied information about the loan project, it is not known how many respondents were actually aware of Connor's and the government's plans or how the attitudes of those who were aware and those who were unaware of them might have differed. This did not deter the *Bulletin* from headlining the story in its September 6 issue, "Connor's Loan Plan Not Wanted."

The final crisis of the loans affair came in early to mid-October and involved Connor, Phillip Lynch (deputy leader of the Liberal party), and a London-based loan broker named Tirath Khemlani, now identified with the government's overseas loan-raising efforts. Lynch played a significant role in unearthing information about Connor's dealings with Khemlani, and early in October Khemlani paid a visit to Australia at the height of Lynch's accusations. His visit provided a tense backdrop to the loans affair controversy. By October 15 Connor had resigned from his ministerial position, the "extraordinary and reprehensible circumstances" were deemed by Malcolm Fraser to have arrived, and the opposition senators commenced blocking the money bills.

The next phase of Labor's horror period covered the month-long Senate stalemate and terminated with the government's dismissal by the governor general. This was a period of rapid recovery in support for the government, and of equally rapid decline in support for the opposition. By early November, the opposition was only four percentage points ahead of the government according to the McNair Gallup voting-intention polls (Figure 8-2). At the same time, however, public approval of the way in which Whitlam was handling his job as prime minister (42 percent) overtook the approval of Fraser, which, at 34 percent, was only a shade above Whitlam's all-time low of 32 percent recorded in August. For the second time in 1975, Morgan and McNair disagreed. On this occasion, however, the polls had been conducted at the same time, and Morgan showed Labor in an election-winning position.

The key to this about-face in public opinion was the apparently hostile public reaction to the opposition's blocking tactics in the

Senate. Findings by McNair Gallup, the Saulwick *Age* Poll, and ANOP support this contention. Considered in sequence, each poll sheds increasing light on the public reaction to the blockage. The McNair Gallup Poll taken on the eve of the government's dismissal showed that, while a majority of people felt the Senate should have a right to reject money bills, a majority also believed the opposition was wrong in exercising this power at the time of the poll.

Table 8-8 reveals that the Senate's blocking tactics polarized the views of intending ALP voters and intending L-NCP voters. A majority of intending ALP voters agreed that the constitution should be changed; a majority of L-NCP voters disagreed with this proposition. Likewise, an overwhelming proportion of ALP supporters felt that the Senate was wrong in blocking money bills, but a lesser majority of L-NCP voters considered the Senate to be right in its action.

Apart from the issue of whether it was right or wrong for the opposition to block the supply bills, a different view of opinion was gathered in the Saulwick *Age* Poll, which explored what the public thought should be done to end the stalemate. On the weekend of

Table 8-8

PUBLIC ATTITUDES TOWARD THE SENATE'S BLOCKING OF SUPPLY BILLS, NOVEMBER 1975

Question		Response (in percentages)		
		Total respondents	Intending ALP voters	Intending L-NCP voters
Do you agree or disagree that the Australian constitution should be changed so as to remove from the Senate the right to reject money bills?	Agree	39	59	21
	Disagree	52	32	70
	Don't know	9	9	9
Do you believe that the federal opposition was *right* or *wrong* in attempting to block the money bills in the Senate at the present time?	Right	29	6	53
	Wrong	64	89	39
	Don't know	7	5	8
				(N = 2,057)

Source: McNair Gallup Poll Press Release, November 14, 1975.

October 25-26, respondents were asked whether the government should back down by calling a general election immediately, the opposition should back down by passing supply, or both sides should compromise by agreeing to pass supply on the condition that an election would be held within the next twelve months. Just under half of the respondents (49 percent) opted for a compromise position, and twice as many respondents thought the opposition should back down (33 percent) as thought the government should back down (16 percent). Once again views were polarized around voting intentions: 62 percent of intending ALP voters felt the opposition should back down, but among intending L-NCP voters, 60 percent preferred a compromise to the government's backing down (33 percent).

ANOP's poll of electors in the six state capitals conducted during the first two weekends of November assessed electors' feelings about who was to blame for the supply crisis. The questioning strategy was different from that of McNair Gallup and Saulwick: an open-ended question was used and the responses were coded after the survey had been completed in the field. The results, given in Table 8-9, point to an awareness among electors of the political opportunism of the opposition and to the public's perception of the blocking as a dispute over power rather than over specific identifiable issues. One illustration of this latter point is that only 2 percent attributed the blocking to the loans affair. The explanations most often given were of a general nature: a quarter of the respondents mentioned reasons connected with the idea that the opposition was anxious for an election, and about the same proportion considered the blocking to be a grab for power by a party unable to accept its role in opposition. Among intending ALP voters, the "grab for power" explanation was that most frequently given to explain the blockage.

It is fortunate that, at one of the most significant moments in Australian political history, the public-opinion-gathering apparatus was elaborate enough to provide these insights. It was certainly not a simple matter in the public mind that the Senate block was either right or wrong; but blockage did have the effect of polarizing the views of ALP and L-NCP supporters. Although a compromise solution may have been preferred overall, there was an almost cynical belief in the community that this was in essence a power play by the government and particularly the opposition. Perhaps this mixture of sentiments explains the views elicited by a final question put to the ANOP sample prior to the government's dismissal:

> There is some comment today about the conventions and
> rules of politics. Some people say one particular party is

Table 8-9

RESPONSES TO ANOP QUESTION:

"Why has the Senate not allowed the Government's Supply bills to pass?"

Response Category	Response (in percentages)		
	Total respondents	Intending ALP voters	Intending L-NCP voters
Liberals are anxious for election, are creating an excuse for an election	25	22	28
Liberals cannot accept opposition, are grabbing for power	24	32	17
Liberals feel Labor has mismanaged the country	12	4	20
Fraser is power hungry, a potential dictator, Hitler	7	11	2
Liberals wish to curb government spending, adopt a different economic strategy	6	2	10
Liberals are obstructionist for obstruction's sake, are blocking everything	6	10	3
Both parties are stubborn, uncompromising; each feels it is right	5	4	5
Senate power is being misused; opposition should not block Senate	5	5	4
Fraser was forced into blockage, by business, by false premises	2	2	1
Whitlam is in the wrong, is dishonorable, could become dictator	2	1	3
Specific cause is loans affair	2	1	3
Blockage is a personal contest between Whitlam and Fraser	2	1	2
			(N = 1,600)

Source: *National Times,* November 17-22, 1975, and Australian Broadcasting Commission, "Four Corners" program, November 15, 1975.

breaking the rules more than the other party. Other people say that both parties are breaking the rules. . . . And other people say that both parties are sticking to the rules of politics. Which do you think is happening?

Fifty-eight percent of respondents thought that both parties were breaking the rules. The opposition parties were blamed by 13 percent, the government was blamed by 9 percent, and 12 percent thought that both parties were sticking to the rules.

At a time when the government was making a strong recovery in public support, especially on the strength of the increasing polarization effects, and when Whitlam's approval ratings were in the ascendancy over Fraser's, the penultimate event of Labor's horror period occurred: Sir John Kerr ended the Senate stalement by sacking Whitlam and the Labor government on November 11 and installed Fraser in his place as caretaker prime minister. Shortly after this, an election was set for December 13, leaving only a few weeks for the campaign to be fought.

The first measure of the public reaction to the governor general's sacking of Whitlam was taken by McNair Gallup among a reduced sample of voters in New South Wales and Victoria eleven days after the incident. Respondents were asked whether the governor general had been right or wrong in terminating the commission of Whitlam as prime minister. Fifty-one percent said he was wrong and 46 percent said he was right, with only 3 percent undecided. Once again, there were great differences in outlook as between the intending ALP and L-NCP voters: 88 percent of ALP supporters thought Kerr was wrong and 81 percent of L-NCP supporters thought he was right. One week later, during the weekend of November 29-30, the Saulwick *Age* Poll conducted a more intensive nationwide poll and found voters to be evenly split over the governor general's action. Respondents were asked whether they supported or did not support the action. With 3 percent undecided, 49 percent were in support and 48 percent were not.

At this stage, the election campaign was already under way. Between the first weekend of November and the first weekend of December, the L-NCP and its leader reversed the downward trends in their public support experienced from September through October. By election eve, the polls were forecasting a landslide victory for Fraser.

Public Opinion during the Election Campaign. The public opinion polls differed in their approaches toward monitoring the election campaign. The most novel departure from the generally accepted pattern of replicated sampling was ANOP's ongoing study of a panel of swinging voters drawn from the sample it had interviewed in the capital cities early in November. During the campaign, panel members were reinterviewed three times. Although ANOP did not issue a formal election-eve forecast, its method yielded a remarkably accurate forecast of the election outcome and a rich source of data covering the impact on public opinion of campaign events.

Of the other polls, only Morgan Gallup did not reinterview subsamples of its last main sample in the week of December 8-12. Both McNair Gallup and the Saulwick *Age* Poll did this, and McNair made a drastic revision of its final forecast. In addition, McNair Gallup conducted on election day a survey of voters at polling booths in some marginal electorates of Sydney, in continuation of a series of similar surveys it had made in the 1972 and 1974 federal elections. Morgan Gallup interviewed its national sample on the weekend of the election, both before and after the outcome was known to respondents.

Another postelection study involving respondents to the preelection Saulwick *Age* Poll was conducted by political scientists at the University of Melbourne, also in continuation of work done by this group in 1974.[23] Particular emphasis was placed on explaining the voting behavior of swinging voters identified in the preelection interviewing program. Although a small, geographically concentrated, and rather tentative study, it provided some new understandings of voter behavior during the campaign and the election.

The results of each poll taken from about the time of the Labor government's dismissal to the election itself are shown in their chronological sequence in Table 8-10. In this comparatively short period, the polls revealed a reopening of the wide pre-October gap in support between the ALP and the L-NCP. Likewise, Fraser's ascendancy in personal approval ratings over Whitlam was restored almost overnight (Figure 8-3). Both trends seem clearly related to the differing ways in which the parties and their leaders conducted their campaigns. Fraser intensified his earlier "competence to govern" and economic mismanagement approach. Whitlam campaigned largely on an "indignity of dismissal" theme, emphasizing constitutional issues and the apparent threat to Australian democracy posed by his government's dismissal. The campaign slogans adopted by each party reflected this fundamental difference in their approaches: for the ALP it was "Shame, Fraser, Shame" and for the L-NCP, "Turn on the Lights."

---

[23] Jean Holmes, "Swingers and Stayers, 1974-75," *Politics*, vol. 11 (May 1976), pp. 47-53.

Table 8-10

RESULTS OF ELECTION AND NATIONAL PREELECTION
POLL FORECASTS, NOVEMBER–DECEMBER 1975

		Vote (in percentages)				
		ALP	L-NCP	DLP	Other	Sample Size
ELECTION RESULTS		42.8	53.0	1.3	2.9	
OPINION POLL FORECASTS						
Morgan Gallup						
November	8– 9	47	43	3	7	(985)
	15–16	44	46	3	7	(1,110)
	22–23	42	48	3	7	(1,314)
	29–30	42	53	2	3	(1,201)
December	6– 7	41	55	2	2	(2,729)
McNair Gallup						
November	8– 9	44	48	3	5	(1,922)
	22–23	42	51	2	5	(1,027)
	29–30	38	55	1	6	(1,062)
December	6– 7	40	53	2	5	(2,168)
	12	42	52	1	5	(157)[b]
Saulwick Age						
November	29–30	44.0	52.3	1.0	2.7	(2,000)
December	6– 7	40.2	52.8	2.0	5.0	(2,000)
	10	40.0	52.8	2.1	5.0	(200)[b]
ANOP[a]						
November	1– 2	46	49	1	2	(800)
	8– 9	51	45	1	2	(800)
December	3– 4	43	52	1	4	(143)[b]

[a] Poll taken in capital cities only—Sydney, Melbourne, Brisbane, Adelaide, Perth, Hobart.

[b] Based on reinterviews with panels selected from earlier samples. Saulwick *Age* and McNair Gallup reinterviewed panels once only; ANOP conducted three successive reinterviews with members of the same panel between November 19 and December 4.

Source: Press releases by Morgan Gallup Poll, November-December 1975, and McNair Gallup Poll, November-December 1975; *Age,* December 6, 10, and 13, 1975; *National Times,* December 8-13, 1975.

The turnaround in support for the parties and their leaders was monitored by the ANOP panel of swinging voters, defined on a series of commitment and party-loyalty scales and demographic measures rather than on the basis of a respondent's past vote versus his intended vote. In the main capital-cities survey taken from November 1-9, 143 of the 1,600 respondents (9 percent) were so defined, and it was found that of these, 47 percent were uncommitted, 28 percent leaned toward Labor, and 25 percent leaned towards the L-NCP coalition. These voters formed the panel and they were all reinterviewed in their homes once a week between November 19 and December 4. In each of the reinterviews respondents were asked for their opinion of the main issue of the election campaign. This was posed as an open-ended question and Table 8-11 shows how the early preoccupations about "rules and conventions" gave way in the minds of these swinging and undecided voters to the "economic management" theme. The leadership theme died in the space of a week, as did criticism of the power of the governor general. Interestingly, the "Labor scandals" theme, particularly the loans affair, never took on any prominence in the swinging voters' nomination of campaign issues.

At the broader level of all electors the Saulwick *Age* Poll on the weekend of December 6-7 asked respondents to rank in order of importance nine election campaign issues. The results revealed a preoccupation with the economic mismanagement theme similar to that found in the ANOP panel study, but further important insights into the differences between intending ALP and L-NCP voters were gained. ALP voters saw the main issues as: the dismissal of the Whitlam government (29 percent), the refusal of the Senate to pass supply (20 percent), pensions and social services (18 percent), and unemployment (9 percent). L-NCP voters saw the key issues as inflation (27 percent), economic management (24 percent), dishonesty and inefficiency in government (15 percent), and strikes (12 percent). According to the McNair Gallup election-day survey, these sentiments pervaded the decisions of those who were interviewed after having cast a vote.[24]

At the time of the last ANOP panel interview on December 3 and 4, a crystallizing of support was found to have occurred among the swingers: the proportion of uncommitted voters had declined from the original 47 percent to 10 percent, those who were leaning towards the ALP accounted for 30 percent, and those leaning towards the

---

[24] McNair Anderson Associates, *Reasons for the Swing Back to the Liberals: The Federal Election December 13, 1975.* Report prepared for the Australian Broadcasting Commission, December 1975.

Table 8-11

MAIN CAMPAIGN ISSUE, PERCEIVED BY ANOP PANEL
OF SWINGING VOTERS, NOVEMBER–DECEMBER 1975

Response Category	Response (in percentages)		
	First reinterview Nov. 19–20	Second reinterview Nov. 26–27	Third reinterview Dec. 3–4
Rules and conventions: respect for rules, the constitution; blockage of supply; sacking of prime minister; unfair tactics; right of an elected government	41	32	27
Economic management: the economy, inflation, Australia's prosperity	21	30	37
Leadership: Whitlam versus Fraser, the better man, the best leader	15	3	2
Stable government: frequency of elections, government's right to see out its elected term	8	17	18
Power of the governor general: limits of vice-regal power	6	1	1
Labor scandals: totality of Labor gaffes	3	3	3
Unemployment	2	5	3
Terrorism: bombings, radical fringe groups	1	1	—
Other	5	6	5
Unsure	6	3	4
	(N = 120)	(N = 143)	(N = 143)

Source: *National Times*, December 8-13, 1975.

L-NCP coalition accounted for 60 percent. This suggests that only about 0.9 percent of the original ANOP sample of 1,600 were approaching the election in a totally uncommitted frame of mind.

The University of Melbourne study conducted the day after the election throws some additional light on the turnaround of voting intentions in the campaign period, but it must be cautioned that this study used a definition of the swinging voter different from the one used by ANOP, and interviewing was conducted by a student group. A swinging voter was defined as someone who had previously voted for a party other than the one he or she had supported in the December 13, 1975 election. Opinion pollsters might take issue with this definition since public opinion polls do not have a good record for eliciting accurate recall of how people voted in previous elections. Some respondents are cagey when asked to state which party they supported, and many are apt to forget or say they don't know.

According to the study, 70 persons (23 percent) out of a sample of 300 Melbourne voters who voted either ALP or L-NCP in 1975 were defined as swinging voters. Minor-party swinging voting was found to be almost entirely negligible. The trend was mainly from an earlier ALP vote to an intended L-NCP vote. Half of those who made the change had reached this decision before the election campaign started, another quarter decided to swing about two weeks before the election, and the remaining quarter about a week before. In fact, of the 70 persons, only one was found to have left his decision to vote L-NCP to polling day itself. Among those interviewed, the swing to the coalition hinged on an unfavorable judgment of the competence of Labor to govern and on Labor's economic mismanagement. This combination of themes occurred repeatedly in the interviews with swinging voters. For the few who claimed to have swung to the ALP, their principal explanation was the constitutional "rules and conventions" theme.

In an attempt to identify the sociodemographic character of swinging voters, measures were made of key variables such as birthplace, education, religion, age, occupation, sex, and social class. The researchers were led to conclude that the sample's responses "demonstrated no link between background social data and the propensity to change a party vote." While this may be in part acceptable, some caution is needed simply on the grounds of the unavoidably small size of the survey sample and the data-analysis strategy employed. One interesting conclusion of the Melbourne analysts was the suggestion that swinging voters were likely to be distinguished from other voters by the level of difficulty they had in deciding how to vote. It was found that the harder the decision for the voter, the later he or she adopted a definite course of action, and this was particularly the case among the small number who swung to the ALP. Three-quarters of those who swung to the L-NCP found the decision relatively easy, but among those who swung to the ALP over half found it a difficult decision to make.

In the course of the Melbourne study, one voter made the response: "I feel sorry for Labor—but they have made a mess of it." Perhaps this person was speaking for a large proportion of the Australian population. Throughout the campaign, ANOP discovered an interesting dichotomy in the attitudes of its panel members. When asked, "Irrespective of which party you support, who deserves to win?" there was a constant, although diminishing, majority view that Labor deserved to win. A second question, along similar lines but with the rider, "Who will win?" produced in the November 1-9 capital-cities survey a majority view (44 percent) that Labor would win, with 40 percent expecting a win by the L-NCP coalition. Sixteen percent were undecided. In the final panel reinterview early in December, only 18 percent expected Labor to win, while 68 percent expected an L-NCP win, with 14 percent undecided. At the same time, however, 47 percent of the same swinging voters thought Labor deserved to win while 39 percent thought the coalition deserved to win.

In what has become widely acknowledged as the most bitter and emotional election campaign in Australia's political history, an almost cynical dissonance was apparent in the voters' views of the recent political events. On the one hand, they were willing to take a sympathetic view of what had happened to Whitlam and the Labor government, but on the other hand they wanted to relegate this to the past and to vote on the basis of competence to govern—with economic management as the key issue. By campaigning on the "indignity of dismissal" theme, Whitlam and the Labor party were backing the loser in the race. In view of the economic events, hierarchical reshuffles, affairs and scandals, Labor was ill-placed to counterattack and defuse the competence-to-govern platform of Malcolm Fraser.

Conclusion

An appreciation of the opinion polls in the 1975 election would be incomplete without a more careful scrutiny of their performance in the campaign period. Although no wrong forecasts appeared in the final poll releases, some curious anomalies among the polls came to light when the results of each successive measure taken during the campaign period are compared. Particular attention should be paid to the measures shown in Table 8-10. They reveal serious disagreement and contradictions about the relative positions of the parties as the election drew nearer. One critic went so far as to state: "It is a misconception to claim that 'the polls were right' in 1975." [25] While this remark might have better applied to certain of the preelection forecasts, there is a need to examine closely the precise trends in opinion depicted by the various polls.

The Morgan Gallup Poll suggested that if an election had been conducted on November 8, Labor might have been in a winning position, particularly with a minimal DLP vote and some favorable preference allocations from the other parties and independent candidates to the ALP. Labor had 47 percent of the vote and the L-NCP had 43 percent. Thereafter, Labor's share of the vote dropped sharply, by five percentage points, in the next two weeks and remained fairly steady until the election itself. The L-NCP improved to 55 percent. McNair Gallup revealed a different progression of events for Labor. It suggested that Labor, at 44 percent, would have been defeated in a November 8 election. It then revealed a serious Labor slump to 38 percent on November 29, whereupon Labor recovered to 40 percent as the election approached. The Saulwick *Age* Polls, taken separately in the last weekend of November and first weekend of December, showed the ALP dropping by a significant four percentage points. This was at a time when McNair Gallup was showing an ALP recovery and Morgan Gallup was showing a slight drop of one percentage point in ALP support.

When examining opinion poll estimates, one must keep survey errors clearly in mind. The fact that these polls were taken largely at the same times probably eliminates many of the problems arising from comparing polls with different fieldwork dates, and the possibility of specific events' affecting one poll and not another. If we assume, however, that the forecasts issued were the best estimates, then the anomaly of the early November Morgan and McNair Gallup readings is hard to explain. Although not strictly comparable in sample coverage, ANOP's findings in the capital cities did lean towards the Morgan Gallup estimates, where Labor was in a strong position to win an election. The other differences in trends between early November and the election may have been chance errors, since several measures were released on the basis of half samples, but the trends in support during the campaign were fundamentally different on each poll from Labor's point of view.

The results of the McNair Gallup reinterviewing program in the week prior to the election are more perplexing. Both Saulwick and McNair Gallup reinterviewed voters on the Tuesday and Wednesday

[25] Rodney Cameron, "Public Opinion Polls and the Federal Election 1975," Press Release by ANOP, December 17, 1975.

of election week. The final Saulwick *Age* Poll released on election day suggested that the situation for the ALP and the coalition had not changed from the previous weekend. McNair Gallup's result published on December 12 ran counter to this and showed that the ALP had gained two percentage points since the previous weekend. Evidence of a change of this magnitude was not apparent in the results of the McNair Gallup reinterviews published during election week. Only 1 percent of the 156 swinging voters who were reinterviewed had shifted their support to the ALP. In terms of the 2,168 persons from whom the swinging voters were originally drawn, this represents a gross shift of less than one-tenth of one percentage point towards Labor. As no other information was published by McNair Gallup to support the two percentage point upward amendment of the ALP voting intention, this anomaly remains unexplained.

Clearly, the new era of opinion polling in Australia has introduced many and divergent perspectives on public opinion. After the long period when the existence of a single opinion poll in a modern democracy was criticized, Australia is now faced with controversy about its polling record and the motives of its pollsters. The apparent success of the polls in forecasting election winners has obscured a number of fundamental contradictions about the status of party support both between elections and in the election campaigns. It has also become easier than ever before for the polls to become pawns in the hands of the country's concentrated publishing empires; this was particularly true in the 1975 election, when the Murdoch press waged its campaign against Labor. As a result, at least some people in the community may become increasingly suspicious of the pollsters' motives and may not cooperate as readily as they have in the past with opinion poll interviewers. On the other hand, there is some hope that a more intensive academic and public interest in the pollsters' craft and in surveys in general is appearing and that this new interest may influence for the good the rules by which the polling game is played.

9

AUSTRALIA'S FOREIGN POLICY AND THE ELECTIONS OF 1972 AND 1975

Owen Harries

Foreign policy was not a decisive issue in the elections which brought the Whitlam government to office in 1972, nor in the elections which settled the question of Labor's removal from office in 1975. In the first, leadership and social policy issues dominated. In the second, despite the fact that the campaign coincided with a difficult local crisis in Portuguese Timor (one which raised delicate questions concerning relations with Indonesia, Australia's most significant neighbor), the management of the economy was clearly the overriding issue.

But to say that foreign policy was not of major importance in the two elections is not the same as saying that the two elections were unimportant for foreign policy. The salience of an issue in an election depends much more on how contentious it is than on its innate importance. It is contention that makes an "issue"; if there is consensus and bipartisanship (or if one party fails to advance a position), then, however serious the matter is considered, it will not provide a ground for battle. Moreover, the priorities and perceptions of the electorate in making its choice are not necessarily those of the leaders it chooses, and after the election the latter are more significant than the former. Certainly in 1972, and probably in 1975, the leaders on the winning sides attached more importance to foreign policy and felt the need for change more urgently than did the electorate at large.

Certainly, too, commentators of various persuasions have concluded that the period 1972–75 was one of enormous significance in Australian foreign policy, involving very substantial discontinuity with the preceding period. The preface of one book published in 1973 begins by stating flatly that "1972 was a watershed in Australian foreign policy,"[1] and one of the academic chroniclers of Whitlam's

---

[1] David Pettit, *Selected Readings in Australian Foreign Policy* (Melbourne: Sorrell Publishing, 1973), p. 7.

foreign policy, writing in 1975, asserted that "Australian foreign policy since 1972 had undergone an alteration in style and direction probably unprecedented in the experience of any sovereign state which had not been subjected to a domestic political revolution."[2] As we shall see, there are many who contest these evaluations. But the very fact that it has been possible to advance them with some plausibility (and, indeed, the fact that they can be contested, which suggests ambiguity and novelty) establishes that, however secondary foreign policy has been as an election issue in recent years, the consequences of the elections for foreign policy have been far from negligible. To understand the nature and significance of these consequences, it is necessary to know something of the situation as it was prior to the Whitlam period.

Background to 1972

By the early 1970s the structure of foreign policy which had been erected by Sir Robert Menzies, and which had survived without serious challenge for the best part of two decades, had been seriously undermined. Menzies's foreign policy had both the virtues and vices of simplicity. Fundamental to it was an acceptance of the cold war as the central fact of international politics, the fact around which policy had to be built. This acceptance was certainly sincere (a history of support for appeasement in the thirties helped to make Menzies, like many others, a vigorous advocate of firm resistance to totalitarian pressures in the fifties), but it was also very convenient in a number of ways.

The central tradition of Australian foreign policy, especially when government has been in non-Labor hands, has been dependence on an identification with one or more of the great Western powers. Until World War II this power had naturally been Great Britain; but that war, and later the withdrawal of Britain from the Indian sub-continent, emphasized Britain's inadequacy as a protector. Attempts immediately after the war to get the United States to assume the role were unsuccessful, but the cold war and America's assumption of the leadership of a global system of anti-Communist alliances solved the problem by making the greatest power on earth available as Australia's ally. Moreover, it did so without necessitating a breaking of the old and emotionally strong link with Britain. In addition, the American emphasis on Asia after the Communist success in China and

---

[2] G. St. J. Barclay, "Problems in Australian Foreign Policy, July-December, 1974," *Australian Journal of Politics and History*, vol. 21, no. 1 (April 1975), p. 1.

the Korean War fitted in well with Australia's needs, for the emergence of postcolonial Southeast Asia as an area of instability and conflict was deeply disquieting for a large, sparsely populated, Anglo-Saxon country in the Pacific. The United States's commitment to the containment of Chinese communism and Australia's concern with "forward defense" and regional stability went hand-in-hand.

In terms of domestic politics, too, the cold war was extremely helpful to Menzies. As long as it was the central issue in foreign policy, his Labor opponents were at an electoral disadvantage. The ALP was divided in its attitudes towards communism and equivocal towards the cold war. The party included many strong and effective anti-Communists, but it also included some who were tolerant and sympathetic towards communism, some who were simply vulnerable to pressure from Communist-dominated trade unions, and others who, while not particularly pro-Communist, were unhappy about having to accept alliance with a capitalist superpower. The result was that the ALP's foreign policy was always something of a balancing act; while it formally accepted the reality of the cold war and the policy represented by the ANZUS and SEATO treaties, it did so in a spirit that emphasized qualifications and reservations. It suffered from the weakness of neither supporting nor opposing the existing policy with any conviction. Menzies was able to exploit this to great effect, and in the process foreign policy tended to become entwined with domestic politics to an unusual, and probably undesirable, degree. After the tensions over communism led to the "split" in the Labor movement in the mid-fifties,[3] he further enjoyed the benefit of the existence of a bitterly anti-Communist DLP, always vigilant in exposing ALP foreign policy equivocations and dependable in delivering its electoral preferences to the Liberal-Country party coalition.

Everything else in Menzies's foreign policy was subordinated to the goal of maintaining and strengthening relations with those he rejoiced in describing as "our great and powerful friends." To this end Australian troops fought in Korea and (along side the British) in Malaya and later in Borneo during Sukarno's "confrontation"; Australia provided communication bases for the United States on its soil; China went unrecognized; and in due time 8,000 Australian troops went to fight in Vietnam. More generally, the Menzies government diligently followed the American and British lead in the councils and forums of international politics. Relations with the new states of Asia

---

[3] See Robert Murray, *The Split: Australian Labor in the Fifties* (Melbourne: Cheshire, 1970) for an account of these events.

were treated mainly as a function of the great-power relationship and were characterized by an uneasy mixture of paternalism and wariness.

For a decade and a half this policy worked well for Menzies and satisfied most Australians. They felt safely insulated from the mess and threats of Asian politics, the cost of the alliances seemed remarkably low, and they had a sense of participating in a great ideological struggle which was important for such an isolated community. But even in the heyday of the Menzies policy, and even if its broad framework were accepted, serious criticisms could be made of the way Menzies implemented it. He assumed too readily not merely a harmony but an identity of interests between Australia and its allies, an identity which could not possibly exist between a smallish regional power and two great powers. His anticommunism became increasingly coarse and facile, uninformed and unargued; and he seemed to proceed on the assumption that international politics had somehow "set" in a permanent pattern, that the cold war could never end. As a result, commitments and rhetoric were shaped in an unqualified and absolute way which showed little appreciation of the possibility of change.

The Changes of the Late Sixties. But from the mid-sixties changes came apace and things began to go seriously wrong. Vietnam, originally a very popular cause in Australia, turned sour.[4] The British, harassed by chronic economic difficulties and uncertain about their international role, announced their withdrawal from Asia. The cold war, already made ambiguous by polycentrism and the Sino-Soviet conflict, became a shaky framework for policy with the advent of détente. Nearer home, the Guam doctrine and Nixon's overtures to China dissolved the familiar scenario and presaged a more complex and uncertain future. Seen in historical perspective, what was happening represented a familiar phenomenon: a small country, having invested heavily in an alliance with great powers, was left embarrassed and unprepared as those great powers made major adjustments and accommodations in terms of their own perceptions and interests and without much sensitivity to the concerns of their smaller partners.

But in this instance the process was made more complicated and difficult because it coincided with significant changes in Australian domestic politics. In January 1966 Menzies retired after seventeen years as prime minister. His going meant not only that men who had

---

[4] For an account of the Vietnam issue in Australian politics, see Henry Abinski, *Politics and Foreign Policy in Australia: The Impact of Vietnam* (Durham: Duke University Press, 1970).

languished in his shadow and were seriously deficient in their knowledge of, and feel for, foreign policy had to face the new problems, but also that serious instabilities and power rivalries began to emerge in the ruling coalition. After being led by one man for the first twenty-two years of its existence, the Liberal party was to have five different leaders in ten years.

In these circumstances it is hardly surprising that there was no convincing and coherent response to the changes occurring in the international environment. Successive leaders wavered among hastily assembled and badly thought out "options"—redoubled loyalty to the American alliance, "fortress Australia," a substitute alliance with Japan, a modified version of forward defense in the company of some Asian states, even the notion of welcoming the Soviet Union as a counterweight to China. Some sensible initiatives were taken— the highly discriminatory "white Australia" immigration policy was modified, for example, and the preparation of the Australian territory of Papua New Guinea for independence was accelerated. Nevertheless, on the central questions there was a failure to find and articulate some organizing concept around which a new foreign policy could be constructed. So the old shibboleths were repeated, with diminishing conviction.

To be fair to the post-Menzies leaders, their task of adjusting to changing circumstances was made more difficult by their dependence on the Democratic Labor party. Cold war anticommunism was the raison d'être of the DLP and was not negotiable. In the old days this had been perfectly acceptable because it had tied the DLP to the coalition. But events in the late sixties brought home the fact that the equation worked both ways: if the DLP, determined to keep an ideologically suspect Labor party out of office, had no option but to support the coalition with its voting preferences, the Liberal and Country parties, dependent on those preferences in an electorally uncertain situation, had little option but to make concessions to the DLP. The concession the DLP wanted was the retention of an inflexible anti-Communist line. Just how serious a constraint this involved became apparent in 1969, an election year, when the minister for foreign affairs tentatively accepted a Russian naval presence in the Indian Ocean as a normal development and showed some interest in Brezhnev's collective security proposal. A sharp DLP reaction caused the government to retreat precipitately. The anticipation of a repetition of such a reaction must have influenced government thinking on a range of issues, including the recognition of China.

The coalition government was thus in something of a trap: if it did not change its policies, it would appear increasingly dated and inflexible; if it did, it would run the risk of alienating DLP electoral support. A government that knew its own mind and was firmly led might have resisted DLP pressure and called its bluff in the belief that the DLP would not dare withdraw support for the coalition and risk letting Labor into office; but for a government which was uncertain and internally divided, the DLP's position was seriously inhibiting. (In fact, it might even have been welcome to some, as an alibi for indecision.)

While these changes were occurring on one side of Australian politics, changes of equal significance for foreign policy were happening on the other. A year after Menzies's retirement Whitlam became leader of the ALP. As well as being an articulate and intelligent man of great energy, who was determined to modernize his party and provide it with a comprehensive program, Whitlam had a particular interest in foreign policy and had gone to great trouble to inform himself about it. The disarray of the government was made-to-measure for a man of Whitlam's debating skill, and he launched a sustained and savage attack on the government's foreign policy as outmoded, ideological, intellectually bankrupt, and subservient. He focused heavily on the Vietnam issue (on which he had earlier taken a rather guarded position) and increasingly on the question of the recognition of China. Quite apart from Whitlam, events were now favoring the ALP in the field of foreign policy more than they had for two decades. Its reservations about the cold war, which had been a serious electoral handicap in the 1950s, were suddenly fashionable. The internal turmoil in the United States and the United States's qualification of its Asian commitments seemed to make more valid the ALP's traditional argument for a more independent foreign policy and a less total identification with the United States.

As so often happens in such a situation, even luck seemed to favor the party whose stocks were rising. In April 1971, in the wake of the loss of a wheat contract with China (Australia had carried on a substantial trade with China for a decade, despite non-recognition), the ALP publicly sought an invitation to send a delegation to Peking. It was a bold and risky move. There was no certainty that the Chinese government would respond and even if it did, China represented such an emotional issue in Australian politics that a visit might end disastrously. After a worrying four weeks' delay, an invitation finally came and Whitlam announced that he would lead the delegation himself. It spent twelve days in China (July 2–14, 1971), was received by Chou En-lai, and had extended discussions not only about trade but also about recognition and general foreign policy issues.

In itself, the delegation's performance was not so unambiguously successful that it guaranteed political advantage. But the opposition had a piece of collossal good fortune that made this unimportant. Unbeknown either to Whitlam or the Australian government, Whitlam's visit coincided exactly with Kissinger's secret visit to arrange the Nixon summit meeting. This only became known when the government had committed itself to an outright attack on Whitlam's performance, claiming that he had been duped and exploited by the Chinese. The effect was devastating. More than anything else, it served to symbolize the government's lack of understanding of and inability to respond to the trend of events; and more than anything else, it vested Whitlam with an aura of statesmanship, the authority of a national leader in tune with the times.[5]

In the light of all this, the fact that foreign policy was not a major issue in 1972 may seem odd. It will seem less so if the following points are kept in mind: (1) The government parties had every reason to play foreign policy down in the campaign, and they did so. In his policy speech, Prime Minister McMahon devoted only a few short paragraphs to it and managed not to mention Vietnam at all. (2) While the initiative in this area had shifted to the ALP, there was still considerable uncertainty as to the electorate's willingness to accept major changes. It was an article of faith among pro-Labor commentators that the Australian people were characterized by a deep-seated "threat mentality" and that the attitudes which had supported the earlier policy were deeply ingrained. There was, therefore, even among the ALP, a sense of caution about pushing too hard on this front. (3) There was no shortage of other issues that carried lesser risks and that were electorally more attractive because they had larger "attentive publics."

To this might be added the final qualification that, while it was not a major issue, foreign policy *was* an issue—not only directly but as a dimension of the "quality of leadership" question, which was major. There is no doubt that Whitlam's stature was significantly enhanced by the assurance he showed in articulating his party's

---

[5] For a sympathetic account of the China visit see Stephen Fitzgerald, *Talking with China: The Australian Labor Party's Visit and Peking's Foreign Policy*, Contemporary China Papers no. 4 (Canberra: A.N.U. Press, 1972). Fitzgerald, an academic with a foreign service background, accompanied the ALP party to China. He was subsequently appointed Australia's ambassador to China by the Whitlam government.

foreign policy and in criticizing that of his opponents. Here, it was widely agreed, was a man of whom Australians need not be ashamed as their spokesman in international affairs. The corresponding uncertainty and lack of aplomb shown by McMahon in the same area contributed to his loss of support.

The Whitlam Years

The Whitlam government began with a flurry of activity in foreign policy. During December 1972 and January 1973, it recognized the People's Republic of China and the German Democratic Republic; it withdrew the remaining 150 Australian military instructors from South Vietnam and foreshadowed aid to North Vietnam; it made an official protest to Washington against the resumption of U.S. bombing of Hanoi and Haiphong (several of its ministers supplemented this with public references to American leaders as "maniacs" and "mass murderers"); it initiated moves to end the remaining ties between the Australian and British legal systems and abolished the system of granting British honors to Australian citizens; it announced a tougher and more hostile policy towards Rhodesia and South Africa; and it made clear its intention of accelerating the independence of Papua New Guinea, whatever the wishes of the territory's own leaders, in order to rid Australia of a colonialist image.

While all this reflected the new government's concern to register its presence and to respond to the expectations which had built up among its supporters after two decades of frustration, it also anticipated what were to be some distinguishing characteristics of the Whitlam government's future conduct of foreign policy: a pronounced concern with being active and taking initiatives, the importance attached to establishing an independent stance, the attention given to projecting a favorable international image, and the playing down of the military power aspects of foreign policy.

Within a year, furious activity and almost perpetual motion were firmly established as part of the Whitlam style. By August 1973 an admiring journalist was writing of the prime minister's international progress in terms of

> a rushing kaleidoscope of events, names, places and faces, hotels and airports, sights, sounds, speeches, impressions, each blurring one into another. It has been a punishing pace. To say that Mr. Whitlam's fifth visit abroad as Prime Minister in eight months has been his most demanding is to

understate the obvious. It almost beggars description. Yet already he talks of his sixth. . . ."[6]

Despite Talleyrand's famous admonition to the contrary, Whitlam seemed to proceed at times on the assumption that zeal and energy would bring their own rewards, that taking initiatives was desirable in itself.

But this activism was also organically connected with other aspects of policy and was functionally necessary in political terms. It was directly related to the concern with independence, or the appearance of independence. In opposition, Whitlam had constantly berated his opponents for their alleged reluctance to make their own judgments and decisions, and in his first press conference as prime minister he declared the establishment of "a more independent Australian stance in international affairs" to be one of the main aims of his foreign policy. The busyness and the initiatives were largely a demonstration of this new independence, a means of asserting that from now on Australia was to be an actor, not merely a passive reactor, in international affairs.

The urge in this direction was strengthened by the view, which was widely accepted at the time, that for the first time in a generation the international scene was fluid and changing, instead of fixed and static. At the beginning of 1973, talk of multipolarity, of new power centers, increasing complexity, and the possibility of realignments was at its height. Détente and the American rapprochement with China, as well as the winding up of the Vietnamese war, lent credence to such interpretations. They were certainly views to which Whitlam subscribed. Writing immediately before the 1972 election, he had asserted, "We are entering a period of unparalleled complexity in international relations" and had presented as his basic theme on Australian foreign policy the opportunity created by this complexity.[7]

The new atmosphere was highly congenial to Whitlam. At home and abroad he was temperamentally drawn towards change and innovation, towards the possibilities of fluidity rather than the advantages of stability and order. Both in terms of personal ambition (and this was largely focused on the international scene) and of finding a role for Australia, a world presumed to be in a state of transition and flux offered more opportunity than a tightly ordered one in which conventional power considerations clearly prevailed.

---

[6] *Australian*, August 14, 1973.

[7] Gough Whitlam, "Australia and Her Region," in John McLaren, ed., *Towards a New Australia* (Melbourne: Cheshire, 1972), pp. 3-4.

Whitlam has often been accused of not paying due attention to power factors in foreign affairs. The London *Economist*, for example, once noted that a characteristic of the key terms he used in relation to foreign policy was "the looseness of their connection with the facts of power and of national self-interest"; [8] and in an article written early in Whitlam's term, this writer observed that the prime minister often proceeded as if "quickness of mind and fleetness of foot, combined with unrelenting busyness, can outwit the logic of power." [9] On reflection, it might be more accurate to say that Whitlam gave great, perhaps inordinate, weight to such things as voting strength in international organizations, moral pressure, and "world opinion" as sources of power, while playing down conventional military strength. During Labor's time in opposition his pleas for more independence had characteristically gone hand-in-hand with demands that Australia should become more in step with world opinion—that is, the independence he was concerned with had been limited to independence from Australia's traditional, great-power allies; it had implied endorsement of greater conformity to the norms of the nonaligned majority. Once Labor was in office, this translated into a concern with being "well regarded"—another of Whitlam's favorite terms—by the nonaligned countries, and consequently into a conspicuous stress on rather moralistic rhetoric and on a conceptualization of the world in terms of the division between the great and the smaller powers. This reflected and satisfied the deep-set distrust of "power politics" which existed in the Labor party, a distrust that could find expression both in nationalistic isolationism and in idealistic internationalism.

The disinclination to give weight to conventional power and military factors was more directly evident in the Labor government's neglect of defense. The election promise to maintain defense spending at 3.5 percent of the GNP was not kept. The defense budget fell below 3 percent. In addition, pay raises and inflation meant that the proportion spent on military capital equipment fell well below 10 percent of the defense budget. The neglect of defense was justified by a strategic assessment which maintained that there were "no foreseeable threats" for ten to fifteen years, an assessment which was often interpreted, at least until public criticism prompted greater caution, as meaning that a threat-free period of that duration could be taken for granted. This interpretation was partly a reaction against the emphasis that had been placed on military threat in the pre-1972

---

[8] *Economist*, June 23-29, 1973.
[9] Owen Harries, "Mr. Whitlam and Australian Foreign Policy," *Quadrant* (Sydney), August 1973.

period—the alleged "threat mentality" of the fifties and sixties which the Labor party had so consistently condemned in opposition. But it also reflected basic ideological attitudes towards international politics which stressed the primacy of economic and social conditions as motivating forces.

All this represented one side of the Whitlam government's foreign policy. But in its totality that policy was to be considerably more complex and ambiguous. For, despite Whitlam's activism, the constraints on Australian foreign policy were considerable; and, despite the government's criticisms of the United States, the alliance with America, embodied in the ANZUS treaty, formed the cornerstone of the country's foreign policy and was supported by most Australians. Furthermore, while Australia was a smallish power, it was also a very rich Western democracy. The result was that the Whitlam government's policy was characterized by what was variously described as a sophisticated balancing act, internal contradictions, or a cynical inconsistency between substance and appearance. These characteristics, as well as the different perceptions and evaluations of the commentators themselves, are what led to the highly contrasting interpretations that have been offered of that policy. Before considering these interpretations it is necessary to describe some of the ambiguities as they developed in key areas between the end of 1972 and the end of 1975.

The United States and the West. As far as relations with Western powers were concerned, the initial public attack on the United States proved not to be an isolated outburst. The flow of criticism that followed reached such proportions that at one point one of the country's soberest newspapers ran an editorial commenting on it under the headline "Bash a Yank a Day." [10] American "militarism" was regularly attacked and the proposed extension of American facilities at Diego Garcia opposed in the interest of the neutralization of the Indian Ocean, which the Australian government supported. American (and other Western) multinational companies became favorite villains and at various times were blamed for most of Australia's economic ills and some of its political ones. The government developed a resource policy aimed at reducing the control of these multinationals over the Australian mining industry and forcing the industrial countries to pay more for Australian mineral resources, in the process lending support to Third World proposals for producer cartels to gain economic and political leverage. In the United Nations,

---

[10] *Australian Financial Review*, June 26, 1973.

Australia's voting pattern changed significantly, moving away from the American and British positions and towards those of the non-aligned nations on issues such as the granting of immediate independence to residual small colonial territories, the granting of observer status to the Palestine Liberation Organization, and the expulsion of South Africa. In the first year relations with France also soured badly, as a major campaign, including recourse to the International Court, was launched to condemn and prevent French nuclear testing in the Pacific (a campaign that stood in sharp contrast to the very muted comments made about the Chinese tests which were proceeding at the same time).

But as against all this, the Whitlam government, like its Liberal and Country party predecessors, repeatedly insisted on the centrality of the ANZUS alliance in its foreign policy. Despite strong and emotional pressure from the left wing of its own party and from the trade union movement, the government honored the agreements under which the United States maintains important tracking, communications, and space research bases in Australia. In the promised renegotiation of these agreements, the government settled for minimal face-saving concessions. Even with SEATO, which Whitlam had strongly criticized and dismissed as moribund, the government responded to American pressure and remained a member of the organization.

Asia. The same tension or ambiguity is apparent in the Whitlam government's relations with Asian countries. Before assuming office, Whitlam had singled out relations with Japan as being of special importance. Indeed, given the dynamic character of the Japanese economy, Japan's potential political importance, and the fact that Japan is Australia's main trading partner, this seemed indisputable. But once in government, Whitlam virtually ignored Japan for most of his first year. For a man who placed such reliance on personal contact, it is significant that not until his sixth journey abroad did he visit that country. Whitlam recognized that "not only Australia but every State in the region has a vital interest in Japanese policies and the way in which Japan conducts its foreign affairs affects every one of us directly."[11] Nevertheless, when he did get there, he approached Australian-Japanese relations essentially in the narrow context of the government's nationalistic resources policy, with Australia taking a very tough negotiating position. When Whitlam

[11] E. G. Whitlam, *Australia's Foreign Policy: New Directions, New Definitions* (Canberra: Australian Institute of International Affairs, 1973), p. 8.

ceased to be prime minister at the end of 1975, the Nippon-Australian Relations Agreement, which he had proposed with considerable fanfare two years earlier, had still not become a reality.

In Southeast Asia, Whitlam supported ASEAN (the Association of South East Asian Nations, comprising Indonesia, Malaysia, the Philippines, Singapore, and Thailand) as a natural grouping concerned with regional development and stability and endorsed its aspiration to make the region a "zone of peace, freedom and neutrality." Australia withdrew the forces it had kept in Singapore under the ANZUK agreement, and it was claimed that never again would an Australian force be sent to fight in an Asian dispute.

But again there was another side. Despite his recognition that "patience, tact and diplomacy" [12] were required in dealing with the countries of Southeast Asia, Whitlam himself did not characteristically manifest these qualities. He had an acrimonious public dispute with Lee Kuan Yew, the prime minister of Singapore, whose views on both the strategic problems of the area and multinational corporations differed from his, and an intervention in Thai affairs brought a sharp and undiplomatic rebuke from a Thai official to the effect that Whitlam should mind "his own bloody business." A grandiose and inadequately thought out proposal for an Asian and Pacific Forum was given a tepid reception. While Whitlam paid particular attention to Indonesia and was prepared to override domestic left-wing opposition to its fiercely anti-Communist military regime, the leaking of secret cables in the spring of 1975 [13] revealed a degree of accommodation to the Communist regime in Hanoi which cast doubt on the claim to "even-handedness" toward the warring governments in Vietnam and strengthened concern about ideological bias. This concern increased considerably shortly afterwards, when Whitlam (who, in opposition, had urged that Australia should offer asylum to Vietnamese refugees) personally insisted on an extremely ungenerous and restrictive policy toward people displaced during the terminal stage of the Vietnam War.

During Labor's three years in government, relations with China cooled perceptibly. At the beginning these were, on Australia's side at least, euphoric. Capitalizing on his triumph while in opposition, Whitlam paid an early visit to Peking and talked of the possibility of Australia's playing the role of "honest broker" between China and the other countries of the region. But well before the end of his term, relations with China had receded into the background. This was

---

[12] Ibid., p. 6.

[13] Melbourne *Age*, April 29, 1975.

probably a result of the very distinct gap between the Chinese appreciation of the post-Vietnam War situation in Southeast Asia, a cold realpolitik assessment that stressed the need for a power balance, and Whitlam's more optimistic and less power-oriented approach. Whitlam refused to concede that the decline of American power and influence created any serious problem and put the emphasis on economic and social factors as the vital forces in shaping the future of the region.

The Nonaligned Movement. If there was one clear theme in Whitlam's foreign policy it was the desire to draw closer to the nonaligned movement. As soon as it came to office, the Labor government began to indicate an interest in attending the conference of nonaligned nations in Algeria as a guest or observer, and by 1975 it had achieved guest status at the Lima conference where it was represented at the ministerial level. Jim Cairns, during his period as deputy prime minister (three different individuals held that post during Whitlam's three years in office), spoke of Australia's aspiration to be "an honorary member of the Third World," and the policies followed by the government bore this out.

At international conferences (notably at the Ottawa Commonwealth Conference in 1973), the Australian government argued the nonaligned case against multinationals and for the merits of producer associations. Labor's policy towards the aborigines and the independence of Papua New Guinea were expressly linked with the need to rid the country of any taint of racism or colonialism. In the United Nations, Australia's votes and rhetoric indicated sympathy, and sometimes identification, with the position of the nonaligned movement. Proposals for the neutralization of oceans and regions received ready endorsement, and African "national liberation movements" were given modest assistance.

But, yet again, in this area there was contradiction, for Australia, with its American alliances and American bases, was *not* nonaligned, nor could it be without a major change of policy. The word "honorary" in Cairns's remark glossed over, but did not dispose of, yet another ambiguity in the Whitlam government's policy.

Interpretations. Given this ambiguous record, it is not surprising that both characterizations and explanations of the Whitlam policy diverged widely. Some saw it as representing a revolutionary change. But others were struck by how continuous it was with earlier policy, arguing that the changes that had taken place were mainly in "means and modalities" or were due to external circumstances and would have occurred whichever party had been in power.[14] Some critics on the right maintained, "we have not even become neutral. We have simply changed sides."[15] But the government's policy was also condemned by left-wing Marxist critics for pretending to make major changes while leaving Australia's position as an instrument of the American-centered neoimperialist hegemony unchanged.[16] (In private, at least, others praised it for precisely the same reason.) It was denounced variously as naive and cynical, doctrinaire and opportunistic, reckless and timid—while its supporters themselves varied between claiming essential continuity and important innovation, depending on the occasion. Sometimes, indeed, they did both at the same time, as when Whitlam, in positively Delphic terms, maintained:

> On 2 December the nation changed its Government, but did not and could not by that act change the essential foundations of its foreign policy. Australia's national interests did not change. Australia's national obligations did not change. Australia's alliances and friendships did not change. Nonetheless, the change is real and deep because what has altered is the perception and interpretation of those interests, obligations and friendships by the elected Governments.[17]

The uncertainty and confusion which surrounded Labor's foreign policy were probably its most important consequences for domestic politics. Enough that was unfamiliar was happening to cause anxiety and concern among conservatives (and in the area of foreign policy these included many Labor supporters), while at the same time there were too many inconsistencies and too much was left unexplained to satisfy liberal opinion. As a result, although foreign policy was not a major issue in the election of 1975, it can plausibly be argued that Whitlam's record in this area contributed to the view, widely held by 1975, that his government lacked consistent purpose and coherent policies, was proceeding on the basis of inadequately considered impulses, and was marked by internal tension. Certainly, the gov-

---

[14] See, for example, Hedley Bull, "The Whitlam Government's Perception of Our Role in the World," in Brian Beddie, ed., Advance Australia—Where? (Melbourne: OUP, 1975), p. 34.

[15] B. A. Santamaria, "Labor's First Six Months," Current Affairs Bulletin (University of Sydney), July 1973, p. 16.

[16] Robert Catley and Bruce MacFarlane, From Tweedledum to Tweedledee: The New Labor Government in Australia (Sydney: A & NZ Book Co., 1974).

[17] Speech at the Australian Institute of Political Science Summer School, January 27, 1973.

ernment showed no inclination to make foreign policy an issue or to push its record in this area to the forefront in the December 1975 election.

The Return of the Coalition

In October 1975, Andrew Peacock, shadow minister for foreign affairs, released the opposition's foreign policy statement for the coming election.[18] It received an extremely good press, though it was noticeable that, while some welcomed it as a sign that bipartisanship had finally been achieved in foreign policy, others praised it as representing a clear and welcome alternative to Whitlam's policy. These different responses may be explained both in terms of the ambiguities of the Whitlam record and of the rather delicate and complex balance which the statement strove to maintain, a balance characterized by the term "enlightened realism" which Peacock repeatedly used to describe it.

In formulating its policy, the coalition faced the problem of coming up with something which was different from both Whitlam's policy and its own pre-1972 policy. It distanced itself from the former by its rejection of the optimistic view of the international environment advanced by the Labor government, its questioning of détente, and its insistence that the international system was under serious strain and was faced with multiple crises. Proceeding from this, it put a firm emphasis on security ("A foreign policy which neglects security is no foreign policy at all") and unambiguously affirmed the centrality of the American alliance. More specifically it supported the American proposal to extend the communications and naval facilities at Diego Garcia on the grounds that a balance of superpower forces in the Indian Ocean was essential. It argued for the restoration of a sense of limitation in international commitments commensurate with the country's power and interests and maintained that Australia's primary relations must be with countries whose interests were compatible with and complementary to its own—the industrially developed democracies on the one hand, and the ASEAN countries on the other. Nonalignment was rejected as a viable option and so was a policy that encouraged Third World "illusions and prejudices."

The emphasis on power and interests represented the realist side of the balance. On the other side, and serving to distinguish the L-NCP's new policy from its pre-1972 one, was the prominence given

---

[18] *Foreign Policy and International Development Assistance Policy*, Liberal Party Federal Secretariat, Canberra, 1975.

to the role that Australia, as a resource-rich country, might play in the solution of such global problems as the food and energy crises and the growing gap between rich and poor countries. The statement argued that Australia must "be prepared to subordinate some short-term economic advantages to the overriding advantages of creating and maintaining a viable international order" and that Australia was well placed to help prevent a polarization between the First and Third Worlds. The question of security was treated not only in the harsh terms of military strength, but also in terms of developing inter-national cooperation and removing the causes of conflict. And the old divisive issue of relations with China was laid to rest by the recognition that the time had come for a nonideological "willingness to respond to China's actions in terms of their merits and relevance to Australia's interests."

At the time of writing, the Fraser government has not been in office long enough to allow any conclusive judgment on how it will translate this general statement into concrete policies, but the first months have not been without interest or significance. As soon as it came to office the new government was faced with a serious crisis over East Timor, which by that time was already reaching its climax. Timor, an island less than 400 miles off the north Australian coast, had been divided politically, the western half being part of Indonesia and the eastern under Portuguese rule. The political crisis in Portugal led to a breakdown of Portuguese control and in August 1975 fighting broke out among three parties competing for control. Indonesia, easily Australia's most significant neighbor, was deeply concerned at the prospect of chronic instability or, even worse, the establishment of a radical left-wing regime in the eastern part of the island. Shortly after the Fraser government came to office, the Indonesians intervened militarily and forcibly suppressed Fretelin, the most left-wing of the parties, which seemed to be gaining the upper hand. Faced with this situation, the government refused to accept either the simple "realist" solution of remaining silent in order to maintain good relations with Indonesia (the policy that the Whitlam government had followed) or the simple "idealist" one of condemning the Indonesians outright, regardless of consequences. Instead it pursued a course of qualified criticism of Indonesia and support for United Nations intervention, while striving to minimize the long-term damage to the relations between the two countries. The criticism was meant to serve notice to Jakarta that Australia was seriously concerned about the use of force to resolve a regional political conflict; and its muted quality testified to the recognition both that the importance of Indonesian-

Australian relations transcended the East Timor issue and that more strident criticism would have made sense only if there had been a willingness on Australia's part to contemplate active intervention—which there was not.

One of the interesting aspects of the Timor crisis was that, contrary to some expectations, Prime Minister Fraser and Foreign Minister Peacock saw the situation in essentially the same terms. Indeed, predictions of a "tough" Fraser's overriding a "trendy" Peacock were not borne out by anything that happened in the coalition's first months in office, though the two men tended to use different language to say similar things.

On great-power issues, the most noticeable early concern focused on the implications of the sustained and formidable buildup of Soviet military power, about which Fraser expressed himself in sharp terms. The government clearly committed itself to supporting efforts to match Soviet power in the Indian Ocean, arguing that this must become a "zone of balance before it could become a zone of peace."[19] Early in 1976 it was announced that work on the Cockburn Sound naval base in Western Australia would be accelerated, that American nuclear-powered ships would be allowed to use Australian ports, and that Australia would participate, by providing a station, in the American Omega navigation system.[20] The Soviet-Cuban intervention in Angola reinforced concern about the implications of the Soviet Union's presence in the Indian Ocean and its increased interest in Southeast Asia. Meanwhile, the commitment to the American alliance was strongly reaffirmed, though the Fraser government also expressed concern about the United States's ability to function effectively as a global power and insisted that Australia must "not be taken for granted."

The critical attention given to the Soviet Union and the related stress on security were warmly received in Peking, and this in turn led to some speculation about a "pro-Chinese" policy, though at the time of writing there is only the "logic of the situation" to support such an interpretation. Steps were taken early to restore stability and "predictability" to Australia's economic relationship with Japan, and the government expressed its determination to bring the interminable negotiations over the Nippon-Australian Relations Agreement to a successful conclusion. It was announced that the prime minister's first major overseas visit would be to Japan and China in midyear.

[19] Andrew Peacock in his address to the Australian-American Association, New York, March 1976.

[20] See Don Hutton, "The Omega Navigational System: Friendly Lighthouse, or Nuclear Target?" *Current Affairs Bulletin* (University of Sydney), May 1, 1976.

As far as the "enlightenment" of the policy is concerned, the domestic economic situation and the government's overriding commitment to tackling inflation have meant that not much has been forthcoming in terms of increased aid or a willingness to subordinate economic advantage to long-term political goals. Papua New Guinea has been generously provided for and assistance to the ASEAN countries is being given a high priority, but beyond that nothing very ambitious can be expected until there is a domestic recovery. At the time of writing, the political stance towards the nonaligned can best be defined as friendly and sympathetic, but stopping well short of Whitlam's attempt at close association.

Conclusion

It is too early to make any definitive pronouncement on the new government's foreign policy. Furthermore, the foreign policy of a country like Australia must always be shaped to a significant extent by events beyond its control. Nevertheless, the indications are that policy is returning to a line of development continuous with the earlier evolution of Australia's external relations, though it takes into account the changes which have occurred in the international environment and on the domestic scene during the first years of this decade. To the extent that these early indications are confirmed, the Whitlam foreign policy is likely to appear in retrospect as one that initially served the useful purpose of challenging and partly dismantling a set of attitudes and prejudices that had become deeply embedded during two decades of Liberal-Country party rule; a policy that subsequently, however—as it seemed to involve a loosening of Australia's ties with the West and the entertaining of ambitions that bore little relation to available power or perceived interests—became increasingly eccentric and aberrant.

10

THE ELECTORATE SPEAKS— AND AFTER

Colin A. Hughes

"Nothing, perhaps, would more surprise the English people," wrote Walter Bagehot in 1867, "than if the Queen by a *coup d'état* and on a sudden destroyed a ministry firm in the allegiance and secure of a majority in Parliament. That power indisputably, in theory, belongs to her; but it has passed so far away from the minds of men, that it would terrify them, if she used it, like a volcanic eruption from Primrose Hill." [1] Yet more than a century later, in a polity presumably more democratic than mid-Victorian England's, the dismissal of a ministry by the Queen's representative in 1975 was accomplished with a reading on the public opinion Richter scale that reached, for the great majority of the population, a point somewhere between disquiet and alarm, but certainly well short of terror. One by one the tops had metaphorically blown off the tawny hills ringing Canberra as senior ministers were flung out of cabinet, the Senate defied time-honored convention to block supply, public servants feared for their salaries, and finally the governor general sacked the prime minister and his government and installed a man in whom the House of Representatives immediately voted no confidence. Yet when Australian voters went to the polls on December 13 they behaved very much as they always had. The evidence suggesting that terror was not present is, first, the absence of physical violence from the election campaign which followed Sir John Kerr's dismissal of the Whitlam ministry and grant of a double dissolution to Malcolm Fraser and, second, the extent to which the 1975 electoral results conformed to well-established patterns.

---

[1] Walter Bagehot, *The English Constitution*, The World's Classics (London: Oxford University Press, 1928), p. 212.

The first point may be made briefly in the absence of evidence to the contrary: compared with the 1966 House of Representatives election fought at the height of bitterness about the Vietnam War, the 1975 campaign was free of violence.[2] Admittedly, following their serious defeat in 1966 most Labor party politicians had drawn the lesson that physical clashes in the streets and at public meetings cost them votes, and in 1975 they did all they could to dampen the exuberance of their more boisterous supporters. Further, in 1966 it was obvious that the ALP was going to be thumped and badly so, which added frustration to the other emotions encouraging physical confrontations, whereas in 1975, at least in the early days of the short campaign, the evidence was uncertain and it appeared possible that Labor could win. But given the potential explosiveness of the situation in 1975, it is still remarkable that heads were counted rather than broken. It is to this second phenomenon, the counting of heads, that the bulk of this concluding chapter is addressed.[3]

Long-Term Electoral Patterns

The patterns of Australian electoral geography and history date from 1910 when, after "the Fusion" of the Protectionist and Free Trade parties in opposition to the rising Labor party, a two-party system was firmly established. Neither the development of the Country party after World War I nor that of the Democratic Labor party in the 1950s affected the character of that system, for each has been essentially a satellite party content to orbit around the principal anti-Labor party of the day. Writing in 1971, Neal Blewett applied the classifications developed by Angus Campbell and associates and V. O. Key to

[2] Pictorial evidence which might suggest a different view is presented in Nick Beame et al., *The Canberra Coup!* (Sydney: Workers News, 1976), produced by the Socialist Labour League.

[3] Australian electoral statistics are available in various forms in Colin A. Hughes and B. D. Graham, *A Handbook of Australian Government and Politics 1890-1964* (Canberra: Australian National University Press, 1968) and *Voting for the Australian House of Representatives 1901-1964* (Canberra: Australian National University Press, 1974); Colin A. Hughes, *A Handbook of Australian Government and Politics 1965-1974* (forthcoming); Malcolm Mackerras, *Elections 1975* (Sydney: Angus and Robertson, 1975) and "Double Dissolution Election, December 13, 1975," Department of Government, University of New South Wales, 1976, mimeographed; and the various editions of the *Commonwealth Parliamentary Handbook* (Canberra: Australian Government Printer). Official returns, showing details at the subdivisional level, are published as *Parliamentary Papers* (Canberra: Australian Government Printer). Unless otherwise attributed, statistics in this chapter derive from the first three works cited above and from the unofficial publications of the Australian Electoral Office in Canberra.

Australian national elections and identified three electoral cycles between 1910 and 1969:

> Three electoral cycles are apparent, each of which can be divided into two phases, an opening and relatively short A.L.P. phase, and a second, more prolonged non-Labor phase. . . . Each phase opens with a realigning election, i.e., two realigning elections in each cycle. The realigning elections are 1910, 1917, 1929, 1931, 1943 and 1949. . . . Although the A.L.P. ascendancies are not maintained for long, thus casting doubt on the nature of the election that originated them, the realigning elections favouring Labor do not come out of the blue but are the culmination of a steady trend towards Labor over the previous decade.[4]

Labor won office in 1910, having had two earlier brief periods of office as a minority government supported by a bloc of Protectionist members; it split over conscription for military service overseas and went out in 1917. It won office again in 1929, split over how to cope with the depression, and went out in 1931. It achieved office in 1941 after the two independents who held the balance of power following the 1940 election switched their support and was defeated at the polls in 1949. It regained office only in 1972 and lost it in 1975, starting what may well be the fourth cycle.

The Stability of the Two-Party Pattern. Over what is now two-thirds of a century, the major parties' bases of electoral support have remained remarkably constant. Neither "side"—that is, the Labor party and the Liberal/Nationalist/United Australia/Liberal party plus Country party coalition—has ever fallen below 40 percent of the total vote. Even more striking to those familiar with other federal party systems in the United States and Canada, the two-party system has remained equally competitive in terms of voting support in each of the six states, despite long periods when one side or the other has held office without interruption—Labor in New South Wales from 1941 to 1965; the Liberals in Victoria from 1955 to the present; Labor in Queensland from 1915 to 1929 and from 1932 to 1957 and the Liberal-Country coalition since 1957; the Liberals in South Australia from 1933 to 1965; and Labor in Tasmania from 1934 to 1969. Some of the stability of governments at the state level can be attributed to electoral manipulation which weighted areas of voting strength, but

---

[4] Neal Blewett, "A Classification of Australian Elections: Preliminary Notes," *Politics*, vol. 6 (May 1971), pp. 87-91.

the fact remains that partisan loyalty, presumably because of its close connection with class identification, has been stable.

This stability can be shown in a variety of ways. One is to compare the division of seats among the parties in the House of Representatives from one election to the next (see Table 10-1).

Another is to examine the competitiveness of electorates individually and collectively. This entails some imaginative arithmetic. In constituencies where there are only two candidates, one from the Labor party and one from the Liberal-Country coalition, or when preferences are distributed so that only two such candidates are left at the final

Table 10-1
PARTY DISTRIBUTION OF HOUSE SEATS, 1949–75

Election	New South Wales			Victoria			Others[a]		
	ALP	Lib	CP	ALP	Lib	CP	ALP	Lib	CP
1949	23	16	8	13	17	3	11	22	8
1951	24	16	7	15	15	3	13	21	7
1954	25	15	7	15	15	3	17	17	7
1955	21	17	8	10	20	3	16	20	7
1958	22	16	8	10	18	5	13	24	6
1961	27	12	7	10	18	5	23	15	5
1963	20	17	9	10	18	5	20	17	6
1966	17	20	9	8[b]	19	5	16[c]	22	6
1969	22	15	8	11	18	5	26[d]	13	7[d]
1972	28	10	7	14	14	6	25[d]	14	7[d]
1974	25	11	9	16	12	6	25[d]	17	6[d]
1975	17	19	9	10	19	5	9[d]	30[d]	9[d]

[a] This includes the four smallest states—Queensland, South Australia, Western Australia, and Tasmania—and the two federal territories as soon as these secured full voting rights.

[b] Plus one Independent Labor.

[c] Including Australian Capital Territory.

[d] Including Australian Capital and Northern Territories.

Source: Colin A. Hughes and B. D. Graham, *A Handbook of Australian Government and Politics 1890-1964* (Canberra: Australian National University Press, 1968) and *Voting for the Australian House of Representatives 1901-1964* (Canberra: Australian National University Press, 1974); Colin A. Hughes, *A Handbook of Australian Government and Politics 1965-1974* (forthcoming).

count, it is possible to speak exactly of a two-party-preferred vote. However, if one candidate has an absolute majority over two or more opponents so that preferences are not counted, or if one of the major parties does not contest the seat, or if only one candidate is nominated for a safe seat and there is, in effect, no poll at all, estimates have to be made as to what the two-party-preferred vote might have been. Such estimates have been made for each election since 1958 by Malcolm Mackerras of the Department of Government, Faculty of Military Studies of the University of New South Wales at Duntroon, A.C.T. (Australia's West Point); these have been employed in the compilation of Table 10-2 and other tables later in this chapter. Using these figures one can classify seats according to their "safeness" on a two-party-preferred vote at each election: ultra-safe, 70 percent or better; safe, 60.0–69.9 percent; marginal, 55.0–59.9 percent; and ultra-marginal, 50.0–54.9 percent. The proportion of House of Representatives seats in each category at each election is shown in Table 10-2.

At each election from 1955 to 1975, between one-fifth and one-quarter of the seats were "ultra-marginal," with a margin of less than ten percentage points of the total vote determining the result; in 1974, one-third of the seats balanced on that knife edge. (That election displayed a quite extraordinary symmetry in the distribution of seats through our categories of "safeness," as a glance down the 1974 column of Table 10-2 will show.) By contrast, relatively few seats are in the "ultra-safe" categories—in 1972 only one in twenty-five. If one supposes that no parliamentarian sleeps well at night unless he had 60 percent of the vote at the previous election, then between 45 and 60 percent of the members of the House of Representatives are constantly sniffing the political wind. With a general election every three years—at the latest—the sensitivity of politicians to any turn in the tides of electoral popularity is understandable, as is the political folk-saying that the biggest party in Parliament is the "No Election party."

Distribution of Electoral Swings. To stress the parameters of stability in Australian politics is not to say that there has been complete uniformity of movements within these parameters on the scale evidenced in, for example, Britain. Table 10-3, using the last seven elections for the House of Representatives, suggests that the several states are, to a limited extent, electoral subsystems with some capacity to deviate from their neighbors' behavior.

It should be remembered that the four smallest states (Queensland, South Australia, Western Australia, and Tasmania) contribute little

Table 10-2

SAFENESS OF HOUSE SEATS, 1955–75

(in percentages)

Safeness Rating	1955	1958	1961	1963	1966	1969	1972	1974	1975
					Election				
Ultra-safe, Labor	4.9	4.9	5.8	3.3	0.8	4.0	4.0	7.1	0.8
Safe, Labor	11.5	12.4	20.6	14.9	8.2	19.2	20.8	17.3	10.4
Marginal, Labor	9.8	9.1	11.6	14.0	14.8	12.0	14.4	10.4	8.7
Ultra-marginal, Labor	12.2	9.9	10.7	8.2	9.9	12.8	13.6	17.3	8.7
Ultra-marginal, Coalition	7.4	8.2	11.6	12.4	9.9	14.4	22.4	17.3	15.7
Marginal, Coalition	16.4	18.2	18.9	14.0	11.5	16.8	11.2	10.4	20.4
Safe, Coalition	26.2	24.8	14.9	28.1	33.5	19.2	13.6	18.1	28.4
Ultra-safe, Coalition	11.5	12.4	5.8	6.6	11.5	1.6	0	2.4	7.1

Note: For explanation of method, see text, pp. 280-81.

Source: For 1958-74, Malcolm Mackerras, *Elections 1975* (Sydney: Angus and Robertson, 1975), and for 1975, "Double Dissolution Election, December 13, 1975," Department of Government, University of New South Wales, 1976, mimeographed; 1955 calculated by author.

Table 10-3

SWING TO THE ALP FROM PREVIOUS HOUSE ELECTION, BY STATE, 1961–75

(in percentage-point gains and losses)

Election	Australia	New South Wales	Victoria	Queensland	South Australia	Western Australia	Tasmania
					State		
1961	4.6	5.0	2.2	9.3	4.4	2.7	6.2
1963	−3.1	−5.5	−2.0	−2.6	−0.9	−0.3	−1.5
1966	−4.3ᵃ	−5.4	−3.2	−3.8	−10.9	1.9	−0.6
1969	7.1ᵇ	7.7	5.6	5.6	11.8	6.9	2.2
1972	2.5ᵇ	3.8	5.5	−0.4	−1.5	−4.3	4.4
1974	−1.0ᵇ	−0.5	0.2	−4.1	−0.2	0.2	−5.1
1975	−7.4ᵇ	−8.1	−6.8	−5.6	−7.6	−7.3	−11.3

a Including the Australian Capital Territory.
b Including the Australian Capital and Northern Territories.
Source: Mackerras, *Elections 1975*, pp. 192-93, and "Double Dissolution," p. 6.

more than one-third of the enrollment (voter registration) and seats in the lower house. Thus, trends for the whole of Australia are affected most strongly by the behavior of the two largest states, New South Wales and Victoria. In 1961 when Labor almost won, there was an exceptionally large swing in Queensland and rather small swings in Victoria and Western Australia. In 1966 and again in 1969 South Australia magnified the national trend noticeably. In 1972 three states moved against the overall trend which finally brought Whitlam to power. In 1974, when there was little change in most areas, Queensland and Tasmania swung away from Labor. However, a slightly longer perspective irons out some of these variations. Thus, if one takes the period from 1966 to 1972, when the ALP national vote increased by almost ten percentage points, the two largest states plus South Australia were slightly above this trend, whereas Tasmania, Queensland, and Western Australia lagged increasingly behind it— and it was in those three states that Labor was virtually wiped out in 1975, electing only two of thirty-three members of the House in place of the sixteen returned in 1974. It has been argued that recent elections have shown a tendency for Labor's support to be concentrated in a southeastern heartland composed of New South Wales, Victoria,

Figure 10-1

DISTRIBUTION OF SWINGS, HOUSE ELECTIONS, 1969–75

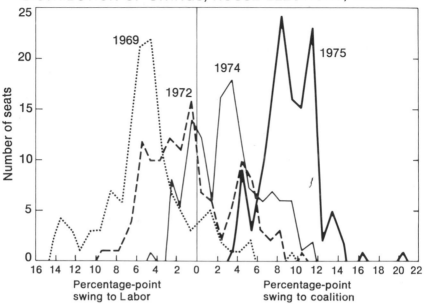

Source: Mackerras, *Elections 1975*, pp. 209, 213, and 217, and "Double Dissolution," p. 5.

and South Australia, and effectively in the three metropolitan centers
of those states—Sydney plus Newcastle and Wollongong, Melbourne
plus Geelong, and Adelaide.

Further light is cast on the distribution of swings in Figure 10-1.
In 1969 the overall movement to Labor covered a wide range of
swings including a few negative ones: as Figure 10-1 shows, the
majority of swings to Labor were on the order of six percentage points,
but four seats swung by over eleven percentage points and in one
seat the swing to the coalition was over nine percentage points. The
further swing to Labor in 1972 was offset by a significant number of
swings away from Labor. In 1974 the small overall swing against
Labor masked a number of swings to Labor and an even greater
number of swings away, some of them substantial. In 1975 we are
back to the 1969 situation, though now all the swings are in the same
direction, against Labor, and the spread is much narrower. The 1975
election was by far the most uniform in its swings, suggesting the
strength of national influences on electoral behavior throughout all
six states and their constituent electorates.

The Urban/Rural Cleavage. Cutting across the long-term stability of partisan voting in Australia since 1910 is the urban/rural division in Australian society. Its electoral significance rests on several connected factors. One of the major parties, the National Country party, draws its support from territory outside the capital cities, and the population, enrollment, and thus eventually number of House seats in that territory are steadily declining relative to the growing major cities. It should be noted that "urban" and "rural" in Australian politics are frequently used loosely as equivalent to "metropolitan," that is, pertaining to capital cities, and "nonmetropolitan," that is, pertaining to the rest of the country. So the National Country party holds electorates containing quite substantial provincial towns or cities with populations of 25-50,000, and yet the close economic and social ties of such towns and cities with their agricultural, pastoral, and mining hinterlands makes the "rural" label applied to these electorates less misleading than might otherwise appear.

In its formative years between 1890 and 1910 the Labor party had a substantial base in rural areas where miners, the migratory or stationary employees of sheep and cattle properties, construction and maintenance workers on the railways, manual workers in service industries in the small towns, and even a substantial proportion of small wheat and sugar farmers regularly voted Labor. Labor's first two prime ministers, Chris Watson and Andrew Fisher, sat for rural electorates in the House. In the House of Representatives Labor held the "outback" electorates which were measured in hundreds of thousands of square miles (in the case of Kalgoorlie, close to one million, or almost a third of the entire country). It also won consistently—or, in some cases, whenever the electoral tide was flowing favorably—a number of other nonmetropolitan electorates each dominated by a largish provincial city. But gradually, partly because of the diminishing proportion of the House coming from rural electorates and partly because of the changing economic and social composition of such electorates, Labor has depended more and more on its urban support. If one looks at the elections won by the Labor party, one discovers that only 37 percent of its members in the House sat for metropolitan electorates in 1910, 43 percent did so in 1914, 48 percent in 1929, 53 percent in 1943 and 1946, and 68 percent in 1972 and 1974. This trend explains the party's growing hostility to any weightage of rural electorates and the Whitlam government's unsuccessful attempts to secure a redistribution (redistricting) of electorates that would increase electoral equality. It also explains the National Country party's insistence on maintaining and increasing the rural weightage, even when the alliance with the Liberals was strained by the vehemence of that insistence.

Labor's dependence on the metropolitan areas is illustrated by the electoral maps in Figures 10-2 and 10-3, which continue the series on the 1955–72 elections published elsewhere.[5] For these figures the Australian electoral map has been redrawn in a schematized form so that each electorate occupies an equal area, just as it has equal representation in the House of Representatives. The shape of the electorates has been altered so that they may fit together, but contiguity has been preserved so that each electorate has its correct neighbors, although not necessarily for the correct proportion of boundary length. The actual contours, as shown on a normal map, are hopelessly misleading, for Sydney and Melbourne, with 40 percent of the voting power in the House between them, shrink to dots, whereas Kalgoorlie, with 0.8 percent of the voting power, occupies almost a third of the map. Electoral politics in Australia is dominated by the capital cities, and novel cartography is required to show this.

The "Fairness" Controversy. There have been frequent complaints that the Labor party has been underrepresented in the House of Representatives and that on occasion it has won a majority of votes without thereby securing a majority of seats. To provide any hard data on this question it is first necessary to "reconstruct" voting figures to a two-party-preferred vote. The next difficulty is to decide what sort of relationship could reasonably be expected between votes and seats, especially if the "cube rule" works in Australia. That rule was stated thus: "when there were two parties, the ratio of seats won by the parties might be expected to be at least the cube of the ratio between the votes cast for them; in other words, if the ratio between votes was A : B the ratio between seats would be at least $A^3 : B^3$."[6] Like the United Kingdom, Australia has single-member constituencies, so an advantage in votes can be expected to produce a larger advantage in the House; moreover, the existence of preferential voting makes it much easier to assign the votes for minor parties or even independents to the two major parties as is required for the formula to work. Table 10-4 sets out the data for such an analysis.

---

[5] Colin A. Hughes and E. E. Savage, "The 1955 Federal Redistribution," *Australian Journal of Politics and History*, vol. 13 (April 1967), pp. 8-20, and Colin A. Hughes, "The 1972 Australian Federal Election," *Australian Journal of Politics and History*, vol. 19 (April 1973), pp. 11-27.

[6] H. G. Nicholas, *The British General Election of 1950* (London: Macmillan, 1951), p. 328.

Table 10-4

TWO-PARTY-PREFERRED VOTES AND SEATS, HOUSE ELECTIONS, 1949–75

| Elec-tion | Estimated Vote | | Seats | | | | | |
| | | | Proportionate | | Cube Rule | | Actual | |
	L-NCP	ALP	L-NCP	ALP	L-NCP	ALP	L-NCP	ALP
1949	51.4	48.6	62	59	66	55	74	47
1951	50.8	49.2	61	60	63	58	69	52
1954	49.2	50.8	60	61	58	63	64	57
1955	54.2	45.8	66	56	76	46	75	47
1958	54.1	45.9	66	56	76	46	77	45
1961	49.5	50.5	60	62	59	63	62	60
1963	52.6	47.4	64	58	70	52	72	50
1966	57.2	42.8	70	52	86	36	80	42
1969	50.0	50.0	62	61	62	61	65	58
1972	47.5	52.5	58	65	52	71	57	66
1974	48.4	51.6	60	64	56	68	60	64
1975	55.6	44.4	69	55	82	42	89	35

Note: For explanation, see text p. 286. The territories have been excluded to preserve continuity.
Source: For estimated vote: 1949-54, Joan Rydon, "The Relation of Votes to Seats in Elections for the Australian House of Representatives, 1949-1954," *Political Science*, vol. 9 (1957), pp. 49-61; 1955 calculated by the writer; 1958-74, Mackerras, *Elections 1975*, pp. 192-93; 1975, "Double Dissolution," p. 6.

It should be noted that the elections shown in the table were conducted on the basis of three different sets of boundaries, one for 1949–54, one for 1955–66, and one for 1969–75, so that bias attributable to boundaries may vary over time.

From Table 10-4 we can extract the figures set out in Table 10-5, showing the disadvantage (or advantage) secured by the Labor party. Only once did the Labor party secure an important advantage: in 1966, when a substantial swing away from Labor was contained by the number of safe Labor seats. Usually the ALP is disadvantaged, and twice, in 1954 and 1961, this disadvantage was sufficient to keep it out of office; in 1969 the even split of the vote (see Table 10-4) gave the coalition a lead of a few hundred votes, not enough to appear

Figure 10-2

AUSTRALIAN ELECTORAL MAP, HOUSE ELECTION, 1974

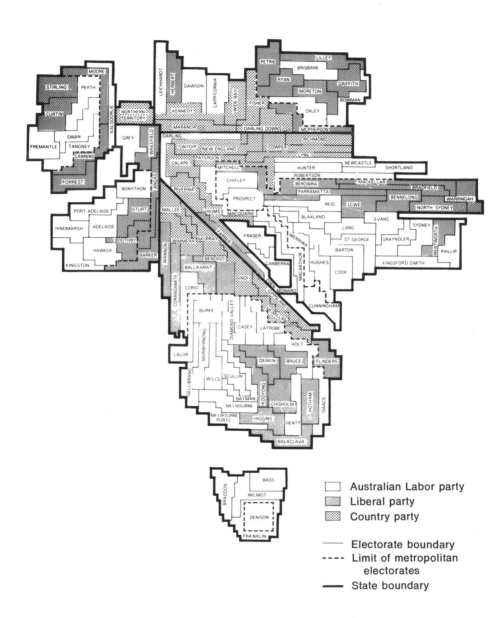

☐ Australian Labor party
▨ Liberal party
▦ Country party

—— Electorate boundary
- - - Limit of metropolitan
     electorates
—— State boundary

Note: For explanation, see text, p. 286.
Source: Colin A. Hughes.

Figure 10-3
AUSTRALIAN ELECTORAL MAP, HOUSE ELECTION, 1975

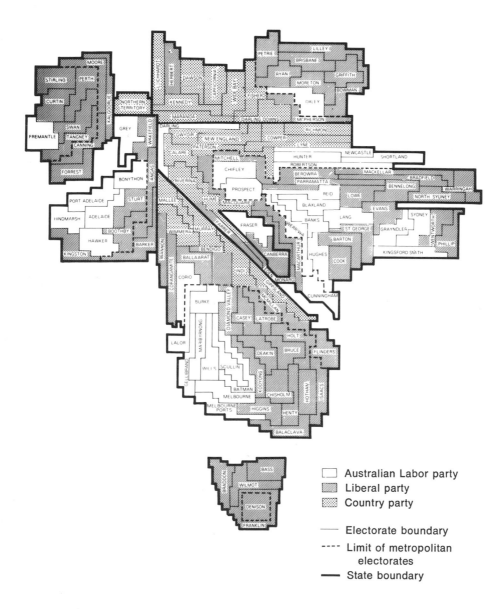

Australian Labor party
Liberal party
Country party

Electorate boundary
Limit of metropolitan electorates
State boundary

Note: For explanation, see text, p. 286.
Source: Colin A. Hughes.

Table 10-5

DIFFERENCE BETWEEN HOUSE SEATS WON BY ALP,
1949–75, AND SEATS IT WOULD HAVE WON UNDER
PROPORTIONATE AND CUBE-RULE SYSTEMS

	Proportionate	Cube Rule
1949	−12	−8
1951	−8	−6
1954	−4	−6
1955	−9	+1
1958	−11	−1
1961	−2	−3
1963	−8	−2
1966	−10	+6
1969	−3	−3
1972	+1	−5
1974	0	−4
1975	−20	−7

Source: See Table 10-4.

at a one-decimal-point division of the national vote but enough to justify retention of office by the coalition under electoral equity. To show that there is a built-in handicap, of course, is not to show what the remedy might be. Thus, one plausible explanation has been that Labor has too many voters locked up in safe industrial, mining, and inner-urban electorates where they produce unnecessarily large majorities; short of complete proportional representation there is no obvious means of unlocking them. Moreover, the classification of seats according to their "safeness" in Table 10-2 suggests that it is only when Labor is polling particularly well, as it did in 1969–74, that its ultra-safe seats outnumber the coalition's. In 1961 and 1969–74 Labor also had more ultra-safe and safe seats combined than did the coalition. This was something of a handicap, but its impact was limited.

It is possible—though any argument would rest on the most conjectural sort of arithmetic—that the weightage given to rural electorates handicaps the Labor party. This is why one of the most urgent priorities of the Whitlam government was to reduce the allowable variation from the state average (called the "quota" for purposes of boundary drawing) from the 20 percent which had prevailed since 1902 to 10 percent, thereby forcing rural electorates closer to urban ones in voter enrollment. The government secured the necessary legislation at the joint sitting of Parliament following the 1974 election, but failed to entrench the new figure in the constitution at a referendum held simultaneously with the election. New boundaries were drawn using the 10 percent formula, but they failed to pass the Senate. Had they been implemented in time for the 1975 election they could not have affected the result, given the landslide swing to the coalition, and it is unlikely that they would have made more than one seat difference in the total. Nevertheless, discrepancies such as appear in Table 10-5 are a source of irritation to Labor supporters and make the "fairness" of the electoral system a matter of continuing controversy in Australian politics.

The Impact of Preferential Voting. The other main area of disagreement relates to the use of the "alternative vote," known in Australia as "preferential voting." Prior to the 1974 election, the Labor party was officially pledged to restore first-past-the-post voting whereby a plurality of formal votes would be sufficient to secure election. Under fire from the opposition, who claimed that this was one more example of Labor's wish to manipulate the electoral system to its own advantage, Whitlam changed the policy to one of making the expression of preferences (in excess of the number of seats to be filled) voluntary rather than compulsory as it had always been for House of Representatives elections. Table 10-6 shows why the Labor party was concerned about the issue and why the abandonment of preferential voting might be expected to advantage Labor.

Of the eighty-four seats in which the result was changed from a first-past-the-post result by the counting of preferences, Labor won only four over the twelve elections between 1949 and 1975. In 1961 and again in 1969 such seats were numerous enough to keep the Labor party out of office. That is not to say, of course, that had there been no preferential voting system in operation Labor would have won those elections, for there can be no certainty that the unsuccessful candidates whose preferences went to the anti-Labor candidates who subsequently won the seats would have run in such changed circumstances. In particular the DLP, which accounted for the majority of such contests, given the choice between standing a candidate so as to record its own support and preventing the ALP from winning the seat on a divided anti-ALP vote, might well have opted for the second alternative and withdrawn from the contest.

Table 10-6

NUMBER OF SEATS AFFECTED BY DISTRIBUTION OF PREFERENCES, HOUSE ELECTIONS, 1949–75

Election	Total Seats		Seats Won by ALP	
	Preferences counted	Result changed	Preferences counted	Result changed
1949	22	9	8	1
1951	6	2	3	1
1954	6	2	0	0
1955	17	1	10	0
1958	31	7	8	0
1961	37	7	10	1
1963	24	8	3	0
1966	31	5	6	0
1969	40	12	5	0
1972	49	14	12	0
1974	33	10	9	1
1975	24	7	6	0

Note: The entries under "Preferences counted" are total numbers of electorates where no candidate won a majority on the first count and thus voters' preferences came into play in subsequent counts. The entries under "Result changed" are total numbers of electorates where the winner after preferences had been counted was not the candidate who received the largest number of first preferences.

Source: Hughes and Graham, *A Handbook of Australian Government and Politics 1890-1964* and *Voting for the Australian House of Representatives;* Hughes, *A Handbook of Australian Government and Politics 1965-1974.*

By the 1975 election the DLP's power to determine the result of elections by assigning its preferences against the ALP had almost disappeared. In only two of the twenty-four contests where preferences were counted did the presence of a DLP candidate prevent the successful candidate from securing an absolute majority on the first count; in one electorate, Corio, there was a sufficient "leakage" of DLP preferences for the Labor candidate to retain his lead, but in the other, Holt, a larger leakage left the Liberal ahead.

Another four of the twenty-four contests in which preferences were counted were occasioned by the presence of Liberal Movement candidates in South Australia; three were won by Labor (Adelaide,

Table 10-7

DISTRIBUTION OF PREFERENCES IN CORIO AND HOLT, HOUSE ELECTIONS, 1975

Candidate and Party	First Count		Second Count			Third Count		
	Votes	Percentage	Preferences	Votes	Percentage	Preferences	Votes	Percentage
CORIO								
Hall (Lib.)	28,907	46.16	211	29,118	46.50	2,184	31,302	49.98
Sahr (Aus.)	604	0.96	a					
Scholes (ALP)	30,688	49.00	340	31,028	49.55	294	31,322	50.02
Timberlake (DLP)	2,425	3.87	53	2,478	3.96	a		
HOLT								
Fidler (DLP)	4,343	5.31	a					
Oldmeadow (ALP)	38,069	46.51	1,538	39,607	48.39			
Yates (Lib.)	39,436	48.18	2,805	42,241	51.61			

a Candidate excluded and his preferences distributed.
Source: Australian Electoral Office.

Grey, and Hawker), one by the Liberals (Kingston, taken from the ALP). Five more were explained by the presence of other minor parties—the Australia party or the Workers party—or of independents; two were won by Labor (Robertson and Maribyrnong) and three by Liberals (St. George, Franklin, and Canberra, all gains from Labor). The other thirteen contests were caused by competition between the coalition partners, and almost half of these occurred in Queensland where there was a deliberate strategy of nominating two candidates, partly in the belief—which had had some reinforcement at the state election a year earlier—that this maximized the anti-Labor vote, and partly in consequence of the National Country party's hope, also supported by the state election, that it could win seats in the metropolitan area. As it was, the National Country party won only four of the thirteen—Calare, which had long been a safe seat, and three seats in rural Queensland taken from Labor, Capricornia, Dawson, and Leichhardt. The demise of the DLP at the 1975 election and the winding up of the Liberal Movement after the election are likely to restore the situation which prevailed before 1955: the counting of preferences allows the coalition partners to compete for their own safe seats and sometimes to contest a marginal seat more effectively; occasionally it allows the intervention of a small, mushroom party or an independent candidate to have an impact on a marginal seat, but it is unlikely to determine who governs Australia.

There is one other matter which warrants attention, not so much for its significance in determining the results of the 1975 election (for then it could not have mattered) but because it is a peculiarity of the Australian electoral system. Australia is unusual among countries holding free elections in that it has made both enrollment and voting compulsory. Thus, at the 1975 election 95.40 percent of enrolled voters went to the polls, and in only two electorates did the proportion fall below 90 percent: Kalgoorlie at 89.70 percent and the Northern Territory at 74.89 percent, both huge electorates with thinly scattered populations and high proportions of aborigines who were recently enfranchised. Because voters are compelled to go to the polls and there are faced with elaborate ballot-papers on which they must express a large number of preferences (for the Senate the number usually runs into two figures and reached a record of seventy-three in New South Wales in 1974), many accidentally or deliberately spoil their ballot-papers and cast what are called "informal" votes. The figures, set out in Table 10-8, show that the proportion of informal votes is consistently and substantially higher for the Senate than for the House, which is understandable given the greater complexity of

Table 10-8
INFORMAL VOTING, 1949–75
(in percentages of ballots cast)

Election	House	Senate
1949	1.98	10.76
1951	1.90	7.13
1953	—	4.56
1954	1.35	—
1955	2.88	9.63
1958	2.87	10.29
1961	2.57	10.62
1963	1.82	—
1964	—	6.98
1966	3.10	—
1967	—	6.10
1969	2.54	—
1970	—	9.41
1972	2.17	—
1974	1.92	10.77
1975	1.89	9.10

Note: Figures are entered in only one column for years when only one house was up for election.

Source: Hughes and Graham, *A Handbook of Australian Government and Politics 1890-1964* and *Voting for the Australian House of Representatives;* Hughes, *A Handbook of Australian Government and Politics 1965-1974.*

the Senate ballot-paper. However, when there have been Senate elections without an accompanying vote for the House of Representatives, the informal vote has dropped noticeably, suggesting that fatigue from filling in two papers is an additional factor.

A comparison of the statistics for different constituencies shows that informal voting tends to be lower in rural electorates than in metropolitan ones and lower in coalition-held seats than in those held by Labor. For the House there is little correlation between informal voting and the number of candidates—that is, the number of preferences that must be expressed—until the number rises above four or five, after which informal voting tends to increase. But for the Senate there is some evidence that the more preferences are required, the more ballot-papers are spoiled, and as there are likely to be more informal votes in Labor areas than elsewhere, the Labor party could be disadvantaged. Thus it was alleged that the exceptionally large number of candidates running in New South Wales in 1974 was the result of a conspiracy to injure Labor's chances. The Whitlam government subsequently sought to require Senate voters to express only a limited number of preferences and make the rest optional; it also sought to increase the deposit required of candidates. Both proposals failed in the Senate.

Electoral Patterns in 1975

Having looked at the working of the electoral system over a number of elections, we can now examine its operation in December 1975 in more detail. Tables 10-9 and 10-10 show the distribution of votes for the House of Representatives and the Senate, respectively, and Table 10-11 the distribution of seats in both chambers.

Table 10-9
RESULTS OF HOUSE ELECTIONS, 1975, BY STATE
(in percentages)

	ALP	Liberals	NCP	Small Parties[a]	Others
New South Wales	45.46	39.71	11.76	1.64	1.42
Victoria	42.09	42.32	8.90	5.90	0.79
Queensland	38.76	32.64	26.74	1.53	0.33
South Australia	42.64	49.29	0.55	7.17	0.34
Western Australia	40.13	53.64	5.05	1.07	0.13
Tasmania	43.50	54.11	1.34	1.05	—
Australian Capital Territory	48.27	47.32	—	3.63	0.78
Northern Territory	43.70	—	53.93	2.37	—
Australia	42.84	41.80	11.25	3.28	0.83

[a] Liberal Movement, DLP, Australia, Communist, and Workers' parties.
Source: Australian Electoral Office.

Table 10-10
RESULTS OF SENATE ELECTIONS, 1975, BY STATE
(in percentages)

	ALP	L-NCP	Small Parties[a]	Others
New South Wales	44.06	49.37	3.63	3.04
Victoria	41.29	50.54	7.70	0.47
Queensland	36.82	57.28	5.22	0.70
South Australia	40.62	51.45	7.19	0.74
Western Australia	36.53	58.57	2.93	1.97
Tasmania	35.22	50.58	0.45	13.74
Australian Capital Territory	37.02	43.57	0.55	18.86
Northern Territory	35.91	54.59	4.15	5.35
Australia	40.91	51.74	5.09	2.26

[a] Liberal Movement, DLP, Australia, and Workers' parties.
Source: Australian Electoral Office.

Table 10-11
PARTY DISTRIBUTION OF SEATS IN HOUSE AND SENATE, 1975, BY STATE

	House			Senate			
	ALP	Liberals	NCP	ALP	Liberals	NCP	Others
New South Wales	17	19	9	5	4	1	—
Victoria	10	19	5	4	4	2	—
Queensland	1	9	8	4	3	3	—
South Australia	6	6	—	4	5	—	1[a]
Western Australia	1	9	—	4	5	1	—
Tasmania	—	5	—	4	5	—	1[b]
Australian Capital Territory	1	1	—	1	1	—	—
Northern Territory	—	—	1	1	—	1	—
Australia	36	68	23	27	27	8	2

[a] Liberal Movement.
[b] Independent.
Source: Australian Electoral Office.

Labor's Losses. Putting the two small territories aside for a moment, Labor's best vote for both House and Senate was in New South Wales, and this was reflected in that state's still substantial bloc of House seats (almost half the parliamentary party in the lower chamber now comes from New South Wales) and the fact that it was the only state in which Labor managed to secure a fifth senator. But in the other states there are some striking discrepancies. In Victoria, Labor won fewer than a third of the House seats, but in South Australia half, although the party's share of the total vote was roughly the same in each state. Labor gained almost as large a share of the total vote in Tasmania, where it won no House seats, as in South Australia, where it won half. The explanation is that in New South Wales the Labor party retained a solid bloc of safe seats in Sydney's inner urban area and western working-class suburbs and in the contiguous industrial and urban mining centers of Newcastle and Wollongong. In Victoria, Labor has been forced back into its old heartland—like Sydney's, composed of inner urban areas and western working-class suburbs in Melbourne west of the Yarra River—but in South Australia Labor managed to maintain a wider representation through much of Adelaide. Sydney, Melbourne, and Adelaide have always had a greater concentration of white- and blue-collar workers in separate zones of the cities than have Brisbane and Perth, and so the two latter metropolitan areas are the more susceptible to swings of the pendulum carrying almost all the seats to either Labor or the Liberals. The remaining state capital, Hobart, is still so small that most of it is contained in a single electorate (Denison), with some suburbs in a second, surrounding electorate (Franklin); both are fairly marginal. Thus, the great majority of Labor's metropolitan seats in those states where the swing against the party was largest were at risk, and only two survived: Oxley, composed of Brisbane's southern industrial suburbs and the contiguous mining and industrial provincial city of Ipswich, retained by the former treasurer, Bill Hayden; and Fremantle, composed of Perth's port area and contiguous suburbs ranging across the socioeconomic spectrum, retained by the former minister for education, Kim Beazley.

The thirty House seats Labor lost in 1975 fall into two main groups. Twenty had been won at recent elections—1969, 1972, or 1974—and were the components of victory in 1972 and survival in 1974. Most were traditionally marginal seats. Eight had been picked up in 1969 in the first surge from the trough of 1966: Barton, Eden-Monaro, and St. George in New South Wales, Bowman in Queensland, Kingston in South Australia, Perth and Swan in Western

Australia, Franklin in Tasmania. Another nine had come with the second surge that carried Labor into office: Cook, Evans, Macarthur, and Phillip in New South Wales, Casey, Diamond Valley, Holt, and LaTrobe in Victoria, and Denison in Tasmania. Finally, in the last stage of the revitalization of the Labor party, in Victoria the ALP had won Henty and Isaacs in 1974, plus the new Western Australian seat of Tangney created just before the election. Disappointing as their loss would be, these were the sort of seats that would go in any significant swing of the pendulum.

Of the other ten seats Labor lost in 1975, seven can to varying degrees be attributed to state peculiarities: Brisbane (held since 1931), Capricornia (1961), Dawson (1966 by-election), and Leichhardt (1951) were part of the steady erosion of Labor support in Queensland that had been going on since the 1961 election, subject to a temporary reversal in 1972. Similarly, Bass (1954—already lost at the by-election of 1975), Braddon (1958), and Wilmot (1946) were casualties of Labor's decline in Tasmania already apparent in 1974 though greatly magnified in 1975. In New South Wales, Macquarie (1940) was especially at risk because of the retirement of a veteran member who had held the seat since 1951. In Western Australia, Kalgoorlie (1961) was a victim of the statewide swing; like Brisbane it had been a marginal seat for many years and had been lost once before, in 1958. In the Australian Capital Territory, Canberra (1951) had an exceptionally large swing attributed to local hostility to both the Whitlam government and to the member whose brief term as minister for the Australian Capital Territory had antagonized many local interests.

In the Senate, Labor lost four seats, one each from Victoria, South Australia, Western Australia, and Tasmania, and gained two of the four new seats from the territories. With only twenty-seven out of sixty-four senators, Labor was much worse off than it had been with twenty-nine of the sixty following the 1974 double-dissolution election. Because of the coalition's strong performance, under the convention whereby after a double dissolution the first five senators elected in the count secure the longer terms (five and a half years) and the other five the shorter terms (two and a half years, the loss of half a year from the normal six/three being caused by the provision of the constitution that all senators elected at a double-dissolution election have their terms dated from the *preceding* July 1), the coalition secured a three-to-two advantage in longer terms in five of the six states. The exception was Tasmania where the independent, Harradine, secured a longer term. Thus at the next half-Senate election, due in 1978, thirteen Labor and sixteen coalition senators will retire, together with Steele Hall, elected for the Liberal movement in South Australia, and the four territorial senators, whose election, not being provided for by the constitution, has been synchronized with House elections by the statute which added them to the Senate. Judging by "normal" Senate results, the average since 1949, Labor can hope to win fifth place in only three states—New South Wales, South Australia, and Tasmania. Thus, the coalition appears to have secured an unbeatable hold on the Senate, whatever might happen at the next House of Representatives election.

Minor Parties and the Solid Party Vote. Closely associated with the Senate's rise in political importance in recent years was the increasing readiness of voters to support minor-party or independent candidates. That development was arrested and sharply reversed at the double-dissolution election in 1974, which wiped out the DLP's Senate representation. Prior to the appearance of the DLP in 1955 it seemed that non-major-party candidates could expect about 5 percent of the Senate vote, as can be seen from the following breakdown:

Election	Percentage of Senate Vote Won by Major Parties
1949	95.30
1951	95.57
1953 [a]	95.04
1955	89.28
1958	87.97
1961	86.78
1964 [a]	90.36
1967 [a]	87.80
1970 [a]	80.40
1974	91.17
1975	92.65

[a] Senate election only

Should Prime Minister Fraser avail himself of the opportunity to dissolve the House six months or so earlier than he need in 1978 and keep House and Senate elections in step thereafter, one might expect that sort of figure to be restored. If he does not and Senate elections return to the "by-election atmosphere" of the 1964–70 period, then maverick candidates might get a larger share of the poll, though it is difficult to imagine who would get the necessary one-sixth of the votes to win a seat in the Senate when only five are at stake from each state.

Perhaps it should be added that even when a substantial proportion of the Senate votes goes to minor-party or independent candidates, the overwhelming majority of voters cast a solid party vote even though the form of the ballot allows them to pick and choose individuals from other tickets for their second and subsequent preferences. This can be illustrated, with 1975 figures, by the destination of coalition preferences in New South Wales, where the size of the state (2.8 million votes cast), the number of candidates (fifty-three), and the absence of any major distraction (the DLP with only 1.75 percent, led the minor parties) combined to concentrate the voters' minds on an either/or choice. The quota for election was 231,796 votes. The leading candidate on the coalition ticket, Cotton (Liberal), received 1,249,256 votes and so, with the quota deducted, had 1,017,460 surplus votes to be distributed. Of these, 99.66 percent went to the second candidate on the coalition ticket, Carrick (Liberal) and a further 0.13 percent to other candidates on the coalition ticket. On the next count, following Carrick's election, he had a surplus of 783,636 votes, of which 99.83 percent went to the third coalition candidate, Scott (Country), and 0.09 percent to others on the coalition ticket.[7] With Scott now elected, 99.90 percent of his surplus of 552,400 went to the fourth candidate, Baume (Liberal), and 0.03 percent to the two remaining coalition candidates. Of Baume's surplus of 323,577,

---

[7] Note that the ballot-papers which gave Carrick 1,329 first preferences would not have been examined to determine the *distribution* of his surplus, only those which had given first preference to Cotton and second to Carrick plus any which had given first preference to the leading Labor candidate, elected at the same time as Cotton, and then second to Carrick. Ballot-papers which give their first preferences to candidates other than those elected first in the "count down" are not reexamined for the purpose of determining the *distribution* of the surplus although they contribute to its *number*. Thus if there had been split-ticket voting by those who gave their first preference to a candidate other than the ticket leader, the consequent leakage would be suppressed by the method of counting. This would be a most unlikely occurrence, but it has been claimed by the fifth-placed candidate on the Labor team in Queensland in 1974, Malcolm Colston, that it cost him election to the tenth and last Senate place. His case was that an unusually high proportion of first preferences had been given to the third member of the coalition team, Neville Bonner, the only aborigine to hold a seat in the federal Parliament; Colston's scrutineers (poll watchers) reported that "half" of these ballot-papers had shown second and immediately subsequent preferences going to Labor candidates, suggesting that a number of Labor supporters wished to show their support for an aborigine. See Malcolm Colston, *The Odd One Out* (Brisbane: Colonial Press, 1975), p. 109. The estimates of Colston's scrutineers have been challenged by other observers.

99.89 percent went to the fifth candidate, Lajovic (Liberal) and 0.04 percent to the sixth and last candidate, Ross (Country); Lajovic's surplus of only 92,240 fell well short of a quota and brought an end to counting "from the top" of the vote. The counting then shifted to "the bottom" with a succession of counts in which the candidate with the fewest votes was excluded and his or her preferences distributed. Ross secured 45 percent of the preferences of forty minor candidates, 70 percent from the leading candidate of the Family Action movement (an anti-permissive-society group which had received 1.8 percent of the total vote) and 84 percent from the last DLP candidate to be excluded, former Senator Kane, but this still left him behind the fifth Labor candidate who secured the tenth and last Senate seat for New South Wales.

That very tight movement of preferences along the party ticket can be compared with the Liberal performance in Tasmania, a much smaller state (247,000 votes cast) with fewer candidates (twenty-eight), several distractions (disputes as to the ordering of candidates on both the Liberal and Labor tickets, the presence of a strong independent candidate in Harradine, and a separate National party ticket), and greater voter sophistication about proportional representation through its use at state lower-house elections for more than sixty years. Here the quota was only 20,211. The first candidate, Rae, had a surplus of 71,492, 93.27 percent of which went to the Liberals' number two candidate, Townley, and 5.98 percent to other Liberal candidates. The leakage may be explained in part by Townley's recent return to the Liberal fold after his success as an independent at the 1974 Senate election. Of Townley's 53,726-vote surplus, 96.97 percent went to number three, Archer, and 2.65 percent to other Liberals; of Archer's 34,816-vote surplus, 98.86 percent went to number four, Wright, and 0.99 percent to the other two Liberals. Of Wright's 20,762-vote surplus, 99.04 percent went to number five and 0.80 percent to number six, but this was not enough to give a quota so the count from the top stopped. Again upwards of 99 percent of the surplus went down the ticket on each count, although there was significantly more leakage to other candidates on the ticket—for the reasons suggested above. A similar pattern is shown by the distribution of Labor surpluses, 99 percent of the ballots indicating straight party preferences but some choosing among the party's candidates in a different order from that recommended by the Labor party. Thus, while the system of proportional representation used for the Australian Senate, unlike the list systems used in Western Europe and just introduced for the South Australian state upper house, offers voters a chance to choose among candidates of their favorite party, very few avail themselves of the opportunity.

Labor's Prospects

The preceding pages suggest that, although the swing produced by the 1975 election was unusually large and exceptionally uniform among electorates, it was far from unique. It closely resembles the picture of 1966 when the Labor party, then in opposition, was handicapped by an unpopular stand—its hostility to the war in Vietnam and consequently, it appeared to many, to the American alliance on which Australian security had rested since 1942. Labor's handicap in 1975 was its administrative record, which combined (1) the highest rate of inflation in more than twenty years and the greatest unemployment in more than thirty-five years, (2) a sudden diversion of resources from the private to the public sector which did more to annoy those who lost than it did to secure the gratitude of those who gained, and (3) a rash of public disputes about policies and personalities in the highest levels of government which recalled the Gorton-McMahon years that had led up to the coalition's defeat and which contrasted unfavorably with the monolithic somnolence of the Menzies era. In the popular phrase, the government was like a bee in a bottle, buzzing but getting nowhere.

Since his rejection at the polls, Whitlam has argued that his party is still in a position to recover by the next election just as it recovered between 1966 and 1969: the 7.1 percentage points it gained then are almost equal to the 7.4 percentage points it lost between 1974 and 1975. Most things are possible, particularly if they have happened once before. Still, there are substantial obstacles to a recovery on that scale in so short a time. The circumstances that produced it in 1966–69 were special. At the leadership level, between 1966 and 1969 the Liberals exchanged a popular prime minister who in 1966 had not yet shown the weaknesses which contributed to the very considerable loss of support he suffered between the House election of 1966 and the Senate election of 1967 (most of the realignment between 1966 and 1969 had already been recorded by the 1967 Senate election) for a new prime minister who by 1969 had been in office long enough to display the weaknesses which contributed to his eventual deposition by his own party. At the same time, the Labor party had exchanged an aging and controversial figure, Calwell, who looked and sounded like the survivor of bygone battles that he was, for Whitlam, who talked about a new set of issues and looked and sounded like Menzies at the height of his powers. The principal issue of the 1966 election, Vietnam, turned from an asset to a liability for the coalition as the war and conscription soured in the public estimation, while Whitlam's "urban strategy" brought forward a new set of issues related to the idea of private affluence and public poverty. Although Gorton's nationalist stance on matters like foreign investment and states' rights moved part of the way towards matching Whitlam's appeal to younger voters, Gorton was unable to record many solid achievements in the face of hostility from within the coalition and from coalition state governments.

Now, in mid-1976, it appears unlikely that the Labor party can secure quick advantages by either changed leadership or new issues. The Liberals, having lost four leaders in rapid succession (Holt, Gorton, McMahon, and Snedden), are unlikely to reject a fifth. Moreover, the one ground on which Fraser might begin to antagonize his supporters, ideological rigidity, gives anyone who seeks to challenge him little leverage. The Fraserism that has emerged is doctrinaire Liberalism as the party has preached it, if not practiced it, since 1945. A prime minister who actively pursues the goals of small government and free enterprise is unlikely to be attacked until the policies directed towards these goals have actually lost his party votes and seats. In the Labor party, the one man who could have replaced Whitlam at once, Bill Hayden, chose not to move. Even if he does succeed Whitlam before the next House election, his considerable virtues as an administrator and an economic pragmatist are unlikely to match Whitlam's charisma on the hustings in securing massive electoral gains in quick time.

Similarly, in the issues area, there is little likelihood that the 1966–69 scenario will recur. Deterioration on the international political scene would favor the coalition with its commitment to greater defense capability and a refurbishing of the American alliance. A continuation of high inflation and unemployment can be blamed on Labor's mismanagement, and, although the evidence of the first months of the Fraser government suggests that things are not going to get much better in the near future, they are not likely to get very much worse. Some of Whitlam's urban strategy will be implemented by the Fraser government and will pass into the area of "settled policies" from which little partisan advantage can be derived. Other parts, which because of their nature or administrative mishandling failed to get off the ground in Labor's three years in office, have to that extent been discredited or at least had their electoral appeal greatly reduced. Others still, borrowed from abroad like the campaign for equality of opportunity in education, have had their theoretical underpinning challenged. The considerable policy advantage which Whitlam held in both 1969 and 1972 will be extremely difficult to recapture by 1978 or maybe even 1981.

The first opinion polls to appear after the December 1975 election suggested that little change was taking place. The *Age-Sydney Morning Herald* poll on the first weekend in April 1976 showed the coalition at 50.4 percent, the Labor party at 43.3 percent, the DLP at 2.2 percent, the Australia party at 1.7 percent, and others at 2.5 percent.[8] The ANOP poll on the last weekend in March and the first weekend in April showed the coalition at 52 percent, the Labor party at 44 percent, the DLP and Australia party at 1 percent each, and others at 2 percent.[9] A better indication of voting intentions for the future is likely to be available after the first Fraser government Budget has been delivered in August 1976. In the meantime responses to two ANOP questions suggest that the coalition may have some difficulties in maintaining that level of support.[10] Asked whether the federal government should be supporting or opposing wage indexation, 62 percent of L-NCP voters and 77 percent of Labor voters favored supporting it, while only 21 percent of L-NCP voters and 13 percent of Labor voters favored opposing. Asked whether governments should allow a relatively high unemployment level in order to bring down the inflation rate, only 21 percent of L-NCP voters and 9 percent of Labor voters agreed, while 72 percent and 87 percent, respectively, disagreed. Now it may be that, should the coalition be perceived to be supporting unpopular policies, its partisans will change their attitude to the policies rather than their voting intentions, or that the coalition will conceal its adherence to such policies, or that it will change or greatly modify its policies.

At the time of the survey, at least, the Fraser government appeared to be out of step in the important area of wages and employment with a majority of its supporters, although the latter remained optimistic. Asked whether the economy was in good shape or bad shape, 73 percent of L-NCP voters and 60 percent of Labor voters answered that it was in bad shape. When those respondents were further asked whether Fraser would be able to restore it to good shape, 75 percent of coalition voters thought he would and only 8 percent said he could not; the Labor voters were less sanguine, with only 19 percent saying he could and 66 percent saying he could not.

---

[8] Melbourne *Age*, April 21 and 22, 1976.

[9] *National Times*, April 12-17, 1976.

[10] Ibid.

According to the *Age-Sydney Morning Herald* poll, Fraser remained solidly popular with Liberal voters: 73 percent gave him a high personal popularity rating, 20 percent an indifferent score, and only 7 percent an unpopular score; his ratings with Labor voters were diametrically opposite—6 percent, 20 percent, and 74 percent respectively. Similarly with Whitlam, his own supporters thought well of him: 67 percent rated him popular, 20 percent were indifferent, 12 percent gave an unpopular rating; among Liberal voters the ratings for Whitlam were 5 percent, 19 percent, and 76 percent respectively. It is worth remembering that we do not know whether the Liberal voters among whom Fraser is unpopular overlap with those among whom Whitlam is popular, though the two small groups are about the same in number. It is quite possible that the same Liberal voters dislike *both* leaders, and maybe *all* political leaders, and so too with the deviant Labor voters. What is certain for the moment is that there is a high positive correlation between voting intention and leadership effect, not surprising in the light of the heightened partisanship induced by the prolonged political crisis in the latter half of 1975.

Following the Labor party's rejection at the 1966 election, there had been considerable speculation that the party was entering a period of decline. Some argued that the defection of a part of its right wing had so tipped the balance of power within the party that doctrinaires on the left would prevent the parliamentary leadership from seeking the middle ground where electoral success lay. Others argued—on the basis of logic and evidence derived from overseas, particularly Britain—that the long-term *embourgeoisement* of the blue-collar worker was nibbling away Labor's electoral base and that Liberal victories in outer suburban electorates in 1966 meant that Labor voters or their children were being converted into Liberals by more consumer goods, better housing, and upwardly mobile neighbors. Internal reforms within the Labor party broke the power of the left in Victoria and produced immediate political gains; a corresponding and deliberately off-setting diminution of the control of the right in New South Wales did the party no obvious harm. Following the 1975 defeat some of the left-wingers who had been pulled into line by Whitlam a few years earlier were among the first to rally to his support and urge his retention as leader.

To that extent the Labor party appears to accept the lesson that domestic harmony helps win power and can be assisted by power-sharing mechanisms which reflect the strengths of different factions or tendencies within the party. And if the handwriting is to be on the wall for the Labor party, it certainly will not spell *embourgeoise-*

ment. The Australian experience of metropolitan sprawl in the post-war years (and indeed for much longer; Australian cities were among the first in the world to undergo suburbanization) is that people take their politics with them and congregate with those of like habits, class, and politics. There can be shifts in the quality and cost of housing as an area fills up which, via the intervening factors of occupation, income, and class, shift its political balance, but these are the exception rather than the rule. Certainly, rapidly growing electorates have bigger swings. If we look at those whose 1975 enrollment was 110 percent or more of their state quota, in only four of the twenty-seven was the anti-Labor swing below the state average, and eight changed hands. (But that is only 30 percent of the group, compared with 24 percent of all electorates—not much of a distinction.) Nine stayed in the Labor camp, and ten were already held by the coalition. So, on balance, it is hard to see the Labor party under challenge from the sort of threat it faced after 1966.

Failures in Office and Internal Party Problems. That is not to say that the ALP is without its problems. If Anthony Downs's view of parties is sound, then in its three years of office the Labor party did not behave rationally in that it placed policy ahead of office. In particular, it failed to identify securing control of the Senate and reform of the electoral system as the two most important goals for political strategy and to subordinate all policy considerations to those goals. Thus, for example, reduction of the quota variation for electoral redistribution from 20 percent to 10 percent first by legislation and then by constitutional amendment was not adequately explained to the electorate. When the referendum was eventually held in 1974 it was muddled with a novel scheme to change the basis for counting heads for the electorate quota from enrollment to population, which would have advantaged Labor to the extent of only three or four seats but was attacked as a sinister attempt to fix the party in control forever. The proposal was then virtually ignored by Labor during the combined election-and-referendum campaign.

The slack staffwork that muffed the resignation of Senator Gair and lost the advantage of what could have been a clever, albeit rather disreputable, move to improve the government's position in the Senate is another instance of the Labor government's incapacity to identify the main chance and to concentrate on it long enough to secure it. Even in individual constituencies electoral advantage was dissipated recklessly. During the Parramatta by-election of 1973, the government's and in particular the prime minister's insistence on an ill-conceived airport siting scheme *may* have lost the by-election and, at the ensuing 1974 election, *may* have also lost an adjacent seat. Similarly the prime minister's failure to pay anything but a fleeting visit to Brisbane after that city's disastrous floods early in 1974 *may* have lost one Labor seat and prevented the party from winning another at the double-dissolution election later in the year. A government with as small a majority as Labor enjoyed after 1972 and a hostile Senate could not afford to ride roughshod over local sensibilities. It must be asked how a major party comes to behave so irrationally (in Downsian terms).

Part of the answer lies in the Labor party's internal constitution, part in Whitlam's personality, and a very large part in the interplay between the two. From its earliest days democracy within the Labor party has meant a nominal and fitful control by the entire parliamentary party, the caucus, over policy and the election of ministers. Throughout the party's history, rather more at the state level than the federal, there have been leaders who bucked the system too blatantly and were deposed, usually with calamitous short-term impact on the party's electoral success. The great leaders in Labor mythology have been those who were prepared to work within the system, to cultivate and conciliate rather than confront backbenchers and the extraparliamentary organs of the party. Within living memory this was the way of John Curtin and Ben Chifley, who between them won a war and implemented a great deal of party policy. As party leader in opposition, Whitlam secured some much needed reforms including the addition of the parliamentary party leadership (the leader and deputy leader from both House and Senate) to the party's leading extraparliamentary organs, the Federal Conference and the Federal Executive, and broke the one-faction domination of the two main state branches. But he failed to obtain the more sweeping reform of the extraparliamentary organization he had sought, and he failed in a crucial attempt to secure a small cabinet to be selected out of the large elected ministry. The first failure was of no consequence in the 1972–75 period, but the second meant that the cabinet never became the sensitive instrument for determining priorities it might have been. Even if Whitlam could have behaved like a Liberal prime minister and selected his own ministers and those he wished to include in an inner cabinet, it is unlikely that many of the disasters which occurred would have been avoided. All of the ministers whose falls from grace contributed to the growing impression of administrative chaos would have been included in his cabinet, and, although Whitlam's own choices for some of the second team might have been marginally better than those elected for him by the caucus, the overall impact of any differences would have been slight.

Here, then, is the Labor party's dilemma. Its traditional processes for working in government failed, but Whitlam's own contribution to that failure refutes any suggestion that the transfer of greater authority to the parliamentary leader—a transfer which many in the party would see as giving in to Caesarist tendencies which have always been resisted—would have been an improvement. The defeat and disintegration of the United Australia party in 1940–41 allowed Menzies, who was then young enough and flexible enough, to rebuild its fragments into the Liberal party which deliberately avoided the organizational faults of the UAP. Labor's defeat in 1975 was not on such a scale. The party's belief in intraparty democracy is too entrenched, in the absence of a clear association between traditional practices and its administrative failure, for any major reform to be acceptable. Whitlam is too near retirement, and no alternative leader has the ascendancy sufficient to tamper with the party machinery. For the foreseeable future one can reasonably expect the Labor party to go on, looking very much as it does now, waiting in a rather Micawberish posture for something to turn up (presumably policy errors by the Fraser government) which will return it to office.

The Broad Implications of 1975

The greater significance of the events of 1975, here taking a much wider focus than the campaign and poll of November-December, lies in their impact on the constitutional structure of Australia. Some consequences flow from the change of government. Thus, Fraser's new federalism seeks to reverse the long drift of power away from the states and to the federal government. The first step is the designation of a specific share of federally collected income tax to go directly to the states (and an additional small share to local government); this the states may increase or reduce by imposing additional taxes or granting rebates. The second step, the transfer of functions from the federal government to the states, could enhance the effectiveness of the states or merely confirm their financial weakness. Which it is to be should be known by the end of 1977. Fraser's parallel campaign to reduce government intervention, to increase the citizen's and taxpayer's capacity to make decisions for himself, runs counter to an even older tendency in Australian politics, one which long antedates the establishment of a federal government. It could prove to be a sloganeering fig leaf for the realities of the welfare state if departmental ministers, anxious backbenchers, and aggrieved interests combine to block the prime minister's ideological thrust. Again, we should know by the end of 1977, for such a bitter pill is certain to require increasingly thick sugar-coatings as the next election nears.

The other consequences come from the Senate's assertion of coequal authority with the House of Representatives and the governor general's enhanced power, which both derive from the possibility of stalemate between the two chambers.[11] What these will be in practice we are most unlikely to know for some years, maybe well into the 1980s. So long as the government of the day retains control of the Senate the Pandora's box opened briefly in 1974 and again in 1975 will remain closed. But once the government loses control of the Senate, whether to the opposition or to a combination of opposition senators and minor-party members or independents, then the implications of the Senate's withholding supply and the governor general's forcing a ministry with a majority in the House to go to the people will move once again from the constitutional law texts to the front pages of the newspapers. Even before then, should the government have only a narrow margin of control in the Senate, the precedents of two state governments' breaches of the convention that casual vacancies should be filled by the nominees of the party previously holding the seats could become important. Further, the attraction of holding the balance of power in the Senate is enhanced by the Senate's new power. This increases the danger of what might be called "constitutional terrorism": sectional interests, which need the support of only one-sixth of the electorate in a small state to win representation in the Senate, might seize both government and opposition by the throat and hold out the prospect of office to whichever would pay the higher price. It may be that the good sense of the Australian voters will work against such an eventuality. The present writer agrees with V. O. Key that the electorate is usually responsible in what it does, in Australia as in the United States. But when the prevailing level of interparty competition keeps the balance so delicately poised, and in particular when the method of electing the Senate differs so substantially from that used for the House of Representatives, responsible electors will have to calculate the effects of their votes very finely.

It has been argued that the coalition's majority in both houses in December 1975 proves that the electorate legitimated the actions of both Senate and governor general. A poll conducted by Australian Public Opinion Polls (the Gallup method) in March 1976 recorded

---

[11] For an extended account, see Colin Howard, "The Constitutional Crisis of 1975," *Australian Quarterly*, vol. 48 (March 1976), pp. 5-25.

that 52 percent of respondents thought that the governor general had been right in bringing about a general election when he did and 53 percent thought that his power to dismiss an elected government should be retained.[12] Only 42 percent thought that he had been wrong, and the same proportion thought that the power should be eliminated. Not surprisingly, 87 percent of coalition supporters thought he had been right and 76 percent thought he should retain the power, while only 9 percent thought he had been wrong and 20 percent thought the power should be eliminated. Among Labor supporters, 83 percent thought Sir John Kerr had been wrong and 70 percent thought the power should be eliminated; 14 percent thought him right, and 26 percent would have him retain the power. However, the respondents drew an interesting distinction between good constitutional theory and wise political practice. In response to the question: "Do you think Mr. Whitlam did himself harm or good by his very strong criticism of the Governor-General's action in the crisis before the election?", 57 percent of Labor supporters thought he had done himself harm, as did 93 percent of coalition supporters; only 35 percent of Labor supporters and 3 percent of coalition supporters thought that Whitlam had done himself good.

In a letter to the editor defending the governor general's action, one Canberra voter wrote: "When the patient survives, who can criticise the surgeon if he dropped a couple of stitches?"[13] This may reflect the common sense approach to the constitutional niceties, but it ignores the possibility that the surgeon also left a sponge inside the patient. For the time being, Australia still enjoys a competitive party system, firm government which rests on an open-ended mandate, a placid electorate, and good political health.

---

[12] *Courier-Mail*, March 25, 1976.
[13] *Canberra Times*, April 15, 1976.

APPENDIX A

Politics and the Constitution:
Twenty Questions Left by Remembrance Day *

David Butler

A constitution is a set of rules designed to provide for orderly government in all foreseeable circumstances. Its strength and viability can be
tested only in crisis—and in most established democracies crises affecting the continuity of government are mercifully rare. The political
scientist must therefore seize on those that occur and analyze them
exhaustively for the light they throw on the generalizations about the
system formulated a priori in more tranquil times. The modern history
of the countries governed on the Westminster model offers no parallel
to the episode in Canberra that reached its climax on November 11,
1975. As a case study in constitutional interpretation and in political
tactics, those events provide a story of remarkable fascination and
complexity. They raise a host of problems for the historian, the
lawyer, and the observer of politics. As long as Australia is governed
under its present constitution, they will be a source of anecdote and
of argument. The Senate's success in forcing an election will be remembered in every future disagreement between the two houses and
the ghosts of Sir John Kerr and Gough Whitlam will haunt every
future meeting between governor general and prime minister.

I returned to Australia in late November to look at the general
election. But since that proved to be the flattest of the four Australian
campaigns that I had watched (as it drifted to the landslide that the
opinion polls predicted), I spent my time trying to sort out for myself

This article was commissioned by *Current Affairs Bulletin*, published by the
Department of Adult Education of the University of Sydney. It is reproduced
here by permission. Details of style and spelling have been changed to conform
with American usage.
* Editor's Note: Remembrance Day is the Australian name for Armistice Day,
November 11—also the date of the governor general's dismissal of Prime Minister
Whitlam.

the rights and wrongs of what happened on November 11. To a few of the most obvious and central questions there will never be a definitive answer and to many more the answer proved too elusive for me, an outsider with all too little time for the task. But friends have encouraged me to set out my questions together with such answers as I could formulate. My readers should certainly disagree with or refine upon those answers and formulate additional questions of their own. During two weeks of listening to the arguments of competent authorities, I was struck by how often new angles and complications emerged which despite a month of hothouse discussion had not occurred to these shrewd and inside observers. This article should be treated as no more than a preliminary report, offering a summary of the problem, perhaps, but only a cursory suggestion of the solutions.

This is not the place to chronicle the detailed events that took place between October 10 and November 11, let alone to write the history of the Labor government. The list on page 318 will remind readers of the key events, and they should turn to the press during and after the crisis for fuller accounts. What follows is an exploration of twenty of the constitutional or political questions raised by the whole affair.

(1) Can the Senate refuse supply?

(2) Must a government have supply or resign?

(3) How long could government have carried on if the Senate had stayed obdurate?

(4) Can a governor general dismiss a prime minister?

(5) Did the governor general deal properly with Whitlam?

(6) Did the governor general deal properly with Malcolm Fraser?

(7) Who was the governor general entitled to consult?

(8) Could Whitlam have called a half-Senate election earlier?

(9) What would a half-Senate election have decided?

(10) What were the electoral deadlines?

(11) Was Whitlam's decision to call a half-Senate election crucial?

(12) Can a prime minister secure the dismissal of a governor general?

(13) Was there anything Labor could have done after Whitlam's dismissal?

(14) Should the governor general have listened to the speaker?

(15) Should the House vote of no confidence in Fraser have made a difference?

(16) Could there have been a referendum to settle the supply issue?

(17) Could the governor general have asked for the issue to be brought to a vote in the Senate?

(18) Would the Senate have given way if the governor general had taken no action on November 11?

(19) Could a governor general dissolve Parliament without the advice of the prime minister?

(20) What general lessons can be drawn?

(1) Can the Senate Refuse Supply? The governor general, the chief justice, and many other authorities agreed that the constitution gives the undoubted right to the Senate to refuse supply. Section 53 reads:

> Proposed laws appropriating revenues or moneys, or imposing taxation, shall not originate in the Senate. . . . The Senate may not amend proposed laws imposing taxation, or proposed laws appropriating revenue or moneys for the ordinary annual services of the government. The Senate may not amend any proposed law so as to increase any proposed charge or burden on the people. The Senate may at any stage return to the House of Representatives any proposed law which the Senate may not amend, requesting, by message, the omission or amendment of any items or provisions therein. And the House of Representatives may, if it thinks fit, make any of such omissions or amendments, with or without modifications. Except as provided in this section, the Senate shall have equal power with the House of Representatives in respect of all proposed laws.

The final sentence might be thought definitive. But there are three plausible objections to accepting the Senate's unfettered power—one textual, one historical, and one constitutional in a wider sense. The textual objection is that rejection is a form of amendment and that the section properly read denies the Senate all control over money bills. Sir Richard Eggleston, a much-respected constitutional authority, argued this in a letter to the *Age* (October 27, 1975). Professor Sawer, while disagreeing with him (*Canberra Times*, December 5, 1975), suggested that if Whitlam had presented the supply legislation to the governor general for signature without the Senate's approval but with the supporting opinion of Sir Richard Eggleston and others, Sir John

Kerr would have had to accede, even if the legality of such a procedure then went to the High Court and was disallowed. It seems that this was in fact considered and rejected by Whitlam and his colleagues. The final outcome—a double dissolution—might still have been the same, but the scenario in early November would have been very different. Moreover, the High Court might have agreed (though it does not seem at all likely) with Sir Richard Eggleston.

The historical objection which Sir Richard Eggleston developed in subsequent correspondence in the *Age* (December 5 and 11, 1975) is that, whatever the letter of the constitution, the founders plainly did not intend that the Senate should refuse supply. This view depends partly on the deliberate omission from the final 1898 draft of the constitution of a clause spelling out such a Senate power and partly on the remarks in Quick and Garran's authoritative commentary on the constitution published in 1901.[1]

But the broadest objection to the Senate's refusal of supply lies not in the letter of the constitution but in the practice. The constitution, after all, represented an attempt to set down formally the customs of British and colonial governments at the end of the nineteenth century. The battle over the powers of the upper house in Britain was not fought out until ten years later, when in 1909–1911 the Commons's ascendancy over the Lords was established. The Australian Senate has a different, democratic basis, but from 1901 until 1974 it never tried to assert its right to bring a government down.[2] Whatever interpretation is made of the text of 1901, the practice of seventy years might be thought to establish unicameral responsibility.

It is worth stressing that the Senate was not objecting to the substance of the Budget (the opposition had not even voted against it in the lower house). Their obstruction was designed solely to force an election—it was a maneuver somewhat analogous to the "tacking-on" procedure of financial amendment to other legislation so explicitly banned in Section 53. The Senate's action was an unequivocal assertion that the Australian government is answerable to both houses. That assertion was endorsed by the highest authorities in the land on November 11 and then by the people on December 13. But we have surely not heard the end of the matter. At some point in the future the two houses will be at loggerheads again and the whole issue will

---

[1] J. Quick and R. R. Garran, *Annotated Constitution of the Australian Commonwealth* (Melbourne, 1901), pp. 663–72.

[2] The Canadian Senate had similar powers vested in it in 1867 but has never used them.

be reopened. For nothing that happened on November 11 settled it definitively.

(2) Must a Government Have Supply or Resign? A. V. Dicey in 1886 developed the doctrine that one of the essential powers of Parliament over the administration was the right to refuse supply.[3] "Grievances precede supply" was one of the great principles on which the Civil War was fought and Charles I lost his head. But essentially in modern times supply is only one among many issues of confidence: it is accepted in all the Westminster model democracies that a cabinet which cannot carry the lower house with it on a major issue of legislation, whether or not supply is involved, must resign or dissolve. Supply is, of course, important because it means that a government cannot rule indefinitely, keeping Parliament adjourned. But there are other annual measures which would deny legality to a cabinet that refused to summon Parliament. Supply is more clearly important in a bicameral situation: a government may ignore votes of no confidence or the defeat of legislation in the upper house but it cannot carry on if the upper house has and exercises the right to refuse money.

But supply is also important if it is thought to be important. One factor that received too little attention in reports of the November crisis was the attitude of senior public servants as they contemplated the subterfuges and potential illegalities in which they would personally be involved if duly authorized monies ran out. Their obligations under the Audit Act and their capacity to place orders and enter into contracts on behalf of the government were in doubt. None of the suggested expedients for carrying on after supply was exhausted about the end of November seemed acceptable. There is little doubt that the honest anxieties of top officials echoed through to Government House and perhaps colored the final decision. Even the governor general has to sign warrants for the expenditure of money, *duly authorized,* and his own conscience may have been exercised on this specific point.

(3) How Long Could Government Have Been Carried on if the Senate Had Stayed Obdurate? It is clear that the available funds would cover expenditure up to the November 27 pay day but that there was grave doubt about meeting public service salaries due on December 11. It is clear too that soundings had been made with Commonwealth and private banks about extending credit to cover routine salaries and other payments but that the legal position about such credit was

---

[3] A. V. Dicey, *The Law of the Constitution,* 7th ed. (London, 1908), p. 450.

SOME KEY EVENTS

1972

Dec. 2   Labor party wins election, 69–58 in House.

1974

May 18   Labor government reelected, 66–61. Senate divided 29 L-NCP, 29 Labor, 2 other.

1975

Mar. 22   Fraser ousts Snedden as leader of Liberals.

Mar. 24   Fraser says government with majority in House has right to govern except in "very extreme" circumstances.

July 2   Cairns dismissed for misleading House (following six weeks of intensive publicity over loans affair).

Aug. 19   Hayden introduces Budget.

Aug. 22   Fraser says Liberals will not vote against Budget.

Sept. 3   Queensland government nominates Field (independent) to succeed Senator Milliner (Labor).

Oct. 9   High Court decides 4–3 that government can call elections for new Australian Capital Territory and New Territory Senate seats.

Oct. 14   Connor dismissed for misleading House.

Oct. 15   Fraser says supply will be refused.

Oct. 16   Senate defers consideration of supply. Whitlam says he will "tough it out."

Oct. 21   Whitlam and Fraser confer separately with governor general.

Oct. 26   Whitlam gets Queen to revoke dormant commission of governor of Queensland.*

Oct. 30   Whitlam and Fraser confer separately with governor general.

Nov. 3   Fraser offers supply in return for election by June and is rebuffed by Whitlam.

Nov. 4   Whitlam seeks help from the banks for credit after supply runs out.

Nov. 6   Whitlam and Fraser confer separately with governor general.
9:15 a.m. Whitlam and Fraser meet and fail to reach agreement.
7:30 p.m. Whitlam tells Labor caucus he is asking for half-Senate election.

Nov. 11   1:10 p.m. Whitlam seeks half-Senate election and is dismissed by governor general.
1:30 p.m. Governor general appoints Fraser as caretaker prime minister.
2:15 p.m. Senate votes supply.
3:15 p.m. House votes no confidence in Fraser.
4:45 p.m. Double dissolution proclaimed.

Dec. 13   Election gives L-NCP coalition 91–36 majority in House, 35–27 majority in Senate (with 2 independents).

* Editor's Note: See discussion of questions 5 and 12.

obscure. There are people close to the Labor cabinet who believe that everything was satisfactorily in train for government to continue up till February: there are people at the top of the public service who believe that the alternatives were proving impossible and this would have become apparent by the middle of November. Australia has a notably tight statutory control over the expenditure of public money. State governments were ready to move writs of prohibition against the auditor general if he sanctioned the expenditure of money not authorized by Parliament. Moreover, depositors and shareholders were ready to take legal steps if their banks made loans secured only by assurances from a government that lacked constitutional supply; some of the banks had by November 11 received legal advice, warning them against giving the government any unsecured credit. It was a complicated situation; there seem to have been no authoritative reports in the press. It is a by-way of the affair that would merit further research. But my impression is that government would have been brought to a standstill by a whole host of court-enforced injunctions, unless, by early December, the Senate had voted supply.

(4) Can a Governor General Dismiss a Prime Minister? There are two relevant sections in the constitution. Section 2 states that a "Governor-General . . . shall have and may exercise in the Commonwealth during the Queen's pleasure, but subject to this Constitution, such powers and functions of the Queen as her Majesty may be pleased to assign to him." Section 64 says: "The Governor-General may appoint officers to administer such Departments of State of the Commonwealth as the Governor-General in Council may establish. Such officers shall hold office during the pleasure of the Governor-General. . . ."

Thus there can be no doubt that the letter of the constitution provided Sir John Kerr with the authority for his action—or indeed for much more arbitrary actions.[4] The issue raised by Whitlam's dismissal was one of propriety, not legality. There are several principles not mentioned in the written document which, it is generally agreed, should guide the governor general in his constitutional role. The most central of these is, surely, that the head of state should do his utmost to preserve his nonpartisan status. Before a governor general intervenes on a matter which is a political issue between the parties, it should be plain first that it cannot be solved without his intervention and second that his intervention shall appear to be as evenhanded as possible. Sir John Kerr was in an extraordinarily difficult situation but

---

[4] Section 58 provides that he can withhold assent to a bill, something which the sovereign in Britain has in fact never ventured to do since 1707.

few people could argue that these conditions were met. A very large number of people saw his action as highly partisan (it could in fact hardly have turned out more unfavorably for the Labor party) and there were, as we shall see, unexplored alternatives.

(5) Did the Governor General Deal Properly with Whitlam? We do not know what went on in the four or five encounters between the governor general and Whitlam during the crisis, and since presumably they were not tape-recorded, we may always be skeptical about any accounts that ultimately appear. Sir John Kerr wrote in the letter of dismissal which he gave to Whitlam on November 11:

> You have previously told me that you would never resign or advise an election of the House of Representatives or a double dissolution and that the only way in which such an election could be obtained would be by my dismissal of you and your ministerial colleagues. As it appeared likely that you would today persist in this attitude, I decided that if you did, I would determine your commission and state my reasons for doing so. You have persisted in your attitude and I have accordingly acted as indicated.

But it appears that Sir John did not offer Whitlam any alternatives when he came to Government House or earlier. Whitlam made the point at his press conference that evening:

> Q: Did you get a chance to offer advice to the Governor-General before getting your dismissal notice?
>
> Whitlam: I had spoken to him on the phone and he knew what my advice was going to be. I had the advice in writing. He didn't accept it. . . .
>
> Q: Are you sure that at no stage of the talks you had with the Governor-General did he give you the impression that he thought a general election was the proper course?
>
> Whitlam: On the contrary he gave me the other impression. He knew I had and was likely to continue to have the majority in the House of Representatives.

However he must have known that the governor general was contemplating this possibility. On November 6 Enderby, the attorney general, had informally communicated to the governor general an opinion on his right to dismiss a government that had been prepared by Byers, the solicitor general. (The opinion had not been signed; Enderby did not agree with Byers's view on reserved powers.) Byers

320

rebutted a press statement released by his precursor, Ellicott (now a Liberal member of the House), who argued that a prime minister who did not advise a dissolution on the refusal of supply would be dismissed. Dismissal was in the air, yet Whitlam was plainly utterly surprised when it turned into reality. It seems that the governor general had never confronted Whitlam explicitly with the stark choice "dissolve or be dismissed" and certainly that he was not confronted with this choice on November 11.

The governor general dismissed Whitlam summarily, it seems, because he thought that any other course would lead to his own dismissal and a continuance of the crisis. There is no doubt that Whitlam had given some grounds for such a belief. His whole approach to the governor general had been truculent and uncompromising. He had spoken in jest perhaps, of the governor general as "My Viceroy"; on October 17 he said, "Unquestionably the Governor-General takes advice from his Prime Minister and no one else." [5] He had moved swiftly to get the Queen to revoke the dormant governor general's commission from Sir Colin Hannah on October 23 after the governor of Queensland had publicly sided with the Senate.[6] And in his press conference on November 11 he was to say, when asked if he would contact London, "The Governor-General prevented me getting in touch with the Queen by just withdrawing the commission immediately. I was unable to communicate with the Queen, as I would have been entitled to if I had any warning of the course the Governor-General was to take."

We shall return later to the possibilities and consequences of an appeal to the Queen. But let us for the moment assume that Sir John's fears on this score were justified and that he acted in an abrupt and arbitrary manner because he felt it necessary to do so if he was to prevent the crisis from spiralling out of control with the possibility of a December election being preempted by the delays of exchanges between London and Canberra. Had he no further options? Once he had given Whitlam the letter of dismissal (thus precluding his own firing) could he not then have offered him the choice either of being recommissioned—with the promise that he would call an election and that he would not interfere with the position of the governor general— or of letting Fraser take office and give the advice for a dissolution?

---

[5] There were well-publicized stories of his speaking jokingly to visitors about how in a crunch it would be a race to the telephone between the governor general and himself to see which could dismiss the other first.

[6] A special aspect of all these assertions of power by an Australian prime minister is that they were seen by state premiers and many others far from Canberra as a threat to established state rights.

It might even have been possible to arrange things so that Whitlam could have taken up Fraser's offer of supply in exchange for a May election.

The governor general was dealing with a tough prime minister and he may have felt that an equal firmness was necessary. But it is not clear that Sir John Kerr had to force on Whitlam both an unwanted general election and the loss of office. Just as Sir John made Fraser's acceptance of office conditional so also he could have made Whitlam's continuance in office conditional.

(6) Did the Governor General Deal Properly with Fraser? In the heated days after November 11 there were accusations of collusion between Government House and the opposition. But no solid evidence was produced. Obviously there may have been inadvertent or even deliberate leaks from one or other of the very few people who could have caught some inkling of how Sir John Kerr's mind was moving. Fraser may have made his own deductions from his official conversations with Sir John. But, until evidence to the contrary is produced, my inclination is to disbelieve conspiracy stories and to accept the word of those who swear that on the morning of November 11 Fraser did not know what was going to happen.

But behind this question a larger one is implied. Was there a coup? In the high-pitched period after November 11, people likened the situation to the Greek Colonels' revolution, or the *Putsch* in Chile and there were shrill suggestions of the possibility of some sort of military takeover.[7] But even on the worst construction of events, the insistence that the public should vote on who should govern Australia could hardly be called undemocratic. In fact, although it is impossible to show that there was no connivance or impropriety, it is perhaps more reasonable to take events at face value. The governor general, deciding that it was necessary to secure legally authorized supply for the continuance of orderly government in Australia, followed what he saw as the only proper route to achieve it. One can fault his judgment, one can even suspect some of his inner motives, but before going further one should invoke William of Occam's razor: as the thirteenth-century sage laid down, "Reasons should not be multiplied beyond necessity." If it is easy to see why a reasonable, conscientious man in the governor general's position might (even though misguidedly) have acted as he did, why introduce further explanations?

---

[7] Wild talk was not confined to one side. I heard a minister in the New South Wales government solemnly telling a campaign rally that if Gough Whitlam won there would "never be another free election in Australia."

(7) Who was the Governor General Entitled to Consult? For his official actions the governor general has normally, like the Queen, to act solely on the advice of his ministers. Section 63 reads: "The provisions of this Constitution referring to the Governor-General in Council shall be construed as referring to the Governor-General acting with the advice of the Federal Executive Council." Most of the substantive provisions about the executive government refer to the governor general in council.* But there are powers reserved to the governor general in his own person and on the exercise of these he plainly has the right to go beyond his ministers for counsel. Unfortunately he is in a very isolated position; he can read the newspapers and receive unsolicited letters from all sorts of people but he cannot easily argue out a hypothetical case in circumstances of total discretion. And he lacks a personal staff of the weight or seniority available to the Queen (his admirable official secretary, David Smith, was a second division, only level 1, public servant of forty-two, and he had been three years in the job). It was difficult for the positive collection of opinions and the assessment of options and personalities to be conducted authoritatively on the governor general's behalf. But of course Sir John Kerr was not without guidance. He said in his explanatory statement of November 11: "I had the benefit of discussions with the Prime Minister and, with his approval, with the Leader of the Opposition, and with the Treasurer and the Attorney-General."

He also said: "Once I had made up my mind, for my part, what I must do if Mr. Whitlam persisted in his stated intentions, I consulted the Chief Justice of Australia, Sir Garfield Barwick. I have his permission to say that I consulted him in this way."

But he was probably ill-advised to turn for support to the chief justice. The advisory opinions decision of 1921 bars the High Court from ruling on hypothetical questions and the chief justice, who might have to preside over litigation arising from a constitutional dispute, should be chary of any personal involvement. Sir Garfield Barwick, moreover, was a former Liberal cabinet minister, as suspicious Labor critics were quick to point out. If Sir John Kerr was intent on avoiding any imputation of partiality, he was surely imprudent to seek guidance in that direction.

(8) Could Whitlam Have Called a Half-Senate Election Earlier? On October 9 the High Court, by a vote of four to three,[8] authorized the

---

* Editor's Note: See discussion of question 19.

[8] The casting vote came from Justice Murphy, who, as attorney general, had helped to prepare the disputed legislation. There are precedents for newly

federal government to go ahead with elections for the newly created Senate seats in the Australian Capital Territory (ACT) and Northern Territory. If Whitlam had gone at once to the governor general to ask for a half-Senate election he could hardly have been refused. The same would have been true even if the request had been made a week or ten days later, after the dismissal of Connor on October 14 or the refusal to consider supply on October 16.

If a half-Senate election had been in progress, the story must have run very differently. Technically it would have been possible for it to be overtaken and cancelled by a double dissolution. It might also have been rendered ineffective by the governors of the non-Labor states refusing to issue writs for Senate contests. But if an election was under way it would have been seen as to some extent a referendum on the issue of whether supply should be passed and it would probably have preempted other action.

(9) What Would a Half-Senate Election Have Decided? If Sir John Kerr had acceded to Whitlam's request on November 11, the half-Senate election had only a limited chance of solving the crisis. Thirty of the thirty-six senators chosen would not have taken their seats until July 1, 1976, and the supply crisis had to be settled long before that. The Northern Territory would presumably have returned one Country party and one Labor senator. The ACT might have returned one Labor senator and one independent sympathetic to Labor, although doubt must be cast on that by the performance of Gorton in the actual contest of December 13 (admittedly in very different circumstances). In both Queensland and New South Wales casual vacancies meant that six seats were at stake and that the candidate who came in sixth would serve the short term till July 1. In normal circumstances it is, paradoxically, the weaker party that gets the sixth seat. Perhaps Labor was most likely to get the sixth seat in Queensland and the Liberals in New South Wales. But it would be conceivable for either side by clever (though potentially double-edged) variation of preferences in different areas to arrange that, although stronger in votes, the sixth seat fell to them.

---

appointed judges' taking part in cases where they have had some prior involvement, though this was a fairly extreme example. However, none of the state attorneys general who were contesting the case objected to Justice Murphy's presence on the bench. If he had disqualified himself, a three-to-three vote would apparently have made it impossible to hold the elections for Australian Capital Territory and New Territory senators and the politics of the next month would have run differently.

It is arguable that if the supply crisis had run on, the anti-Liberal trend shown by the polls [9] would have produced a Senate landslide to Labor. But except in the ACT that would probably not have helped them at all in the short term. On November 11 the Senate contained thirty coalition members, twenty-seven Labor members and three independents (two, Steele Hall of South Australia and Bunton of New South Wales, voted with Labor on supply and one, Field of Queensland, was absent, sub judice). On the most optimistic of Labor assumptions the Senate that would have existed from the declaration of the results (which would not be till late January) until June 30 would not have been better than thirty-one Labor, thirty-one coalition, and two independent (Gorton and Steele Hall). But since Labor would be unlikely to win the sixth seat in both Queensland and New South Wales, a more probable outcome would be thirty-two coalition, thirty Labor, and two independent. And if Gorton failed, it would be thirty-three coalition, thirty Labor, and one independent. The half-Senate election was not very likely to give Labor a complacent Senate.

But of course the half-Senate election would have served as a plebiscite. If the votes on December 13 had gone decisively Labor's way, it is overwhelmingly probable that the continuing Senate would not have kept its stomach for the fight.

(10) What Were the Electoral Deadlines? Sir John Kerr, Whitlam, and Fraser had been made aware by the Electoral Office of the legal and technical constraints that would limit the calling of an election. It seems to have been universally accepted that the Australian Christmas set a deadline.* If there were not an election before then there could hardly be one before well into February (July and August in Britain are just as barren electorally). The election had to be on a Saturday. December 20 was almost impossible—it was too near Christmas and it would be hard to muster the school teachers who normally man the booths. December 13 seemed the natural terminus.

In theory, with House elections, only seven days have to elapse between the issue of writs and the close of nominations and only seven days between nominations and polling day. But the need to wait till nominations close to print ballot-papers and to circulate them to absent voters makes the Electoral Office demand more time. The

---

[9] An *Age* poll showed that 70 percent of voters disapproved of the Senate's action and the Morgan Gallup poll recorded a 5.5 percent swing to Labor between October 18 and November 8.

* Editor's Note: Christmas comes at the beginning of summer in Australia.

twenty-two days of 1931 and the twenty-five days of 1940 are the shortest gaps yet between dissolution and polling day.[10]

In crisis that period could surely have been abbreviated by a day or two. For a House of Representatives election on December 13 (and in a real crisis December 20 would not have been impossible) a dissolution could presumably have waited till, say, November 20, even if the rush led to one or two administrative slip-ups on polling day. But it was the Senate that complicated the issue. It is up to state governors to issue writs and, by Section 9 of the constitution, states are allowed, subject to federal law, to make laws prescribing the method of choosing senators. It seems that the timetable under the South Australian Election of Senators Act, 1903, requires nine days to elapse between the dissolution and the issue of writs; effectively that was considered to mean that not less than twenty-nine days would have to elapse between dissolution and a poll for the Senate in South Australia.[11] It would not, of course, be necessary for all Senate elections to take place simultaneously but the force of custom and convenience is very strong. If, therefore, there was to be either a half-Senate election or a full Senate election (following a double dissolution) on December 13, the choice had to be made by November 13 or 14 at the latest. All concerned knew that the week was critical. If the supply issue was to be settled by an election in 1975, the decision could not be delayed.

(11) Was Whitlam's Decision to Call a Half-Senate Election Crucial?

It seems plain that Sir John Kerr had decided to intervene, irrespective of whether Whitlam chose to advise a half-Senate election or not. He had consulted Sir Garfield Barwick and prepared his explanatory statement before Whitlam phoned at 10 a.m. on November 11 to ask for an appointment to recommend a half-Senate election on December 13.

Whitlam's request was seen as rendering it unavoidable for the governor general to make a decision one way or the other; but Sir John showed no wish to avoid it. It is, however, interesting to speculate on whether, had there been no half-Senate request, the governor general could have waited till supply was finally exhausted at the end of the month. It is true that by then it would have been too late for an election to be held until well into the new year. But the Senate's nerve

---

[10] See "The Timing of Australian Elections," in David Butler, *The Canberra Model* (Sydney, 1973), pp. 99-104.

[11] It was considered by the competent authorities that for a Senate election to take place in South Australia on December 13 the South Australian Executive Council had to act before midnight on November 11 and due contacts had been made between Canberra and Adelaide to ensure the necessary arrangements.

might have cracked in the course of November or Whitlam might have been persuaded that he had to consent to an election. And if neither of those eventualities occurred, it would still be possible to call on Fraser, who had committed himself to ensuring supply as soon as an election was announced. If the choice that was put to him on November 11 had been put to him at the end of November, he would undoubtedly have consented and got the Senate to put an immediate end to the supply crisis while waiting for a February election.

From Sir John Kerr's point of view, presumably, the objections to such a pause would have been, first, the inconveniences that were already occurring through the running down of supply; second, the damage to Australia's prosperity and reputation that was being inflicted by the continuing crisis; third, the fact that a final resolution might be delayed from December until February; and fourth, the fear that the ingenious Whitlam might find some new way to complicate or extend the constitutional crisis. One cannot presume to judge which factors were uppermost in Sir John Kerr's mind. But he seems to have made it up.

For, in theory at least, he could have granted the half-Senate election on November 11 and still have been free to impose a double dissolution later in the month.[12] Some cost and inconvenience would have been incurred by the half-Senate candidates already launched on their campaigns. But that would have mattered little if it had produced a more patently just outcome to the crisis. There would have been a chance that the issue would have settled itself by then; if not, it

---

[12] It is ironic that the governor general was in fact able to call a double dissolution. Of course a House election, with or without a half-Senate election, would not have offered a solution since only six of the new senators would have taken office before July 1 and, whichever side won the House, the chances of a continued conflict with the Senate would have been considerable. However, double dissolutions were devised to enable governments to appeal to the people against the obstruction of the Senate. It was odd for a double dissolution to be invoked by those who were doing the obstructing. Moreover the issue at stake, the refusal of supply, had not taken place in a way that justified a double dissolution. (Section 57 provides that a measure has to be rejected twice, with a three-months interval before a double dissolution can be called.) In November 1975 it was only because 21 Labor bills (which Fraser had no intention of passing) had satisfied the necessary conditions that Fraser would recommend a double dissolution. The scenario in November 1975 would have been very different if, almost coincidentally, the possibility of a double dissolution had not been lying around. Yet it could be argued that the governor general was acting in favor of Labor by insisting that the 21 Labor bills rejected by the Senate should be mentioned explicitly in the proclamation of a double dissolution. If Labor had won the House but lost the Senate it could then instantly have enacted these 21 measures in a joint sitting.

would have been apparent that the governor general had waited to intervene till almost every expedient had been exhausted.

(12) Can a Prime Minister Secure the Dismissal of a Governor General? There has been only one recorded instance of this happening: in 1932 Eamon de Valera, the newly elected prime minister of Ireland, asked the Crown to change the governor general of Ireland who had been appointed on the advice of the previous government and who had protested publicly about being treated with discourtesy. But the opinion is strongly held that the Queen ought to accede promptly to almost any request from a Commonwealth prime minister for the dismissal of a governor general. It is open to question whether "promptly" means that if Whitlam had been able to get to the phone at 1 p.m. on November 11, he could have insisted that the Queen (at 2 a.m. English time) should have agreed on the spot to his request and taken immediate action. If she had asked for time, the governor general could, of course, have dismissed Whitlam in the interim (though she might have asked for a truce while she considered the matter).

She would have been in a great difficulty in seeking advice. Her British ministers and the British high commissioner in Canberra would be scrupulously anxious to keep out of an Australian domestic concern. The Australian high commissioner in London could only speak as the mouthpiece of the Canberra government. Her own palace advisers, skilled though they may be about British politics, would hardly be able to help on the Australian scene. The natural contact, the governor general, though he might have a right to give his side of the story, could hardly guide her on the proper action. She would be under great pressure to give a speedy answer—and it is hard to see how she could prudently refuse such a request.

But if that is so, it raises a specter to hover over any future Australian crisis. Will every governor general carry a letter of dismissal in his hand when he confronts a prime minister? Will every prime minister carry a radio telephone with an open line to Buckingham Palace?

It makes nonsense of any picture of the governor general as an umpire, if he can be first dismissed by any batsman whom he thinks of declaring out. But there is, of course, a qualification to this picture. Even if the prime minister technically has the power to get rid of an uncooperative governor general, from a political point of view it would usually be very rash to invoke such a power. Certainly if Whitlam, after dismissing Cairns and Connor, were to have dismissed the governor general, his own appointee, the howls of indignation, the innuendos of dictatorship, would have been overwhelming. Despite his remarks on November 11 about contacting the Queen (quoted on page 321) Whitlam himself later indicated that in the last resort he would have chosen an election.

But it is worth pursuing the question of what might have followed if Whitlam had secured the dismissal of Sir John Kerr. To provide for the absence of a governor general, it has been customary for some of the state governors to be entrusted with a dormant commission to act as governor general. Until ten years ago the task seems always to have been allotted to the senior of the governors of New South Wales and Victoria largely because of geographical convenience, and only these two governors held a dormant commission. Although practice has changed somewhat, it seems that in 1975 the task would naturally have fallen to Sir Roden Cutler, governor of New South Wales since 1966. But it could have been transferred to, say, Sir Mark Oliphant of South Australia, a Labor-appointed governor.[13] Yet there can be no certainty that he or any other governor would have proved more cooperative with Whitlam than Sir John Kerr—if each in turn was obdurate, are we to envisage the successive dismissal of one acting head of state after another? Even to outline this fantasy underlines the hazardousness, perhaps even the unlikelihood, of an actual dismissal of the governor general.

(13) Was There Anything Labor Could Have Done after Whitlam's Dismissal? It seems that at 1:30 p.m. on November 11 Whitlam drove from Government House to the Prime Minister's Lodge where he discussed the situation with a few colleagues. He did not get in touch with members of his party in Parliament House, who were having their lunchtime recess.

Consequently when the Senate reassembled at 2 p.m. most senators, including the Labor leaders, Senator Wriedt and Senator Doug McClelland, were unaware of what had happened. After ten minutes or so of routine business, the supply measures came up for discussion. To the general surprise Senator Withers, the Liberal leader, made no objection to their passage and within minutes they were enacted. Some Labor senators thought they had actually won but almost immediately news of Whitlam's dismissal spread through the chamber.

If the Labor senators had realized what was up, they could easily have delayed the passage of supply for hours—or perhaps days. The

13 It can readily be argued that the process of appointing a new governor general would involve no more delay than the routines of swearing in an acting governor general and that Whitlam could in a matter of hours have got into office some immediately available outsider. But that is by no means certain.

procedural facilities for filibustering are very considerable. The questions without notice which were still under way at 2 p.m. could have been continued for a long time. The formal motions which followed could have been made subject for debate. Unless closure is moved senators can speak for an hour. The Liberal-Country party senators did not command the absolute majority—thirty-one—needed to enforce closure, and it is unlikely in the circumstances of the day that the independents, Steele Hall and Bunton, would have given them the necessary majority. Parliament could not be dissolved until supply was voted. And much could have happened while Parliament still sat. There were indeed public servants who genuinely feared violence— even the sacking (in the medieval sense) of Government House.

Equally the Labor members of the lower house may have missed a propaganda opportunity by adjourning at 3:15 p.m. If they had continued in session, passing declaratory motions, the affront of the dissolution at 4:45 would have been much greater. Not since Cromwell in 1655 has a British or Australian parliamentary session been forcibly ended by intrusion from the head of state.

Probably nothing that might have been done in either chamber on the afternoon of November 11 would in fact have altered the final outcome. It is likely that the eventualities discussed here would only have heightened the drama of a wildly overdramatic day. But it is possible, if the drama had been thus extended, people would have said and done things which would have changed the way in which the whole situation came to be regarded.

(14) Should the Governor General Have Listened to the Speaker? At 3:15 p.m. on November 11 the House of Representatives by sixty-four to fifty-four passed a vote of no confidence in Fraser as prime minister. The speaker sought an interview with the governor general to convey this information. He was told that the governor general was busy and was unable to see him before 4:45—by which time the House had been dissolved. In the Labor indictments of Sir John Kerr, his refusal to see Scholes, or to take cognizance of the fact that Fraser lacked the confidence of the House, loomed large.

In the Westminster tradition the speaker is a key figure of high precedence. He speaks to the Crown on behalf of the lower house and he has the highest claim on the attention of the head of state. The Australian speaker is a more partisan figure, but it was still a needless discourtesy for the governor general to keep him waiting for an hour and a half. But that is not to say that he should have acted on the speaker's demand for the reinstatement of Whitlam.

(15) Should the House Vote of No Confidence in Fraser Have Made a Difference? If the governor general had changed course because of the House vote at 3:15 (on the ground that the supply problem had been solved by the Senate vote at 2:15 and that there was evidence that Whitlam still could call on a working majority in the lower house), he would surely have brought down even more obloquy on his head than he actually received—though from the other side. To ask Fraser to get supply in exchange for a dissolution and then to double-cross Fraser as soon as he had carried out his part of the bargain would have appeared as an utterly devious intervention on behalf of the Labor party.

It can be argued that Fraser was only carrying out the established constitutional principle—a prime minister defeated in the lower house must resign or seek a dissolution, and he was seeking a dissolution.[14] But that is not an altogether satisfactory argument. Fraser, after all, had never had the confidence of the lower house. The Westminster system certainly does not enshrine the view that any minority leader who is asked to try to form a government that can command a majority, and who fails when it comes to a vote, can then ask for and expect a dissolution. Acceptance of that principle would greatly add to the difficulties of forming a government in any multiparty situation.

Despite that reservation, in the circumstances that he had got himself into by midafternoon of November 11, it is hard to see that the governor general could have abandoned the dissolution because of any vote in the House of Representatives.

(16) Could There Have Been a Referendum to Settle the Supply Issue? A proposal for a referendum, if approved by only one House, cannot be put to the people until it has been approved again three months later (Section 128). Therefore this conflict between Senate and House could only have been settled by referendum, either by mutual consent or if the House had had the forethought to pass a referendum proposal back in August (when the refusal of supply was not a live issue). And the referendum would have had to be on a formal proposal to change the constitution.

(17) Could the Governor General Have Asked for the Issue to Be Brought to a Vote in the Senate? It was crucial to the whole situation that the Senate never voted to refuse supply but only to defer con-

---

[14] In fact Fraser had advised a double dissolution and announced the fact to the House an hour before the vote of no confidence.

sideration of the matter. If the Senate had once voted down the supply measures, the initiative would have passed back to the lower house, for the Senate could no longer have cleared the way for an election by ending the supply crisis on its own. It was also much easier in party terms to vote for deferral. Several Liberal senators had expressed unhappiness about voting against supply and had publicly or privately implied that in the last resort they would not do so, although they were quite willing to go along with their party on procedural matters like deferral.

After seeing the governor general on October 21, Fraser said: "If he gives a decision we would respect and accept it absolutely. If he gives advice we would give the greatest possible weight to it because of the respect we have for the office and the man." It was widely suggested that the governor general should have asked Fraser or Senator Withers to let the substantive issue come to a vote. But on October 23 Fraser said explicitly that he did not think the governor general could request the Senate to pass supply: "That is not part of the Constitutional powers of the governor-general."

It is hard to find fault with Fraser on that proposition. Obviously the governor general ought to know what is going on in the Parliament, but it is doubtful whether he should take public cognizance of parliamentary tactics or procedure to the point of interfering in so specific a matter. He could well be portrayed as intervening directly on behalf of the Labor party. Moreover his intervention might not be effective since he would have no power to force senators to pay heed to his suggestion. If he was snubbed he would plainly have diminished the authority of his office.

(18) Would the Senate Have Given Way if the Governor General Had Taken No Action on November 11?

Some commentators stressed the unhappiness of at least four Liberal senators and suggested that the business interests which had done so much to encourage Fraser to a showdown were losing their nerve as the opinion polls showed how unpopular the confrontation was proving to be. Others insist that pressures had been brought to bear on the weaker brethren and that the Liberal senators would have stood firm, despite the heat which would certainly have increased as supply ran out. This hypothetical but vital question will probably remain a riddle for all time. People who were likeliest to know gave categorical but totally contradictory answers to it. It is to be hoped that those concerned have tape-recorded frank accounts of their own attitudes and intentions for the benefit of posterity.

(19) Could a Governor General Dissolve Parliament without the Advice of the Prime Minister? Dissolution is the prerogative of the governor general (Section 5), but writs for a new election can be issued only by the governor general in council (Section 32). It has been the invariable rule for those summoned to constitute an Executive Council to be current ministers, but that seems to be a matter of custom, not law.[15] It would in theory be possible for the governor general to seek advice from an Executive Council composed of elder statesmen, retired ministers or governors general and to put an election irrevocably in motion. Such action might set awkward precedents but it might also enable a prime minister who had injudiciously said "never" to climb down gracefully.

(20) What General Lessons Can Be Drawn? "Happy the country that has no politics." Today such a sentiment is eighteenth-century dreaming. Yet none can deny that Australia suffered a surfeit of politics in 1975. Issues of constitutionality that bore only incidentally on the November crisis had stolen headlines all the year. The right to issue writs for the new Senate seats, the right to depart from tradition in the nomination of senators, the legality of the Electoral Act—all these and other issues had been debated at length; for example, the loans affair turned in part on the interpretation which the governor general in council had put on the phrase "short-term." Constitutional wrangling was the order of the day.

But that was only a fragment of the hyperpolitical scene. During 1975 four leading figures had left the cabinet with more or less éclat, while others had been forcibly demoted, all with the traditional background of Labor party infighting, extensively reported in the media. The Liberals also experienced some savagery in the process of acquiring their fourth leader in four years. Meanwhile the country was suffering record inflation and record unemployment and looking vainly to its politicians for a remedy.

Australians, according to surveys, were evenly divided on the rights and wrongs of what Sir John Kerr did on November 11. But few seem to have let the constitutional issue influence their votes on December 13. It has been suggested that one reason why the election produced so big a swing, so decisive a majority, was that Australians

---

[15] Quick and Garran in their *Annotated Commentary on the Australian Constitution* take it for granted (p. 707) that Sections 61-63 are designed to establish cabinet government and that the members of the Executive Council shall be ministers, but the point is nowhere specified, except perhaps in the official Australian order of political precedence, which puts "Executive Councillors under Summons" well ahead of "Executive Councillors not under Summons."

wanted to escape from Canberra's freneticisms of 1975 to a quiet life and that a coalition vote looked like the best way to achieve it.

But if the public turned away from the events of November 11, many politicians and political analysts stayed locked up in them, seeking to assess rights and wrongs both in terms of legal proprieties and political tactics. For them Australian politics will never be the same again.

As the election result became inevitable one encountered honest but embittered Labor enthusiasts who saw in the crisis of November 11 proof that the whole system was stacked against them. They had won two elections and each time they had been forced to go to the country before half their term was up. A nineteenth-century elitist constitution had been twisted by the lawyers to do down the people's government. Obsolete monarchical powers had been invoked on behalf of conservatism. The business establishment and the farmers[16] had combined with a totally one-sided press cartel to destroy and discredit the Labor party. There was no justice in the system, no balance by which the same restraints and opportunities were applied to left and right equally. It seemed that a party seeking fundamental social change in a democratic way, abiding by the rules, would inevitably be frustrated by the forces of privilege.

It was hard not to sympathize with elements in this grievance. Some parts of the establishment had played rough and despite the effort of a predominantly Labor-sympathizing press gallery, the columns of the newspapers were more blatantly partisan than in any recent contest.

Perhaps there never can be balance between governments of right and left. Those who seek change inevitably make more obvious mistakes than those who preserve the status quo—and governments are judged by their mistakes. The Labor government, totally lacking in ministerial experience, came to power at a time of world slump and world inflation, whose unpleasant consequences no government could

---

[16] The Country party at no point secured the limelight. Yet it was at the center of the affair. Country people felt peculiarly alienated and threatened by the trendy and urban-dominated Labor government. Country party members had little to fear from an election (for they mostly held safe seats) but much to fear from the absence of an election or from a half-Senate contest that gave Labor a temporary majority in the upper house. The electoral and redistribution bills which the Senate was holding up threatened to cut Country party representation by a third. Anthony and his colleagues were among those pressing hardest for a confrontation over supply. It was a nice irony that they were in the end all too successful. The coalition won a majority so large that in the House the Liberals had a majority on their own, denying the Country party the leverage which they had traditionally used to extract attention to their special interests from Liberal prime ministers.

have neutralized. At the same time it intervened vigorously in a large number of social fields, often where intervention was long overdue and its activities, sometimes its bungles, worried a lot of ordinary people almost as much as the "big interests" that were so patently threatened. Labor's loss of support was not surprising—and to some extent it was self-invited: it was not a capitalist conspiracy that made people aware of and dismayed by the conduct of Cairns or Connor. Even a good socialist could be disturbed by some of the stances taken up by Whitlam.

Yet, given another eighteen months, the economy might have turned around, the Hayden Budget might have worked, the fresh and more acceptable team at the top of the cabinet might have earned new respect, and public opinion polls might have shown a swing back. Labor was denied those eighteen months because of the acceptance by the governor general (and others) of the Senate's right to force an election by refusing supply, by an assertion (never before acted upon) that Australia has a system of bicameral responsibility. Anyone who had been caught up in the hopes of 1972 could not escape the feeling that Labor had been cheated of its just chance to prove itself.

The Australian constitution showed its limitations—or did it? A Liberal could say that its provisions were properly invoked; the Senate enabled the voters to pass judgment on a government that, as it proved, had lost public confidence. But even those who sided with Sir John Kerr could not deny the constitutional ambiguities which the debates over the events of October and November had highlighted: the precedents of 1975 may prove to be dragon's teeth that will rise and slay future governments of any complexion.

Certainly the controversy highlighted the basic dilemmas of a constitution that depends half on law and half on custom. The lawyers who prefer to rely on the text as laid down in 1901 prevailed over those who argued that conventions had changed and that even the drafters of the constitution would not have expected the head of state to take advantage of their attempt to set down the unrepealed powers still left to a nineteenth-century sovereign. An unwritten constitution or even a semiwritten constitution can work well only if those who operate it show great self-restraint and respect for convention.

The affair specifically highlighted the issue of the governor general's reserve powers and the tradition that the head of state should, if possible, avoid intervention in politics that could be seen as partisan. But intervention of a significant sort is almost necessarily partisan; it can hardly avoid helping one side more than the other. The head of state can try to be an honest broker (and in the early stages Sir John

Kerr made some attempt at this). But when he takes action that is not strictly along conventional lines he inevitably becomes the subject of controversy.

But the moral of the affair is political as much as constitutional. It highlighted the importance of good intelligence in political strategy making. Throughout the early stages Fraser seemed substantially to have miscalculated public opinion. At the end Whitlam seemed absolutely to have misjudged Sir John Kerr's likely course of action.

It also highlighted the danger of overplaying politics. It would seem that all the parties to the dispute operated a bit more toughly than the Westminster system allows. Ultimately parliamentary government demands a degree of mutual forbearance and respect between the contending parties, a willingness to compromise. On this occasion forbearance and compromise were lacking. Entrenched behind their dead-end positions of "no supply" and "no election," Fraser and Whitlam each strained the established conventions of Australian government.

In the outcome Fraser came out resoundingly on top but it was a near-run thing. Politics is the art of the possible and Whitlam must deeply regret that, going for total victory, he did not take advantage of Fraser's November 3 offer of supply in exchange for an election by June 1976. Using that as a basis for negotiation he might have got some of the twenty-one bills that the Liberal senators were blocking—as well as six more months in office and an election in what might have proved more favorable circumstances.

APPENDIX B

The Vote and the Count

Senate Elections. The scrutiny of ballot-papers, culminating in the filling of vacancies in the Senate election, is effected under a system of *Proportional Representation*, based on preferential marking of the ballot-papers for all the candidates. Under this system where there are two or more vacancies to be filled, it is not necessary for a candidate to obtain more than half of the votes to be elected—a candidate is elected when he receives a number of votes equal to the quota. The quota is determined by dividing the total number of first preference votes in the count by one more than the number of candidates required to be elected and by increasing the quotient so obtained (disregarding any remainder) by one. For example, where there are five candidates to be elected, the quota is one-sixth of the total first preference votes, plus one.

When all the Senate ballot-papers recorded at all polling booths in any Division have been returned to the respective Divisional Returning Officer, he will open the parcels and make a fresh scrutiny of the ballot-papers, thus carrying out a complete recheck of the counting which was done at the counting centres.

The total number of all first preference votes recorded for each candidate will then be tabulated and the results transmitted to the Australian Electoral Officer for the State. When final figures have been received from each Divisional Returning Officer, the Australian Electoral Officer will determine the quota for election in the manner previously described.

This appendix consists of excerpts from Frank L. Ley, *Commonwealth Electoral Procedures*, Australian Electoral Office (Canberra: Australian Government Publishing Service, 1976), pp. 34-36 and 71-79. Ley is chief Australian electoral officer. The 1975 ballots have been substituted for the 1974 ballots reproduced in Ley's booklet.

Any candidate who has then received a number of first preference votes equal to or greater than the quota is deemed to be elected. Where an elected candidate has received a number of votes in excess of the quota, a number of votes equal to the surplus will be transferred to the other candidates remaining in the count in the manner described in the next paragraph.

All of the ballot-papers of the first elected candidate are then sorted into parcels according to each voter's next preference indicated thereon to determine the proportion in which the surplus votes are to be transferred. The surplus votes are then transferred in their correct proportion to the continuing candidates (the actual ballot-papers being taken at random), and the remainder (i.e. the number of ballot-papers of the elected candidate equal to the quota) are set aside as finally dealt with. After the surplus votes have been distributed, any candidate who has reached the quota is deemed to be elected and his surplus votes (i.e. that portion he received from the previously elected candidate over and above the number which was required to reach the quota) are distributed to the remaining candidates in the order of the voters' preferences. If, after the distribution of the surplus votes of all elected candidates, fewer candidates than the number of vacancies to be filled have been elected, the candidate with the least number of votes in the count at that stage is excluded and the ballot-papers which have been sorted to him are transferred, in accordance with the next preferences thereon, to the candidates still remaining in the count (i.e. to those candidates who have not been elected or excluded up to that stage).

If no candidate is then elected, or fewer than the required number have been elected, the process of excluding candidates is continued until a further candidate is elected, in which case (unless all vacancies have been filled) the surplus votes of that elected candidate are then transferred. If necessary, the process of excluding candidates one by one is continued until all the vacancies have been filled.

If on any count two or more candidates have an equal number of votes, the Australian Electoral Officer decides which shall be excluded or the order of their election, as the case may be. If in the final count for filling the last vacancy two candidates have an equal number of votes, the Australian Electoral Officer exercises his casting vote but, except in these circumstances, he does not vote at the election.

House of Representatives Elections. The *Alternative Vote* system used for a House of Representatives election also relies upon the preferential marking of the ballot-papers by the voters to indicate their order of preference for all the candidates. This method of marking the ballot-papers affords the voter an alternative choice of candidates or indeed several alternatives should his earlier choices become ineffective due to the exclusion of candidates at various stages of the count.

In a House of Representatives election, if the number of first preference votes recorded in favour of a candidate is greater than one-half of the total number of formal votes in the election (i.e. an absolute majority of the formal votes), that candidate is elected. If no candidate has received an absolute majority of the votes, the candidate who has received the fewest first preference votes is excluded from the count and each ballot-paper counted to him is transferred to the candidate next in order of the voter's preference. This process of excluding candidates one by one is continued until a candidate receives more than half the number of votes in the count, when he is elected.

If on any count two or more candidates have an equal number of votes and one of them has to be excluded, the Divisional Returning Officer decides which shall be excluded, or, if in the final count two candidates have an equal number of votes, the Divisional Returning Officer will record his casting vote to decide the result of the election but otherwise he does not vote in the election.

Recount of Ballot-Papers. At any time before the declaration of the result of an election, the officer conducting the election may, if he thinks fit, at the written request of a candidate, or of his own volition, recount the ballot-papers. A recount is generally undertaken only where the closeness of the final result makes it desirable.

Declaration of the Poll. As soon as possible after the scrutiny of the ballot-papers has been completed the result of the election will be declared. This is called the "Declaration of the Poll." In the case of a Senate election, the poll is declared at the office of the Australian Electoral Officer and, in the case of House of Representatives elections, the declaration of the poll is made at the offices of the respective Divisional Returning Officers.

Court of Disputed Returns. A candidate at an election or a person who was qualified to vote thereat may dispute the validity of the election by addressing a petition to the High Court sitting as the Court of Disputed Returns.

Example Showing the Application of Proportional Representation

(As used in Senate elections)

Say, 4 candidates to be elected; 610 votes recorded of which 15 are informal, i.e. there are 595 formal votes:

$$\text{Quota for election} = \left(\frac{595}{5}\right) + 1 = 120$$

	A	B	C	D	E	F	G	H	I	J	Total votes in count
Candidates											
First preference votes	30	10	20	320	5	150	40	∴	10	10	= 595

D 1st elected with a surplus of 200 votes
F 2nd elected with a surplus of 30 votes

D's first preference votes are now sorted to continuing candidates, according to next available preference thereon (this is to ascertain the proportion in which surplus votes are to be transferred). Say they go:

	A	B	C	E	G	H	I	J
∴	. .	300	16	. .	. .	. .	. .	4

Transfer value of D's surplus votes $= \frac{200}{320}$ (i.e. surplus ÷ 1st preferences) ∴ actual votes to be taken at random and transferred =

$$\left. \begin{array}{l} \text{to B } \dfrac{200}{320} \text{ of } 300 = 187 \\[2mm] \text{to C } \dfrac{200}{320} \text{ of } 16 = 10 \\[2mm] \text{to J } \dfrac{200}{320} \text{ of } 4 = 3 \end{array} \right\} = 200$$

340

F's 150 1st preference votes sorted to continuing candidates according to the next available preferences thereon. Say they go:

A	B	C	E	G	H	I	J
100	15	10	15	6	1	—	3

$\therefore$

Transfer value of F's surplus votes $\frac{30}{150}$ (i.e., surplus ÷ 1st preferences)

$\therefore$ actual votes to be transferred:

$$\text{to A } \frac{30}{150} \text{ of } 100 = 20$$

$$\text{to B } \frac{30}{150} \text{ of } 15 = 3$$

$$\text{to C } \frac{30}{150} \text{ of } 10 = 2$$

$$\text{to E } \frac{30}{150} \text{ of } 15 = 3$$

$$\text{to G } \frac{30}{150} \text{ of } 6 = 1$$

$$\text{to H } \frac{30}{150} \text{ of } 1 = 0$$

$$\text{to J } \frac{30}{150} \text{ of } 3 = 1$$

$= 30$

Tally sheet now reads:

Candidates	A	B	C	D	E	F	G	H	I	J	Total votes in count	Number of elected candidates' votes set aside
First preference votes	30	10	20	320	5	150	40	..	10	10	= 595	
D's 200 surplus votes transferred ..	..	187	10	1st Elected	..	2nd Elected	..	..	..	3	..	120 ⎫ i.e.
F's 30 surplus votes transferred ..	20	3	2		3		1	..	..	1	..	120 ⎭ 2 quotas
Progress totals	**50**	**200**	**32**		**8**		**41**	..	**10**	**14**	**= 355**	

B 3rd elected with a surplus of 80 votes.

The 190 votes received by B from D and F now sorted to continuing candidates. Say they go:

A	C	E	G	H	I	J
..	..	..	..	187	3	..

Transfer value of B's surplus votes $= \dfrac{80}{190}$ (i.e. surplus votes ÷ votes received by B at the previous stage of the count)

∴ actual votes to be transferred:

$$\left. \begin{array}{l} \text{to H} \quad \dfrac{80}{190} \text{ of } 187 = 79 \\[2mm] \text{to I} \quad \dfrac{80}{190} \text{ of } 3 = 1 \end{array} \right\} = 80$$

342

Tally sheet now reads:

Candidates	A	B	C	E	G	H	I	J	Total votes in count	Number of elected candidates' votes set aside
Progress totals, brought forward	50	200	32	8	41	..	10	14	= 355	120 (i.e. 1 quota)
B's surplus votes transferred	..	3rd Elected	..	..	..	79	1	..	.	
Progress totals	50		32	8	41	79	11	14	= 235	

No further candidate now having a quota, E with the fewest votes, is excluded and his 8 votes are transferred. Say they go:

	A	C	G	H	I	J
	2	..	..	..	5	1
Progress totals	52	32	41	79	16	15 = 235

J with the fewest votes, is now excluded and his 15 votes are transferred. Say they go:

	A	C	G	H	I
	..	..	..	12	3
Progress totals	52	32	41	91	19 = 235

I with the fewest votes, is now excluded and his 19 votes are transferred. Say they go:

	A	C	G	H
	..	..	9	10
Progress totals	52	32	50	101 = 235

343

C with the fewest votes, is now excluded and his 32 votes are transferred. Say they go:

	A	G	H	
	12	10	10	
Progress totals	64	60	111	= 235

G with the fewest votes, is now excluded and his 60 votes are transferred. Say they go:

	A	H	
	55	5	
Progress totals	119	116	= 235

A 4th elected.

Complete tally sheet would read:

Candidates	A	B	C	D	E	F	G	H	I	J	Total votes in count	Number of elected candidates' votes set aside
First preference votes	30	10	20	320	5	150	40	..	10	10	= 595	
D elected, 200 surplus votes transferred	..	187	10	1st Elected	..	2nd Elected	..	..	..	3	.	120
F elected, 30 surplus votes transferred	20	3	2		3		1	..	..	1	.	
Progress totals	50	200	32	3rd Elected	8		41	..	10	14	= 355	120
B elected, 80 surplus votes transferred	..				..		..	79	1	..		120
Progress totals	50		32		8		41	79	11	14	= 235	

E excluded, 8 votes transferred	2	..	Excluded	..	..	5	1	
Progress totals	**52**	**32**		**41**	**79**	**16**	**15**	= **235**
J excluded, 15 votes transferred	..	..		..	12	3	Excluded	
Progress totals	**52**	**32**		**41**	**91**	**19**		= **235**
I excluded, 19 votes transferred	..	..		9	10	Excluded		
Progress totals	**52**	**32**		**50**	**101**			= **235**
C excluded, 32 votes transferred	12	Excluded		10	10			
Progress totals	**64**			**60**	**111**			= **235**
G excluded, 60 votes transferred	55			Excluded	5			
Progress totals	**119**				**116**			= **235**
	4th Elected							

Example Showing the Application of the Alternative Vote
(As used in House of Representatives elections)

Let it be assumed that there are 5 candidates for which 610 votes were recorded and of these 10 are informal, i.e. there are 600 formal votes. For election a candidate must receive an absolute majority of the formal votes—i.e. 301 votes.

Candidates	Adams	Brown	Grey	Jones	White	Total
First preference votes	150	200	70	100	80	600

No candidate having received an absolute majority of the votes, candidate GREY, with the least number of votes, is excluded. His 70 ballot-papers are now sorted to continuing candidates according to the next available preference thereon. Say they go:

Adams	Brown	Jones	White
10	..	40	20

Tally sheet now reads:

	Adams	Brown	Grey	Jones	White	Total
First preference votes	150	200	70	100	80	600
GREY excluded—70 ballot-papers transferred	10	..	Excl.	40	20	
Progressive totals	160	200	..	140	100	600

No candidate yet having received an absolute majority of the votes, candidate WHITE with the fewest votes is now excluded and the 100 ballot-papers which were previously sorted to him are transferred to the next continuing candidates. Say they go:

Adams	Brown	Jones
15	30	55

This will give ADAMS (160 + 15) 175 votes, BROWN (200 + 30) 230 votes and JONES (140 + 55) 195 votes. ADAMS is now excluded and his 175 ballot-papers are transferred. Say they go:

	Adams	Brown	Grey	Jones	White	Total
	Brown 60	Jones 115				
Tally sheet now reads:						
First preference votes	150	200	70	100	80	600
GREY excluded—70 ballot-papers transferred	10	..	Excl.	40	20	600
Progressive totals	160	200	..	140	100	600
WHITE excluded—100 ballot-papers transferred	15	30	..	55	Excl.	
Progressive totals	175	230	..	195	..	600
ADAMS excluded—175 ballot-papers transferred	Excl.	60	..	115	..	
Progressive totals	..	290	..	310	..	600

Candidate JONES having received an absolute majority of the votes in the count is elected with 310 votes.

Examples of Ballots

(These 1975 ballots are substituted for the 1974 ballots reproduced in the Australian Electoral Office booklet.)

Form F

BALLOT-PAPER

COMMONWEALTH OF AUSTRALIA
STATE OF NEW SOUTH WALES

(To be initialed on back by Presiding Officer before issue.)

Electoral Division of SYDNEY
Election of One Member of the House of Representatives

DIRECTIONS:—Mark your vote on this ballot-paper by placing the numbers **1, 2, 3, 4** and **5** in the squares respectively opposite the names of the candidates, so as to indicate the order of your preference for them.

CANDIDATES

☐ **AARONS, Laurence**

☐ **GIESEKAM, Merilyn**

☐ **MacNEIL, Roderick**

☐ **McMAHON, James Leslie**

☐ **WALLACE, Janis Joye**

Form E

BALLOT-PAPER   (To be initialed on back by Presiding Officer before Issue.)

COMMONWEALTH OF AUSTRALIA.   STATE OF NEW SOUTH WALES

ELECTION OF TEN SENATORS.

DIRECTIONS.—Mark your vote on this ballot-paper by placing the numbers 1, 2, 3, 4, 5, 6, 7, 8, 9, 10, 11, 12, 13, 14, 15, 16, 17, 18, 19, 20, 21, 22, 23, 24, 25, 26, 27, 28, 29, 30, 31, 32, 33, 34, 35, 36, 37, 38, 39, 40, 41, 42, 43, 44, 45, 46, 47, 48, 49, 50, 51, 52 and 53 in the squares immediately to the left of the names of the respective candidates so as to indicate the order of your preference for them.

CANDIDATES

A | JARVIS Helen Myfanwy
A | ADLER Gordon Frank

B | COTTON Robert Carrington
B | CARRICK John Leslie
B | SCOTT Douglas Barr
B | BAUME Peter Erne
B | LAJOVIC Milivoj Emil
B | ROSS Dorothy Dickson

C | BROWN Frieda Jessie
C | NILE Frederick John
C | HARRISON Kenneth Brian

D | KELLY Ron
D | KHOURY Robert Omar

E | KANE John Thomas
E | DALY Peter Francis
E | McCOSKER Anne Therese
E | CASEY William Denis
E | KEOGH James Clement
E | WESTMORE Peter Anthony

F | GREEN Ross Winston
F | WILSON Lyn

G | MORGAN Terence Paul
G | PAYNE Bill

H | McCLELLAND Douglas
H | McCLELLAND James Robert
H | MULVIHILL James Anthony
H | GIETZELT Arthur Thomas
H | SIBRAA Kerry Walter
H | RENSHAW Emily Anastasia

I | HILL John Sinclair Leslie
I | TIER Mark Douglas John
I | O'SULLIVAN Susan Joan
I | KENNARD Neville John
I | GRANT John McDonald Falconer
I | EDMONDS John Hanbury

J | MASON Colin Victor James
J | NEWMAN Robert Stanley
J | McMILLAN Mavis Alexandra

MARTIN Athol James
ALLE Adrian Frederick
HOWARD Noel Anthony
POURSHASB Darius
WOODS Lawrence William
BURKE Kenneth
BECHER Luciano George
McPHERSON David Brian
TABER Bruce Murray
GUY Thomas Edward
APPLEBY Reginald Thomas
BOYTON Andrew Barclay
STEUART Michael Gordon
WOJESZLOVSZKY Michael
BREEN-HEMINGWAY John Christopher Roc

NOTE.—The letter "A" or "B" or "C" or "D" or "E" or "F" or "G" or "H" or "I" or "J" appearing before the square immediately to the left of a candidate's surname indicates that that candidate and each other candidate who has the same letter appearing before the square immediately to the left of his surname have been grouped by mutual consent.

The fact that no letter appears before the square immediately to the left of a candidate's surname indicates that the name of that candidate has not been included in any group.

APPENDIX C

A Summary of Australian
National Election Results, 1972-75

Compiled by Richard M. Scammon

1972 ELECTION RESULTS, AUSTRALIAN HOUSE OF REPRESENTATIVES

State	Total	Labor	Liberal	Country	Democratic Labor	Australia	Other[a]
New South Wales	2,411,592	1,252,047	722,937	235,132	84,322	80,662	36,492
% of state vote	100	51.9	30.0	9.8	3.5	3.3	1.5
Seats	45	28	10	7	—	—	—
Queensland	952,901	449,620	242,752	187,057	53,319	15,741	4,412
% of state vote	100	47.2	25.5	19.6	5.6	1.7	.5
Seats	18	8	6	4	—	—	—
South Australia	627,366	317,646	259,341	13,991	23,052	6,418	6,918
% of state vote	100	50.6	41.3	2.2	3.7	1.0	1.1
Seats	12	7	5	—	—	—	—
Tasmania	210,057	123,814	73,166	—	10,086	1,076	1,915
% of state vote	100	58.9	34.8	—	4.8	.5	.9
Seats	5	5	—	—	—	—	—
Victoria	1,806,530	854,201	606,273	134,158	150,824	38,743	22,331
% of state vote	100	47.3	33.6	7.4	8.3	2.1	1.2
Seats	34	14	14	6	—	—	—
Western Australia	490,969	226,398	193,060	40,831	22,054	5,618	3,008
% of state vote	100	46.1	39.3	8.3	4.5	1.1	.6
Seats	9	4	3	2	—	—	—
Australian Capital Territory	77,003	40,147	17,556	—	2,758	10,529	6,013
% of territory vote	100	52.1	22.8	—	3.6	13.7	7.8
Seats	1	1	—	—	—	—	—
Northern Territory	24,632	9,676	—	11,657	—	1,129	2,170
% of territory vote	100	39.3	—	47.3	—	4.6	8.8
Seats	1	1	—	1	—	—	—
Total, Australia	6,601,050	3,273,549	2,115,085	622,826	346,415	159,916	83,259
% of total vote	100	49.6	32.0	9.4	5.2	2.4	1.3
Seats	125	67	38	20	—	—	—

[a] Communist, 8,105; miscellaneous, 75,154.
Source: Australian Electoral Office.

1974 ELECTION RESULTS, AUSTRALIAN HOUSE OF REPRESENTATIVES

State	Total	Labor	Liberal	Country	Australia	Democratic Labor	Other[a]
New South Wales	2,658,092	1,400,255	887,202	282,169	77,507	—	10,959
% of state vote	100	52.7	33.4	10.6	2.9	—	.4
Seats	45	25	11	9	—	—	—
Queensland	1,083,283	476,710	330,365	255,659	18,808	—	1,741
% of state vote	100	44.0	30.5	23.6	1.7	—	.2
Seats	18	6	7	5	—	—	—
South Australia	702,123	341,563	256,904	28,903	14,267	—	60,486
% of state vote	100	48.6	36.6	4.1	2.0	—	8.6
Seats	12	7	5	—	—	—	—
Tasmania	233,678	128,787	103,701	—	423	—	767
% of state vote	100	55.1	44.4	—	.2	—	.3
Seats	5	5	—	—	—	—	—
Victoria	2,027,260	970,236	738,236	151,707	50,025	104,974	12,082
% of state vote	100	47.9	36.4	7.5	2.5	5.2	.6
Seats	34	16	12	6	—	—	—
Western Australia	563,414	261,107	233,240	—	7,016	—	62,051
% of state vote	100	46.3	41.4	—	1.2	—	11.0
Seats	10	5	5	—	—	—	—
Australian Capital Territory	93,688	52,055	33,320	3,300	4,130	—	883
% of territory vote	100	55.6	35.6	3.5	4.4	—	.9
Seats	2	2	—	—	—	—	—
Northern Territory	29,468	13,397	—	14,514	—	—	1,557
% of territory vote	100	45.5	—	49.3	—	—	5.3
Seats	1	—	—	1	—	—	—
Total, Australia	7,391,006	3,644,110	2,582,968	736,252	172,176	104,974	150,526
% of total vote	100	49.3	34.9	10.0	2.3	1.4	2.0
Seats	127	66	40	21	—	—	—

[a] National Alliance, 60,325; Liberal Movement, 57,817; miscellaneous, 32,384.

Source: Australian Electoral Office.

1975 ELECTION RESULTS, AUSTRALIAN HOUSE OF REPRESENTATIVES

State	Total	Labor	Liberal	Country	Democratic Labor	Australia	Other [a]
New South Wales	2,772,120	1,260,335	1,100,672	326,124	—	10,931	74,058
% of state vote	100	45.5	39.7	11.8	—	.4	2.7
Seats	45	17	19	9	—	—	—
Queensland	1,133,594	439,405	370,041	303,107	—	—	21,041
% of state vote	100	38.8	32.6	26.7	—	—	1.9
Seats	18	1	9	8	—	—	—
South Australia	741,168	316,006	365,353	4,070	—	525	55,214
% of state vote	100	42.6	49.3	.5	—	.1	7.4
Seats	12	6	6	—	—	—	—
Tasmania	242,125	105,324	131,003	3,248	—	—	2,550
% of state vote	100	43.5	54.1	1.3	—	—	1.1
Seats	5	—	5	—	—	—	—
Victoria	2,097,697	882,842	887,685	186,667	101,750	21,473	17,280
% of state vote	100	42.1	42.3	8.9	4.9	1.0	.8
Seats	34	10	19	5	—	—	—
Western Australia	609,050	244,404	326,679	30,727	—	—	7,240
% of state vote	100	40.1	53.6	5.0	—	—	1.2
Seats	10	1	9	—	—	—	—
Australian Capital Territory	107,204	51,744	50,727	—	—	—	4,733
% of territory vote	100	48.3	47.3	—	—	—	4.4
Seats	2	1	1	—	—	—	—
Northern Territory	29,621	12,944	—	15,976	—	701	—
% of territory vote	100	43.7	—	53.9	—	2.4	—
Seats	1	—	—	1	—	—	—
Total, Australia	7,732,579	3,313,004	3,232,160	869,919	101,750	33,630	182,116
% of total vote	100	42.8	41.8	11.3	1.3	.4	2.4
Seats	127	36	68	23	—	—	—

[a] Workers, 59,434; Liberal Movement, 49,484; Communist, 9,393; miscellaneous, 63,805.
Source: Australian Electoral Office.

1974 ELECTION RESULTS, AUSTRALIAN SENATE

State	Total	Labor	Liberal-Country-National[a]	Liberal Movement	National Alliance	Country	Other[b]
New South Wales	2,370,085	1,184,993	987,711	—	—	—	197,381
% of state vote	100	50.0	41.7	—	—	—	8.3
Seats	10	5	5	—	—	—	—
Queensland	1,032,460	451,623	519,851	—	—	—	60,986
% of state vote	100	43.7	50.4	—	—	—	5.9
Seats	10	4	6	—	—	—	—
South Australia	640,243	303,461	224,049	63,032	—	19,959	29,742
% of state vote	100	47.4	35.0	9.8	—	3.1	4.6
Seats	10	5	4	1	—	—	—
Tasmania	211,225	97,861	77,961	—	—	10,459	24,944
% of state vote	100	46.3	36.9	—	—	5.0	11.8
Seats	10	5	4	—	—	—	1
Victoria	1,840,419	859,078	791,254	—	—	—	190,087
% of state vote	100	46.7	43.0	—	—	—	10.3
Seats	10	5	5	—	—	—	—
Western Australia	517,953	230,181	214,909	—	55,301	—	17,562
% of state vote	100	44.4	41.5	—	10.7	—	3.4
Seats	10	5	4	—	1	—	—
Total, Australia	6,612,385	3,127,197	2,815,735	63,032	55,301	30,418	520,702
% of total vote	100	47.3	42.6	1.0	.8	.5	7.9
Seats	60	29	28	1	1	—	1

a On the Senate ballot in most states, Liberal-National Country party coalition candidates are grouped in the same column. The name used by the coalition varies somewhat from state to state. In South Australia and Tasmania in 1974, Country party candidates were listed in a separate column.

b Democratic Labor, 235,343; Australia, 92,107; Liberal National, 23,965; Communist, 20,583; miscellaneous, 148,704 (one seat won by an independent).

Source: Australian Electoral Office.

1975 ELECTION RESULTS, AUSTRALIAN SENATE

State	Total	Liberal-Country-National[a]	Labor	Liberal Movement	Country	Other[b]
New South Wales	2,549,748	1,258,859	1,123,462	6,218	—	161,209
% of state vote	100	49.4	44.1	.2	—	6.3
Seats	10	5	5	—	—	—
Queensland	1,053,209	603,228	387,740	4,709	—	57,532
% of state vote	100	57.3	36.8	.4	—	5.5
Seats	10	6	4	—	—	—
South Australia	683,829	351,818	277,800	44,136	—	10,075
% of state vote	100	51.4	40.6	6.5	—	1.5
Seats	10	5	4	1	—	—
Tasmania	222,319	108,853	78,310	—	3,611	31,545
% of state vote	100	49.0	35.2	—	1.6	14.2
Seats	10	5	4	—	—	1
Victoria	1,966,077	993,634	811,773	16,279	—	144,391
% of state vote	100	50.5	41.3	.8	—	7.3
Seats	10	6	4	—	—	—
Western Australia	556,112	287,358	203,151	5,084	38,366	22,153
% of state vote	100	51.7	36.5	.9	6.9	4.0
Seats	10	5	4	—	1	—
Australian Capital Territory[c]	104,992	45,743	38,867	—	—	20,382
% of territory vote	100	43.6	37.0	—	—	19.4
Seats	2	1	1	—	—	—
Northern Territory[c]	28,427	—	10,207	—	15,519	2,701
% of territory vote	100	—	35.9	—	54.6	9.5
Seats	2	—	1	—	1	—
Total, Australia	7,164,713	3,649,493	2,931,310	76,426	57,496	449,988
% of total vote	100	50.9	40.9	1.1	.8	6.3
Seats	64	33	27	1	2	1

a On the Senate ballot in most states, Liberal-National Country party coalition candidates are grouped in the same column. The name used by the coalition varies somewhat from state to state. In Tasmania, Western Australia, and the Northern Territory in 1975, Country party candidates were listed in a separate column.

b Democratic Labor, 191,049; Workers, 62,385; Australia, 34,632; miscellaneous, 161,922 (one seat won by an independent).

c The Senate (Representation of Territories) Act, passed at the joint sitting of Parliament in July 1974, gave the Australian Capital Territory and the Northern Territory the right to representation in the Senate. In 1975, for the first time, the territories voted to elect two senators each.

Source: Australian Electoral Office.

CONTRIBUTORS

TERENCE W. BEED is director of the University of Sydney Sample Survey Centre, which was set up in 1975. As managing director of Australian Nationwide Opinion Polls from its inception in 1970, he was coeditor of the *Australian Public Opinion Newsletter*.

DAVID BUTLER, a fellow of Nuffield College, Oxford, since 1951, has studied and lectured widely in the United States. He has written extensively on British politics and elections and is the author of *The Canberra Model* and coauthor of *Political Change in Britain*.

MARGARET BRIDSON CRIBB is a senior lecturer in political science at the University of Queensland. A specialist in Australian national and state government and in industrial relations, she has published numerous articles and is now preparing a major work on the National Country party.

LEON D. EPSTEIN, Bascom professor of political science at the University of Wisconsin at Madison, is the author of works on American and British parties and of a comparative study, *Political Parties in Western Democracies*. He spent the last four months of 1975 at the Australian National University.

MICHELLE GRATTAN is chief political correspondent in Canberra for the Melbourne *Age*. She also teaches politics at the Centre for Continuing Education at the Australian National University. Before joining the *Age*, she was a senior teaching fellow in the politics department at Monash University in Melbourne.

Owen Harries is associate professor at the School of Political Science, University of New South Wales. He has contributed to numerous scholarly journals and recently edited *Liberty and Politics: Studies in Social Theory*. At present he is on a two-year leave from the university while serving as policy adviser to the Department of Foreign Affairs, Canberra.

Colin A. Hughes is a professorial fellow in political science at the Australian National University. He is joint editor of half a dozen volumes of Australian electoral statistics and editor of a series on Australian state government. His most recent book is *Mr. Prime Minister*.

C. J. Lloyd has just completed a year as a visiting fellow in the urban research unit at the Australian National University. He is the joint author of three books on Australian politics and public administration and is now working on a study of the National Press Gallery in Canberra.

D. W. Rawson is a senior fellow in political science at the Australian National University. His books include *Politics in Eden-Monaro*, *Australia Votes*, and *Labor in Vain? A Survey of the Australian Labor Party*.

Paul Reynolds is a lecturer in Australian politics and political sociology at the University of Queensland. He is the author of *The Democratic Labor Party* and of articles on Australian and New Zealand politics.

Richard M. Scammon, coauthor of *This U.S.A.* and *The Real Majority*, is director of the Elections Research Center in Washington, D.C. He has edited the biennial statistical series *America Votes* since 1956.

R. F. I. Smith is a research fellow in the Department of Political Science at the Australian National University. He is the author of several recent articles on Australian political institutions and public policy.

Patrick Weller is a research fellow in the Department of Political Science at the Australian National University. He is the editor of *Caucus Minutes 1901–1949* and coauthor of *Treasury Control in Australia* and *Public Servants, Interest Groups and Policy-making*. Recently he has published several articles on parties, political institutions, and public policy in Australia.

INDEX

Academic opinion polls: 215, 251–253
Advertising:
    bias in: 207
    Liberal party use of: 132–133
    "machinery" advertising: 206
    national campaign: 204–205
    response advertising: 206–207
    by state and local campaigns: 204–
       206
    third-party endorsements: 206
    use in campaigns: 204–206
Age: 186, 200
    description: 173
    opinion poll interests: 213, 217
    see also: Saulwick *Age* poll
Airlines, ALP attempt to nationalize: 79
ALP: *see* Australian Labor party
"Alternative vote": 31, 291–294, 338–
    339
ANOP poll:
    1972 election forecast: 213
    1975 election forecasts, table: 249
    on campaign issues: 251
    description: 213
    forecast errors: 221, 222
    as Gallup Poll competitor: 213
    House election forecasts, 1972–75,
       table: 221
    on Senate blocking of supply: 245–
       247
    survey methods: 222, 248
    on swinging voters: 248, 250–253
    see also Opinion polls
Anthony, Doug: 53, 65, 114, 148
    policy speech: 153
ANZUS treaty: 259, 267–269
Appropriation and taxation measures,
    Senate powers: 12

ASEAN: 269
Asia, Whitlam government relations
    with: 268–270
ASRB poll:
    1972 election prediction: 213
    description: 213
    on economy: 239
    forecast errors: 221, 222
    House election forecasts, 1972–75,
       table: 221
    see also Opinion polls
Australian: 176, 180, 185, 190, 191
    bias charges against: 182–183, 186
    description: 173–175
    editorial policy, alleged bias in:
       182–195
    journalists' strike: 181–195
"Australian ballot": 27
Australian Broadcasting Commission
    (ABC):
    bias allegations: 171, 196–198
    description: 174
    free campaign time provided: 207
    news distribution among parties:
       196
Australian Council of Trade Unions:
    83, 84, 97
Australian Financial Review: 173, 175,
    176
Australian Journalists' Association
    (AJA): *see* Journalists' strike
Australian Labor party (ALP):
    1972 elections, role of Whitlam
       policies: 55
    ABC news coverage: 196
    airlines, attempt to nationalize: 79
    "Arab loans affair": 70–71, 74, 99–
       101

banks, nationalization attempt: 79
campaign financing: 98–102
campaign issues: 93–94
campaign strategy: 89–102
China, delegation to: 262–263
condition of party in 1975: 88
cube rule, impact of: 287, 290
decline: 68–76
defeat: 94–96
election forecasts: 221, 222
electoral alignment: 20–22
electoral image: 73
failures in office: 307–308
foreign policy: 262–275
future prospects: 303–307
history: 77–79
House elections, two-party preferred votes and seats, 1949–75,
  table: 287
House seats, party distribution,
  1949–75, table: 280
ideology: 73
internal problems: 307–308
leadership: 85
media advertising: 204–206, 207
media coverage: 196, 201–203
membership organization: 23–25
ministerial successes: 73
Murdoch group newspapers, relationship with: 179–181
office, approach to: 56–58
opinion polls: 249, 305
overseas campaign contributions:
  70–71, 74, 99–101
party discipline: 86–87
party machinery: 87
preferential voting, impact: 291–
  294
professional background of leaders: 85
proportionate and cube-rule systems, impact of: 287, 290
radio and television campaign expenditures: 134
"Rally for Democracy": 95
rank-and-file sovereignty: 86
rise under Whitlam: 54 et seq.
rural base of support, 1890–1910:
  285
safeness of House seats, 1955–75,
  table: 282
and socialism: 79–81, 87
surveys, campaign use of: 227–228
swing to, from previous House
  election, by state, 1961–75, table:
  283

underrepresentation in House of
  Representatives: 286
union affiliation: 81–86
union support: 96–98
urban support: 285–286
votes: 69, 72, 140, 221, 287–289,
  296–302
white-collar workers' support: 83
see also Whitlam ALP government
Australian Nationwide Opinion Polls:
  see ANOP poll
Australian party (AP):
  constituency: 163–164
  as minor party: 160
  radio and television campaign ex-
    penditures: 134
  votes: 166–168
Australian Sales Research Bureau: see
  ASRB poll
Australian Women's Weekly: 174

Ballots:
  formal and informal: 28, 294–296
  party labels, absence of: 29
  recounts: 339
  samples: 348–349
  secret: 27
  tabulation, examples: 341–347
  valid and invalid: 28, 294–296
Banks, ALP attempt to nationalize: 79
Barnard, Lance: 56, 72
Bass by-election: 72–73, 89, 127, 241
Blockage of supply: see Supply, blockage of
Boswell, Brian: 190
Bowen, Nigel: 120
Bowman, D. N.: 192
Britain: see Great Britain
British National Opinion Polls (NOP):
  212
Budget:
  as campaign issue: 127–129
  Whitlam government disputes: 67,
    68
  see also Supply, blockage of
Bulletin: 174
  circulation: 214
By-elections: 72–73, 89, 120, 241, 307–
  308

Cabinet:
  appointment by prime minister: 11,
    19

authority, basis of: 10
background and parliamentary service of members: 19
responsibility to Parliament: 10
size variations: 19
state representation: 19
tenure: 11–14
Whitlam cabinet: 59–60
Cairns, Jim:
budget policies: 68
dismissal: 38, 71–72
"loans affair" involvement: 70–71
Morosi appointment: 68
opinion poll on dismissal: 241–242
as Whitlam rival: 55
Cairns, Phillip: 241
Calwell, Arthur A.: 86
Cameron, Clyde: 96
Campaign advertising: see Advertising
Campaign financing:
ALP: 98–102
"Arab loans affair": 99–101
disclosure of sources: 98–102
overseas contributions to ALP: 99–101
union donations to ALP: 98
Campaign headquarters, role in Liberal party campaign: 134–136
Campaign issues:
ALP: 93–94
opinion poll: 251
Campaign strategy:
ALP: 89–102
Country party: 152–154
Liberal party: 121, 131–134
Campaign violence, 1975 absence of: 278
Canberra press gallery: 171, 177
Fraser campaign coverage: 199–201
Fraser criticism: 198–199
Whitlam campaign coverage: 201–202
Canberra Times: 173, 186
Candidate selection: 25–27
Country party: 151
plebiscite method: 26, 27
state party organizations, role of: 25–27
Carleton, Richard: 198
Carlton, J. J.: 112
China, People's Republic of,
ALP delegation: 262–263
Fraser government policy: 274
Whitlam government recognition of: 264

Whitlam government relations with: 269–270
Coalition government: see Liberal-National Country party (L-NCP)
Cold war as foreign policy issue: 258–264
Combe, David: 99–101, 207
Commonwealth of Australia, establishment: 5
Communism as foreign policy issue: 258–262
Communist parties: 160
Company profits and dividends, opinion poll: 240
Comparisons with American and British governmental systems: 1 et seq.
Compulsory voting: 28–29
and opinion polls: 224–225
Connor, Rex:
"loans affair": 70, 74, 130
opinion poll on: 242–243
resignation: 38
Constitution:
amendment proposals: 8
appropriation and taxation measures, Senate powers: 12
background: 6
changes in federal relationships: 8 et seq.
conflict with parliamentary conventions: 37 et seq.
dissolution of House of Representatives: 14–16
dissolution of Senate: 15
"double-dissolution" provisions: 15
governor general, powers: 10
ministers and: 10
model: 9
House of Representatives: 9
Senate: 9, 12
states' rights, residual strength: 7
working rules of national government: 10
Constitutional crisis: 37–47, 77, 129–131
as campaign issue: 93–94
legal proprieties and political tactics, issue of: 333–335
questions raised: 314–336
see also Supply, blockage of
Corio, distribution of preferences, House elections, 1975, table: 293
Council for the Defence of Government Schools (DOGS), election participation: 161

Country party (NCP):
    ABC news coverage: 196
    Anthony policy speech: 153
    break with Liberal party: 114
    campaign issues and tactics: 152–
        154
    candidate selection: 151
    candidates' background, change in:
        152
    demographic changes affecting base
        of support: 145
    electoral alignment: 21
    financial support: 150
    history: 143–145
    House seats, party distribution,
        1949–75, table: 280
    ideology: 144
    leadership: 147–148
    Liberal party, relations with: 114,
        147–148, 150, 156
    McEwen retirement, transfer of
        power: 53
    media coverage: 196
    membership organization: 23–25
    ministerial positions in Fraser gov-
        ernment: 156
    as opposition party: 148
    organization: 23–25, 145–147
    radio and television campaign ex-
        penditures: 134
    self-reappraisal: 148, 157
    Senate budget denial, role in: 149
    state campaigns: 154
    support: 145–146, 155, 157
    votes: 287–289
    Whitlam government reaction to:
        148
    see also: Liberal-National Country
        party (L-NCP)
Courier Mail: 172
Court of Disputed Returns: 339
"Cube rule": 286–287, 290
Cusick, Pat: 191

Daily Mirror: 173, 182, 186, 188
Daily News: 173
Daily Telegraph: 173, 174, 182, 185, 188
    journalists' strike: 182–195
Deakin, Alfred: 6
"Declaration of the Poll": 339
Defense, Labor government neglect of:
    266
Democratic Labor party (DLP):
    and cold war issue: 259, 261, 262
        constituency: 162–163
        election forecasts: 221, 222
        electoral alignment: 22, 23
        formation: 159, 161
        opinion poll, preelection forecast:
            249
        radio and television campaign ex-
            penditures: 134
        support: 162
        votes: 167, 221
Dicey, A. V.: 317
Dissolution of House of Representa-
    tives: 14–16, 333
DLP, see Democratic Labor party
Double dissolution: 15, 75–76
    Kerr's action of November 11,
        1975: 43–46
    Whitlam call for in 1974: 65
Downs, Anthony: 307

East Timor: 273
Economic policy:
    as campaign issue: 93–94, 136–139
    conflict between public service and
        Labor government ministers: 67
    Labor campaign issue: 93–94
    Labor campaign strategy: 91
Economy:
    as 1975 campaign issue: 257
    as cause of Labor government's
        downfall: 66
    development of: 4
    effect on Senate actions: 66
    Labor approach to: 58
    opinion polls on: 238–240
Eggleston, Sir Richard: 315–316
Election deadlines: 325–326
Election procedures: 337–348
    "Australian ballot": 27
    ballots, absence of party labels: 29
    ballots, valid and invalid: 28
    compulsory voting: 28–29
    "cube rule": 286–287, 290
    district system elections: 30–31
    "fairness" controversy: 286–287,
        290–291
    how-to-vote cards: 29, 30, 206
    secret ballot: 27
    see also House elections; Preferen-
        tial voting; Senate elections
Election results: 66, 69, 140–141, 154–
    155, 249, 296–297, 298–302, 352–357
    see also: House elections; Prefer-
        ential voting; Senate elections

Electoral alignment of parties: 20–23
Electoral districts, maps: 288–289
Electoral patterns:
    in 1975: 296–297
    long-term: 278–279
Electoral swing distribution, by state,
    1961–75: 281–284
Electorates:
    characteristics: 3–6
    districts, maps showing winners in
        1974 and 1975 House elections:
        288–289
    enrollment: 294–307
    geographic distribution: 145
    informal voting, impact of: 294–
        296
    preferential voting, impact of: 291–
        294
    proportionate and cube-rule sys-
        tem, impact of: 287, 290
    redistricting: 285, 307
    urban/rural cleavage: 285–286
"Electronic blackout": 95
Electronic media:
    campaign coverage, political bias:
        196–198
    Liberal party advertising expendi-
        tures: 134
    news distribution among parties:
        196
    paid campaign advertising: 204–
        206
    see also Mass media; Radio broad-
        casting; Television broadcasting
Ellicott, Robert: 130

Fairfax papers:
    AJA House Committee statement
        against bias of: 192–193
    description: 173
    election coverage, memo to staff:
        192
Federal Parliamentary Gallery: 177
Federalism: 6–10, 309
Fischer, Henri: 100, 101
Fisher, Andrew: 285
Foreign policy:
    as 1972 and 1975 campaign issue:
        257–258, 263
    ANZUS treaty: 267, 268
    Asia, Whitlam government rela-
        tions with: 268–270
    China, ALP relations with: 262–
        263

complexity of: 265–267
defense, Labor government neglect
    of: 266
DLP influence on: 259, 261–262
Fraser government: 273–275
interpretations of Whitlam policy:
    270–271
of Liberal party: 258–264
L-NCP's 1975 policy statement:
    272–275
of Menzies: 258–260
nonaligned movement, Whitlam
    policy: 270
party advantage, shift of: 53
pre-1972: 258–264
of post-Menzies leaders: 260–262
SEATO treaty: 268
Western powers, Whitlam govern-
    ment relations with: 267–268
"White Australia" immigration
    policy: 261
of Whitlam and ALP government:
    262–275
"Formal" ballot: 28
Fraser, Malcolm: 38–46, 73, 106
    budget crisis, role in: 127–131
    campaign policy speech: 138–140
    Canberra press gallery, criticism
        of: 198–199
    "caretaker" prime minister, ap-
        pointment as: 75
    foreign policy of Fraser govern-
        ment: 273
    governor general's dealings with:
        322
    media coverage of campaign: 199–
        201
    media management by: 171
    new federalism and Fraser govern-
        ment: 309
    no confidence vote: 277, 330, 331
    opinion polls on: 237, 243, 247–
        248, 305–306
    personal and political background:
        123–124
    political style: 124–125
    rise to power: 123–126
    Senate power, use to force elec-
        tion: 38, 39

"Gair affair": 65, 120, 121, 148
Gallup polls: see McNair Gallup poll;
    Morgan Gallup poll; Opinion polls

German Democratic Republic, Whitlam government recognition of: 264
Gorton, John: 52, 105, 147
Governor general:
appointment: 10
authority to ask for Senate vote on supply: 331–332
constitutional powers: 10, 14–16, 323, 333
dismissal by prime minister, issue of: 328-329
dismissal of prime minister, authority: 319–320
dissolution powers: 14–16, 333
opinion poll: 310–311
powers: 10, 323
sources of guidance: 323
see also Kerr, Sir John
Great Britain, ties with: 258, 264

Half-Senate elections: 75, 323–328
Harradine, Brian: 55
Hartley, Bill: 99, 100–101
Hayden, Bill: 73, 96, 127
"Hayden Budget": 91
Herald: 172–173, 175
Heroes, absence of in Australia: 6
Hewitt, Sir Lennox: 70
Hogben, Brian: 188–190
Holt distribution of preferences, 1975 House elections, table: 293
Holt, Harold: 52, 105, 147
House elections:
1972 results, by state: 352
1974 results, by state: 353
1975 results, by state: 296, 354
ballot, 1975 sample: 348
counting of ballots: 339
cube rule, impact on elections: 286–287, 290
districts, results by, 1974 and 1975 elections, maps: 288–289
informal voting, election impact of: 294–296
opinion poll forecasts: 221–222
party distribution of seats, 1975 election, by state: 297
preferential voting system: 30–33, 338–339
procedures: 30–33
proportionate and cube-rule election systems, impact on seats won, 1949–75, tables: 287, 290
swing distribution, 1969–1975: 284

swing to ALP from previous election, by state, 1961–75, table: 283
tabulation of preferences, sample application: 246–247
two-party-preferred votes and seats, 1949–75, table: 287
see also Senate elections
House of Representatives:
dissolution of: 14–16
Liberal members' occupations, 1949–75, table: 107
party discipline: 18
party distribution of seats, 1949–75, table: 280
party majority, significance: 11
as "people's house": 13
"popularly elected house": 11, 12
safeness of House seats, by party, 1955–75: 281–282
underrepresentation of Labor party: 286
vote of no confidence in Fraser: 277, 330–331
How-to-vote cards: 29, 30, 206

Immigrants to Australia, origins: 5
Independent: 175
Indonesia, Fraser government relations with: 273
Inflation:
Labor government's approach to: 58
Liberals' campaign attack: 121
opinion poll on: 240
Informal voting: 28, 294–296
Inland Australia, economic importance: 3
Interest rates, opinion poll on: 240
International affairs: see Foreign policy
Investigative journalism in 1975 election: 178

Japan, Whitlam government relations with: 268–270
John Fairfax group: see Fairfax papers
Joint parliamentary sitting: 16, 66, 120
Journalists' strike:
AJA Code of Ethics: 184, 188
AJA structure: 181
bias, News Ltd. examples: 186
editorial policy as basis: 182–185

grievances: 182–185
management's response: 188–192
NSW branch of AJA, strike meeting statement: 188

Kerr, Sir John: 319–323, 325–327, 330–332
  dismissal of Whitlam: 43–45, 75, 320–322
  double dissolution forced: 43–46
  Fraser appointment as caretaker prime minister: 322
  speaker of House, postponement of interview with: 330
  see also Governor general
Khemlani, Tirath: 70–71, 74–75
Killen, James: 112

Labor party: see Australian Labor party (ALP)
Lang Labor party: 161
Legislative-executive relations: 10
Lewis, Thomas: 109
Liberal Country League (LCL): 163
Liberal Movement (LM):
  constituency: 163
  formation: 159, 161
  radio and television campaign expenditures: 134
  support: 162
  votes: 166–167
Liberal-National Country party (L-NCP):
  1972 defeat, impact: 112–114
  adaptability after Menzies's retirement: 52
  election forecasts: 221, 222, 249
  electoral alignment: 21–22
  foreign policy: 258–264, 272–275
  government of: 17
  House elections, two-party-preferred votes and seats, 1949–75, table: 287
  internal friction: 113
  opinion polls on: 247, 249
  as opposition party: 65, 112–119
  policies, 1973–75: 114–119
  safeness of House seats, 1955–75, table: 282
  unity problems: 52–54
  votes: 140, 221, 296–297
Liberal party:
  1974 campaign strategy: 121
  ABC news coverage: 196

break with Country party: 114
budget crisis, role in: 127–131
campaign issues and techniques: 136–140
campaign planning: 131–134
conservative nature: 20
decline after 1967: 52
electoral alignment: 20–22
headquarters, role in campaign: 134–136
history: 103–106
House seats, party distribution, 1949–75, table: 280
ideology: 106–110
leadership problems: 52, 53, 119–123
legislation blockage: 119–121
media advertising by: 204–206
media coverage: 196
membership and staff of party branches, table: 108
membership organization: 23–25
Menzies's role: 104–105
name changes: 20
occupations of Liberal members of House of Representatives, 1949–75, table: 107
opinion poll ratings: 235–238
as opposition party: 110, 112–114, 119, 120, 235–238
organization: 109, 110, 111
platform revision: 115–118
radio and television campaign expenditures: 134
Snedden leadership and defeat: 119–123
supply, denial by: 119–121, 127–131
surveys, campaign use of: 238
votes: 140, 288–289
see also Liberal-National Country party (L-NCP)
"Loans affair": 70–71, 74, 99–101
  opinion polls on: 241–243
London Economist: 266

Macdonald, Ranald: 208
Major parties:
  bases of electoral support: 279–281
  Senate elections, percentage of votes won, 1949–75: 300
  see also names of individual parties
Map of population distribution: 219
Maps of electoral districts: 288–289

Mass media:
bias charges against: 171, 196–198
campaign coverage: 196–204, 208–209
campaign strategy and: 176–178
Fraser use of: 171
opinion polls, media coverage: 202–203, 226–227
paid campaign advertising in: 207
structure: 172
see also: Canberra press gallery; Electronic media; Journalists' strike; Newspapers; Radio broadcasting; Television broadcasting
May, Ken: 189–190
McClelland, James: 96
McEwen, John: 53, 147–148
McMahon, William: 53–54, 55, 105, 114, 147
McNair Gallup poll:
approval ratings of Whitlam, Snedden, and Fraser, 1974–75: 237
on company profits and dividends: 240
on economy: 240
election forecasts, November–December 1975, table: 249
forecast errors: 221, 222
on Fraser: 237
on inflation: 240
on interest rates: 240
on Labor government and opposition: 235–238
on party preferences: 230
on Senate blocking of supply: 244–247
on shortage of goods: 240
on Snedden: 237
on strikes: 240
survey methods: 222, 248
on unemployment: 240
on voter intentions: 230–232
on Whitlam: 237, 247
see also Opinion polls
Media: *see* Electronic media; Mass media; Newspapers; Radio broadcasting; Television broadcasting
Medibank: 66
Melbourne, population: 2
Melbourne *Herald* group: 172–173, 175
Menadue, John: 63
Menzies, Sir Robert: 52, 54, 104, 105
foreign policy: 258–260
Mercury: 173

Metropolitan centers, population statistics: 2
Mini-budget of Whitlam government: 67
Ministers:
appointment by prime minister: 19
membership in House of Representatives or Senate, constitutional requirement: 10
see also Prime Minister; Cabinet
Minor parties:
1975 election, share of Senate vote, by state, table: 168
alliances with majority parties: 165
DLP share of Senate vote, by state, 1974 and 1975 elections, table: 167
election forecasting and: 225–226
formation: 159–161
as ideological alternative: 160
impact on 1975 election: 165–169
as major party offshoot: 159
as political embodiment of particular interests: 160
preferential voting, impact of: 164–165, 292–294
and solid party vote: 300–302
support: 161
votes: 166–169, 296–297
Mirror: 180
Morgan Gallup poll:
1972 election prediction: 213
approval ratings for Whitlam and Fraser: 140
ASRB poll and: 214
bias and: 234
on Cairns's dismissal: 241–242
competitor: 212–213
on Connor's Loan Plan: 242–243
election forecasts, November–December 1975, table: 249
forecast errors, House elections, 1958–1975, tables: 221, 222
House election results and poll forecasts compared, table: 221
on Labor government and opposition: 235–238
on "loans affair": 241–243
ownership: 211–212
questions used, type of, 1974–75: 232
survey methods: 223, 248
on voter intentions: 231–234
see also Opinion polls
Morgan, Roy: 212–213
Morosi, Juni: 68

Murdoch group:
    circulation: 213
    description: 173
    journalists' strike: 181–195
    Labor party, relationship with:
        179–181
    opinion poll interests: 212
Murdoch, K. R. (Rupert): 173–175, 179,
    180, 181, 183–184, 190, 195, 209
Murdoch, Sir Keith: 175, 194
Murphy, Lionel: 17, 56, 119

Nation Review: 175
National Country party: *see* Country
    party
National heroes, absence of: 6
National party: 20
National Press Gallery: *see* Canberra
    press gallery
National Star: 174
National Times: 173, 175
NCP: *see* Country party
New Guinea: *see* Papua New Guinea
New Journalist: 182
New South Wales, 1975 coalition pref-
    erences: 301–302
New York Magazine: 174n
New York Post: 174n
News: 173, 180
News, Ltd.:
    bias, journalists' charges: 182–183,
        186
    circulation: 212
    strike by journalists: 182–195
News of the World: 174
Newspapers:
    bias, examples of: 186–187
    campaign coverage: 202–204, 208–
        209
    concentration of control: 175
    description: 172–175
    editorial policy, bias charges: 182–
        195
    management: 175–176
    management's response to strike:
        187 et seq.
    opinion polls, use of: 202–203
    paid campaign advertising: 204–
        206
    strike by journalists: 181–195
    Whitlam government, coverage:
        178–181
    see also Canberra press gallery

Non-Labor coalition: *see* Liberal-
    National Country party (L-NCP)
Nonaligned movement, Whitlam for-
    eign policy: 270
NOP: 212
Northern Territory News: 174, 191

Observer: 175
Opinion polls:
    1972 election prediction: 213
    academic polls: 215, 251–253
    accuracy: 220–222, 226
    bias and: 234
    on campaign issues: 250–251
    and compulsory voting: 224–225
    on confidence in press coverage of
        politics: 209
    disagreement of: 235–236, 243, 251–
        253, 254–255
    on economy: 238–240
    election forecasts, November–
        December 1975, table: 249
    forecast errors, House elections,
        1972–75, table: 222
    on Fraser: 237, 243, 247–248, 305–
        306
    on Governor general's action: 310–
        311
    history: 211–214
    on Labor government and opposi-
        tion: 235–238
    on Labor government's "horror
        period": 230, 238–247
    media coverage of data: 202–203
    minor parties, election forecasting
        and: 225–226
    organizations operating polls in
        1975, table: 216–217
    political parties' use of: 227–229
    and preferential voting: 225
    problems of geography and: 218
    role in election campaigns: 255
    on Senate stalemate and Labor
        government's dismissal: 243–247,
        310–311
    on social issues: 226–229
    structural changes in polling orga-
        nizations: 213–215
    survey methods: 223, 248
    "swinging voters," polling of: 224,
        225
    techniques: 247–253
    types of: 212–215

on voter intentions: 231, 235–238, 242–243, 305

see also ANOP poll; ASRB poll; McNair Gallup poll; Morgan Gallup poll; Saulwick *Age* poll

Overseas loan-raising: see "Loans affair"

Packer group, description: 174

Packer, Sir Frank: 174

Papua New Guinea, foreign policy on: 264, 270, 275

Parliament: see House of Representatives; Senate

Parliamentary conventions:
conflict with constitution: 37 et seq.
legislative-executive relations: 10

Parliamentary democracy: 10–14

Parramatta by-election: 120

Party caucus: 19

Party distribution in House and Senate, 1975 election, by state: 297

Party leadership: 85

Party membership: 23–25
Liberal party branches, table: 108

Party system:
absence of majority in Senate, effects of historically: 16–18
based on lower house: 9–14
candidate selection: 25–27
control of both houses, difficulty of: 17
stability: 279–281
state party organizations, role of: 23–27

Pascoe, Timothy: 117, 135

Peacock, Andrew: 272, 274

Plebiscite method of candidate selection: 26–27

Population:
geographic distribution: 145, 215–218
map of population distribution: 219
origins: 4, 5
prosperity of workers: 3
statistics: 2

Preferential voting:
Corio and Holt, distribution of preferences, House elections, 1975, table: 293
in House elections: 31–33, 338–339
impact of: 31–33, 164, 291–294
minor parties, impact on: 164
and opinion polls: 225

sample showing application in House election: 346–347

seats affected by distribution of preferences, House elections, 1949–75, table: 292

in Senate elections: 33–37, 337–338

Press: see Canberra press gallery; Mass media; Newspapers; Radio broadcasting; Television broadcasting

Prime minister:
authority, basis of: 10
dissolution powers: 14–16
Governor general, appointment by: 10
Governor general, dismissal of and by, issue of: 319–320, 328–329
majority party, leader of: 10, 11
member of House of Representatives: 9, 14
parliamentary support, importance of: 11
responsibility to Parliament: 10
supply, denial of: 11, 12
tenure: 11–14
see also Fraser, Malcolm; Whitlam, Gough

Prime Minister and Cabinet, Department of:
Whitlam reorganization attempt: 63
see also Cabinet; Ministers

Pringle, R.: 194

PR-STV, Senate election method: 33–36

Public opinion polls: see ANOP poll; ASRB poll; McNair Gallup poll; Morgan Gallup poll; Opinion polls; Saulwick *Age* poll

Public service, relations with Whitlam government: 61–64, 67–68

Radio broadcasting:
1975 campaign coverage: 203–204
ABC, political bias attacks: 196–198
ALP use of: 95
"electronic blackout": 95
expenditures, by party, table: 134
free campaign time: 204, 207
news distribution among parties: 196
see also Mass media

"Rally for Democracy": 95

Recounts: 339

Referendum as solution to supply issue: 331

Reporters: *see* Journalists' strike
Rhodesia, Whitlam government's policy
 on: 264
Rural/urban cleavage of electorate:
 285–286

Saulwick *Age* poll:
 of campaign issues: 250
 on economy: 239
 election forecasts, November–
  1975, table: 249
 forecast errors: 221, 222
 on Fraser government: 305–306
 House election results and forecasts, 1975, table: 221
 L-NCP and ALP approval ratings,
  1975 campaign: 140
 survey methods: 222, 248
 on voter intentions: 305
 on Whitlam dismissal: 247
 see also Opinion polls
Scarf, Reuben F.: 100
Schildberger, Michael: 179n, 195n
SEATO treaty: 259, 268
Secret ballot: 27
Senate:
 abolition desired by ALP: 46
 constituency: 9
 constitutional model: 9
 constitutional right to refuse supply: 314–317
 dissolution of: 15
 governor general's authority to ask
  for vote on supply: 331–332
 legislative powers: 9, 12
 opposition, pattern of: 17
 party discipline, lack of: 17, 18
 party majority different from
  House of Representatives: 11
 power, historical survey: 16–18
 supply, blockage by: 12, 243–247,
  310–311, 314–317, 331–332
 U.S. Senate as model: 9, 13
Senate elections:
 1974 results, by state: 355
 1975 results, by state: 297, 356
 ballot, 1975 sample: 349
 counting of ballots: 337–338
 informal voting, impact of: 294–
  296
 party distribution of seats, 1975
  election, by state: 297
 preferential voting system: 337–338

procedures: 33–37
 proportional representation: 17
 PR-STV method: 33–36
 single transferable vote: 33–36
 tabulation of preferences, sample
  application: 340–345
 see also House elections
Shortage of goods, opinion poll on: 240
Snedden, Bill: 65, 108, 113
 defeat: 119–123
 opinion poll ratings: 236–237
Socialism, ALP and: 79–81
South Africa, Whitlam government's
 policy on: 264
Southeast Asia, Whitlam government
 relations with: 269
Soviet Union, Fraser government relations with: 274
State party organizations:
 Liberal party membership and
  staff, table: 108
 role in candidate selection: 25–27
States:
 1972 House election results, by
  state: 352
 1974 House election results, by
  state: 353
 1975 House election results, by
  state: 296, 354
 1974 Senate election results, by
  state: 355
 1975 Senate election results, by
  state: 297–356
 House of Representatives, two-
  party-preferred votes and seats,
  1949–75, table: 287
 party distribution of Senate seats,
  1975 election, by state: 297
 swings to ALP from previous
  House election, 1961–75, table:
  283
Strikes:
 opinion poll on: 240
 see also Journalists' strike
Sun: 173, 174, 200
Sun Herald: 173
Sun News Pictorial: 172
Sunday Australian: 173
Sunday Mail: 172, 173
Sunday Mirror: 173, 182, 187
Sunday Press: 172
Sunday Telegraph: 173, 174, 182, 187
Supply, blockage of: 11–12, 73–75
 constitutional language: 12
 continuation of government with-
  out supply, issue of: 317–319

Country party's role: 149
Fraser use to force election: 39
government's duty to resign: 317
Governor general's interference, issue of: 331–332
half-Senate elections as means of resolution: 323–325
implications for future: 310
Liberal party actions: 119–121, 127–131
opinion polls on: 243–247
referendum as solution: 331
Senate firmness on issue: 332
Senate powers: 12, 314–317
Whitlam government's crisis, summary: 37–47
Surveys: see Opinion polls
Swinging voters:
academic opinion poll: 251–253
ALP, swing to, from previous House election, by state, 1961–75, table: 283
distribution in House elections, 1969–75: 284
main campaign issue perceived by, poll: 251
Sydney, population: 2
Sydney Morning Herald: 173, 192

Tasmania, 1975 voting preferences: 302
Telegraph:
bias charges, News Ltd. journalists' letter: 182–183
editorial policy as basis for journalists' strike: 181–185
see also *Daily Telegraph*
Television broadcasting:
1975 campaign coverage: 203–204
ALP use of: 95
"electronic blackout": 95
expenditures, by party, table: 134
Fraser campaign coverage: 198
free campaign time: 204, 207
news distribution among parties: 196
paid campaign advertising: 204–206
see also Mass media
Timing of election: 325–326
Trade unions: see Unions
Treasury Department, Labor's problems with: 63, 67–71
Truth: 173, 180
"Turn on the lights" campaign: 132–133
Two-party pattern, stability: 279–281

Unemployment, opinion poll on: 240
Unions:
affiliation with ALP: 81–86
Australian Council of Trade Unions: 83, 84, 97
Australian Journalists' Association (AJA), strike by: 181–195
donations to ALP: 98
numerical strength: 82
support for ALP: 91–98
wage demands as campaign issue: 91
United Australia Party (UAP): 20, 104, 309
United States:
Fraser government relations with: 274
Whitlam government relations with: 267–268
United Tasmania Group (UTG): 161
University of Melbourne poll of swinging voters: 251–253
Urban/rural cleavage of electorate: 285–286

Valid ballot: 28
Vietnam as foreign policy issue: 259–260, 264
Violence, absence of in 1975 campaign: 278
Vote of no confidence in Fraser: 277, 330–331
Voting, compulsory: 28–29
and opinion polls: 224–225

Watson, Chris: 285
West Australian: 173
Western powers, Whitlam government relations with: 267–268
"White Australia" policy: 5, 116, 261
Whitlam ALP government: 54–76
blockage of supply crisis: 37–47
budget disputes: 67, 68
cabinet-caucus relations: 59–60
constitutional crisis, summary: 37–47
Country party reactions: 148
economic decisions: 64
editorial opinion against: 178–179
failures in office: 307–308
foreign policy: 264–275
"horror period": 230

"loans affair": 70–71
"mini-budget": 67
ministerial successes: 73
opinion poll ratings: 235–238
public service, relations with: 61–64
Whitlam, Gough: 17, 38–46, 53–55, 65
1975 campaign, press coverage:
201–202
China visit: 262–263
dismissal by Kerr: 43–45, 75, 320–
322; options after: 329–330
duumvirate rule with Barnard: 56
foreign policy: 262–275
half-Senate election, call for: 323,
325, 326–328
media coverage of campaign: 201–
202

Murdoch, interpretation of rift
with: 180
opinion polls on: 236, 237, 242,
243, 248
Parliament House, description by:
177
personal characteristics: 54–55
policies: 54, 55
speech: 90–93
style of governing: 56–58
Workers' party (WP): 160–161
constituency: 163–164
votes: 167

Yew, Lee Kuan: 269

Cover and book design: Pat Taylor